Handbook on Household Hazardous Waste

Edited by

Amy D. Cabaniss

Government Institutes
An imprint of
The Scarecrow Press, Inc.
Lanham, Maryland • Toronto • Plymouth, UK
2008

Government Institutes

Published in the United States of America
by Government Institutes, an imprint of The Scarecrow Press, Inc.
A wholly owned subsidary of
The Rowman & Littlefield Publishing Group, Inc.
4501 Forbes Boulevard, Suite 200
Lanham, Maryland 20706
http://www.govinstpress.com/

Estover Road
Plymouth PL6 7PY
United Kingdom

British Library Cataloguing in Publication Information Available

Library of Congress Cataloging-in-Publication Data

Cabaniss, Amy D., 1961–
   Handbook on household hazardous waste / Amy D. Cabaniss.
      p. cm.
   Includes bibliographical references and index.
   ISBN-13: 978-0-86587-163-2 (pbk. : alk. paper)
   ISBN-10: 0-86587-163-9 (pbk. : alk. paper)
   1. Hazardous wastes. 2. Consumer goods—Environmental aspects. 3. Refuse and refuse
disposal. 4. Waste products—Environmental aspects. 5. Chemicals—Environmental aspects.
I. Title.
TD1030.C33 2008
363.72'87—dc22   2007042316

♾™ The paper used in this publication meets the minimum requirements of
American National Standard for Information Sciences—Permanence of
Paper for Printed Library Materials, ANSI/NISO Z39.48-1992.
Manufactured in the United States of America.

Contents

Acknowledgments

I wish to acknowledge and give my sincerest thanks to the authors who have contributed to this book. Countless hours have gone into this. Without your contributions to the book and the field in general, we would be far less fortunate. A hearty thank-you to Sue Bruning, Scott Cassel, Philip Dickey, Dana Duxbury-Fox, Dave Galvin, Jim Hanna, Bill Lafield, Bill Lewry, Dave Nightingale, Mike O'Donnell, Jim Quinn, Anne Reichman, Wes Schultz, Jennifer Tabanico, and Mike Wilson.

Thank you also to the reviewers for their time and application of expertise. These include Pam and Paul Bergstrand, Deanna and Ray Carveth, Annette Frahm, Eric Laut, and the many individuals who provided comment on Chapter 7 to Scott Cassel.

And for their support and expertise, thank you to Kolin Anglin, Cheryl Clofrano-zaske, Ryan Kellogg, Kelby Neal, Jennifer Volkman, and Diana Whitelaw.

The North American Hazardous Materials Management Association has been supportive of this effort and it is from the NAHMMA conferences and Board of Directors that I identified contributing individuals. My thanks to the Board and members.

Special thanks to Dave Galvin for inspiring me to create this book, and to Michael Bender for encouraging me many years ago to join the NAHMMA Board and conferences; it continues to be a great professional and personal affiliation. CRERPA—The practical experience was tremendously helpful—thank you. Thank you as well to Sarjit Rattan and Doug English for their interest and their expert assistance in manuscript preparation. Thank you also to my family for their support.

Last but not least, thank you to all "in the trenches"—we owe you a great debt.

Amy Cabaniss, *Editor*

Preface

This book is about capturing information and expert recommendations from people "in the know,"—active, busy practitioners and visionaries. It was easy to identify the leaders from NAHMMA (the North American Hazardous Materials Management Association) conferences and colleagues on the NAHMMA Board of Directors; the hard part was limiting it to these few outstanding individuals, as we are blessed with many in this arena. My inspiration for this book came from the realization that while the annual conference proceedings document much of the how-to and forward thinking, there is not a single repository of the history, present, and anticipated future of the field. This book represents an assemblage of wisdom that we hope will serve you well.

The purpose of the book is to inform professionals working for government and businesses, as well as students and interested others about household hazardous waste, a topic that affects each and every individual and community given the nearly universal use, storage, and disposal of chemical consumer products such as cleaners, pesticides, paint-related products, automotive products, and others. The field of household hazardous waste management has experienced tremendous growth over the past 25 years as the public has demanded greater protection of health and environment. Still, many communities lack the basic information, guidance, and planning support for HHW collection and management so that struggles (*e.g.,* to gain politicians' and residents' support, host a collection, build a facility, affect behavior change, and encourage extended producer responsibility) continue on a regular basis. More and more communities host HHW collections and build permanent facilities to accommodate the amount of material received from residents and the increased demand for this disposal option.

This handbook offers perspectives based on many collective years of accrued insight. While readers will need further study before fully delving into this field, we hope that on these pages you will find a wealth of information that prompts questions and ideas and inspires plans and progress.

This book offers some answers to many questions:

- What is household hazardous waste and why do we collect it?
- What is the evolution of HHW management and what are the salient issues of concern?

- How are HHW collections held and collected materials managed?
- What are some best management practices?
- What types of factors should be considered when hosting an HHW collection or building a permanent facility?
- What are some effective ways to motivate behavior change?
- How can a product stewardship approach increase collections, cover costs, and promote non-hazardous consumer products?
- What is an example of the industry perspective on HHW?

In Chapter 1, Dave Galvin, an early and continuing maverick in the field, presents the case for why public health and the environment need to be protected and HHW properly managed, and presents a timeline and current status of the industry along with Philip Dickey of the WA Toxics Coalition, in Chapter 2. Sue Bruning and Mike O'Donnell, both managers for household hazardous waste services companies, have organized, staffed, and cleaned up after 2,300 mobile collection events and worked in 250 permanent facilities. They write about their experiences and offer insight into managing operationally effective HHW programs, in Chapter 3. Sue shares further insight by highlighting creative collection options in Chapter 5.

HHW facilities are familiar territory to two government officials, Dave Nightingale and Bill Lewry, who share their expertise in Chapter 4. Both are recognized for their design and operation of cost-effective and safe facilities. The compelling story is that a safe place to hold a truckload of waste for a single shipment saves money, no matter how a program chooses to process waste. While this is not a chapter with HHW facility layouts (there are many reasons not to provide cookie-cutter designs), it is one that will aid you in designing a well-working facility.

Wesley Schultz is an applied social psychologist and professor with extensive research and publication. Among other psychological interests, Wes has focused on behavior change theory and interventions. He and his research colleague, Jennifer Tabanico, have seen the usefulness and further promise of community-based social marketing (CBSM) in achieving desired behavior changes. They share the results of their applied research on using CBSM for motor oil waste collection, in Chapter 6.

Scott Cassel, Executive Director and founder of the Product Stewardship Institute, explores the shared responsibility for managing HHW at the end of their useful lives and along the entire product life cycle. In Chapter 7, Scott explains why product stewardship represents a worldwide paradigm shift in managing waste among manufacturers, retailers, government agencies, and other key stakeholders. He presents a history of the movement and outlines key issues for consideration.

Jim Hanna has a broad, experienced perspective, having worked as a county HHW program manager, HHW services manager, and as an environmental manager for Yellowstone National Park and now, Starbucks. In this concluding chapter, Jim offers, among other suggestions, the wisdom of the Precautionary Principal.

Appendices are provided on green chemistry, an industry perspective, and a vast listing of resources for more information. These reflect the expertise of other individuals including Bill Lafield, VP of Communications for the Consumer Specialty Products Association, Mike Wilson, a research scientist at University of California-Berkeley, School of Public Health, and Anne Reichman, Director of Public Affairs and former Director of Earth 911.

Some of the relevant topics not covered in this book, that are worthy of reader investigation are:

- Waste exchange programs—how-to's and the pro's and cons
- Contractor management—liability, selection of disposal facilities, etc.
- Detailed specifics of running a collection program
- Conditionally exempt Small Quantity Generator (CESQG) waste management
- Ways in which regulations (*e.g.,* RCRA, DOT, OSHA, TSCA, FIFRA, NPDES, Universal Waste) impact HHW programs
- Training staff for maximum program impact
- Funding mechanisms

We hope that reading this book provides you with a good vantage point from which to see the small and big pictures, serving as a guidepost for future HHW-related activities.

It is important to note that this is a relatively new field; this is the first handbook on HHW. The field will grow rapidly over the next 5–10 years, particularly with developments in product stewardship, green chemistry, etc. Thus, readers will want to seek updates on the information provided herein. The resource section will aid in this pursuit.

Amy Cabaniss
with contribution from Deanna Carveth

About the Authors

Amy Cabaniss has provided household hazardous waste education—through products and programs she developed, consulting and conference presentations on HHW—since 1990. She worked as a regional recycling coordinator for six years during which time she was in charge of hosting HHW and consumer electronics collections and overseeing the design and construction of a permanent HHW facility. Amy is currently on the Board of Directors of the North American Hazardous Materials Management Association (NAHMMA) and has served many terms. She is the Campus Environmental Coordinator for Connecticut College (New London, CT) and a doctoral candidate in environmental studies.

Deanna Seaman Carveth is a 20-year solid waste professional with 15 years specifically related to managing household hazardous waste programs—mobile and permanent events as well as small business programs. She has personally organized and staffed over 1,000 mobile events and worked in 25 permanent facilities in three states. She started at the San Francisco Household Hazardous Waste Collection Facility after obtaining a chemistry degree from San Francisco State University. Deanna was a founding member of NAHMMA and currently serves on the board for the Washington State Recycling Association.

CHAPTER 1

What Is Household Hazardous Waste?*

Dave Galvin
Philip Dickey

Introduction

When Alice followed the white rabbit down its hole, she found a small bottle with a simple instruction tied to its neck: "DRINK ME," it said. Alice hesitated, recalling one of the simple rules that she had been taught, "If you drink much from a bottle marked 'poison,' it is almost certain to disagree with you, sooner or later." But this bottle had no such label, so Alice proceeded to drink heartily, showing a naïve trust for what labels say and, maybe more importantly, what they don't say. And, as we know, things proceeded to get "curiouser and curiouser."[1]

In another childhood classic, Curious George, the little red monkey, encountered a bottle labeled, "ETHER," in his second of many adventure books. Being always curious, he opened the cork and took a big whiff. "It smelled funny. Suddenly his head began to turn. Then he felt as if he were flying. Then rings and stars danced before his eyes. Then everything went dark."[2] Luckily, little George recovered and went on to many more monkeyshines. There are too many statistics, however, of people—children in particular—who have not been so lucky.

These early tales are part of folklore now, part of our collective wisdom that some products are poisonous or can be dangerous. We don't find too many bottles marked, "Drink Me," but we do see many labeled "Poison." Household hazardous waste programs regularly get calls regarding dusty old bottles marked, "Ether," which we calmly advise not to touch while the nearest bomb squad is called. As consumers we have tolerated a remarkable array of products around us that contain toxic or otherwise hazardous chemicals. Not only are there concerns about their direct effects on us through use and exposure, but also there are concerns about what happens to these chemicals when the products are used up or thrown away.

---

*An industry perspective on household hazardous waste management appears in Appendix A on page 223.

Some consumer products have contained hazardous chemical ingredients or exhibited hazardous properties throughout history. The number and variety of such products exploded following World War II as American households followed the industrial slogan, "better living through chemistry."[3] It wasn't until the early 1980s that local environmental, health, and safety interests began to wonder about what happens when all of these hazardous products are used or thrown away – maybe in individually small amounts, but what about the cumulative impacts? The term, household hazardous waste ("HHW"), was coined in 1981 to capture the burgeoning interest in these problematic leftovers from the home.

This chapter presents a few definitions of household hazardous waste. Various product lists are examined that catalog types of consumer products that fall into this category when disposed. This chapter also discusses the ongoing evolution of the HHW concept, as more focus is placed today on exposures to hazardous chemical ingredients contained in a wide variety of consumer products.

Federal Exemption, Local Action

When the Resource Conservation and Recovery Act ("RCRA") was passed in 1976, it strengthened solid waste management requirements in the U.S. (such as requiring lined landfills), in Subtitle D, and created a "cradle to grave" management system for those solid wastes that are considered hazardous, in Subtitle C. The law was clearly aimed at industrial and other large quantity producers of hazardous wastes. While the law itself (PL 94-580; 48 USC 6901) was silent on the household/consumer product topic, the accompanying Senate Report signaled congressional intent at the time:

> "[The hazardous waste program]…is not to be used to control the disposal of substances used in households or to extend control over general municipal wastes based on the presence of such substances."[4]

This was a practical policy decision at a time when most environmental laws were new and systems needed to be developed for the major wastes of concern. Referencing this intent, U.S. EPA created the official household waste exemption when it developed the first RCRA regulations in 1980, codified in *40 CFR 261.4(b)(1)*:

(b) *Solid wastes which are not hazardous wastes.* The following solid wastes are not hazardous wastes:

(1) Household waste, including household waste that has been collected, transported, stored, treated, disposed, recovered (e.g., refuse-derived fuel) or reused. "Household waste" means any material (including garbage, trash and sanitary wastes in septic tanks) derived from households (including single and multiple residences, hotels and motels, bunkhouses, ranger stations, crew quarters, campgrounds, picnic grounds and day-use recreation areas).

The U.S. Environmental Protection Agency supports state and local programs that address hazardous household products and their wastes, while acknowledging the federal regulatory exemption. In an important policy directive in 1988,[5] U.S. EPA acknowledged that, because of the household exemption, HHW can legally be discarded with municipal solid waste under Subtitle D of RCRA. However, "EPA recommends that sponsors of HHW collection programs manage the collected HHW as a hazardous waste." Furthermore, the policy directive noted, "EPA believes that these programs are important because they:

(1) promote citizen awareness regarding proper handling of HHW;
(2) reduce the amount of HHW in the municipal waste combustors or landfills;
(3) limit the amount of HHW which is dumped down a drain and ultimately discharged to a publicly-owned treatment works (POTW), or is dumped indiscriminately;
(4) remove a greater amount of HHW from the home, thereby reducing potential safety hazards; and
(5) help to reduce the risk of injuries to sanitation workers."

In the same policy directive, U.S. EPA noted that communities should recognize that potential Superfund (Comprehensive Environmental Response, Compensation and Liability Act, or "CERCLA") liability applies regardless of whether a substance (such as HHW) is exempt under the hazardous waste law (RCRA). "The additional safeguards provided by HHW collection and Subtitle C management may reduce the likelihood of environmental and human health impacts and, therefore, may also reduce potential CERCLA liability."[6]

Hazardous waste regulations center on "solid" wastes, and do not directly address toxic or otherwise hazardous chemicals that are discharged down the drain into a municipal wastewater treatment system either in normal use or disposal. Clean Water Act and local sewerage regulations mirror the exemption for household (on the water side usually referred to as "domestic") substances, assuming that whatever consumer products go down the drain are part of the normal domestic sewage mix. As we note later, this can present separate concerns, especially in cases where wastewater discharges go to on-site (septic tank and drain field) systems. HHW programs often recognize these concerns with liquid household products, many of which should be subject to alternative, safer management.

State Rules

Most states mirror the federal exemption for HHW in state laws and regulations. California and Minnesota are examples of states that go beyond federal laws to partially or fully regulate HHW. Those two, plus Washington, are examples of states with much broader definitions of what designates as hazardous, especially in what qualifies as "toxic," and thus encompasses many more materials as "hazardous wastes." It is important to check with the state environmental or health agencies to confirm the legal as well as practical context for handling HHW before launching any local program.

U.S. EPA offers a very useful website to link to state environmental agencies regarding hazardous waste issues, including HHW. Check out: http://www.epa.gov/epaoswer/osw/stateweb.htm#maincontent.[7] The National Center for Manufacturing Sciences, an industry association, provides another very helpful site with hazardous waste, universal waste, mercury, lead-abatement, and other links to all 50 states, at: http://www.envcap.org/state-tools/index.cfm.[8]

Rather than attempting to assemble a list here for all 50 states, which would be outdated before publication, it is best to acknowledge the variation that exists among the states as well as the likelihood of ongoing changes and refinements. The reader should go directly to state and/or local sources. In addition to the valuable sites noted above, use an Internet browser and search for "HHW" and your state; in almost all cases multiple links will be found that get you closer to the action than we can do in this handbook.

Definitions and Lists

There is no definitive definition of household hazardous waste, nor is there a uniform list of waste products that are considered HHW. Definitions and lists vary by state and even within states. Programs include different wastes depending on their local concerns (for example, groundwater protection, "problem" wastes in garbage, water quality issues); how their solid waste is managed (for example, landfilled vs. combusted); and if health concerns are factored in (for example, poisoning reduction, toxic chemical exposure reduction, drinking water contamination, pesticide handling in agricultural areas).

Some HHW programs include small household batteries, especially those regions that combust their solid waste and are thus concerned about certain heavy metals in the waste stream, air emissions, and subsequent ash. But many other HHW programs do not collect non-automotive batteries. (Note that small button batteries containing mercury or silver are collected more often than alkaline.) Many programs include latex (water-based) paint even though relatively new (in the last decade at least) latex does not designate as hazardous under federal criteria. Many states do *not* include latex paint in their HHW definitions. Some programs focus on unique issues associated with wastewater treatment plants or on-site septic tank concerns, including high nutrient sources, certain detergent ingredients, pharmaceuticals, and personal care products not typically thought of as hazardous. Most programs include harsh cleaners such as strong acids (for example, toilet bowl cleaners) and strong bases (for example, drain openers), even though their use (and their disposal) into large municipal wastewater systems is not usually an environmental concern; they do remain a concern for the risk of skin or eye burns for the consumer, and in disposal to on-site septic tank systems.

The U.S. EPA's informal definition of household hazardous waste (on its website) is, "Leftover household products that contain corrosive, toxic, ignitable, or reactive ingredients…. Products, such as paints, cleaners, oils, batteries, and pesticides that contain potentially hazardous ingredients require special care when you dispose of them."[9]

EPA's official definition of HHW was promulgated in 1986:

> "Household hazardous waste: Solid wastes discarded from homes or similar sources as listed in 40 CFR 261.4(b)(1) that are either hazardous wastes as listed by EPA in 40 CFR, Parts 261.33(e) or (f), or wastes that exhibit any of the following characteristics as defined in 40 CFR, Parts 261.21 through 261.24: ignitability, corrosivity, reactivity, and EP toxicity."[10]

Table 1.1 describes the RCRA Subtitle C lists and characteristics, with examples of consumer products or their contents that would designate as hazardous were it not for the household source exemption. The federal list of common HHW products is shown in Table 1.2.

Table 1.1. Lists and Characteristics that Define Hazardous Wastes. It summarizes federal RCRA criteria (identified on a specific list or meeting certain characteristics), with examples of household products that fit these criteria if they were to be discarded as waste.

List or characteristic	Definition	Household product examples
"P-list" – acute hazard	Acutely hazardous – specific chemicals listed in 40 CFR 261.33(e)	Warfarin, epinephrine, aldrin, dieldrin, endosulfan, endrin, other banned pesticides
"U-list" – otherwise toxic	Toxic – specific chemicals listed in 40CFR 261.33(f)	Xylene, toluene, methanol, ethyl ether, cresol, methyl ethyl ketone, acetone, ethyl acetate, Freon-12, creosote, formaldehyde, DDT, lindane, pentachlorophenol
Ignitable	Catches fire readily. Flash point less than 60° C. (140° F.). Includes all flammable ("class I") and some ("class II") combustible liquids as defined in fire codes.	Gasoline, lighter fluid, alcohol, oil-based paints, organic solvents, petroleum distillates, mineral spirits
Corrosive	Causes skin or eye burns. Strongly acidic (pH less than or equal to 2) or alkaline (pH greater than or equal to 12.5)	Acids: Toilet bowl cleaner, masonry wash (muriatic). Bases: Drain openers, some oven cleaners (lye)
Reactive	Causes chemical reactions. Explosive, unstable, or readily undergoes violent change when combined with other common products.	Chlorine bleach, ammonia, acids/bases, peroxide, cynanide-containing, many old legacies (which have dried out and formed unstable crystals).
Toxic	Poisonous or causes illness. Several criteria based on tests of an extract ("EP"), now Toxicity Characteristic Leaching Procedure ("TCLP").	Most pesticides, solvents, many adhesives, paint strippers, mercury-, silver-, cadmium, arsenic- or lead-containing products.

Source: Developed from U.S. EPA regulations and other sources.

[As noted earlier, the federal RCRA toxicity definition is limited to a relatively short list of heavy metals and pesticides that leach according to a certain test. While many states mirror the federal definitions, some, such as California, Minnesota, and Washington, have much broader and more encompassing definitions of toxicity.]

Earth 911, a non-profit organization that operates a comprehensive locator of state and local HHW services, defines household hazardous waste as, "A product that is discarded

Table 1.2. Common Household Products Considered to be HHW by the U.S. Environmental Protection Agency When Thrown Away. These common household items containing potentially hazardous ingredients might be found in your garage, basement, or other storage space in your home.

Category	Items
Cleaning Products	Oven cleaners, drain cleaners, wood and metal cleaners and polishes, toilet cleaners, tub, tile, shower cleaners, bleach (laundry), pool chemicals
Indoor Pesticides	Ant sprays and baits, cockroach sprays and baits, flea repellents and shampoos, bug sprays, houseplant insecticides, moth repellents, mouse and rat poisons and baits
Automotive Products	Motor oil, fuel additives, carburetor and fuel injection cleaners, air conditioning refrigerants, starter fluids, automotive batteries, transmission and brake fluid, antifreeze
Workshop/Painting Supplies	Adhesives and glues, furniture strippers, oil or enamel based paint, stains and finishes, paint thinners and turpentine, paint strippers and removers, photographic chemicals, fixatives, and other solvents
Lawn and Garden Products	Herbicides, insecticides, fungicides/wood preservatives
Miscellaneous	Batteries, mercury thermostats or thermometers, fluorescent light bulbs, driveway sealer
Other Flammable Products	Propane tanks and other compressed gas cylinders, kerosene, home heating oil, diesel fuel, gas/oil mix, lighter fluid

Source: U.S. EPA, *List of Common HHW Products,* www.eps.gov/msw/hhw-list.htm

from a home or a similar source that is either ignitable, corrosive, reactive, or toxic (*e.g.,* used motor oil, oil-based paint, auto batteries, gasoline, pesticides, etc.)."[11]

The Pollution Prevention Regional Information Center ("P2RIC"), which hosts the valuable national HHW listserv, defines HHW as follows: "*Household hazardous waste* consists of the unwanted or unusable portion of consumer products that contain substances that can harm human health or the environment. Hazardous products are often found in the categories of automotive and home improvement products, cleaners, and pesticides. A product is *hazardous* if it exhibits one or more of the following properties: flammable/ignitable, explosive/reactive, corrosive, toxic, and radioactive."[12]

Note that this last definition includes "radioactive" (discarded smoke detectors are the main culprits), yet most state and local programs refuse to accept smoke detectors in their collection services due to unique regulatory and handling concerns. Other states (*e.g.,* Kentucky) include "irritant" as a characteristic, while others (*e.g.,* Washington and California) expand the toxicity characteristics well beyond federal definitions to include more stringent toxicity tests as well as carcinogenicity and persistence.

In summary, *household hazardous waste* can be defined as a loose category of wastes from residential sources that contain chemical ingredients or properties that present one or more concerns due to hazards in their use or storage, in their handling in municipal waste streams, or in their ultimate disposal in the environment.

Universal Waste

An interesting subset of hazardous wastes was created by U.S. EPA in 1995 as a way to promote recycling of certain problem wastes, especially those containing heavy metals such as mercury, cadmium, and lead. Universal waste rules streamline regulatory requirements for batteries, certain pesticides, mercury-containing equipment (such as thermostats), and lamps (especially fluorescent bulbs that contain mercury). These rules promote greater proper handling of these widely generated ("universal") wastes by, for example, making it easier to accumulate them on-site and to ship through a common carrier, as well as simplifying the associated paperwork. Note that states may add to the federal list as they incorporate universal wastes into state-level regulations; Maine, Maryland, and Vermont, for example, include PCB-containing light ballasts. Many states now include cathode ray tubes and a wide range of consumer electronics; New Jersey and Texas include oil-based paints; New Hampshire includes antifreeze; Michigan includes pharmaceuticals. The federal regulations for universal wastes are set out in *40 CFR 273*. While universal wastes directly address regulated sources such as small businesses, programs that manage these wastes often include households as well as other sources.

Product vs. Waste

An important distinction that has already been woven into this chapter is that of *hazardous household product* vs. *household hazardous waste*. Officially, a household substance does not become an HHW until it is discarded. Hazardous products abound, however, and are clearly the subject of this book and its concerns. Many "HHW" programs around the country include issues related to hazardous product use, storage, exposure and safety, in addition to management of the unused residuals at the time of discard. Subsequent sections of this chapter make a case for broadening the purview of HHW programs to include "HHP" and the whole range of chemical exposure issues.

Signal Words: Poison, Danger, Warning, Caution

Two federal laws unrelated to hazardous waste require certain signal words and other hazard warnings to appear on consumer product labels if the contents exhibit hazardous properties. These warning statements are intended to alert consumers to health or environmental hazards primarily during use of the product rather than concerns related to disposal of unwanted product. For products other than pesticides, these signal words are required under the Federal Hazardous Substances Act (administered by the Consumer Product Safety Commission). For pesticides, some of the same signal words are used with a slight variation on their definitions, under the Federal Insecticide, Fungicide and Rodenticide Act. Table 1.3 shows these important words and their different meanings. While these

Table 1.3. Signal Words on Consumer Product Labels. Important signal words are required on some, but not all, consumer products in the U.S. These words offer clues to the hazardous nature of the products or to their ingredients.*

Label	Requirements
Non-pesticide label requirements**	Danger: the product is extremely flammable, extremely corrosive, or highly toxic.
	Poison: the product is highly toxic.
	Warning or Caution: indicates products with lesser hazards; used interchangeably.
	Must contain statement "Keep out of reach of children" or its practical equivalent.
	Must contain description of the principal hazards involved in using the product. Words and phrases used to describe these hazards include: Flammable, Corrosive, Vapor harmful, Harmful if absorbed through skin.
Pesticide label requirements	Danger or Poison: the product is highly toxic or corrosive.
	Warning: the product is moderately toxic or irritating.
	Caution: the product is slightly toxic or irritating.
	Must contain the statement "Keep out of reach of children" on the front label. All registered pesticide labels must at a minimum bear the signal word "caution."
	Must contain information on any fire, explosion, or chemical hazards the pesticide poses.
	Must contain information on how to avoid the product's hazards.

Source: Compiled from various sources.

  *It should be noted that the Consumer Product Safety Commission refers to a "hazardous product" as anything that can cause harm, including chain saws, nail guns, poorly designed items that can injure children, electric fans, and small parts that can choke infants, not just chemicals. Regarding HHW, we refer to household products that contain hazardous chemicals or that present a chemical-related hazard in use or disposal.

**These signal words are not required on food, drugs, or cosmetics, which are regulated under different rules by the U.S. Food and Drug Administration.

signal words offer clues for certain products, and are often referenced in public information regarding HHW, they do not exactly match the suite of products considered HHW and should be used carefully when defining what is in and what is out of consideration.

The information available on labels has significant limitations. All ingredients are not listed (although foods, drugs, and personal care product labels do list most ingredients). Pesticides only name and quantify the "active" ingredients, those directly responsible for pesticidal action; the rest of the ingredients (which often account for 90+ percent of the product) go unidentified under the catch-all "inert" or, more recently, "other." Only pesticides are required to include disposal and environmental hazards information, and until recently (about 2001) recommended disposal methods often ran contrary to current local or state guidelines. Signal words are linked to acute human health hazards only; the signal words do not address chronic health hazards and they do not correlate with environmental hazards. Some chronic health hazards are now required to be listed separately by the Consumer Product Safety Commission, but such information is entirely risk-based and does not routinely identify the presence of carcinogens or other chronic hazards.

Small Business/"CESQG" Waste

Federal and most state rules recognize a category of hazardous waste generated by entities other than households that are in many ways similar to HHW (in some cases the very same product purchased at the big-box hardware store) and often disposed in municipal solid waste facilities due to their small quantities. These commercial (non-household generated) wastes are conditionally exempt from RCRA and most state regulations, and are referred to as "Conditionally Exempt Small Quantity Generator" ("CESQG") wastes. (Some states refer to them as "SQG," "VSQG," "moderate risk," or a variety of other titles.)

Officially (by federal and most state regulations), conditionally exempt small quantity generators produce no more than 100 kilograms (about 220 pounds or 25 gallons) of hazardous waste, and no more than 1 kilogram (about 2.2 pounds or less than 1 quart) of acutely hazardous waste in any calendar month *and* never accumulate more than 1,000 kilograms of hazardous waste or 1 kilogram of acutely hazardous waste on-site at one time.

CESQGs typically include such commercial entities as automobile service stations, small auto body or collision repair shops, dry cleaners, sign painters, printers, landscapers, small laboratories, medical clinics—a wide variety of businesses (or governmental shops) that generate relatively small amounts of wastes that designate as hazardous. The key is the amount of waste generated—even some large businesses can be CESQGs if they manage their hazardous materials carefully.

This is an important category of wastes of which to be aware. State rules vary widely on how these wastes should be handled, or even if this conditional exemption exists. Many state and local programs collect these CESQG wastes with, or in parallel with, HHW services. It is very important to make distinctions and to follow state rules to the letter. If CESQG wastes are co-mingled with HHW, all of the resulting wastes must be handled as hazardous following state and federal requirements—the mixed waste loses its household exemption. Practically, that is often not a big deal if all HHW is handled as hazardous waste anyway. It is worth repeating that some states do not recognize the small-quantity exemption at all and "regulate to zero." Check out this category carefully with your state regulators before launching any CESQG services.

Agricultural Pesticide Wastes

Another interesting category to consider is waste pesticides from small farms. The first officially recognized HHW service in the U.S. was a pesticide-only collection event held in Kentucky in 1981 (see next chapter). It is noteworthy that farm pesticide collections and HHW collections sprang up at the same time in history, and have been closely intertwined in many areas.

Most states or regions with significant agriculture sponsor or help to coordinate agricultural pesticide collection services, often in partnership with private companies and associations. Contact your state department of agriculture to inquire about such services. The Pesticide Stewardship Alliance[13] is a non-profit organization that coordinates these programs across the United States.

Hazardous Ingredients vs. Hazardous Products

A household product is not necessarily hazardous because it contains a hazardous ingredient. In most traditional situations, the amount of the hazardous ingredient has a lot to do with how hazardous the product is itself. Some ingredients, but certainly not all, can be diluted to a point where their hazard becomes negligible.

Lye (sodium hydroxide), for example, is an extremely corrosive chemical when concentrated. Drain openers such as Drano® contain almost 100% lye and are extremely dangerous as an immediate or acute hazard. Some products that contain only a small percentage of sodium hydroxide, on the other hand, are not corrosive. Similarly, concentrated acetic acid is corrosive, but vinegar, which is about 5% acetic acid, is generally regarded as non-corrosive and is used in foods. Acids and bases are good examples of chemicals for which the hazard is directly related to concentration.

In contrast, other ingredients are so toxic or otherwise dangerous that even small amounts can be hazardous in consumer products. Lead, for example, is an extremely toxic metal, which even in small amounts causes central nervous system damage and loss of intelligence in children. Since lead is accumulated in the body, even small additional doses are of great concern and no safe dose of lead is recognized. Substances that cause cancer are also still of concern even in tiny amounts because even though the cancer risk decreases with concentration, for some types of carcinogens it never goes to zero, according to current theories.[14] Although the risk to a particular individual might be fairly small, if a large number of people use the product, some of them will get cancer. To those unlucky individuals, the small degree of their predicted risk is no consolation.

Ingredients that are known endocrine disruptors are also of concern even at very low concentrations, and particularly for exposure to pregnant women, fetuses, and very young children. These substances interfere with hormonal processes, some of which are critical during pregnancy and early development. Some endocrine disruptors display inverted dose-response relationships, so that over certain dose regions, smaller doses are actually more dangerous than larger doses. Inverted dose-response curves turn on its head the traditional adage "the dose makes the poison," meaning that small enough doses are always harmless.

Finally, worldwide attention has focused on toxic chemicals that are persistent and accumulate in animal tissues. These so-called "PBTs" (persistent, bioaccumulative, toxic chemicals) or "POPs" (persistent organic pollutants) include older organochlorine pesticides such as DDT and chlordane, as well as newer ingredients such as PBDE (poly-brominated diphenyl ether) flame retardants and PFOAs (perfluoro-octanoic acids) used in the manufacture of non-stick surfaces such as Teflon®.[15] PBTs are of concern even in small concentrations because their residues can build up continuously in the environment and in animals, eventually reaching levels that produce adverse effects. Even management of these products as hazardous waste at the end of their lifecycle may not be sufficient to prevent damage because off-gassing of hazardous components during use may cause them to build up in indoor air, house dust, food, or users' bodies. Products containing these ingredients are a whole new can of worms often unrelated to the traditional HHW.

Why HHW Is Considered a Problem

It is important to describe in general terms why small amounts of hazardous household products can cause problems either in their use or storage or when they are disposed (known then as household hazardous waste).

Household products contain many of the same toxic chemicals used in industry, small businesses, and agriculture. While consumer products often come in smaller sizes or contain lower concentrations of hazardous ingredients, the shelves of grocery and hardware stores contain a wide variety of extremely hazardous products and products with high concentrations of hazardous ingredients. For example, one can buy 100% petroleum naphtha (spot remover, paint thinner, or charcoal lighter fluid), 100% sodium hydroxide (drain opener), 100% paradichlorobenzene (mothballs), 100% naphthalene (mothballs), 100% methyl ethyl ketone (solvent), 85% methylene chloride (paint remover), 50% malathion (garden insecticide), 12% sodium hypochlorite (pool chemical), and 4 molar hydrofluoric acid (rust remover). These products exhibit all of the properties of industrial hazardous waste and need to be handled with extreme care during use, storage, and disposal in order to avoid potentially serious health or environmental damage. Even products that contain only small amounts of hazardous ingredients can sometimes be hazardous themselves, sometimes because of undisclosed ingredients such as so-called "inert" ingredients in pesticides, the designation of which is purely a technicality and does not indicate safety or lack of hazardous properties.

Home Poisoning Incidents

Accidental exposures to chemical products in the home are fairly common and, about half of the time, involve children under six years of age. Over the years 2000 to 2005 the number of cases handled by U.S. poison control centers ranged from about 2.2 to 2.4 million per year, or 8.0 to 8.3 exposures per thousand population.[16] Roughly half of these exposures were to household pharmaceuticals, the other half to all other types of products such as cleaners, cosmetics, paints, and pesticides. By far, the majority of reported exposures were acute (91.5% in 2005) rather than chronic. Poison Control Center data include deliberate exposures as well, but they are a small fraction of the total. The three product categories most often involved in human exposures in 2005 were analgesic medications (11.7%), cosmetics/personal care products (9.2%), and household cleaners (9.0%). These figures reflect the availability of the substances rather than their toxicity. In 2005 there were 1,352,831 reported non-pharmaceutical exposures, resulting in 54,635 moderately serious outcomes, 4,783 major outcomes, and 464 deaths. In addition, there were 1,412,834 reported pharmaceutical exposures, resulting in 129,026 moderate outcomes, 29,171 major outcomes, and 2,598 deaths. From an acute outcome perspective, corrosives are especially likely to cause serious injuries, with moderate to lethal outcomes at 14.9% for alkaline oven cleaners, 13.8% for alkaline drain cleaners, 8.97% for acid rust removers, and 6.8% for acid toilet cleaners. By contrast, all cleaning products together averaged only 3.8% and all non-pharmaceutical products 4.4%. Pharmaceutical products averaged 11.4% moderate to lethal outcomes.[17] Also extremely dangerous are solvent products, which if ingested, can be aspirated into the lungs causing potentially fatal pneumonitis. Exposures to household chemicals are exacerbated by improper storage, hazardous products that resemble candy or food containers, hazardous products with pleasant odors, and failure or inability to read labels.

Chronic Health Effects

Unlike acute health effects, effects from chronic exposures can seldom be attributed to particular products because symptoms are delayed and an association is difficult to establish long after the fact. It is well known, however, that consumer products contain a host of ingredients that may be carcinogens, reproductive and developmental toxicants, endocrine disruptors, neurotoxicants, etc., as shown in Table 1.4. U.S. EPA's TEAM (Total Exposure Assessment Methodology) studies in 1987 found that indoor concentrations of a dozen common organic pollutants were 2 to 5 times higher than in air outdoors.[18] The risk of health effects depends on ingredient toxicity and exposure partly during product use, which can vary widely depending on frequency and duration of use, ventilation, and compliance with label warnings. However, ongoing exposure also occurs from contaminants in both indoor air and house dust.[19, 20, 21] Although risk assessment is fraught with uncertainties and is often controversial, a few better known examples are worth mentioning.

In 2002 the U.S. EPA cancelled all consumer uses of the popular arsenic-treated wood called CCA (chromated copper arsenate). It was used for building decks, railings, fences, posts, and other outdoor wooden structures. Although the agency stopped short of concluding that the wood posed unreasonable risk, EPA did state that "phase-out of these uses will reduce the potential exposure risk to arsenic, a known human carcinogen, thereby protecting human health, especially children's health and the environment."[22] Risk assessments by the states of Maine[23, 24] and California,[25] as well as the University of Florida, had found high cancer risks. This was in contrast to studies by the wood preservative industry[26] and the Consumer Product Safety Commission.[27] It had long been clear that exposure to CCA sawdust was hazardous and that burning the wood was unacceptable. Billions of board feet of CCA-treated lumber remaining in service will be discarded over the next 20+ years.[28] Arsenic-treated wood is exempt from federal regulation as a hazardous waste but may be subject to more stringent regulation in some states. Concerns have been raised about the disposal of arsenic-treated wood in landfills,[29, 30] and some studies and calculations indicate that it would fail the Toxicity Characteristic Leaching Procedure (TCLP) leaching test and the more stringent Waste Extraction Test (WET) required in California.[31, 32]

Lead from household paint remains a significant risk to children long after its use was discontinued in 1978. Even today, children suffer loss of intelligence from ingesting peeling paint chips or the dust in pre-1978 homes, and are threatened by remodeling projects that release lead that is buried under subsequent coats of paint. Since 1973, the action level of lead in children's blood (the point at which exposure reduction is recommended) has been lowered from 40 to 10 micrograms/deciliter, and the argument has been made

Table 1.4. Chronic Hazards Associated with Selected Ingredients in Consumer Products.

Ingredient	Found in	Qty	Health Effect
Arsenic[a]	CCA-treated wood	.6–6 kg/m^3	known carcinogen
Carbaryl[b]	Sevin® insecticides	1–22.5%	likely carcinogen
Lead	progressive hair dye[c]	3,000–6,000 ppm	carcinogen, neurotoxic
	paint (pre-1978)[d]	1–50%	
	solder, electronics[e]	37–40%	
	some vinyl products[f]	2,000–12,000 ppm	
Mercury[g]	thermometers, thermostats	.5g, 3g average	neurotoxicant
	fluorescent light bulbs	10–50 mg	
Methylene chloride[h]	paint removers	<85%	possible carcinogen
p-dichlorobenzene	mothballs, toilet deodorizers	~100%	possible carcinogen
bisphenol A[i]	polycarbonate plastic		endocrine disruptor
DEHP[j]	vinyl tile, shower curtains	6–40%	endocrine disruptor
			possible carcinogen
			developmental toxicant
permethrin[k]	household insecticides	<2.5%	likely carcinogen

[a] Arsenic as As2O5 in outer portion of wood. Lower range is typical for above-ground uses. (American Wood-Preservers Association, *Standards 2001* (Granbury, Tex.: American Wood-Preservers' Association, 2001).

[b] Carbaryl percent active ingredient from labels of typical consumer-use products.

[c] Results from paper published by Mielke in 1997 and cited by Howard W. Mielke, Myiesha D. Taylor, Chris R. Gonzales, M. Kelley Smith, Pamala V. Daniels, and Ayanna V. Buckner, "Lead Based Hair Products: Too Hazardous for Household Use," www.uwsp.edu/geo/courses/geog100/MielkeHairLead1. htm (17 Apr. 2007). In 1997, the Center for Environmental Health filed suit against the manufacturers. The suit was settled in January 1998 with an agreement by the manufacturer to attempt to reduce the amount of lead acetate by 50%. Thus, current product would be expected to contain approximately the concentration listed.

[d] Cushing N. Dolbeare and Don Ryan, *Getting the Lead Out: Controlling Lead Paint Hazards in Housing*, National Housing Institute, Shelterforce Online. September/October 1997. www.nhi.org/online/issues/95/lead.html (17 Apr. 2007).

[e] Eutectic (the lowest melting temperature) tin/lead solder is 37% lead. Typical commercial electronic solders were 40% lead before the introduction of lead-free solders.

[f] Clifford Rechtschaffen and Patrick Williams, "The Continued Success of Proposition 65 in Reducing Toxic Exposures," *ELR News and Analysis* 35 (December 2005): 10850–10856.

[g] Purdue University, *What Devices Contain Mercury?* www.purdue.edu/dp/envirosoft/mercbuild/src/devicepage.htm (17 Apr. 2007).

[h] Methylene chloride content from material safety data sheets for typical products.

[i] Polycarbonate plastic is a polymer of bisphenol A.

[j] 6–23%: Jane Poors and René Fuhlendorff, Survey No. 1. Phthalates and Organic Tin Compounds in PFC Products. http://glwww.mst.dk/chemi/01080100.htm (17 Apr. 2007). Up to 40%: Jouni J.K. Jaakkola, Leif Øie, Per Nafstad, Grete Botten, Sven Ove Samuelsen, and Per Magnus, "Interior Surface Materials in the Home and the Development of Bronchial Obstruction in Young Children in Oslo, Norway," *American Journal of Public Health* 89, no. 2 (February 1999): 188–192.

[k] Permethrin concentrations determined from product labels of typical consumer insecticides.

that it should be lowered even further to 2 micrograms/deciliter.[33] Toxicologist Steve Gilbert notes, "Currently, there appears to be no safe level of lead exposure for the developing child."[34] Lead-based paint turns up regularly at HHW collection sites and is a serious potential source of contamination of recycled paint.

Widespread mercury contamination of certain types of fish has resulted in numerous local health advisories and recommendations that pregnant women and young children avoid consuming some kinds of fish and limit consumption of others.[35] According to the National Research Council, more than 60,000 children born each year are at risk from neurodevelopmental effects due to methylmercury.[36] The sources of this contamination are myriad, and include mines, coal-power plants, refineries, laboratories, garbage incinerators, municipal sewage plants, auto wreckers and repair shops, cement plants, and printing industries.[37] Household products including batteries, thermometers, thermostats, switches, fluorescent bulbs, and other devices also contribute to mercury entering the environment through incineration, deposition, and evaporation. The Washington State Department of Ecology estimates that of the 3,900–5,000 pounds of mercury released into the environment each year from human activities within the state, nearly 2,000 pounds could be prevented by improving waste-separation and disposal methods in dentistry, households, medical facilities, and other product-based sources.[38] Washington as well as a number of other states has banned the sale or distribution of thermometers, manometers, and novelty items such as toys, games, or jewelry that contain mercury. Mercury fever and air thermometers, that are still in many homes, and fluorescent bulbs also pose a risk to consumers if the mercury is released through breakage and not properly cleaned up and disposed.[39]

Polyvinyl chloride (PVC) is not a material currently considered hazardous and collected by most HHW programs, but evidence is accumulating of harmful effects not only from its production, but also from its use and disposal. DEHP (di (2-ethyl-hexyl) phthalate) is a plasticizer used in many PVC plastic applications. In the home, DEHP and other phthalate esters can be found in articles such as floor tiles, plastic shower curtains, and other objects[40] not usually considered hazardous by existing definitions. DEHP has been frequently identified in indoor air and house dust,[41, 42, 43] and is a common contaminant of wastewater.[44] The CDC found nearly universal exposures to DEHP in the American population, with higher exposures in children than in adults.[45] The National Toxicology Program has expressed concern about current DEHP exposures to infants and toddlers due to possible effects on the developing reproductive system.[46] The source of residential DEHP exposures has not yet been quantitatively attributed to specific household products, but studies have identified DEHP in emissions from PVC flooring[47] and correlated dust concentrations with the presence of PVC in building materials.[48] Vinyl products pose other risks as well, especially if burned in a house or car fire or incinerated in garbage. Burning PVC produces dioxins as well as hydrochloric acid mist, a major concern for firefighters.[49] Even under ordinary circumstances, some PVC products may pose health risks. Young children exposed to PVC flooring had nearly twice the risk of developing bronchial obstruction (a mechanism of asthma) as did those not exposed[50] and, in another study, exposure to DEHP in house dust was correlated both with the amount of PVC in homes and with asthma.[51] Equilibrium concentrations of toluene and methyl isobutyl ketone off-gassed from new vinyl shower curtains surpassed short-term occupational exposure limits and can elevate indoor air toxic concentrations for more than a month.[52] High levels of lead have also been found from time to time in a variety of PVC products, including lunch boxes, window blinds, toys, and clothing. A report for the European Commission estimated that 28 percent of the lead in municipal waste landfills might be attributed to PVC products.[53]

Para-dichlorobenzene (p-DCB) is used in some kinds of mothballs and toilet deodorizers and is a possible human carcinogen. It sublimates directly from solid to gas continuously when in use, causing an immediate and long-lasting effect on indoor air quality. In a monitoring study,[54] when a single block of p-DCB deodorant was placed in a toilet bowl in a home with no other known sources of p-DCB, the indoor air concentration increased from 1 ug/m3 to between 100 and 600 ug/m^3. The compound also increased in the breath of residents of the home, from 1 ug/m3 to 40 ug/m^3. Although far below workplace exposure limits, typical p-DCB concentrations may significantly increase cancer risk. Based on the cancer potency and typical indoor air concentrations in California studies, lifetime cancer risk for indoor exposure to p-DCB would range from 44 to 1,750 per million people.[55] (An "acceptable" cancer risk is usually considered to be 1 per million). The lower estimate is based on lowest mean summer indoor concentrations, while the upper estimate uses 90th percentile winter concentrations. Actual risk would be reduced slightly because outdoor air has much lower concentrations of p-DCB. A person who spent on average 75% of his or her time indoors would have three-quarters of the estimated risk, or approximately 33 to 1,300 times the acceptable risk. All consumer products containing paradichlorobenzene were banned in California on December 31, 2006. Other states have yet to follow.

Environmental Risks from Product Use

Many household products pose risks to pets, birds, aquatic life, beneficial insects, and other environmental species. Metaldehyde-based slug baits are especially dangerous to dogs. The number of poisonings is impossible to estimate because there is no comprehensive publicly available database comparable to Poison Control Center statistics. EPA reports 285 calls regarding metaldehyde exposure to domestic animals from 2001 through mid-2004,[56] but this figure is surely a small fraction of the total. According to Dolder,[57] if a 10-pound dog ingests a typical 2% metaldehyde bait, about 4 ounces of bait can be fatal and a dose of as little of one-tenth of a teaspoon warrants decontamination and possible treatment, although no antidote exists.

Dogs and cats are also at high risk from antifreeze left unattended in a garage or spilled on the floor, driveway, or street. Based on lethal doses for cats (1,650 mg/kg) and dogs (5,500 mg/kg),[58] approximately 7 ml and 22 ml of ethylene glycol (essentially pure antifreeze) would be fatal to a 10 pound cat or dog, respectively. Since a 1:1 dilution with water is standard in use, discarded radiator fluid would be half as toxic based on the ethylene glycol, but may have additional additives or leached metals that could increase its toxicity. Dogs are more likely than cats to ingest significant amounts of antifreeze because they eat large, infrequent meals and because the sweet taste appeals to them, whereas cats cannot detect sweet substances.[59] Propylene glycol, with a lower toxicity, is in some cases a substitute.

stormwater runoff from urban landscapes is an important source of pesticides and fertilizers in small streams. U.S. Geological Survey studies in western Washington in the 1990s identified more than 20 separate pesticides in urban streams.[60] In the Seattle/King County area, five ingredients in common lawncare products were detected at all sites studied.[61] Five insecticides were sometimes measured at concentrations that posed potential risks to aquatic life. Three of those ingredients (diazinon, chlorpyrifos, and lindane) have been phased out or highly restricted since the studies were done, in part because of aquatic toxicity concerns, but replacement pyrethroid insecticides have caused aquatic toxicity in urban California streams.[62] Sources of the pesticides in both the Washington and California studies could include both consumer and professional landscape applications.

Widely available rodenticide baits, especially those containing the active ingredient brodifacoum, are disproportionately implicated in the death of wildlife. Such incidents can occur from direct ingestion of bait by birds or mammals, but also from secondary poisoning, in which a predator eats a poisoned rodent and is then killed by the toxic residue in the dead animal's body. Here again, incident reports drastically underestimate the magnitude of the problem because most carcasses are never found, much less analyzed. However, the reports are useful in identifying the particular chemicals most responsible. Residues of anticoagulant rodenticides have been detected in 27 species of wild birds and 17 species of wild mammals. Brodifacoum was found in 87% of 290 dead birds and 83% of 218 dead mammals.[63] It is impossible to know how many of these incidents involved homeowner use of rodenticides as opposed to professional use, but EPA has stated that professional applicators are much more likely to know when to use the products and how to use them in order to limit risks. EPA has proposed making single-feeding anticoagulant baits such as brodifacoum restricted-use pesticides in order to prevent consumer misuse.[64]

Health Hazards from Improper Disposal

One of the classic hazards associated with improper disposal of HHW involves injuries to solid waste workers. While these workers in the U.S. suffer one of the highest injury rates for any occupation, mostly based on direct physical or impact hazards, chemical exposures to ingredients in the trash play a part.[65] Such injuries are anecdotal yet widespread among trash haulers. One of the most widely publicized tragedies occurred in New York City in 1996, when sanitation worker Mike Hanly was killed from exposure to concentrated hydrofluoric acid that had been left at the curb for residential garbage pick-up.[66] In another tragic incident in Paterson, New Jersey, in 1997, aerosol hairspray cans burst in a recycling facility and the fumes ignited, killing one worker and severely burning another.[67]

Explosions and fires in solid waste handling are widespread, although data are mostly anecdotal and not systematically documented. Reactions of common household products such as chlorine bleach with soda pop or bases with acids result in fires inside solid waste trucks, at transfer stations, in shredders, and at landfills.[68] Cans with even small amounts of gasoline or paint solvents may explode, damaging equipment as well as endangering workers.

Similar hazards are present in sewers when volatile organic solvents such as paint thinners, degreasers, or paint strippers are disposed down the drain. In one memorable incident in Seattle in 1982, solvent fumes in a residential sewer were ignited by a furnace pilot light, resulting in damage to a full block of utilities and street surface.[69] In a similar incident in Laurens, Iowa, in 2005, an ignitable product in a neighborhood sewer caused explosions, fire damage, and noxious fumes over a three-block area.[70]

Environmental Risks from Improper Disposal

Fully 25% of the United States' population uses on-site (septic tank and drainfield) systems for their wastewater treatment.[71] This translates into more than four billion gallons of wastewater per day dispersed below the ground's surface.[72] Domestic sewage includes whatever goes down the drain or toilet in use or in direct disposal, including potentially any and all consumer products. On-site systems are particularly sensitive to, and not designed to treat, toxic or otherwise hazardous chemicals. Cleaning solvents have been well documented to pass through on-site systems and contaminate groundwater.[73–76] Chlorine bleach, disinfectant, and lye-based drain opener have all been documented to "destroy" the bacteria in a domestic septic tank at very low concentrations;[77] of particular note, it took only 0.4 ounce of the drain opener to kill all of the bacteria in a 1,000 gallon tank. U.S. EPA notes, "Flushing household chemicals, gasoline, oil, pesticides, antifreeze, and paint can stress or destroy the biological treatment taking place in the system or might contaminate surface waters and groundwater."[78]

Domestic sewage has been found to contain a wide variety of heavy metals and organic compounds.[79, 80, 81] While many of these chemicals come from leaching of pipes, from food sources, and even from the drinking water inflow, some are added from consumer products in normal use (*e.g.,* laundry detergents, automatic dishwashing detergents, bleaches, cleaners, drain openers), from the house dust found on clothing that washes off in the laundry, and from direct disposal of unused products. A surprising amount of arsenic comes from detergents.[82] Some other metals such as chrome and zinc are unusually concentrated in cosmetics and personal care products. Zinc has even been implicated in permit violations in small treatment plants from baby diaper ointments.[83]

Some of the "emerging" chemicals of concern to wastewater treatment agencies include nonylphenol ethoxylate, a surfactant (surface-active agent) still used in many detergents, of which the breakdown product, nonylphenol, is a known endocrine disruptor; triclosan, a nearly ubiquitous antimicrobial additive in soaps and other products; antibiotics, antidepressants, analgesics, and a wide range of other pharmaceuticals; bisphenol-A, another known endocrine disruptor that leaches out of polycarbonate plastics; and ethynylestradiol, synthetic estrogen from birth control pills.[84, 85] Many of these emerging compounds have also been documented in septic tank effluents.[86]

In 2005 Americans produced 245 million tons of municipal solid waste (also known as trash, garbage, refuse, rubbish, "MSW"), which is approximately 4.5 pounds of waste per person per day. Of this total, 32 percent is recovered and recycled or composted, 14 percent is burned at combustion facilities, and the remaining 54 percent is disposed in landfills.[87]

Various MSW characterization studies have documented household hazardous wastes to represent between 0.3 and 0.6 percent by weight.[88–96] This range has not seemed to change noticeably in the past 20 years, which might be due to the relatively small amounts of HHW involved when compared to the large volumes of paper, food waste, plastics, and other main MSW constituents. Even though roughly one-half-of-one percent does not sound like much on a relative basis, the size of the numbers involved on an absolute basis show that the HHW that is thrown away in residential trash represents more than one million tons per year in the municipal solid waste stream of the U.S.[97] (Nighingale and Donnette cite a figure of 1% HHW in MSW as a general average, and note that such an amount represents 2.75 million tons per year in American solid waste.[98])

Concerns about the combustion of solid waste center on heavy metals, particularly mercury but also lead and cadmium. This has been a major issue for those areas using waste-to-energy ("WTE") or other combustion technologies. Mercury in MSW combustors peaked in the late 1980s and has since been declining. Mid-1990s estimates still showed MSW combustors to be one of the largest identifiable sources of mercury (at 19% of total national emissions),[99] but trends since then have continued to decrease, both due to reductions of sources from MSW (such as from batteries) and improved treatment technologies. Even with these reductions and improvements, when judged on an energy-generating basis, "WTE plant's mercury emissions compare with coal plants on the basis of each kilowatt-hour-generated by a facility."[100] Production of various chlorinated dioxins and furans are another major concern within MSW combustors. PVC plastics are implicated as a major chlorine source and precursor within MSW.[101] Tremendous improvements in control technologies in recent years have resulted in an estimated 99% reduction in the dioxin emissions from MSW combustors in the U.S. between 1987 and 2000; they still represent the third largest quantifiable source as of EPA's year-2000 estimates.[102] Ash management (bottom ash at 90–95% by volume, plus fly ash at 5–10%) is a related concern for combustors, since the ash, especially fly ash, concentrates metals (cadmium, copper, lead, zinc) as well as captured dioxins.[103]

In an interesting parallel with on-site wastewater systems in rural areas, use of backyard burn barrels for household solid waste is a major issue when it comes to release of hazardous chemicals to the environment. An estimated 28% of people living in rural and non-urban areas in the U.S. (which include 21% of the total U.S. population as of the 2000 census) burn their household refuse in backyard barrels. EPA notes, "The low combustion temperatures and oxygen-starved conditions associated with the burning of household refuse in 'burn barrels' results in poor and uncontrolled combustion conditions."[104] These backyard barrels now represent the single largest estimated source of dioxins in the U.S. —fully one-third of all emissions.[105, 106] Emissions from burn barrels also have been documented to include lead, mercury, and hexachlorobenzene,[107] the elements presumably from constituents in consumer products or packaging, the chlorinated benzene likely as a result of the combustion process.

Landfills present different issues from combustion. Today's practices attempt to "entomb" MSW in dry, airtight cells within a landfill, and include bans on the disposal of liquids and capping efforts to prevent water from getting in. Leachate (the liquid that does drain out of a landfill – "garbage soup"[108]) is collected and, in many areas, sent to a municipal wastewater treatment plant for management. Many metals and organic compounds show up in MSW landfill leachate.[109–112] Certain chlorinated volatile organic compounds ("VOCs") have been documented both in leachate and in landfill gas, including trichloroethane, perchloroethane, and vinyl chloride.[113–114] Many of the same "emerging" contaminants as mentioned above have also been detected in landfill leachate.[115–116] Production of chlorinated dioxins and furans is also a concern in landfill gas.[117] HHW likely represents the major remaining source of VOCs in landfills after full implementation of the screening and regulated hazardous waste exclusion requirements of 1991. "Diverting HHW and CESQG wastes in significant proportions from MSW could reasonably be expected to further reduce VOCs in landfill gas."[118] An excellent review paper by Slack *et al.* (2005) presents a thorough overview of hazardous chemicals in municipal landfills, including detailed tables of organic compounds and metals documented in MSW leachate and possible sources of these materials in HHW.[119] Efforts to reduce or eliminate hazardous chemicals in the MSW will assist in long-term management of landfills, leachate, gas production, and eventual closure of these facilities.[120]

The Range of Product Categories Considered HHW

Old Legacies

Many old chemical products no longer sold today remain ubiquitous, collecting dust on grandpa's shelves in the basement, garage, shed, or barn. Every program in the country that has collected HHW from the public over the past 27 years has experienced receipt of products that are 50 or more years old. The pesticide dichloro-diphenyl-trichloroethane ("DDT"), for example, was surprisingly common as a consumer product until its cancellation in the early-to-mid 1970s. It still routinely shows up in HHW collections across the country. Arsenic trioxide, carbon tetrachloride, strychnine, white lead, picric acid, ethyl ether, and many, many other hazardous chemicals are still out there, in need of safe handling and proper waste management. This is a very important category of HHW and represents significant human health and safety concerns in addition to environmental concerns. Old legacy products are reason enough to provide some minimal level of HHW collection services in any community.

These old legacies include the following examples:

- *Banned pesticides.* DDT, aldrin, dieldrin, chlordane, arsenicals, strychnine, pentachlorophenol—the list is long and is continuously added to as more of these highly hazardous chemicals are removed from the market.[121]

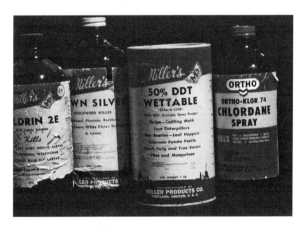

Figure 1.1. Old Legacies I. (*Photo by Dave Galvin*)

- *Leaded paints.* Before 1978, many household paints contained white lead as a pigment and drying agent. Old cans of lead paint are still part of the HHW inventory in many older homes.

Figure 1.2. Old Legacies II. (*Photo by Dave Waddell, used with permission*)

- *PCB ballasts*. Polychlorinated Biphenyls were used in fluorescent light ballasts until 1977. Any old ballast that does not have a clear label saying "contains no PCBs" must be assumed to have this persistent, bioaccumulative, toxic chemical. Ham radio testing oils, contained in a pail or drum known as a "dummy-load," also often used PCBs and have shown up at collections.
- *Aerosols with CFCs*. Chlorofluorocarbons were commonly used as propellants in aerosol products, but have been phased out since the mid 1990s. Old aerosol cans still linger. (Note, that until very recently asthma inhalers were exempted as an essential use for CFCs, but most have now changed to other propellants).

Figure 1.2. Old Legacies III. (*Photo by Doug Wechsler, used with permission*)

- *Exotics*. Gunpowder ingredients such as picric acid, old cleaning solvents such as ethyl ether and carbon tetrachloride, odd explosives, World War II ordnance, … you name it, we have seen it at HHW collections.

"Core" Hazardous Materials

A number of currently available household products classify under everybody's definitions as HHW when disposed, and have been at the core of all HHW programs over the past two decades. These include the following items:

- The *"old legacies"* noted above.
- *Most pesticides*. Insecticides, herbicides, fungicides, and other –cides are all designed to kill or repel some organisms. It is a complex group of products. While some "alternative" pesticides such as the 25(b) products[122] are much more benign than the rest, it is simpler to collect all unused pesticides rather than to try to tease out the variations one by one.
- *Oil-based paints, varnishes, and stains*. Petroleum distillates, mineral spirits, and other organic solvents form the base for these architectural coatings. They present flammability and toxicity concerns and, as liquid leftovers, are not usually allowed in regular municipal solid waste.
- *Organic-based solvents and cleaners*. Paint thinners, paint strippers, spot removers, degreasers, parts cleaners, and other organic solvents need special handling.
- *Harsh cleaners*. Many toilet bowl cleaners and masonry washes are strong acids such as hydrochloric (also known as muriatic) acid. On the other end of the pH scale, many lye-based drain openers and some oven cleaners are strong bases. To protect users as well as municipal solid waste workers, products with these pH extremes need to be handled very carefully.
- *Pool chemicals*. Products used to clean, sanitize, and balance swimming pools, hot tubs, and spas contain a range of acids and bases, oxidizers, and other hazardous chemicals. These products are generally recognized as hazardous (corrosive and/or reactive) and are routinely collected at HHW services.
- *Reactive chemicals*. Chlorine bleach, ammonia, and peroxides are all problematic products due to their tendencies to react with each other or with other common household items, often with explosive or toxic results.

Additional Hazardous Materials

Due to varying local conditions, regulations or historical quirks, a number of hazardous substances are often separately managed or subject to different waste management strategies in various state or local programs. These include some of the following materials:

- *Used motor oil*. Many do-it-yourself ("DIY") mechanics change their automotive lubricating oil. Used oil does not designate as a hazardous waste under federal RCRA characteristics, but it is included in the EPA generic HHW list (see Table

1.2) and is so designated by at least three states (California, Massachusetts, and Rhode Island). Various state and local programs throughout the country are well established to recycle this waste separately, such as at auto service stations, retail auto parts stores, even through curbside collection, but many HHW services do accept motor oil if it is brought in.

- *Oil filters*. Oil filters changed at the same time as lubricating oil often contain surprising amounts of remainder oil unless they are well drained (*i.e.*, hot-drained for 24 hours). Some filters used in heavy-duty pickup trucks or off-road vehicles used to be terne-coated, which presented extra concerns due to this tin-lead alloy; current filters no longer use this coating.

- *Antifreeze*. Ethylene glycol, the most commonly used antifreeze in radiator systems, is toxic to people and animals. Drained radiator fluid may also contain a number of heavy metals from the engine block and equipment, including high lead levels.[123] It should be recycled. Most states require special management.

- *Automotive (lead-acid) batteries*. The lead as well as the hazards of the sulfuric acid have compelled most states to set up separate recycling systems for car batteries. These systems often include a deposit upon purchase (known as an advance recycling fee) in order to encourage proper return of old batteries through service stations or automotive supply shops. The recovery rate for automotive batteries was estimated at 98% in 2005.[124]

- *Household (A-, C-, D-cell) batteries*. Most current general purpose batteries (the typical AA, AAA, C, and D cells) are "alkaline," composed of a zinc-manganese dioxide combination. Alkaline batteries now have the lion's share of the market over the older carbon zinc or zinc chloride cells. Lithium batteries are very long-lasting, and are becoming very common in these various cell sizes to fit digital cameras and other small electronic devices, as well as in 9-volt sizes for smoke detectors and other devices. Alkaline and zinc batteries are usually not considered hazardous since mercury was removed from them in the mid 1990s. Lithium batteries, on the other hand, are considered toxic and reactive. These small batteries are everywhere and so disposal is a common issue; many HHW programs accept them.

- *Button cell batteries*. The small round batteries used in watches, calculators, and many other small gadgets are typically mercuric-ozide or zinc-air, although lithium is gaining share in this market. These tiny batteries need special collection due to their mercury or lithium content. Silver-oxide buttons also require special collection to keep silver out of the environment.

- *Rechargeable batteries*. The traditional rechargeable battery has been the nickel-cadmium (NiCad). The market is being taken over by nickel-metal hydride (NiMH) batteries that seem to be a great improvement in both utility and reduced hazard. Many rechargeable devices such as cellphones and cameras use lithium-ion batteries. A national take-back system operated by the Rechargeable Battery Recycling Corporation ("RBRC")[125] safely collects and recycles rechargeable batteries. Local programs should promote this service and do not need to duplicate it.

- *Consumer electronic wastes*. Cathode ray tubes from televisions and computer monitors are heavy with lead. Many computers, cellphones, VCRs, radios, and a wide variety of other electronic gadgets contain sufficient amounts of mercury, cadmium, copper, beryllium, or other chemicals to qualify them as hazardous waste. Many also are treated with PBDE flame retardants. This "e-waste" stream has garnered increased attention in recent years, but has not been a traditional part of HHW programs. Some producer- or retailer-sponsored (or state-mandated) take-back systems are being set up. Encourage such comprehensive approaches to consumer electronics collection rather than taking on this complex and expensive waste handling at local HHW services.

- *Latex (water-based) paint.* Older latex paints (20+ years old) show up at many HHW collection services. These pre-1988 paints often contained mercury as a mildewcide and preservative. Modern latex paints are mercury-free, made with very low volatile organic compound (VOC) content, and use polymer-based pigments. They are usually considered non-hazardous. Many states do not consider latex paint as HHW, while many do; check out local conditions.
- *Fluorescent lamps.* All fluorescent lighting lamps, whether tubes or compacts, contain small amounts of mercury. Even the "green end cap" or "low mercury" lamps that do not designate as hazardous under RCRA's standard TCLP test still contain 3–4 mg of mercury, as do the compact "curly" bulbs. All fluorescent lamps need to be handled separately from municipal solid waste in order to capture this mercury rather than release it into the environment. Some state-mandated take-back systems are being set up; more are needed.
- *Other mercury-containing products.* Thermostats, thermometers, sphygmomanometers, auto tilt-switches, and many other devices contain elemental mercury, often in large individual amounts. All of these legacy uses of mercury need to be carefully swept out of homes for safe handling, to remove the safety hazard of exposure in the home through breakage as well as the long term environmental hazard of mercury releases in solid waste management systems. A national thermostat product stewardship system, the Thermostat Recycling Corporation ("TRC"),[126] is available.
- *Propane gas cylinders.* Small (*e.g.,* five-gallon/20-pound) gas cylinders that are typically used for outdoor grills present explosion concerns even when essentially empty. Fire code changes in 2002 resulted in overnight obsolescence for millions of these tanks. They continue to present challenges to solid waste management systems. Check with propane tank rental companies for take-back programs.
- *Aerosol cans.* Pre-1990s aerosol products often used chlorofluorocarbons ("CFCs") as propellants. Even modern aerosols present ongoing challenges for solid waste and HHW services due to explosion hazard as well as flammability of many of the contents (such as isobutyl propane).

Problem Wastes

The following types of wastes from households arise, but for one reason or another present operational challenges that usually prevent them from being accepted at typical HHW collections:

- *Asbestos.* Fibers of asbestos were commonly used in home, pipe, and duct insulation, wall and ceiling surfaces, tiles, and electrical equipment. Asbestos should only be removed by certified asbestos abatement contractors. Do-it-yourself removal is fraught with hazard and should be strongly discouraged. Small quantities that have been properly handled, wetted, sealed in thick plastic bags, etc., are sometimes accepted at some community HHW collections.

- *Leaded paint.* Remodeling projects in homes older than 1978, and especially in homes built before 1940, often involve removal of old paint that contains high concentrations of lead. As with asbestos, this is a significant health issue in the home. Such lead abatement should be left to certified professionals. If it is too late and leaded paint chips have been generated as a do-it-yourselfer waste, some HHW services will accept them.

- *Ammunition, fireworks, flares, explosives.* Old bullets and gunpowder, road or marine flares, fireworks, and other explosive materials are almost universally *not* accepted at HHW services. Local bomb squads operated by police or sheriff departments are the best option.

- *Radioactive substances.* Most household smoke alarms use an ionization detector which contains a small amount (1–2 microcuries) of Americium 241, a synthetic isotope that emits both alpha and gamma rays. They are not a hazard in use, unless the devices are broken apart. Manufacturers are required to take them back. Most local programs simply provide the addresses to homeowners for ground (*e.g.,* UPS) shipping.

- *Dioxin-containing wastes.* A few old phenoxy herbicides, such as Silvex and 2,4,5-T, were known to have significant contamination with dioxins. This situation has presented challenges in many states due to restrictions on handling dioxin-bearing wastes.

- *Unknowns.* Many old houses have a few unlabeled, unknown materials that are brought into HHW collections. Unknown contents of old, dusty bottles, jars, or bags need to be handled very carefully, as previously noted regarding legacy chemicals that include shock-sensitive crystals. These wastes drive up the cost of HHW services due to the time involved in careful chemical identification.

Unique Wastes

Unique wastes or new items not often thought about 10 or 20 years ago; a whole new world awaits HHW programs as the perception of what is hazardous continues to grow. Amongst the product categories are:

- *Pharmaceuticals.* A wide range of medications are found in most homes. While roughly 10% will designate as an RCRA hazardous waste, all are biologically active and present disposal problems as well as concerns about poisoning and misuse/ abuse.[127] There are very limited safe, effective options for handling these wastes today. Few HHW services want to accept the safety risks, and most programs are not set up to handle the subset of medications that are strictly regulated as controlled substances by the U.S. Drug Enforcement Administration.

- *Personal Care Products.* A surprising number of cosmetics, shampoos, and other personal products contain heavy metals, phthalates, organic solvents, and other hazardous chemicals in hazardous amounts.[128] This is an area of growing concern, but few if any HHW services have addressed these products or their wastes.

- *Many electronic wastes.* As previously addressed, the need for separate e-waste collection is increasing. For many HHW programs this is a new and challenging, as well as costly, waste stream to manage.
- *Treated wood.* Pressure-treated, preserved woods have been widely used in house buildings, decks, fences, picnic tables, and children's play structures. The most common ingredient was CCA (chromated copper arsenate); other treatments included pentachlorophenol and creosote. All are now restricted from use as consumer products, yet much CCA-, penta-, and creosote-treated wood remains in use. When this wood is removed, should it be handled as HHW? Some HHW collections accept it; most do not at this time. The replacement products, copper quat and copper azole, tend to be safer, yet use much higher concentrations of copper and might yet present challenges for disposal.
- *Flame retardant-treated materials.* Brominated flame retardants such as poly-brominated di-phenyl ethers ("PBDEs") have been widely used in mattresses, furniture, carpets, draperies, and electronic equipment. Should all of these materials be considered HHW now?
- *PVC plastic.* Many products in the home as well as home-construction materials are made of polyvinylchloride plastic. These PVC materials also often contain high concentrations of phthalate esters such as di (2-ethyl-hexyl) phthalate ("DEHP"). When incinerated, PVC forms highly toxic dioxins. Should all of these materials be considered HHW in order to protect public health and the environment? The State of Maine HHW plan recommends that PVC be separated from residential waste and collected with other HHW.[129]

Tomorrow's Concerns/Evolving Concepts

Since the first HHW collection programs in the 1980s, the availability of collection services has grown, the programs have become more sophisticated, and priorities have changed. Waste streams, such as electronic waste, that were not foreseen at the outset, have become important priorities. There has been an increasing desire on the part of government HHW programs to see product manufacturers and retailers take responsibility for their products at end of life, with some resulting initiatives. While HHW programs could continue this gradual process of evolution, there are reasons why bigger and more rapid changes are needed.

Scalability of Collection Services

HHW collection services have grown from single events to annual events and, in many places, permanent, ongoing services that are available 52 weeks a year. However, even the most active programs around the country find that they are serving no more than 5 or at the very most 10% of the service-area population. Budgets are stretched to meet even these meager service levels. For example, the HHW collection services of the Local Hazardous Waste Management Program in King County (the greater Seattle area in Washington state) are among the longest running in the country. In 2006 the LHWMP collected 3,037 tons of HHW from 52,810 customers.[130] While this is no small feat and serves to remove those hazardous materials from further human exposure as well as unsafe disposal, such services cost King County citizens $4.2 million in 2006, while only accommodating 7% of the available population (1.8 million people in 740,000 households).[131] Is this success? To scale up to 100% would cost $60 million for this one metropolitan area, a sum considered unattainable as well as unsustainable. If we really want to sweep out all of the HHW generated, or even a significant (say, greater than 50%) share, a different model will be needed. Communities should strive for greater than 5–10% participation of their populations in order to substantially divert HHW from landfilling, combustion, wastewater, or other concerns; the challenge we all face is how to do so most efficiently and economically.

Emerging Issues and Chemicals

In the past ten years, a wealth of new research has identified new chemicals of concern, new exposure pathways, and new health effects. The appearance of these new aspects of consumer products challenges the existing definitions of hazardous chemical products and the boundaries of who should have responsibility for them. Products that are not currently considered hazardous by conventional criteria, such as polycarbonate water bottles, vinyl shower curtains, and furniture containing brominated flame retardants, contain varying amounts of hazardous substances. These compounds can leach into drinking water or contaminate indoor air and house dust, providing pathways for human exposures that may be harmful by themselves or in combination with those from other products. Human body burden testing has revealed that some people have potentially harmful levels in their bodies of certain chemicals such as phthalates, lead, and pesticides that are ingredients in common household products,[132–135] although other sources of these chemicals also exist. Wastewater effluent and receiving waters have been shown to contain countless chemicals that originate from cosmetics, prescription and over-the-counter medications, cleaning products, human hormones, and even beverages such as coffee.[136] Estimating the toxicity of such complex mixtures is difficult, but the results may well dictate the need to improve wastewater treatment processes to remove some of these chemicals before they reach receiving waters.

In the mid 1990s, endocrine disruption made headlines with the publication of the book *Our Stolen Future*, written by Theo Colborn, Pete Myers, and Diane Dumanosky.[137] This seminal work, much like its predecessor, *Silent Spring* by Rachel Carson,[138] sounded a warning that a group of chemicals was having profound consequences on wildlife and perhaps also on human beings. Attacked, like its predecessor, by the chemicals industry, the thesis of *Our Stolen Future* has largely held up to subsequent research. Chemicals *can* interfere with hormonal processes, sometimes at astoundingly low levels of exposure. In addition, the timing of exposure can be critical, and sometimes lower doses are more toxic than higher ones.[139] Evaluation of risk requires detailed knowledge of the timing and magnitude of exposures, and the results are not necessarily what one would expect based on extrapolation from high doses to adults.

Whether these emerging new pollutants are harmful in landfills or incinerators is one question, but their safety in the home is quite another. As non-profit organizations, farsighted local and state government programs, and European counterparts take aim at such chemicals and the products that contain them, what should be the role of HHW programs, both in managing existing flows of waste products and in taking leadership to help shape the laws and regulations that will define products of the future?

The authors would argue that HHW programs, collectively at the national level, should first reconsider the definition of HHW based on the reality of materials both in commerce and in waste streams. A definition based purely on the traditional hazardous waste characteristics (*i.e.,* designation based on federal RCRA criteria) is arguably too narrow for all of the activities and concerns currently encompassed by HHW programs. As early as 1995, Dana Duxbury argued, "Today, 'household hazardous waste' may be a misnomer because HHW programs no longer focus exclusively on households, on items defined by RCRA as hazardous, or on waste…. It may be time to either change the acronym 'HHW' or let manufacturers and the public know [the] diverse nature of these programs: education, reduction and collection programs concerned about the use, storage and disposal of products with hazardous constituents."[140]

In particular, the definition of toxicity should be extended to effectively identify materials containing small amounts of toxic materials with characteristics that allow for transport and accumulation to potentially dangerous levels in humans, ecosystems, or particular environments. For example, a future definition of HHW should include persistent, bioaccumulative, toxic chemical ("PBT") characteristics as a criterion. Only by including the product constituents in their field of view can HHW programs play a significant role in removing unacceptable ingredients from consumer products "upstream" instead of solely focusing on waste management downstream.

Second, at the state and national level, HHW programs and their professional organizations should get more involved in policy decisions related to registration and labeling of products. In 2001, the North American Hazardous Materials Management Association and several state and local HHW programs succeeded in convincing EPA to change the disposal instructions on consumer pesticide products, removing the outdated recommendation to dispose of partially full containers in the trash (wrapped in newspaper, which effectively hid them from collection workers). Despite strong opposition from the pesticide industry, current labels now direct consumers to contact their local health or environmental agency for disposal instructions and refer them to Earth 911 for locally appropriate information.[141] This victory was important not only because it resolved a labeling issue that had been problematic for years, but also because it demonstrated that HHW programs have the power to make changes at the federal level.

More recently, some HHW programs and city governments have submitted comment letters to EPA on the re-registration of individual pesticide active ingredients, on the problem of undisclosed "inert" ingredients in pesticide products, and on other issues. In some cases incremental improvements in product labeling and use restrictions have occurred, perhaps due in part to this form of local program advocacy. King County (Wash.)'s collaboration with the U.S. Geological Survey on pesticide monitoring in streams resulted in a joint report highlighting the widespread contamination of local streams with toxic concentrations of the insecticide diazinon, data that were considered by EPA in its eventual decision to end virtually all urban uses of the chemical.[142] In Washington state, local HHW programs have worked closely with the Department of Ecology and non-profit organizations to restrict uses of mercury and to establish a regulatory structure to phase out PBTs.

These kinds of activities go beyond the traditional education and collection roles and can have the benefit of reducing or ending the use of specific problematic chemicals.

Stemming the Tide of New Chemicals at the Source

Despite the important but scattered successes described above, simple mathematics shows that an even more proactive approach to HHW management is needed. The California Department of Toxic Substances Control notes, "The U.S. currently has more than 85,000 chemicals in commerce. There are approximately 2,500 'high production volume' (HPV) chemicals, which are manufactured at a rate of more than one million pounds annually, with nearly 45 percent of these HPV chemicals lacking adequate toxicological studies conducted to evaluate their health effects on humans and wildlife. Further, about 2,000 new chemicals are introduced into commerce annually in the United States at a rate of seven new chemicals a day."[143] On the other hand, the number of chemicals that have been banned from specific consumer products in the last ten years can be practically counted on two hands (e.g., diazinon, chlorpyrifos, chromated copper arsenate, etc.). EPA's reregistration program for pesticides has examined 271 active ingredients in 15 years[144] and intends to increase that rate to 70 per year for the next 15 year cycle.[145] At the same time, EPA registers new active ingredients, having registered 11 new conventional active ingredients in 2006.[146] It is apparent that current evaluation and registration processes are not adequate to keep up with the entry of new chemicals on the market, much less ensure that chemicals already in commerce are safe for their intended uses.

It is unlikely that most of the chemicals in commerce today are so hazardous that their use in consumer products should be curtailed. However, the problem is that we do not know, either because the toxicology data do not exist or because they are not publicly available. Clearly, there needs to be more scrutiny and transparency in the regulation of chemicals. However, a risk assessment–based process such as that used by EPA for regulating pesticides is far too onerous for the job. Fortunately, a model is provided by the new regulation process in Europe called REACH (Registration, Evaluation and Authorization of Chemicals.) "Adopted in December 2006, REACH will require producers and users of an estimated 30,000 chemicals in commerce in Europe to register them and provide information on their production, use, hazard and exposure potential. For chemicals identified as substances of very high concern REACH will allow their use only if explicitly authorized."[147]

Green chemistry approaches are growing, both in the chemistry departments of universities and in industry.[148–149] A more proactive, greener chemicals policy is needed at the national level as well as in the states. Wilson has proposed such a framework for California.[150] Governor Baldacci of Maine has initiated a process to promote formulation with safer chemicals in consumer products and services.[151] It is critical to our future that such efforts blossom, be supported, and spread. See also Appendix B.

Product stewardship is also an approach that is nascent and overdue in the United States. Extended producer responsibility or "EPR," a term first coined in 1990 by Thomas Lindhqvist of Lund University in Sweden, is "an environmental policy approach in which a producer's responsibility, physical and/or financial, for a product is extended to the post-consumer stage of a product's life cycle."[152] Examples in the U.S. of product stewardship/EPR programs include the Rechargeable Battery Recycling Corporation and the Thermostat Recycling Corporation at the national level (both previously referenced), plus various state-level programs, either voluntary or mandated. A more comprehensive approach is taken by the Province of British Columbia in Canada.[153] The Product Stewardship Institute and the Product Policy Institute are two non-governmental organizations that promote this approach. It is time for this model to take over the way we manage end-of-life products in the U.S.

In Summary: Beyond Waste, Toward a Solution

It is no longer acceptable to operate a small HHW collection service that is used by 5% of the target population and claim success. A comprehensive approach based on new models is essential.

The authors believe that HHW programs should move from their traditional rather narrow focus on disposal of residual hazardous products and put more emphasis and resources into proactively shaping future products that will eventually end up as recyclables or waste. Obviously, not all of this work must happen at the local level. We would expect national professional organizations such as the North American Hazardous Materials Management Association ( ) to take a lead role with support from key local programs. First, we suggest that the term household hazardous waste be replaced by language that better describes the future direction toward a wider view of hazardous products, with a positive view. How about: *Healthy, Environmentally-Safe Products* (*"HESP"*) programs? Second, the definitions of products encompassed by those programs should be redefined as discussed earlier to include hazards related to product use (the *hazardous household products* or *"HHPs"*) as well as disposal (the *household hazardous wastes* or *"HHWs"*). Third, programs should engage and support efforts to reform chemical regulation policies at the state and federal levels. Fourth, waste management technologies should be periodically reviewed in light of new scientific evidence to ensure that they adequately protect against health and environmental risks. Fifth, HHW programs should creatively engage with both manufacturers and retailers to explore new possibilities for promoting safer alternative products and techniques, reducing the sales of inappropriate or particularly hazardous products, manufacturer-funded and manufacturer- or retailer-operated take-back programs (product stewardship or EPR systems), and other innovative partnerships. Sixth, consumer education programs should be designed to include well researched social marketing techniques and carefully evaluated to measure both behavior change and resulting health or environmental improvements attributable to that behavior. Many of these themes are examined further in subsequent chapters of this handbook.

We should work toward a world where the old, nasty household chemicals are all safely swept out and dealt with properly; where no household products need signal words such as DANGER or POISON to warn of potential harm; where young children are free to explore their homes and environs safe from exposures to any problematic consumer chemicals.

About the Authors

Dave Galvin is program manager for King County Water & Land Resources Division's office of the Local Hazardous Waste Management Program, a regional partnership addressing HHW and well as CESQG hazardous materials in the metropolitan Seattle area.

Philip Dickey is staff scientist for the Washington Toxics Coalition, a non-profit organization that protects public health and the environment by eliminating toxic pollution.

Notes

1. Lewis Carroll [pseudonym of Charles Lutwidge Dodgson], *Alice's Adventures in Wonderland* (London: Macmillan, 1865); illustrations by John Tenniel.

2. H.A. Rey and Margret Rey, *Curious George Takes a Job* (Boston: Houghton-Mifflin, 1947).

3. This is a variation of the DuPont Company's advertising slogan, "Better Things For Better Living...Through Chemistry," used from 1935 until the early 1980s.

4. U.S. Senate, *Senate Report 94–988, 94th Congress, 2nd Session, at 16* (Washington, D.C., 1976).

5. Winston Porter, *Clarification of Issues Pertaining to Household Hazardous Waste Collection Programs* (OSWER Policy Directive No. 9574.00-1) (Washington, D.C.: U.S. Environmental Protection Agency, 1988).

6. Porter, *Clarification of Issues*.

7. U.S. EPA, "Wastes, States" (with links to hazardous waste-related sites in all 50 states), www.epa.gov/epaoswer/osw/stateweb.htm#maincontent (7 Apr. 2007).

8. National Center for Manufacturing Sciences, "Gateway to State-by-State Resource Locators," www.envcap.org/statetools/index.cfm (7 Apr. 2007).

9. U.S. EPA, "Municipal Solid Waste, Household Hazardous Waste," www.epa.gov/msw/hhw.htm (7 Apr. 2007).

10. U.S. EPA, *A Survey of Household Hazardous Wastes and Related Collection Programs* (EPA/530-SW-86-038) (Washington, D.C.: U.S. EPA, 1986).

11. Earth 911, "Household Hazardous Waste," www.earth911.org/master.asp (4 Apr. 2007).

12. Pollution Prevention Regional Information Center, "P2RIC topic hub: Household Hazardous Materials," www.p2ric.org/TopicHubs/toc.cfm?hub=16&subsec=7&nav=7 (7 Apr. 2007).

13. The Pesticide Stewardship Alliance website can be found at www.tpsalliance.org/.

14. U.S. EPA, *Guidelines for Carcinogen Risk Assessment* (EPA/630/P-03/001F), March 2005, 3–20 to 3–24; www.oaspub.epa.gov/eims/eimscomm.getfile?p_download_id=439797 (29 March 2007).

15. Dupont, *About PFOA*, www2.dupont.com/PFOA/en_US/about_pfoa/index.html (29 May 2007).

16. Melisa W. Lai, Wendy Klein-Schwartz, George C. Rodgers, Joseph Y. Abrams, Deborah A. Haber, Alvin C. Bronstein, and Kathleen M. Wruk, "Annual Report of the American Association of Poison Control Centers' National Poisoning and Exposure Database," *Clinical Toxicology* 44 (2006): 803–932.

17. Lai *et al.,* "Annual Report," 803–932.

18. Lance A. Wallace, "The TEAM Study: Personal Exposure to Toxic Substances in Air." *Environmental Research* 43 (1987): 290–307; see also Wayne Ott, Anne Steinemann, and Lance Wallace, *Exposure Analysis* (Boca Raton, Fla.: CRC Press, 2007).

19. John W. Roberts and Philip A. Dickey, "Exposure of Children to Pollutants in House Dust and Indoor Air," *Reviews of Environmental Contamination and Toxicology* 143 (March 1995): 59–78.

20. Ruthann A. Rudel, David E. Camann, John D. Spengler, Leo R. Korn, and Julia G. Brody, "Phthalates, Alkylphenols, Pesticides, Polybrominated Diphenyl Ethers, and Other Endocrine-Disrupting Compounds in Indoor Air and Dust," *Environmental Science and Technology* 37, no. 20 (2003): 4543–4553.

21. Wayne R. Ott, Anne C. Steinemann, and Lance A. Wallace, *Exposure Analysis* (Boca Raton, Fla.: CRC Press, 2007).

22. U.S. EPA, "Manufacturers to Use New Wood Preservatives, Replacing Most Residential Uses of CCA," U. S. Environmental Protection Agency press release, February 12, 2002 (Washington, D.C.: U.S. EPA, 2002).

23. Heather Carlson-Lynch and Andrew E. Smith, *Evaluation of Children's Health Hazards from Arsenic Exposure Associated with the Use of CCA-Treated Wood in Residential Structures and Municipal Playgrounds (Draft),* (Augusta, Maine: Maine Department of Human Services, August 1998).

24. Stephen M. Roberts and Hugo O. Ochoa, Letter to John Ruddell, Division of Waste Management, Florida Department of Environmental Protection, April 10, 2001.

25. California Department of Health Services, *Evaluation of the Hazards Posed by the Use of Wood Preservatives on Playground Equipment*, Office of Environmental Health Hazard Assessment, Department of Health Services, Health and Welfare Agency, State of California, (Sacramento, Calif.: CDHS, 1987).

26. Gradient, *Focused Evaluation of Human Health Risks Associated with Exposure to Arsenic from CCA-treated Wood* (Cambridge, Mass.: Gradient Corporation, July 6, 2001).

27. U.S. CPSC, *Playground Equipment: Transmittal of Estimate of Risk of Skin Cancer from Dislodgeable Arsenic on Pressure Treated Wood Playground Equipment* (Washington, D.C.: Consumer Product Safety Commission, 1990).

28. Carol A. Clausen, James H. Muehl, and Andrzej M. Krzyski, "Properties of Structural Panels Fabricated from Bioremediated CCA-treated Wood: Pilot Scale," *Forest Products Journal* 56, no. 3 (March 2006): 32–35; www.fpl.fs.fed.us/documnts/ pdf2006/fpl_2006_clausen001.pdf (12 Apr 2007).

29. Maine State Legislature, *An Act to Protect Public Health by Reducing Human Exposure to Arsenic* (H-490), passed June 4, 2003 (Augusta, Maine: Maine State Legislature, 2003).

30. Helena Solo-Gabriele, Timothy Townsend, Monika Kormienko, Kelvin Gary, Kristin Stook, and Thabet Tolaymat, *Alternative Chemicals and Improved Disposal-End Management Practices for CCA-treated Wood* (Final Draft – Report #00-03) (Gainesville, Fla.: Florida Center for Solid and Hazardous Waste Management, University of Florida, 2000).

31. Timothy Townsend, Kristin Stook, Thabet Tolaymat, Jim Kun Song, Helena Solo-Gabriele, Naila Hosein, and Bernine Khan, *New Lines of CCA-Treated Wood Research: In-Service and Disposal Issues* (Report #00-12) (Gainesville, Fla.: Florida Center for Solid and Hazardous Waste Management, State University System of Florida, 2001).

32. Philip Dickey, *Guidelines for Selecting Wood Preservatives*, Report for the San Francisco Department of the Environment, September 9, 2003 (Seattle: Washington Toxics Coalition, 2003).

33. Steven G. Gilbert and Bernard Weiss, "A Rationale for Lowering the Blood Lead Action Level from 10 to 2 ug/dL," *NeuroToxicology* 27 (June 29, 2006): 693–701.

34. Steven G. Gilbert, *A Small Dose of Toxicology* (Boca Raton, Fla.: CRC Press, 2004), 92.

35. U.S. EPA, *What You Need to Know about Mercury in Fish and Shellfish*, www.epa.gov/ waterscience/fishadvice/advice.html (30 Mar. 2007)

36. U.S. Geological Survey, *Mercury in the Environment* (Fact Sheet 146-00, October 2000), www.usgs.gov/themes/factsheet/146-00/#sources (30 Mar. 2007).

37. U.S. EPA, *Mercury*, www.epa.gov/mercury/ (14 June 2007).

38. Washington State Department of Ecology, *Summary of Washington's Mercury Reduction Strategy*, www.ecy.wa.gov/programs/eap/pbt/hgreductionstrategy.html (30 Mar. 2007).

39. U.S. EPA, *Mercury Spills*, www.epa.gov/epaoswer/hazwaste/mercury/faq/spills.htm (30 Mar. 2007).

40. Agency for Toxic Substances & Disease Registry, *ToxFAQs™ for Di(2-ethylhexyl)phthalate (DEHP)*, www.atsdr.cdc.gov/tfacts9.html#bookmark02 (13 Apr. 2007).

41. Rudel *et al.*, "Phthalates, Alkylphenols, Pesticides, Polybrominated Diphenyl Ethers, and Other Endocrine-Disrupting Compounds in Indoor Air and Dust," 4549.

42. T. Otake, J. Yoshinaga, and Y. Yanagisawa, "Exposure to Phthalate Esters from Indoor Environment," *Journal of Exposure Analysis and Environmental Epidemiology 14*, no. 7 (November 2004): 524–528.

43. Carl-Gustaf Bornehag, Bjorn Lundgren, Charles J. Weschler, Torben Sigsgaard, Linda Hagerhed-Engman, and Jan Sundell, "Phthalates in Indoor Dust and Their Association with Building Characteristics," *Environmental Health Perspectives* 113, no. 10 (October 2005): 1399–1404.

44. F. Alatriste-Mondragon, R. Iranpour, and B.K. Ahring, "Toxicity of Di-(2-ethylhexyl) phthalate on the Anaerobic Digestion of Wastewater Sludge," *Water Resources* 37, no. 6 (March 2003): 1260–1269.

45. U.S. CDC, *Second National Report on Human Exposure to Environmental Chemicals* (Atlanta: Centers for Disease Control and Prevention, 2003).

46. National Toxicology Program Center for the Evaluation of Risks to Human Reproduction, *Expert Panel Report on Di(2-ethylhexyl)phthalate"* (Alexandria, Va.: National Toxicology Center, 2000).

47. A. Afshari, L. Gunnarsen, P.A. Clausen, and V. Hansen, "Emission of Phthalates from PVC and Other Materials," *Indoor Air* 14, no. 2 (April 2004): 120–128.

48. Bornehag *et al.*, "Phthalates in Indoor Dust and Their Association with Building Characteristics," 1403.

49. Sandra Steingraber, *Update on the Environmental Health Impacts of Polyvinyl Chloride (PVC) as a Building Material: Evidence from 2000–2004—A Commentary for the U.S. Green Building Council*, www.healthybuilding.net/pvc/steingraber.pdf (13 Apr. 2007).

50. Jouni J.K. Jaakkola, Leif Øie, Per Nafstad, Grete Botten, Sven Ove Samuelsen, and Per Magnus, "Interior Surface Materials in the Home and the Development of Bronchial Obstruction in Young Children in Oslo, Norway," *American Journal of Public Health* 89, no. 2 (February 1999): 188-192.

51. Caro-Gustaf Bornehag, Jan Sundell, Charles J. Weschler, Torben Sigsgaard, Bjorn Lundgren, Mikael Hasselgren, and Linda Hagerhed-Engman, "The Association between Asthma and Allergic Symptoms in Children and Phthalates in House Dust: A Nested Case-Control Study," *Environmental Health Perspectives* 112, no. 14 (October 2004): 1393–1397.

52. J.C.S. Chang, R. Fortmann, and N. Roache, "Air Toxics Emissions from a Vinyl Shower Curtain," *Proceedings Indoor Air* (2002): 542–547.

53. ARGUS, *Behavior of PVC in a Landfill—Final report for the European Commission, February, 2000*, http://ec.europa.eu/environment/waste/studies/pvc/landfill.pdf (13 Apr. 2007).

54. Lance A. Wallace, "Major Sources of Benzene Exposure," *Environmental Health Perspectives* 82 (1989):165–169.

55. Green Media Toolshed, *Scorecard Chemical Profile for Paradichlorobenzene*, www.scorecard.org/chemical-profiles/html/14dichlorobenzene.html (30 Mar. 2007).

56. U.S. EPA, *Level I Screening Ecological Risk Assessment for the Reregistration of Metaldehyde* (Washington, D.C.: U.S. EPA, Office of Pesticide Programs, Environmental Fate and Effects Division, 2006).

57. Linda K. Dolder, "Metaldehyde toxicosis"—Toxicology Brief (peer reviewed), *Veterinary Medicine* (March 2003): 213–215.

58. U.S. National Institutes of Health, "Hazardous Substances Data Bank," *National Library of Medicine*, toxnet.nlm.nih.gov/ (5 Apr. 2007).

59. J.W. Bradshaw, "The evolutionary basis for the feeding behavior of domestic dogs (Canis familiaris) and cats (Felis catus)," *Journal of Nutrition* 136 (7 Suppl, 2006): 1927S-1931S.

60. G.C. Bortleson and D.A. Davis, *Pesticides in selected small streams in the Puget Sound Basin, 1987–1995* (U.S. Geological Survey fact sheet 067-97) (Tacoma, Wash.: U.S. Geological Survey, National Water Quality Assessment Program, Puget Sound Basin, 1997).

61. F.D. Voss, J.C. Ebbert, D.A. Davis, A.M. Frahm, and G.H. Perry, *Pesticides detected in urban streams during rainstorms and relations to retail sales of pesticides in King County, Washington* (USGS fact sheet 097-99) (Tacoma, Wash.: U.S. Geological Survey, National Water Quality Assessment Program, 1999).

62. D.P. Weston, B.W. Holmes, I. You, and M.J. Lydy, "Aquatic Toxicity Due to Residential Use of Pyrethroid Insecticides," *Environmental Science and Technology* 39, no. 24 (2005): 9778–9784.

63. U.S. EPA, *Rodenticide Incidents Update,* EPA Docket OPP-2006-955 (Washington, D.C.: U.S. EPA, 2006).

64. U.S. EPA, *Proposed Risk Mitigation Decision for Nine Rodenticides,* EPA Docket OPP-2006-955 (Washington, D.C.: U.S. EPA, 2007).

65. Laura Fleming, Melissa Danits, Judy Bean, James Englehardt, Jeff An, Nicolette John, and Jeffrey Rogers, "Solid Waste Workers: Occupational Exposures and Health," *Journal of Solid Waste Technology and Management* 28, no. 2 (May 2002).

66. John Aquino, "You Only Live Once: Solid Waste Safety," *MSW Management* 12, no. 5 (July/August 2002).

67. Aquino, "You Only Live Once."

68. Mary Butler, "Small but loud explosion at landfill alarms neighbors," *Tacoma News Tribune*, 7 January 2001, B1.

69. "Blast damage," *Seattle Times*, 19 July 1982, C2.

70. Lynn Freehill, "Residents leery after incidents in basements," *Des Moines Register*, 4 February 2005, 3B.

71. National Small Flows Clearinghouse, "Septic System Information," www.nesc.wvu.edu/nsfc/nsfc_septicnews.htm (10 Apr. 2007).

72. U.S. EPA, *A Homeowner's Guide to Septic Systems* (EPA/832-B-02-005) (Washington, D.C.: U.S. EPA, 2002).

73. Richard Noss, Robert Drake, and Christopher Mossman, *Septic Tank Cleaners: Their Effectiveness and Impact on Groundwater Quality* (Amherst, Mass.: University of Massachusetts, 1987), #87–3.

74. John Kolega, *et al.,* "Goundwater quality studies at land septage disposal facilities," in *Proceedings of the Third National Symposium on Individual and Small Community Sewage Treatment* (St. Joseph, Mich.: American Society of Agricultural Engineers, 1982), 332–45.

75. John Kolega, "Household hazardous wastes in septic systems: types, quantities and impacts," in *Proceedings of the Fifth National Conference on Household Hazardous Waste Management*, ed. Dana Duxbury (Andover, Mass: Dana Duxbury and Associates, 1990), 481–88.

76. F. DeWalle, D.A. Kallman, D. Norma, J. Sung, and G. Plews, *Determination of Toxic Chemicals in Effluent from Household Septic Tanks* (EPA/600-2-85-050) (Cincinnati: U.S. EPA, 1985).

77. Mark A. Gross, *Assessment of the Effects of Household Chemicals upon Individual Septic Tank Performance* (Little Rock, Ark.: University of Arkansas, Arkansas Water Resources Research Center, 1987), pub. no. 131.

78. U.S. EPA, *A Homeowner's Guide*, 8.

79. David V. Galvin, "Household hazardous waste in municipal wastewaters and storm drains: An important target for comprehensive pollution prevention programs," in *Proceedings of the 64th Water Pollution Control Federation Annual Conference* (Alexandria, Va.: Water Pollution Control Federation [now, Water Environment Federation], 1991), 1–17, #AC91-068-004.

80. U.S. EPA, *Report to Congress on the Discharge of Hazardous Wastes to Publicly Owned Treatment Works* [known as the "Domestic Sewage Study"] (EPA/530-SW-86-004) (Washington, D.C.: U.S. EPA, 1986).

81. D. Jenkins and L. Russell, *Contribution of Heavy Metals to Wastewaters from Household Cleaning Products* (New York: Soap and Detergent Association, 1990).

82. Philip Dickey, *A Database of Safer Substitutes for Hazardous Household Products – Phase One Report* (Seattle: Washington Toxics Coalition, 1990); Philip Dickey, *A Database of Safer Substitutes for Hazardous Household Products – Phase Two Report* (Seattle: Washington Toxics Coalition, 1991); Philip Dickey, *A Database of Safer Substitutes for Hazardous Household Products – Phase Three Report* (Seattle: Washington Toxics Coalition, 1992).

83. Massachusetts Executive Office of Environmental Affairs, *Customer Education and Zinc Use Reduction at Dydee Diaper Service, Inc., Toxics Use Reduction Case Study* (Boston, Mass.: Office of Technical Assistance, 1993).

84. Dana Kolpin, Edward Furlong, Michael Meyer, Michael Thurman, Steven Zuagg, Larry Barber, and Herbert Buxton, "Pharmaceuticals, Hormones, and Other Organic Wastewater Contaminants in U.S. Streams, 1999–2000: A National Reconnaissance," *Environmental Science and Technology* 36, no. 6 (2002): 1202–11.

85. Christian Daughton and Thomas Ternes, "Pharmaceuticals and Personal Care Products in the Environment: Agents of Subtle Change?" *Environmental Health Perspectives* 107, suppl. 6, (December 1999): 907–38.

86. K.E. DeJong, R.L. Siegrist, L.B. Barber, and A.L. Wren, "Occurrence of Emerging Organic Chemicals in Wastewater Effluents from Onsite Systems," in *Proceedings of the Tenth National Symposium on Individual and Small Community Sewage Systems* (St. Joseph, Mich.: American Society of Agricultural Engineers, 2004), 400–7.

87. U.S. EPA, *Municipal Solid Waste in the United States – 2005 Facts and Figures* (EPA/530-R-06-011) (Washington, D.C.: U.S. EPA, 2006).

88. Cal Recovery Systems, Inc., *Characterization and Impacts of Non-regulated Hazardous Wastes in Municipal Solid Waste of King County* (Seattle, Wash.: Puget Sound Council of Governments, 1985).

89. William Rathje, Douglas Wilson, V.W. Lambou, and R.C. Herndon, *Characterization of Hazardous Household Wastes in Marin County, California, and New Orleans, Louisiana* (Las Vegas, Nev.: U.S. EPA, 1987).

90. State of Minnesota, *Statewide MSW Composition Study—A Study of Discards in the State of Minnesota* (Minneapolis, Minn.: Solid Waste Management Coordinating Board, 2000).

91. Alameda County, *2000 Waste Characterization Study* (Alameda County, Calif., 2001).

92. Wisconsin Department of Natural Resources, *Wisconsin Statewide Waste Characterization Study* (Madison, Wis.: DNR, 2003).

93. California Integrated Waste Management Board, *Statewide Waste Characterization Study* (Sacramento, Calif.: CIWMB, 2004).

94. King County, *Waste Monitoring Program: 2002/2003 Comprehensive Waste Stream Characterization and Transfer Station Customer Surveys* (Seattle, Wash.: King County Solid Waste Division, 2004).

95. City and County of San Francisco, Waste Characterization Study (San Francisco: City and County of San Francisco, Department of the Environment, 2005).

96. New York City Department of Sanitation, *Final Report: 2004–05 NYC Residential and Street Basket Waste Characterization Study* (New York, 2006).

97. U.S. EPA, *Household Hazardous Waste*, www.epa.gov/epaoswer/non-hw/househld/hhw. htm (14 June 2007).

98. David Nightingale and Rachel Donnette, "Household Hazardous Waste," in *Handbook of Solid Waste Management,* 2nd Edition, eds. George Tchobanoglous and Frank Kreith (New York: McGraw-Hill, 2002), 10.6.

99. U.S. EPA, *Mercury Study Report to Congress, Volume II: An Inventory of Anthropogenic Mercury Emissions in the United States* (EPA/452-R-97-004) (Washington, D.C.: U.S. EPA, 1997).

100. PowerScorecard, *Electricity from: Municipal Solid Waste* (2003), powerscorecard.org/ tech_detail.cfm?resource_id=10 (13 Apr. 2007).

101. Bjorn Hedman, Morgan Naslund, and Stellan Marklund, "Emission of PCDD/F, PCB, and HCB from Combustion of Firewood and Pellets in Residential Stoves and Boilers," *Environmental Science and Technology* 40, no. 16 (2006): 4968–75.

102. U.S. EPA, *The Inventory of Sources and Environmental Releases of Dioxin-Like Compounds in the United States: The Year 2000 Update* (External Review Draft, March 2005) (EPA/600-P-03-002A), www.epa.gov/ncea/pdfs/dioxin/2k-update/ (13 Apr. 2007).

103. Chris Chi-Yet Chan, *Behavior of Metals in MSW Incinerator Fly Ash During Roasting with Chlorinating Agents* (Toronto, Ontario, Canada: University of Toronto, 1997).

104. U.S. EPA, *Inventory of Sources and Environmental Releases of Dioxin-Like Compounds*, 6–18.

105. U.S. EPA, *Inventory of Sources*, xlii–xliii.

106. P.M. Lemieux, C.C. Lutes, J.A. Abbott, and K.M. Aldous, "Emissions of Polychlorinated Dibenzo-p-dioxins and Polychlorinated Dibenzofurans from the Open Burning of Household Waste in Barrels," *Environmental Science and Technology* 34, no. 3 (2000): 377–84.

107. U.S. EPA, *The Hidden Hazards of Burn Barrels* (EPA/530-F-03-012) (Washington, D.C.: U.S. EPA, 2003).

108. G. Fred Lee and Anne Jones-Lee, *Flawed Technology of Subtitle D Landfilling of Municipal Solid Waste* – a white paper (El Macero, Calif.: G. Fred Lee & Associates, 2007).

109. Gretchen Sabel and Thomas Clark, "Volatile organic compounds as indicators of municipal solid waste leachate contamination," *Waste Management and Research* 2 (1984): 119–30.

110. M. Reinhard, N. Goodman, and J. Barker, "Occurrence and Distribution of organic chemicals in two landfill leachate plumes," *Environmental Science and Technology* 18 (1984): 953–61.

111. D.R. Reinhart, "Review of recent studies on the sources of hazardous compounds emitted from solid waste landfills: A U.S. experience," *Waste Management Research* 11 (1993): 257–68.

112. N. Paxeus, "Organic compounds in municipal landfill leachates," *Water Science Technology* 47, no. 7–8 (2000): 323–33.

113. Gregory Vogt, "Landfill Gas as a Source of Low-Level Volatiles in Groundwater," *Waste Age* (January 1995): 91–2.

114. N. Praxeus, "Organic compounds," 323–32.

115. A. Coors, P. Jones, J. Giesy, and H.-T. Ratte, "Removal of estrogenic activity from municipal waste landfill leachate assesses with a bioassay based on reporter gene expression," *Environmental Science and Technology* 37 (2003): 3430–4.

116. Kimberlee Barnes, Scott Christianson, Dana Kolpin, Michael Focazio, Edward Furlong, Steven Zaugg, Michael Meyer, and Larry Barber, "Pharmaceuticals and Other Organic Wastewater Contaminants Within a Leachate Plume Downgradient of a Municipal Landfill," *Ground Water Monitoring and Remediation* 12, no. 2 (Spring, 2004): 119–26.

117. U.S. EPA, *The Inventory of Sources and Environmental Releases of Dioxin-Like Compounds*, 6–1.

118. Nightingale and Donnette, "Household Hazardous Waste," 10.9.

119. R.J. Slack, J.R. Gronow, and N. Voulvoulis, "Household hazardous waste in municipal landfills: Contaminants in leachate," *Science of the Total Environment* 337 (2005): 119–137.

120. R.J. Slack *et al.,* "Household hazardous waste in municipal landfills," 133.

121. U.S. EPA, UN PIC ["Prior Informed Consent"] and US PIC-Nominated Pesticides List, www.epa.gov/oppfead1/international/piclist.htm (12 Apr. 2007).

122. The FIFRA Section 25(b) pesticides are those products considered by U.S. EPA to have "minimum risk," and are exempted from most pesticide registration and related rules. They include products with active ingredients such as herbs or spices, mint oils, corn gluten, and table salt. For a complete list, see www.epa.gov/oppbppd1/biopesticides/regtools/25b_list.htm (9Apr. 2007).

123. Greentruck, How do I dispose of used antifreeze?, www.greentruck.com/waste/antifreeze/1102.html (14 June 2007).

124. U.S. EPA, Municipal Solid Waste, 10.

125. The Rechargeable Battery Recycling Corporation collects rechargeable batteries throughout the country at many retail venues. Get more information at www.rbrc.org/call2recycle/ (9Apr. 2007).

126. The Thermostat Recycling Corporation collects old household as well as commercial thermostats throughout the country at a variety of outlets. Get more information at www.nema.org/gov/ehs/trc/ (12 Apr. 2007).

127. Christian G. Daughton and Thomas A. Ternes, "Pharmaceuticals and Personal Care Products in the Environment: Agents of Subtle Change?" *Environmental Health Perspectives* 107, suppl. 6 (December 1999): 907–938.

128. Daughton and Ternes, "Pharmaceuticals and Personal Care Products," 907–938.

129. Maine Department of Environmental Protection, *Plan for Statewide Collection of Household Hazardous Waste* (Augusta, Maine: DEP, 2001).

130. Trudy Rolla, evaluation coordinator, Local Hazardous Waste Management Program in King County, personal communication (13 April 2007).

131. Rolla, personal communication.

132. Benjamin C. Blount, Manori J. Silva, Samuel P. Caudill, Larry L. Heedham, Jim L. Pirkle, Eric J. Sampson, George W. Lucier, Richard J. Jackson, and John W. Brock, "Levels of Seven Urinary Phthalate Metabolites in a Human Reference Population," *Environmental Health Perspectives* 108 (2000): 979–982.

133. Environmental Working Group, *Body Burden: The Pollution in People,* www.ewg.org/reports/bodyburden/ (11 Apr. 2007).

134. U.S. CDC, *Second National Report on Human Exposure to Environmental Chemicals* (Atlanta: Centers for Disease Control and Prevention, 2003).

135. Toxic Free Legacy Coalition, *Pollution in People: A Study of Toxic Chemicals in Washingtonians,* www.pollutioninpeople.org/ (11 Apr. 2007).

136. Dana W. Kolpin *et al.,* "Pharmaceuticals, Hormones, and Other Organic Wastewater Contaminants," 1202–1211.

137. Theo Colburn, Diane Dumanosky, and John Peterson Myers, *Our Stolen Future* (New York: Penguin Books USA, 1996).

138. Rachel Carson, *Silent Spring* (Boston: Houghton Mifflin, 1962).

139. Frederick S. vom Saal and Claude Highes, "An Extensive New Literature Concerning Low-Dose Effects of Bisphenol A Shows the Need for a New Risk Assessment," *Environmental Health Perspectives* 113, no. 8 (August 2005): 926–933.

140. Dana Duxbury, " 'HHW' Today," *Household Hazardous Waste Management News,* no. 25 (June, 1995), 1,7–8.

141. U.S. EPA's Read the Label First Campaign, www.epa.gov/oppt/labeling/pubs/articles.htm (12 May 2007).

142. U.S. EPA, EFED Chapter for Re-Registration Eligibility Decision (Washington, D.C., EPA, 1999), 36.

143. California Department of Toxic Substances Control, *Emerging Chemicals of Concern,* www.dtsc.ca.gov/AssessingRisk/EmergingContaminants.cfm (28 Mar. 2007).

144. U.S. EPA, "Pesticide Reregistration Performance Measures and Goals," *Federal Register* 71, no. 121 (Friday, June 23, 2006), www.epa.gov/fedrgstr/EPA-PEST/2006/June/Day-23/p9956.pdf (28 Mar. 2007).

145. U.S. EPA, Registration Review Process, www.epa.gov/oppsrrd1/registration_review/reg_review_process.htm (28 Mar. 2007).

146. U.S. EPA, Registration Activities in the Office of Pesticide Programs (2006), www.epa.gov/opprd001/workplan/bird2006.pdf (28 Mar. 2007).

147. Richard A. Denison, *Not That Innocent: A Comparative Analysis of Canadian, European Union, and United States Policies on Industrial Chemicals* (Washington, D.C.: Environmental Defense and Pollution Probe, 2007); www.environmentaldefense.org/documents/6149_NotThatInnocent_Fullreport.pdf (5 Apr. 2007).

148. Terrance J. Collins and Chip Walter, "Little Green Molecules," *Scientific American* (March 2006): 82–90.

149. Paul T. Anastas and John C. Warner, *Green Chemistry: Theory and Practice* (New York: Oxford University Press, 1998).

150. Michael P. Wilson, Daniel A. Chia, and Bryan C. Ehlers, *Green Chemistry in California: A Framework for Leadership in Chemicals Policy and Innovation* (Berkeley, Calif.: University of California, California Policy Research Center, 2006).

151. Governor John E. Baldacci, An Order Promoting Safer Chemicals in Consumer Products and Services, February 22, 2006, www.maine.gov/tools/whatsnew/index.php?topic=Gov_Executive_Orders&id=21193&v=Article (12 Apr. 2007).

152. Organization for Economic Co-operation and Development, *Extended Producer Responsibility: A Guidance Manual for Governments* (Paris, France: OECD, 2001).

153. British Columbia, Ministry of the Environment, British Columbia's Product Stewardship Programs, www.env.gov.bc.ca/epd/epdpa/ips/ (12 Apr. 2007).

CHAPTER 2

The History and Current Status of Household Hazardous Waste Management

Dave Galvin

Introduction

The term household hazardous waste was coined in 1981 to address a new concern over the impacts and proper management of old, unwanted hazardous products. In a true grassroots manner, local waste-handling officials in a few states independently noted problems caused by hazardous household product leftovers and the lack of any infrastructure to safely handle them. Early single-day household hazardous waste collections sprang up at the local level throughout the 1980s. A new movement blossomed. Single-day HHW collections were followed by more creative mobile services and then permanent programs that included fixed collection sites open year-round. Public education, waste reduction campaigns, and other related elements were part of the collection efforts. In 1986, the first national conference addressing this topic was held and continues to be hosted annually as a key way to share experiences and expand the movement. Today, HHW collection, reduction, and related management programs are operating in all 50 states as well as in remote territories such as Guam. These programs have become institutionalized in many parts of the country as a core service provided by local government.

This chapter describes the origins and development of HHW programs across the United States from the early days of scattered, single-day collection events to full-service programs that include such elements as public education, use reduction, waste collection, recycling and product stewardship. The evolution of this movement is demonstrated in this chapter by reference to the numbers of programs offered at state and local levels, and the changes shown in the proceedings of over 20 years of national HHW conferences. I conclude with a reflection on the current status of HHW management, as pressure mounts for HHW programs to address a much wider range of hazardous chemicals and to move toward incorporation of a more comprehensive product stewardship model.

Origins

As described in Chapter 1, consumers have always been exposed to some hazardous chemicals, going back a hundred years or more when lead and arsenic were common in a variety of products used around the home. However, with the advent of organochlorine pesticides in the 1940s and the explosion in variety of products marketed in the United States following the second World War, household products containing hazardous chemicals became commonplace. Paints, batteries, pesticides, cleaners, automotive supplies, plastics, glues, detergents—any number of products in the modern home came to contain hazardous chemicals. Rachel Carson wrote in her landmark work, *Silent Spring*, in 1962, "A few minutes' research in any supermarket is enough to alarm the most stouthearted customer—provided, that is, he has even a rudimentary knowledge of the chemicals presented for his choice."[1]

So what happens when all of these hazardous products are used and/or thrown away? Not much thought went into this question through the middle decades of the 20th century. In *Silent Spring,* Carson focused on the *use* of pesticides such as DDT and their wide, unintended impacts. She did not directly address the topic of how to dispose of the leftover cans of DDT, chlordane, dieldrin, or lindane from one house, nor the potential multiplied effect of the 80 million households in the United States at that time.

What Carson did do, was to jump start the environmental movement in a decade that began to question authority. In 1970, the year of the first Earth Day, the U.S. Environmental Protection Agency was established, as well as the vanguard of the core American environmental laws, the National Environmental Policy Act, and the Clean Air Act. These were followed soon thereafter by the Clean Water Act, Consumer Product Safety Act, and a major update of the Federal Insecticide, Fungicide and Rodenticide Act, all in 1972. It was not until 1976 that the Resource Conservation and Recovery Act ("RCRA," PL94-580, 48 USC 6901) was enacted, which established more exacting standards for municipal solid waste management and that set up a national system for dealing with hazardous wastes. The first regulations for implementing RCRA were promulgated by the U.S. EPA in 1980. As described in Chapter 1, household products were exempted from the hazardous waste management requirements of this new law.

The question of how to handle these domestic hazardous wastes first surfaced in the early 1980s in local programs scattered across the country. This was a time when most of the national environmental laws were relatively new, and when the RCRA regulations were just starting to go into effect. Working independently, local waste management officials in Massachusetts, California, Washington, Kentucky, New York, and Alaska began to wonder about some of these toxic or otherwise hazardous products and the problems they could be causing in municipal solid waste, wastewater systems, or the environment.

The Term Household Hazardous Waste

The term "household hazardous waste" was coined in 1981 by Dave Galvin in Seattle, Washington, to describe leftover and discarded consumer chemical products with various hazardous properties. Partial credit for the term also goes to Gina Purin, who was concurrently working on the subject in Sacramento, California. The earliest document the

Figure 2.1. The First HHW Publications from Seattle, 1979–1981. (*Photo by Ned Ahrens, used with permission*).

author can find that contains the term household hazardous waste is a project work plan from Galvin's agency, [Seattle] Metro, dated January 12, 1981. That project had previously developed a public information brochure, *Toxic Substances in Your Home*, in 1979, and a technical report in 1980 compiling what information could be found.[2] These three documents are shown in Figure 2.1 as the earliest publications specifically aimed at this topic.[3]

Gina Purin, one of the pioneers in the movement, chose to call her early effort in Sacramento the "Household Poison Project" in order to avoid the term hazardous waste, since regulations in California did not recognize the federal household exemption and nobody knew what to do with these wastes without getting into a bureaucratic tangle. This was sorted out soon thereafter and by 1983 she and others were using the term household hazardous waste in all of their materials.

In Seattle, Galvin and Susan Ridgley catalogued their pioneering Household Hazardous Waste Project in a series of five reports,[4] published in 1982, that were widely used by others as key early references. Purin compiled the first nationally available handbook on the subject in 1984. *Household Hazardous Waste: Solving the Disposal Dilemma*[5] was an instant classic in this new grassroots movement. It was considered to be "the word" on the topic and was used as the main reference in the field through the mid to late '80s. Purin and colleagues followed in 1987 with a second handbook, *Alternatives to Landfilling Household Toxics*,[6] that provided valuable updates based on the extensive experience that had developed in just a few years. Figure 2.2 illustrates these two influential early handbooks.

Another very useful early summary of the HHW movement was the report by Rachel Laderman and her colleagues at the University of Massachusetts, Amherst, *Toward a Comprehensive Program for Management of Household Hazardous Wastes in Massachusetts*,[7] published in 1985. It contained summaries of most of the early HHW programs around the country, including notes from interviews that contain some of the only remaining details pertaining to early efforts in this field.

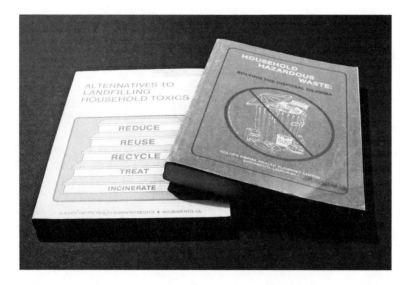

Figure 2.2. Gina Purin's *Handbook* (the 1984 "bible"), plus her 1987 *Alternatives to Land-filling* update. (*Photo by Ned Ahrens, used with permission*).

The First HHW Collection Events

Obsolete agricultural pesticides came to the attention of agricultural and solid waste officials at about the same time as interest was first expressed about HHW. A number of widely used pesticides (such as DDT, dieldrin, and lead arsenate) had been suspended or cancelled in the 1970s, leaving stockpiles at many farms. Bill McClellend in North Carolina was the first to organize an agricultural pesticide collection in 1980, soon followed by Rob Denny in Maine in 1981 and by projects in Michigan, Wisconsin, Kentucky, and other states thereafter.[8] This early attention to cleaning out the residue of recently de-registered agricultural pesticides might hold one of the keys to explaining the rise of interest in HHW as well.

Ron West of Chemical Processors, Inc., a visionary businessman in Seattle, Wash., opened his industrial treatment, storage, and disposal facility ("TSDF") to the public on an unadvertised, as-needed basis beginning in 1980. This low-key public service likely represents the first "HHW" collection program in the U.S., even before the name was coined. (North Dakota also appears in Dana Duxbury's tallies of early HHW collection programs with a single project in 1980, likely a pesticide collection event.)[9]

The first well-documented HHW collection event was a pesticide "and other chemicals" recall involving households as well as farms, schools, and businesses, held in Lebanon, Marion County, Kentucky, (population 17,900) in 1981.[10] Marion County Health Department's Keith Brock accepted old pesticides for one week in January 1981. Nineteen hundred pounds of pesticides were collected. In nearby Lancaster, Garrard County, Kentucky, (population approximately 3,000), the West Bluegrass District also held a pesticide collection in either late 1981 or early 1982, but details are now lost. Marion County has been generally recognized as the first collection event aimed at hazardous household products, albeit almost exclusively focused on pesticides.[11, 12]

Efforts to collect a full range of HHW began in earnest in 1982, springing up independently in Seattle, Washington; Sacramento, California; Lexington, Massachusetts; and Oswego and Broome Counties in New York. These pioneering projects were generally small events aimed at both providing some type of collection service for these newly identified, problem wastes, and learning about all of the challenges inherent in handling these wastes for the first time.

In Seattle, Dave Galvin and Susan Ridgley set up a pilot collection project that ran for three weeks in February 1982, at a fire station and nearby auto service businesses; 56 households participated.[13] Simultaneously, Wally Swofford developed a pesticide-only collection network in the Seattle area through the Public Health district offices in conjunction with Chemical Processors, Inc. Rick Pierce set up a small call-up service for HHW disposal in Tacoma, Washington, around the same time. Dave Bader in Whatcom County, Washington, also began accepting paints for special disposal at around this time.

Spurred by early work on waste disposal by the Massachusetts League of Women Voters, George Smith in Lexington, Massachusetts, organized the first-in-the-nation, one-day HHW collection event on October 30, 1982, that attracted 93 participants.[14] With help from the League of Women Voters, knowledge gained through this Lexington experience was captured in a "how-to kit"[15] that included educational materials and recommendations on event logistics. The availability of these kits, coupled with the League's network, sparked the quick spread of this new idea to many more communities in Massachusetts and other New England states.

This early focus by the League of Women Voters, a group known for its careful research as well as its grass-roots projects and its ability to spread well-researched information widely through its network of local and state offices, also provides one key to the early interest in and explosion of action regarding HHW in the 1980s.[16]

In Sacramento, the first California HHW project was run on ten consecutive Saturdays in October through December 1982; 250 households participated.[17] This experience led organizer Gina Purin to not only host subsequent events in Sacramento, but to develop "the bible" handbook on the issue, as noted above.

The state of Oregon experimented with a door-to-door HHW collection project in Gresham in conjunction with the local fire department beginning in 1982. Oswego County, New York, (at Fulton, on Lake Ontario) and/or Broome County, New York, (at Binghamton) also held early events in 1982, as did a project in Maine, but details are now lost.

Interest in HHW collection for proper management grew quickly and more special projects sprang up: 31 programs in seven states in 1983; 94 programs in 18 states in 1984; and 175 programs in 25 states by 1985.[18] This explosion of local HHW efforts was led by towns in Massachusetts that had 14 collection events in 1983 and 30 in 1984. Most of these early efforts were single-day collection events, known by such titles as "toxics collection days," "clean sweeps," "amnesty days," or "round-ups."

The state of Florida entered the arena in a big way with passage of its Water Quality Assessment Act in 1983. This occurred after a grand jury in Dade County that had been investigating toxic chemical contamination of the Biscayne Aquifer in South Florida came to the conclusion that the problem was not the result of any single or small group of large sources, but rather "individual and invisible, seemingly minute, acts of contamination such as a single can of paint poured in a single backyard, when multiplied thousands of times over in a community such as ours, in the last analysis poses the greatest threat to our water supply."[19] The resulting "Amnesty Days" program was the first large-scale, mobile collection service in the country, set up as a two-year initial sweep-out of small quantity hazardous wastes from households, small businesses, farms, and schools. Frank Walper of the Florida Department of Environmental Protection helped to get the Amnesty Days program established, which was soon picked up by Jan Kleman, who shepherded Florida's subsequent and significant HHW efforts through the DEP over the next 20 years.

In California, following quickly on the heels of Sacramento's pioneering project, services sprang up in Palo Alto, San Diego, Redlands, and San Bernardino in 1983–84. In Alaska, one-week events were held in Anchorage and Fairbanks in 1983; these included small businesses in addition to households. In Madison, Wisconsin, the first "clean sweep" event was held in 1984. Dow Chemical Company organized an HHW collection event in Midland, Michigan, in 1984, linked to its industrial incinerator facility. In Albuquerque, New Mexico, one of the largest early events was held in 1985, collecting HHW from more than 1,000 households over a five-day period. San Francisco also held a large event in 1985 to kick off its HHW activities. By this time, the San Bernardino project had become the first "permanent" program (other than very small, on-demand efforts elsewhere) with services located at a few fire stations. They accepted a full range of HHW, year-round.

Figure 2.3 and Table 2.1 illustrate the mushrooming activity to address this emerging issue Duxbury's tallies showed growth from two collection programs in 1980 to 273 programs in 29 states by 1986.[20]

In addition to Purin's 1984 handbook, other useful tallies of early HHW history can be found in two *Waste Age* articles: "'White Hat' Hazwaste Programs Target Homeowners, Small Shops"[21] from 1984, and "Programs to Collect Household Hazwastes Experience a Boom"[22] from 1985.

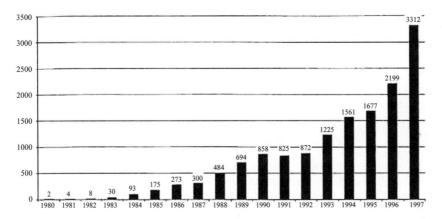

Total Number of HHW Collection Events in the U.S., by Year   Waste Watch Center

Figure 2.3. Growth of HHW Programs in the U.S. 1980–1997. (Dana Duxbury, "A 97 Percent Increase 1995!," *Household Hazardous Waste Management News,* no. 35 (August 1998), 1. This chart represents the lastest available summary of Duxbury's "National Listing of Household Hazardous Waste Collection Programs," which she kept at the Waste Watch Center and reported annually at the national conferences.)

Table 2.1. HHW Collection Programs by State by Year 1980–1993.

State	1980	1981	1982	1983	1984	1985	1986	1987	1988	1989	1990	1991	1992	1993	Total
Alabama						1				1	2	2	2	4	12
Alaska				2	3	4	7	2	6	10	9	15	16	20	94
Arizona								1	1	2	2	4	3	1	14
Arkansas								1				1			2
California			1	5	12	37	28	81	99	113	181	149	231	227	1164
Colorado					4	1				3	3	3	5	12	31
Connecticut					1	9	25	24	38	37	49	42	28	34	287
Delaware								1			1	2	1	1	6
Florida					21	22	16	13	18	72	85	95	61	116	519
Georgia												2	2	2	6
Hawaii							1	1	2	9		9	8	0	30
Idaho										2	3	2	4	6	17
Illinois							1		6	1	10	19	15	32	84
Indiana						2	1	2	5	4	10	3	9	16	52
Iowa							2		3	12	6	9	18	31	81
Kansas							3				16	12	11	22	64
Kentucky		2		1							4	4	6	6	23
Louisiana						1	1	1	2	2	2	2	1	1	13
Maine					2		1	1	1	3	6	2	2	3	21
Maryland			1					2	3	5	10	5	6	2	34
Massachusetts			1	14	30	33	78	51	101	102	78	63	62	149	762
Michigan					2	8	14	11	23	30	51	60	35	19	253
Minnesota						7	10	9	33	56	31	41	49	52	288
Mississippi												2		1	3
Missouri									2	1	5		3	17	28
Montana					1									4	5
Nebraska						3		1	3	3	6	1	1	7	25

Continues on next page

Table 2.1. (continues).

State	1980	1981	1982	1983	1984	1985	1986	1987	1988	1989	1990	1991	1992	1993	Total
Nevada											2			1	3
New Hampshire			1		4	11	22	19	27	23	19	35	35		196
New Jersey						8	7	3	13	33	39	47	54	74	278
New Mexico						1			3	3	2	3	2	2	16
New York			1	4	2	8	21	28	44	62	73	57	55	61	416
North Carolina						2				5	6	6	5	10	34
North Dakota	1										1	3	3	5	13
Ohio				1	2		1			2	4	7	6	4	27
Oklahoma				1					1	1	1	7		1	12
Oregon			1		1	1	2	2	3	3	6	16	15	10	60
Pennsylvania						1	1	2	5	6	3	4	5	12	39
Rhode Island					5	4	4	7	5	5	5	2	1	1	39
South Carolina									1		3		1	1	6
South Dakota							1					2	2	5	10
Tennessee											1	1	2	5	9
Texas							6	2	5	3	12	5	7	28	68
Utah									1	2	2	6	2	4	17
Vermont				1		2	5	3	2	6	14	7	14	9	63
Virginia						1	3	7	15	10	13	11	9	15	84
Washington	1	2	3	4	3	8	12	12	17	37	63	55	42	99	358
West Virginia						1		1		1	1		1	1	6
Wisconsin				2		6	9	9	7	18	16	16	27	43	153
Wyoming										1	1	2	3	5	12
Total/Year	2	4	8	31	94	175	273	300	484	692	859	825	867	1223	5837
Total States	2	2	6	7	18	25	28	28	31	38	43	46	43	48	50

Source: Dana Duxbury, "The National Listing of Household Hazardous Waste Collection Programs – 1993," in *Proceedings of the Eighth National Conference on Household Hazardous Waste Management, November 6-10, 1993, Burlington, Vermont,* ed. Dana Duxbury (Andover, Mass.: Dana Duxbury and Associates, 1994), Appendix VI, 618.

What explains the origin of HHW programs in the early 1980s and their explosive growth through independent initiatives across the country? There does not appear to be a single clear answer. Federal and state hazardous waste regulations were new and only beginning to go into effect. As they did so, they tended to focus on large quantity generators: industries and large business wastes. Environmentally concerned state and local agencies as well as non-governmental groups such as the League of Women Voters, well experienced in organizing recycling events in the 1970s, turned to hazardous chemicals as one of the next concerns on which to focus. The League in particular provided key impetus as well as organization, beginning in Massachusetts and quickly connecting with colleagues from Connecticut to California. As noted, agricultural pesticide collections offered an early on-ramp for household pesticides, too. Local concerns regarding sources of chemicals to groundwater and to wastewater treatment plants also drove a number of early efforts. Many factors contributed and interest clearly mushroomed across the country.

U.S. EPA Viewpoint

Since the regulations that were developed to implement RCRA exempted household wastes unconditionally (as described in Chapter 1), the U.S. EPA did not anticipate the sudden rise in interest in what had come to be called "HHW." In 1984, Assistant Administrator Lee Thomas wrote in a memo, "I fully agree that disposal of household hazardous waste in Subtitle C facilities is preferable to disposing of these materials in sanitary landfills and that EPA should support these programs to the greatest extent practical."[23] He left it to the states to oversee the burgeoning HHW activities.

At the first HHW national conference in late 1986 (discussed further below), Marcia Williams, director of EPA's office of solid waste, echoed this view, "EPA supports and encourages household hazardous waste (HHW) collection programs. The agency views these programs as a way of ensuring the safe disposal of these products and of educating the public."[24] At this gathering, EPA unveiled its first major publication on the subject, *A Survey of Household Hazardous Wastes and Related Collection Programs*."[25]

In 1988, Deputy EPA Administrator Winston Porter issued a "policy directive" clarifying EPA's position on, and support of, HHW programs.[26] This directive is discussed in more detail in Chapter 1. In 1993, EPA produced a general guidance document for organizing local HHW collection events.[27] Since most of the action on HHW was happening in the states and at the local level, one of the key roles that EPA played in the growth of the movement was to sponsor the first 13 national conferences on the subject (see below).

Early Workshops/Conferences

The state of California hosted the first conference aimed at HHW, in twin sessions. Held in Berkeley on December 11, 1984, and in Los Angeles on December 13, 1984, the "Household and Small Business Hazardous Waste Collection Symposium" included presentations about the pioneering projects in Florida, Seattle, Sacramento, Palo Alto, and San Diego, as well as some early research on small business generators.

The Ecology Center in Ann Arbor, Michigan, organized the first regional conference on the topic of HHW in April 1985. It featured presentations from the Seattle, Sacramento, and Wisconsin early events and helped to kick-start projects throughout the Great Lakes region.[28]

The National Conferences

The first national conference to share information on this emerging waste management issue was convened in Arlington, Virginia, in 1986, sponsored by the U.S. Environmental Protection Agency and organized by Dana Duxbury, who worked out of the Tufts University Center for Environmental Management.[29] The event signaled that a critical mass of local, independent projects had been reached and that a national movement was born. Presentations covered a wide range of topics related to the early collection projects from around the country. U.S. EPA's new report was issued and discussed, the definition of HHW and whether or not it posed a problem were debated, and "how-to" sessions were held on organizing collection events and public education.

Annual meetings have continued since. The first eight were organized by Dana Duxbury, with sponsorship from the U.S. EPA and in partnership with the American Public Works Association and the Government Refuse Collection and Disposal Association. Later conferences were organized under the aegis of the North American Hazardous Materials Management Association (NAHMMA), initially in partnership with the International City/County Management Association, then with the Solid Waste Association of North America, then (beginning in 2001) on its own. Appendix 2-A provides a synopsis of these annual events. The conference agendas and proceedings, available through NAHMMA[30], catalog better than any other resource the development and evolution of this field, which is only briefly presented in this chapter.

Early conferences focused on arguments about what is HHW (mainly between product manufacturers and proponents of HHW programs); clarifications from U.S. EPA about HHW's regulatory status with respect to both RCRA and CERCLA; and descriptions of ever-more-complex examples of local HHW collection events and services. Public education was always a theme along with the dominant focus on collection, at first aimed at marketing the collection events but later expanding to look at behavior change and source reduction.

Early "special waste" categories that received the most attention included batteries (primarily for their mercury content), used motor oil, paints, and pesticides. Early "problem wastes" included dioxin-containing herbicides and wood preservatives, PCB contamination in paints, and unknown chemical products received at collections.

One vivid feature of many early conferences was a "live demonstration of incompatibles" conducted outside the venue by Larry Sweetser from Sanitary Fill Co. of San Francisco. Larry was mixing incompatibles, torching aerosols and otherwise demonstrating some of the immediate safety concerns associated with hazardous household products.

By 1991, Duxbury's database of programs across the country had documented at least one HHW collection event or service in all 50 states, with the arrival of Georgia, Mississippi, and Nevada in that year. Collection programs of one kind or another had grown to more than 800 per year. "Permanent" programs (providing ongoing, at least once-per-month service) had grown to 96 in 16 states.[31]

In addition to names already mentioned, a host of people across the country provided key leadership, expertise, and experience at the national, state, or local level, from government, from businesses (product manufacturers as well as waste contractors), and from NGOs. Appendix 2-B to this chapter presents a chronology of names that the authors recognize as providing key leadership on the HHW issue over these decades.

In the mid to late 1980s, Bill Rathje and Doug Wilson from the "Garbage Project" at the University of Arizona conducted a series of important studies quantifying household hazardous waste in municipal solid waste, both through sorts of garbage at the time of disposal and through archaeological digs of municipal landfills.[32–34] Their presentations at the annual conferences provided useful data and insights, as well as humorous anecdotes.

Agricultural/farm pesticide collection programs represented some of the first collection efforts and have been a mainstay throughout the country, often combined with HHW programs in rural areas or predominantly agricultural states. Chuck Cubbage of Michigan catalogued these pesticide collection efforts all through the 1990s, state by state, as recorded in the annual HHW conference proceedings. Cubbage's 1999 summary is the most recent.[35] The large state-sponsored collection programs in the mid to late 1980s in Michigan, Minnesota, and Washington brought in impressive quantities of old pesticides (more than 300 pounds per participant on average); among the most common products received were lead arsenate and DDT.[36] In 2000, the National Pesticide Stewardship Alliance, now called the Pesticide Stewardship Alliance, was formed.[37]

Product stewardship is an approach to extend or share responsibility for products and their wastes among manufacturers, retailers, governments, consumers, and others. This issue was first addressed at the national NAHMMA conference in Austin, Texas, in 1994. Groundbreaking North American product stewardship requirements were established at that time in British Columbia, Canada, for a wide variety of product categories including paints, pesticides, solvents, motor oil, and other typical HHW. Canada was ahead of the U.S. on product stewardship and remains so today.[38]

EPA's "consumer labeling initiative" ("CLI") started in 1996 to clarify and simplify the pesticide label for consumers. Label considerations included readability, ingredient information, hazard identification, precautionary statements, and overall utility to the consumer to make informed product choices and to use products safely.[39] The disposal recommendation on the label turned out to be the most contentious issue. The wording of pesticide labels had for years been along the lines of, "Securely wrap original container in several layers of newspaper and discard in trash."[40] In 2001, EPA at last came out with the compromise language, "For disposal of partially-full containers, call your local solid waste agency or 1-800-CLEANUP for disposal instructions."[41] This compromise language was in part due to the recognition that many state and local regulations prohibited the old label wording, and that many HHW programs existed (although not universally) to safely manage waste pesticides as HHW rather than trash.

Consumer electronic wastes came into their own in the late 1990s and have been a dominant part of conference discussions and special collections since then, as state and local programs grappled with heavy metals and later the issue of brominated flame retardants in these ubiquitous products. Pharmaceuticals as a household waste problem first surfaced in conference discussions in 2003. Product stewardship discussions became more detailed, children's health and environmental health issues in general took on greater prominence, and the conversation among HHW professionals has in recent years clearly shifted "upstream" to products and ingredients not even on the horizon 20 years earlier, such as Teflon®-coated materials, CCA-treated wood, personal care products, and endocrine disrupting chemicals. Green chemistry, chemical policy, community-based social marketing, environmental justice, and environmental health are the themes moving forward as of 2007.

International HHW Conference in Vienna

While the national hazardous materials management conferences have always enjoyed participation by Canadian colleagues, Prof. Gerhard Vogel organized the first truly international conference focused on HHW, which was held in Vienna, Austria, on May 16-17, 1991.[42] Speakers from eight European countries, the United States, South Africa, Hong Kong, and Japan presented a wide range of systems and levels of experience with consumer products and wastes containing hazardous chemicals (known as "problemstoffe" in Vienna). Even Denmark's system, the earliest organized and most comprehensive in the world, only reported collecting between 10 and 20% of the estimated generation of HHW at that time. Dr. Vogel emphasized that to be truly successful, source reduction will be much more important than separate (and very costly) waste collection.

Formation of the Waste Watch Center, NAHMMA, and Earth 9-1-1

Dana Duxbury formed the non-profit Waste Watch Center in 1988 as "an environmental education organization devoted to educational projects in the areas of solid, hazardous and household hazardous waste management, reduction, reuse, recycling and pollution prevention."[43] The Center operated until 2000.

Via the Waste Watch Center, the first issue of *Household Hazardous Waste Management News* came in Spring 1989. A roughly quarterly publication, it served to share valuable national information and updates and provided a forum for Duxbury to editorialize on topics of HHW importance. A total of 39 issues were printed over 11 years, the final issue coming in October 1999. The first and last issues of this important communication vehicle had a mailing list of over 8,000 in its heyday.[44] Second only to the national conference proceedings, these newsletters provide one of the best sources of historical information on the growth of HHW programs and key HHW issues through the 1990s.

NAHMMA, the North American Hazardous Materials Management Association, was formed in 1993 by a caucus of attendees at the eighth national conference in Burlington, Vermont. This meeting was organized by Michael Bender (VT) who became the NAHMMA Executive Director. NAHMMA was established as a membership-based professional organization that was "dedicated to pollution prevention and reducing the toxicity of municipal waste streams." Dave Galvin was the first president.

NAHMMA has matured in recent years into an active organization serving state and local programs that address HHW, Conditionally Exempt Small Quantity Generators (CESQG) and related issues. In addition to hosting the long-running national conference, NAHMMA supports professional training, policy development, education and outreach, and a growing number of active state or regional chapters. Information is available at www.nahmma.org.

Following are members of the Founding Board of Directors for the North American Hazardous Materials Management Association 1993–1994.

1. Annie Berthold-Bond, *Green Alternatives* magazine, Rhinebeck, New York
2. Ned Brooks, Minnesota Pollution Control Agency, St. Paul, Minn.
3. Scott Cassel, Massachusetts Executive Office of Environmental Affairs, Boston, Mass.
4. Thomas Dewhirst, Kalamazoo Human Services Dept., Michigan
5. Dana Duxbury, Waste Watch Center, Andover, Massachusetts
6. Karen Feeney, Santa Barbara Public Works Dept., California
7. Judi Frantz, California Dept. of Health Services, Sacramento, California
8. Michael Frishman, Sec.-Treas., Massachusetts Office of Technical Assistance, Boston, Massachussets
9. Dave Galvin, Pres., Local Hazardous Waste Management Program in King County, Seattle, Washington
10. W. Robert Kelly, Kelly Green Environmental Services, Exeter, New Hampshire
11. Eric Laut, Chemical Waste Management, Inc., Napierville, Illinois
12. Claudia Marsales, Woodington Systems, Inc., Thorold, Canada
13. Elizabeth McCormick, Laidlaw Environmental Services, Inc., Columbia, South Carolina
14. Bill Quan, San Francisco Hazardous Waste Program, California
15. Deanna Seaman, Norcal Waste Systems, Inc., San Francisco, California
16. Marie Steinwachs, Vice Pres., Household Hazardous Waste Project, Springfield, Missouri
17. Ann Thorsen, Washington County, Stillwater, Minnesota
18. Mike Winka, New Jersey Department of Environmental Protection, Trenton, New Jersey

Another organization, Environmental Recycling Hotline, was established in 1991 by Chris Warner, a visionary who saw ways to use technology to provide a central, convenient source of information about state and local environmental services, first via a 1-800 telephone hotline and soon after via the Internet. The ER Hotline grew into "Earth 911," the best source of up-to-date, specific information on local HHW and other recycling services throughout the country. It is as simple as entering one's zip code into the website (www.earth911.org) or the current telephone line (1-800-CLEANUP) to find details on local services for general HHW, batteries, electronic waste, and a variety of other topics, as well as a wealth of background information on these topics.

From Events to Permanent Programs

Single-day or short-duration collection events evolved into ongoing program services, including permanent or fixed collection sites, mobile collection operations, satellite services, and other variations. Duxbury defined "permanent program" as a program that accepts HHW at least once per month. Today, permanent refers more to permanent structures that accept HHW either seasonally or year-round and can store HHW on-site in compartments to separate incompatible materials, for up to 90 days by law. This type of facility that has become more common provides greater convenience to residents by offering more collection opportunities. It also can save the operator money by permitting the bulking and temporary storing of materials instead of sending partial drums off-site.

San Bernardino County, Calif., is generally regarded as the first permanent collection program in the U.S., begun in 1985 with drop-off sites located at fire stations. Martha's Vineyard, Mass., developed the first small-scale permanent facility in 1988—a trailer, with two-times-per-month collections. San Francisco in 1988 was the first program to build a large-scale, specially designed, permanent collection facility for HHW. Anchorage, Alaska, soon followed in early 1989 with one of the first specially built facilities designed to collect CESQG wastes as well as HHW. Hennepin County, Minn., built the first permanent facility in the U.S. that was designed into (as part of) an MSW transfer station; it began operations in 1990.[45]

Door-to-door services have been offered to home-bound individuals on a small scale, and to all households in some areas, focused primarily on used motor oil and batteries, but in some places covering the full range of HHW. Special (limited product) drop-offs have been set up for some of the less-hazardous, readily recyclable wastes such as used motor oil, latex paint, batteries, and antifreeze. California authorized such drop-off sites in 1990, and they became known as "ABOPs" for the wastes usually accepted there (antifreeze, batteries, oil, paint).

As HHW programs developed, they primarily were associated with solid waste services at the state and local levels. Over time they have become more and more integrated into solid waste systems, including recycling services. In some areas, wastewater treatment authorities have been a driving force in their efforts to keep HHW out of the wastewater, but these have remained clearly in the minority.

Contractors

Private hazardous waste haulers have been an integral, essential part of the movement since day one. As noted earlier, one of the very first HHW collection services in the country was offered by Chemical Processors, Inc., in Seattle, which opened its doors to general public customers on a free, voluntary basis in 1980. Contractors have honed their expertise in assisting local governments to run HHW collection services as well as in the recycling or disposal of the wastes collected. Services run the gamut from selective handling of individual waste types, to turnkey, comprehensive event or facility operations, to door-to-door (*i.e.,* curbside) pick-up.

The role of waste-handling contractors in the growth and development of the HHW movement cannot be overstated. These companies have provided expertise to state and local program sponsors. They helped to evolve the way events, facilities, and recycling options operate, based on real-world experience, adaptability to different state laws, and business competition. They were involved in organizing as well as helping to sponsor all of the national conferences. They have served in leadership roles in NAHMMA. They continue to offer proactive, efficient services while helping to change the very nature of those services over time.

An alphabet soup of companies has worked with state and local government programs since 1981. Mergers, buy-outs, and consolidation have occurred within the industry over the past few decades to the extent that it is difficult to follow the trail.

Some of the major companies that were instrumental in the early years included Chemical Processors, Inc. in Seattle, beginning in 1980; Northeast Solvents in Massachusetts; SCA Chemical Services, Inc., which was the contractor for the first event in Lexington, Mass., in 1982 and also had the first Amnesty Days contract in Florida, which became GSX and operated throughout the East Coast and Midwest in the early to mid 1980s, which was acquired by Laidlaw Environmental Services in the late '80s; BKK Corp. in California, which operated the early San Diego door-to-door services; Northwest EnviroService in Seattle, which also ran the early HHW and CESQG collections in Alaska; American Environmental and Safety Specialists in California; Sanitary Fill Company, which operated San Francisco's HHW services, and later became part of Norcal Solid Waste Systems, Inc.; Chemical Waste Management, which was involved in New England collections in the early 1980s as well as sites throughout the country by the mid '80s; Clean Harbors, Inc., in New England beginning around 1985; Crosby & Overton on the West Coast; Rollins Environmental Services in Delaware; and CECOS-BFI in Texas in the late '80s.

Major players through the 1990s included many of the above companies plus Aptus in Minnesota (later acquired by Rollins); MSE Environmental in California and the Midwest; Burlington Environmental in Washington, later acquired by Philip Environmental; Advanced Environmental Technology Corporation (AETC) which merged with Chemical Waste Management (a subsidiary of Waste Management Services) to form Advanced Environmental Technical Services (AETS); Clean Harbors with an expanded range across the East Coast; Heritage Environmental in Indiana and Washington; Amazon Environmental in California; and Curbside, Inc. (a Safety-Kleen subsidiary).

In the new century, key contractors included, in the Midwest, Onyx Environmental Services that later became Veolia; EQ in Florida; Care Environmental in NJ and the Southeast; and the expansion of Philip Services, MSE Environmental, and Clean Harbors across the country. As a handful of waste companies now dominate the field, an apparent result of the merging and consolidation in the HHW management field, there appears to be a leveling off of costs to communities.

Individuals who played key leadership roles in the evolution of HHW programs across the country are noted in Appendix 2-B.

Product Manufacturers

Product manufacturers reacted to the emergence of the HHW movement in a major way in the mid-to-late 1980s and throughout the 1990s. They are less involved in dialogue on HHW issues today. At first, manufacturers of products that were considered hazardous debated the definitions of HHW and disagreed with the need for special disposal of any residuals of their products. Presentations and major discussions with contrasting opinions punctuated the first five national hazardous materials management conferences in the late '80s and continued in some topic areas throughout the '90s.

The Chemical Specialties Manufacturers Association (CSMA), which represented manufacturers of household cleaners, disinfectants, antimicrobials, automotive specialty products, polishes, floor maintenance products, home, lawn, and garden pesticides, and personal care products, contended that, "household products are not a threat to human health or the environment, can safely be disposed of through normal collection procedures, [and] will not, even in significant amounts, pose an environmental threat at landfills."[46] CSMA members argued that only the following items should be separated from the municipal waste stream: certain banned pesticides such as DDT, used motor oil, old gasoline, car batteries, ammunition and explosives, and unidentified materials of a suspicious nature.[47] An affiliate group, the Household Products Disposal Council, later named the Household and Institutional Product Information Council, was involved in creating public information campaigns regarding these messages and in the later peer review processes presented below. CSMA changed its name in 2000 to the Consumer Specialty Products Association. Many in the organization continue to argue against "green" trends today.[48] Some companies, however, appear to have begun to embrace the concept due to consumer market interest.

The National Paints and Coatings Association (NPCA) was also involved in dialogues early on, agreeing that solvent-based paints should be considered HHW while excluding water-based (latex) paints. NPCA promotes a "six-point program for leftover paints"[49] that emphasizes careful purchase and use, safe storage, and managing left-over solvent-based paints via HHW collections. NPCA is directly involved in the Paint Product Stewardship Initiative, a multi-stakeholder dialogue aimed at the establishment of a national system for the management of leftover paints.

The Soap and Detergent Association was active in discussions regarding hazardous consumer products and HHW from the very beginning. The SDA represents major cleaning product manufacturers and has often joined CSMA (now CSPA) in challenging the need for special collection of cleaning product wastes or the need for "alternative" product suggestions (discussed in more detail below). SDA continues today to argue against "green" trends.[50]

Key industry participants who were directly involved in the national conferences or other dialogues regarding hazardous household products and HHW included the Clorox Company (makers of sodium hypochlorite bleach and disinfecting cleaners), Eveready and Spectrum Brands/Rayovac® (makers of household batteries), the Drackett Company (makers of Drano®), Church & Dwight Company (manufacturers of Arm & Hammer® baking soda products), Reckitt & Coleman (Lysol®, Black Flag®), S.C. Johnson (Raid®, Windex®, later Drano®), Proctor & Gamble (Tide®, Mr.Clean®, Febreze® and many other brands), Solaris (Ortho® products at the time) and Rochester-Midland (makers of commercial cleaners).

Manufacturer involvement in discussions regarding product waste disposal recommendations, label wording, and product reformulation was a key part of the early national conferences and is essential if product stewardship is to be further advanced. Thus, it would be beneficial to bring industry players back to the table at NAHMMA conferences to advance discussions on HHW management, chemicals policy, and further development of less hazardous products.

Household batteries were one of the biggest issues in the first ten-plus years of HHW development, due mainly to their mercury content and, for rechargeable batteries, their cadmium content. The Eveready and Rayovac companies were regular participants in the national conferences until after the development of the Rechargeable Battery Recycling

Corporation and the successful reduction of mercury levels in household batteries in the mid '90s.

Mercury issues also brought fluorescent lamp manufacturers such as Philips Lighting Co. into conversations on waste management and the importance of reducing the mercury content of lamps. Later, general electronic products and thermostats became a focus of concern and continue to be items addressed today in direct dialogues between product manufacturers and HHW interests.

CESQGs

The handling of conditionally exempt small quantity generator ("CESQG") business wastes has been intertwined with HHW services since the early days of the movement. Many of these wastes from small businesses such as auto shops, janitorial services, sign makers, painting contractors, and many other businesses are similar to, or even the same product residuals as, HHW. Most CESQG businesses produce too small volumes of such wastes to make commercial collections economical. Chapter 1 provides background on the legal definition of these small-quantity generators.

As HHW programs developed, many have addressed the CESQG realm. The national hazardous materials management conference has, for example, grown to include an almost equal focus of attention on small business services as on households. By offering a range of technical assistance, incentives, and waste collection services to CESQG businesses, communities benefit from proper waste management and these small businesses benefit from services to which they might not otherwise have easy access.

Alaska's early collection events in Anchorage and Fairbanks in 1983 represent the first documented collections for a wide range of small quantity generator business wastes. Amnesty Days in Florida, which began in 1984, launched a large-scale, mobile service that included CESQGs as well as households right from the beginning.

The Association of Bay Area Governments did an important early study in 1985 that detailed the types of hazardous wastes coming from a variety of CESQGs by standard industrial classification ("SIC") code.[51] These wastes included chlorinated solvents such as perchloroethylene, 1,1,1-trichloroethane and methylene chloride; paints, inks, and dyes; pesticides; motor oil; brake fluids; antifreeze; acids, bases; heavy metals; and essentially every other type of hazardous waste generated by industries in large (fully regulated) quantities.

Santa Barbara, Calif. started collecting CESQG wastes in 1985. Counties across the state of Florida began addressing CESQGs in the local program development that followed the Amnesty Days' sweep-out in the mid '80s. Marin County, Calif., started in 1991. The Local Hazardous Waste Management Program in King County, Wash., also kicked off major CESQG programs in the Seattle area in 1991. Vermont developed small business programs at about the same time.

It was not until 1989 that CESQGs were addressed in the national hazardous materials management conference sessions. Eventually the national conference name changed to include "small business and universal wastes" in 1995.

HHW Education and Outreach

Complementary to the rise of HHW collection services over the past 25 years, public outreach and educational efforts have aimed at both raising awareness about the issue in order to foster appropriate participation in collections, and encouraging changes in consumer behavior. Public education campaigns have run the gamut from telephone hotlines to brochures, media advertisements, workshops, garbage-can stickers, utility bill inserts, displays, speakers' bureaus, shelf-labels, and school programs, to name a few.

The first publication aimed at the general public to raise awareness about hazardous household products, including promotion of caution in their use and recommendations for disposal, was a small brochure produced by Galvin's program in Seattle in 1979: *Toxic Substances in Your Home*.[52] (See Figure 2.1) Many others began to proliferate in the early 1980s. Duxbury and others in the League of Women Voters of Massachusetts produced an early video regarding HHW, called *Beginning at Home: Tackling Household Hazardous Wastes*,[53] as a way to encourage new HHW collection programs. Jack Lord of Santa Monica, Calif., produced an early, glossy, widely circulated booklet, *Hazardous Wastes from Homes*,[54] in 1986, which also had a companion teachers' guide for schools. The Environmental Hazards Management Institute (EHMI) produced the popular *Household Hazardous Waste Wheel*®[55] beginning in 1987, which was widely distributed by state and local programs, HHW contractors, and community organizations across the country. A few of these influential early publications are shown in Figure 2.4.

In 1985, the Washington Toxics Coalition developed an open house tour that led attendees through a home in Seattle, with examples of hazardous products and safer alternatives in each room. It was called *Home Safe Home*, and was a seminal event in the development and promotion of recommendations for alternatives to hazardous products. A segment about this tour was aired on National Public Radio.

The Household Hazardous Waste Project in Missouri was started in 1986 by Sondra Goodman and Marie Steinwachs at the Southwest Missouri State University in Springfield. It was an educational program designed to supplement and complement collection services, aimed at "help[ing] people to identify risks, make informed decisions, and to use, store, and dispose of products safely."[56] The HHW Project is still going strong 21 years later, as part of the University of Missouri Extension (see www.extension.missouri.edu/owm/hhw. htm). It is a useful resource for educational materials and expertise on this subject.

The Environmental Health Coalition in San Diego is another long-standing group involved with HHW education that started the first door-to-door pilot HHW collection program in the early 1980s in San Diego. EHC produced one of the earliest, detailed fliers on the topic, *The World Is Full of Toxic Waste – Your Home Shouldn't Be*,[57] as well as an early, 29-minute video, *Toxics in Your Home*, and an early hazard rating system for household products. This organization continues to work on toxic chemical reduction and environmental justice issues today (see www.environmentalhealth.org).

Shelf-labeling at retail stores emerged as one on-site strategy to raise awareness on the part of the consumer at stores, and to possibly promote a shift to consumer purchases of less hazardous products. Iowa was the first state to attempt this directly, as part of its Groundwater Protection Act in 1987. Retail outlets were required to post information materials in the stores in order to educate consumers about the "danger incurred in disposal of products, the proper disposal of the products and the use of alternative products which do

Figure 2.4. Examples of Early HHW Education Materials. (*Photo by Ned Ahrens, used with permission*).

not present as great a disposal danger as the products specified."[58] Vermont followed soon afterward, as part of its Toxic Use Reduction Act of 1990, requiring that "shelf talkers" be posted in retail stores. Both programs have had mixed response and results over the years.

Early HHW educational programs were primarily aimed at raising awareness and advertising the availability of the collection services offered in the community. Much of the effort followed a linear "knowledge-attitude-behavior model," that predicted if information was provided, attitudes would change and in turn, people would perform the desired behavior. Behavior change is much more complex.

While informational campaigns remain necessary, there has been a move toward motivating consumers to buy less hazardous products as well as to minimize the generation of wastes that need special handling, or, in the case of wastes such as do-it-yourself (DIY) used motor oil, to encourage proper recycling of the oil and oil filters. In the early to mid 1990s, frustration with the lack of results from informational campaigns caused some involved in HHW programs to look for a better model. Michael Dennis' presentation[59] at the Vermont conference in 1993 caught the interest of HHW practitioners. Behavior change became the rallying cry, using techniques adapted from social marketing efforts and topics such as smoking cessation, seat-belt promotion, and other health-based issues.

Annette Frahm and colleagues in King County, Wash., presented these techniques in 1995 in the guidebook, *Changing Behavior: Insights and Applications.*[60] Douglas McKenzie-Mohr from the University of New Brunswick, Canada, introduced community-based social marketing in his book, *Fostering Sustainable Behavior.*[61] (See also Chapter 6)

Many programs encouraged citizens to use "less toxic alternatives," either certain specific products or, more frequently, generic recipes such as the combination of vinegar and baking soda to unclog a drain pipe, or baking soda as a general purpose scouring powder. The primary focus on these alternative recommendations tended to be cleaning products. Many grew out of old wives' tales and were not well researched or based on careful analysis. Manufacturers of products for which alternatives were being suggested countered the claims of undue hazard of their products and efficacy of the alternative recipes, and expressed concerns about the promotion of consumer mixing of materials to create alternative products.

The Washington Toxics Coalition produced the first rigorously researched rating system for name-brand products in 1994, based on criteria covering human health and safety as well as environmental concerns. Modeled after *Consumer Reports*, Philip Dickey's *Buy Smart, Buy Safe*[62] guide was widely circulated and served to fuel the concerns of some product manufacturers, as well as put pressure on them to consider reformulation. Some companies did reformulate products, removing certain problematic ingredients. Whether this was in response to such pressures or part of ongoing changes within the industry is unclear. Dickey produced a companion guide, *Grow Smart, Grow Safe*,[63] focused on lawn and garden products, which is still in such demand that it is now in its fifth edition.

A lengthy series of well-researched fact sheets on a wide variety of products, issues, and "safer" alternatives was developed by the Washington Toxics Coalition beginning in the late 1980s. Dickey collated these into a single publication in 2006 called, *Safer Alternatives for the Home and Garden*,[64] which is one of the best publications on products and alternative options available. The Washington Toxics Coalition (www.watoxics.org) continues to be a national leader in toxic chemical reduction.

The Waste Watch Center convened a "Cleaning Products Summit" meeting in March 1995 to bring key product manufacturers together with state and local HHW program managers. Representatives from Clorox, S.C. Johnson, Reckitt & Colman, Dow Chemical, Proctor & Gamble, Rochester Midland, and other chemical product manufacturers pressed for clarity regarding the definition of HHW, which products were of highest concern to HHW program managers, and the need to eliminate or at least improve alternative product suggestions, including some that were clearly wrong, useless, or unhealthy. The "Andover Principles" were agreed upon by consensus at that meeting:

- "No one wants to distribute inaccurate or misleading information regarding 'alternatives' or commercial cleaning products.
- No product or recipe should be recommended as a disinfectant unless it is registered with the EPA.
- There is unanimous concern about unsubstantiated environmental claims ("green," "earth friendly," etc.) as they relate to all cleaning products.
- Both industry and non-industry groups agree that there is a need to educate one another on issues related to products with hazardous constituents, product development, and HHW program mandates; and the attendees pledge to do so.

- There is a need to review existing information on alternatives.
- The non-industry representatives need to develop a comprehensive list of their specific and actionable (by all parties) concerns."[65]

To address the last principle, a white paper[66] was written by a group of program participants that served to crystallize many of the concepts important to HHW programs, with an underpinning of documented reference citations. Representatives of the CSMA and the Soap and Detergent Association (SDA) intended to produce a parallel paper, but none was forthcoming and the dialogue ended.

Bills requiring that public information about products be "competent and reliable" began appearing in various state legislatures or administrative proceedings in 1996. California, for example, adopted a source reduction policy that called for "relevant and accurate data" and "reliable evidence" to support public information materials.[67] Agreements were reached in California and Washington to develop peer review processes to assess alternative product, recipe, or ingredient recommendations. The Washington effort foundered after attempting too complex a process. On the other hand, the California peer review project, sponsored by the California HHW Information Exchange, produced valuable documentation and advice via an Internet-based, refereed, collaborative process. It reviewed the following materials for frequently-cited household uses: boric acid, vinegar, baking soda, borax, diatomaceous earth, pyrethrins, piperonyl butoxide, tri-sodium phosphate, d-limonene, hydrogen peroxide, and linseed oil. The general-use guide, *Alternatives to Household Chemicals*,[68] that was produced as a result of the technical reviews is still a valuable reference in the field.

In the mid to late 1990s, a separate approach unfolded in the Southeast. Under the auspices of the Southern States Energy Board and its Waste Management Coalition, a Task Force on Household Hazardous Waste was initiated in 1996 to "help local solid waste officials provide guidance on the management of household product waste (HPW) and household hazardous waste (HHW) to residents who have limited or no access to HPW and HHW collection programs."[69] The task force involved representatives of state agencies as well as individuals from the Household and Institutional Product Information Council, the National Paints and Coatings Association, the Soap and Detergent Association, and other product manufacturers. After four years of hammering out recommendations, this group produced its *Resource Guide*[70] which in most cases recommended solid waste or sewer disposal options, and included special procedures for reconditioning old gasoline, handling HHW during transport, disposal down the drain, solidification, and proper storage. Such recommendations were not widely supported by state and local programs that already had active HHW collection services.

Product and Ingredient Changes

Looking back over nearly three decades provides a useful perspective on the topic of hazardous household products. While much is generally the same for HHW programs, many product manufacturers have changed product formulations for the better and some quite significantly. New issues continue to emerge.

Pesticides

Almost all organochlorine pesticides, such as DDT, aldrin/dieldrin, endrin, chlordane, and heptachlor, have been eliminated from sale and use in the United States over the past thirty years. Only lindane (the gamma isomer of benzene hexachloride) is still sold, and, ironically (or appallingly, depending on one's point of view), its one remaining use is in direct application to people (mostly children's scalps) to kill lice. Other old pesticides have also joined the banned or cancelled lists, such as the phenoxy herbicides 2,4,5-T and Silvex, lead arsenate, pentachlorophenol (some non-household uses remain), strychnine, and, more recently for most home and landscape uses, chromated copper arsenate, chlorpyrifos, and diazinon. It is progress that these particular poisons are no longer available for sale in consumer products. Still, old stocks continue to show up at collections, some in astounding quantities even in the year 2007 (35 years after the final cancellations of DDT, for example).

Modern pesticidal products continue to evolve. Use of the chrysanthemum extract pyrethrum and, more abundantly today, the synthetic substitute pyrethroids, continues to grow. While thought to be safer than some of the older products that they substitute, new studies are noting unforeseen sediment toxicity in urban streams likely caused by widespread pyrethroid use.[71] Many modern pesticides are more targeted to particular pests (*i.e.,* less broad-spectrum products are available). They are generally less persistent in the environment, but sometimes have other toxicity concerns.[72]

Alternative products such as the "25(b)" pesticides (*e.g.,* certain herbs, spices, mint oils, corn gluten, and table salt) are considered of such minimum risk that they are exempted from most federal registration requirements. The growth of baits, traps, and other innovative products continues the move away from broadcast applications of broad-spectrum poisons. The more targeted approaches often minimize unintended exposures or, in many cases, may not use poisonous chemicals at all. Use of Integrated Pest Management (IPM) continues to spread, as does demand for organic foods. (IPM employs a whole-system perspective including establishment of pest tolerances, careful monitoring, up-front design aimed at minimizing pest issues, and various biological, mechanical, and other tactics that result in minimal pesticide use.) Despite these improvements, products such as "weed and feed" herbicide/fertilizer mixtures are still heavily used on lawns in broadcast applications. Continued progress is needed and major changes are likely to continue in the product realm of household pesticides.

Batteries

Significant changes have been made in battery handling and content over the past few decades. Lead-acid batteries, primarily used in automobiles, were an early target of hazardous product recycling efforts, with great success. In 1986, lead-acid auto batteries represented 65% of the lead in municipal solid waste (MSW), even with a claimed recovery rate in the 70% range.[73] Since then, most states enacted legislation requiring an advance fee and recycling incentives. Recent studies show a 98% recovery rate.[74]

Nickel-cadmium (NiCad) rechargeable batteries represented more than half of the cadmium in MSW in the 1980s[75] and 75% of all the cadmium in MSW in the mid 1990s.[76] After a push in Minnesota, New Jersey, and other states in the early 1990s to reduce NiCad disposal and to promote recycling, the Rechargeable Battery Recycling Corporation (RBRC) was formed in 1994, followed by the federal Battery Act in 1996. Newer rechargeable batteries are using nickel-metal hydride (NiMH) as well as lithium ion technology, further reducing disposal of cadmium into MSW.

Mercury levels in household batteries used to be high. In 1989, household batteries accounted for 89% of the mercury in MSW even though they made up only 0.005% by volume.[77] This was a big issue at that time, especially for those areas that combusted their MSW. Led by Minnesota, a variety of states put pressure on manufacturers to reduce the mercury content of household batteries. By the end of 1993, the four dominant battery manufacturers (Duracell, Eveready, Panasonic/Kodak, and Rayovac) converted to "no mercury added" designs for alkaline and zinc-carbon batteries. This approach was reinforced in the federal Battery Act of 1996. Mercury levels have gradually declined in battery discards as the older batteries are removed from use.

Paints

From the late 1800s until World War II, essentially all commercial paints were "oil" or solvent-based. These products could release significant amounts of volatile organic compound (VOC) vapors when they dried and required organic solvent thinners for mixing and clean-up. The first commercially viable, water-based ("latex") paint, called Kem-Tone®, was developed by Sherwin-Williams in 1941. It did not capture significant shares of the market until the 1960s. The slogan, "No muss, no fuss, no bother," helped to propel the shift from oil to latex in household paints.[78–79] The shift to latex use continued steadily over the second half of the 1900s, and by 2007 the National Paints and Coatings Association estimated that of all architectural coatings (including house paints, stains, and related products) sold in the United States, "over 85 percent ... are now water-based; the remaining 15 percent or so are considered solvent-based. This is in response to consumer demands for paints that are easier to apply while being environmentally friendly."[80]

White lead was widely used in household paints as a pigment and drying agent. It was significantly reduced in many paints starting in the 1950s and it was eliminated nearly three decades later by a Consumer Product Safety Commission rule in 1978. Old cans of paint with high lead content continue to show up at HHW collections, although their numbers are beginning to dwindle. Old leaded paints continue to present significant health issues in homes built before 1978 as old paint peels and as remodeling projects redistribute the lead in house dust, which is then easily taken up by young children. Lead abatement by professionals is a far better option than DIY remodeling in these older homes, especially where young children are living.

Mercury was also widely used in paint as a fungicide/mildewcide until the late 1980s. In May 1991, the last pesticide registration for mercury in paint was cancelled. Latex paint batching and recycling efforts have been haunted by this legacy throughout the history of HHW services for programs that have collected water-based paints. As with lead, the end appears to be in sight as most batched drums of collected latex paint no longer have mercury levels that would designate them as a hazardous waste.

Volatile organic compounds (VOCs) in the solvent portion of paints have decreased significantly over the past decades due to pressure from air regulators, especially in California (and in particular driven by the South Coast Air Quality Management District). Today, low VOC and ultra-low VOC paints and coatings are common.[81]

Manufacturers are stepping up to the plate and progress seems imminent on the development of a national product stewardship solution for waste paint.[82]

Other Mercury-Containing Products

Fluorescent tube lamps contained on average 35–50 mg of mercury in the early 1990s. The small or compact fluorescent lamps (CFLs) had about 20 mg.[83] Due to pressure from state and local solid waste managers, especially in areas where MSW is incinerated, manufacturers have been steadily reducing the mercury content. In 1995, Philips Lighting came out with a 40-watt lamp that contained less than 10 mg mercury and would pass the RCRA Toxic Characteristic Leaching Procedure (TCLP) test. Other "green" lamps have followed from most manufacturers so that today's "green end-cap" or similar tube lamps typically contain less than 10 mg of mercury and the compact fluorescent lamps contain 3–5 mg. While this is an improvement from 10-plus years ago, a mercury-free fluorescent lamp does not yet exist. With concerns about climate change pushing greater use of fluorescent lamps to reduce carbon emissions, safe handling of used CFLs, such as via a product stewardship take-back system, remains a priority for HHW programs.

Flashing lights in the heels of sneakers attracted consumer interest when first introduced in 1992 by L.A. Gear. However, to light up the sneakers the manufacturer used mercury switches and an instant controversy arose. These products were short-lived; manufacturers suffered significant costs in the recalls that followed their introduction. Numerous state laws now ban mercury in clothing and other similar items. Uses of mercury in thermometers, thermostats, tilt-switches, novelties, and other products continue to get attention, including state legislation, and efforts are increasing to phase out essentially all uses of this toxic element.

Used Motor Oil

In 1988, do-it-yourself (DIY) oil changers generated 193 million gallons of used motor oil in the U.S., of which only 9% was properly recycled.[84] The number of U.S. drivers who change their own oil has decreased markedly since then, as "quick lube" services increase and as the population ages.[85] Recycling of DIY used oil has improved, mostly due to significant increases in convenience. According to Earth-911, there are now more than 12,000 community-based oil recycling locations across the country provided by either local government or private businesses such as auto parts stores or service stations.[86]

Cleaning Products

Early concerns with household cleaners focused mainly on corrosives (including caustics), reactives, products containing phosphates, and biodegradability issues. Considerable effort was made by HHW programs to promote alternatives to corrosive products such as drain openers, oven cleaners, and toilet-bowl cleaners. These products remain ubiquitous today although some less-hazardous products in these categories are available from manufacturers such as Seventh Generation and others. Chlorine bleach remains a staple item and is now widely available in concentrated "ultra" formulations that are labeled as corrosive, representing an increase in hazard potential over the older product which was a strong oxidizer but not considered corrosive. The 1990s saw a gradual reduction in the use of phosphates, particularly in laundry detergents, as a result of a patchwork of state and regional bans that eventually became sufficiently widespread to render impractical the manufacture of both phosphate and phosphate-free formulas. More recently, attention has turned to automatic dishwasher (AD) detergents that had, by the late '90s, become the primary source of phosphates in domestic wastewater.[87] Despite earlier industry contention that effective AD products could not be made without phosphates, a number of smaller companies have been producing such products for years and their availability is increasing. Washington State began a phase-out of phosphate in AD detergents in 2006 and other states may follow. It is noteworthy that some of the alternative products do not contain chlorine.

Biodegradability of surfactants (surface-active agents) in cleaning products literally became visible in the late 1940s, when newly designed surfactants quickly began to replace soap in products. The principal emerging surfactant at that time, alkylbenzene sulfonate (ABS), had a highly branched molecule that was resistant to degradation in wastewater treatment processes or receiving waters. After widespread appearance of sudsy foam in rivers, manufacturers realized that the problem could be solved simply by a minor rearrangement of the molecules to a linear form. The entire industry shifted quickly to *linear* alkylbenzene sulfonate (LAS) and the foaming problem was solved,[88] although aquatic toxicity of surfactants can still be a problem in certain situations. Interest in surfactants revived in the 1990s, when research showed that another group of surfactants, alkylphenol ethoxylates (APEs), were resistant to biodegradation[89] and became increasingly toxic to fish as they broke down.[90] In addition, it was found that several partial breakdown products of two types of APEs were estrogenic and could cause feminization of male fish.[91] It was later found that other chemicals such as ethinyl estradiol could have the same effect. In 1997, Philip Dickey (WA Toxics Coalition) published a report called *Troubling Bubbles*[92] that summarized the research against APEs and recommended substituting alternative surfactants in cleaning and personal care products. Dickey tested representative products and identified the kinds of products most likely to contain APEs. Since that time, APEs have been removed from most consumer cleaning products and many institutional cleaners, although some other uses remain and the surfactant industry largely continues to defend the ingredients. EPA's Design for the Environment Program has actively worked to promote reformulation of products to less-harmful ingredients via partnerships with industry. Their laundry detergent program identified APEs as having characteristics of concern.[93]

Constituents of Concern

As progress continues to be made on improving many of the classic HHW products and their contents, there is a growing concern focused on toxic or otherwise hazardous constituents in products, many of which have not traditionally been considered within the HHW purview. Chapter 1 highlights these issues for such chemicals as the brominated flame retardants (PBDEs) in furniture, bisphenol-A in polycarbonate plastics, phthalate esters in cosmetics, heavy metals in computers and other consumer electronics, and even the chlorine and reactivity associated with the pervasive plastic, polyvinyl chloride (PVC), in a wide range of building as well as consumer products. HHW programs of the future will need to look beyond the surface hazards of the product categories to identify problem constituents. The manufacture of products with newer, safer, "greener" ingredients will help to lessen the burden.

Today's Programs

HHW programs of one type or another are now considered a core local governmental service in more than half the states in the country, and are provided in at least some communities in all 50 states, as well as some of the territories. Most programs focus on collection services, from simple events to permanent facilities with satellite depots or events, even curbside collection, supplemented by commercial handling of certain wastes such as used motor oil or batteries at retail outlets.

The Earth 911 program offers the best snapshot of services offered today. Table 2.2 provides summary data from Earth 911 showing the total number of HHW service listings by state, those that are considered "permanent," and those that are offered by municipalities (and tend to be the more comprehensive HHW collections) vs. those offered by commercial entities (that tend to be single-material collections such as used motor oil at a service station, or rechargeable batteries at an electronics store). While these data demonstrate a broad mix of services, they represent the best available snapshot of currently operating HHW collections in all 50 states.

The last column in Table 2.2 shows a crude ratio of each state's 2006 population divided by the number of HHW service listings. The variety of listings runs the gamut, from an oil depot to a full-service HHW facility serving tens of thousands of customers. Still, this calculation gives a very rough comparison of the level of services available in the 50 states. Iowa and Minnesota have the lowest ratios of population per service listing (theoretically reflecting the most available services), while New York State and the District of Columbia have the highest ratios.

The following list is of all HHW materials tracked in the Earth 911 system, and the top 20 searches in 2006 (Table 2.3).*

Service

Used Motor Oil	Used Oil Filters
Antifreeze	Car Batteries
Used Tires	Single-Use Batteries
Transmission Fluid	Brake Fluid
Paint Donation/Exchange	Fluorescent Bulbs
Paint Recycling	Paint Disposal
Freon Removal	Propane Tank Recycling
X-rays	Pesticides

---

*Ann Reichman, Earth 911, personal communication, 26 Apr. 2007.

Table 2.2. Earth 911 Household Hazardous Waste Listings by State in 2007*

State	Total HHW Service Listings	Permanent	Temporary (current)	Temporary for 2006	Municipal	Commercial	Population per service Listing
AK	36	36	0	0	9	27	18,613
AL	722	718	4	0	38	684	6,370
AR	130	130	0	0	30	100	21,622
AZ	401	401	0	3	92	309	15,377
CA	4696	4693	3	184	654	4042	7,764
CO	270	269	1	7	37	233	17,605
CT	177	177	0	1	156	21	19,801
DC	10	10	0	0	2	8	58,153
DE	189	189	0	2	113	76	4,516
FL	1807	1791	16	23	276	1531	10,011
GA	654	654	0	1	155	499	14,318
HI	71	71	0	0	9	62	18,106
IA	784	784	0	4	75	709	3,804
ID	112	112	0	0	42	70	13,093
IL	543	525	18	15	138	405	23,632
IN	584	581	3	7	289	295	10,811
KS	390	390	0	0	144	246	7,087
KY	312	312	0	0	51	261	13,093
LA	184	184	0	1	6	178	23,303
MA	844	831	13	67	614	230	7,627
MD	302	302	0	0	147	155	18,595
ME	90	90	0	0	60	30	14,684
MI	418	414	4	20	119	299	24,152
MN	1246	1246	0	1	113	1133	4,147
MO	430	430	0	0	34	396	13,588
MS	315	315	0	0	44	271	9,240
MT	91	91	0	0	41	50	10,381
NC	331	330	1	2	144	187	26,757
ND	41	41	0	0	5	36	15,509
NE	149	149	0	14	17	132	11,868
NH	212	212	0	0	172	40	6,202
NJ	416	405	11	3	222	194	20,972
NM	110	110	0	0	10	100	17,769
NV	170	170	0	6	26	144	14,680
NY	313	313	0	1	112	201	61,681
OH	872	866	6	10	242	630	13,163
OK	162	162	0	0	27	135	22,094
OR	192	192	0	0	64	128	19,275

Continues on next page

Table 2.2. *(continued)*

State	Total HHW Service Listings	Permanent	Temporary (current)	Temporary for 2006	Municipal	Commercial	Population per service Listing
PA	1621	1620	1	3	195	1426	7,675
RI	29	29	0	0	7	22	36,814
SC	700	700	0	1	440	260	6,173
SD	66	66	0	0	6	60	11,847
TN	1018	1018	0	2	407	611	5,932
TX	2973	2971	2	99	559	2414	7,907
UT	146	146	0	3	12	134	17,466
VA	1408	1403	5	3	195	1213	5,428
VT	85	84	1	0	72	13	7,340
WA	749	749	0	5	218	531	8,539
WI	373	373	0	6	165	208	14,897
WV	117	117	0	2	18	99	15,542
WY	69	69	0	0	34	35	7,464
Total	28,130	28,041	89	496	6,857	21,273	10,643

Source: Ann Reichman, Earth 911, personal communication, 16 Apr. 2007.

*These data were pulled from the Earth 911 database in April 2007. The number of temporary listings is not indicative of what is normally within the Earth 911 system for HHW (the number is VERY low); also, April is early in the "event" season, as most HHW collections run in the spring, summer, and fall; Earth 911 constantly receives updates from coordinators across the country and, as a result, its database is constantly in flux. These data are from the Earth 911 database, with the following explanation and qualifiers:

The sites by state are broken out by permanent listing, temporary listings, municipal sites and commercial sites;

"Permanent" means listings of all sites/programs that accept one or more HHW materials and the listing is provided on the Earth 911 system on a continuous manner; this could include curbside programs, municipal drop-off programs and commercial listings;

"Temporary" means listings of all events or collections accepting one or more HHW materials that have a beginning and an end date associated with the collection; generally special event collections are included in this category and they can be both municipal and commercial; "Temporary (Current)" means listings in 2007; "Temporary 2006" means listings still in the system from 2006 events (numbers are very low – many had been removed as the database is regularly updated);

"Municipal" means listings of any collection or program associated with or run by a municipality; in certain cases this includes commercial companies (such as a Waste Management, Inc.) that may provide a contracted service for a municipality;

"Commercial" means any listing provided by a private company (*i.e.,* not a municipality or contracted with a municipality); many of these listings represent retail take-back services;

"Population per service listing" is based on the state's July 1, 2006, population estimate (from U.S. Census Bureau, www.census.gov/popest/states/tables/NST-EST2006-01.xls) divided by the total HHW service listings; this is an attempt to normalize the data to compare relative service levels in different states.

Insecticides	Herbicides
Fungicides	Fertilizers
Household Cleaners	Solvents
Degreasers	Adhesives
Gasoline and Unwanted Fuels	Pool Chemicals
Photographic Chemicals	Paint Thinners
Mercury-Containing Items	Unwanted or Outdated Medications
Ammunition	Explosives
Asbestos	Smoke Detectors
Fire Extinguishers	Mercury-Containing Thermostats

As can be seen from the Table 2.3, automotive wastes (used motor oil, car batteries, antifreeze, used tires, gasoline, used oil filters, transmission fluid and brake fluid) make up the largest volume of inquiries, followed closely by paint and related products (paint disposal, paint recycling, paint donations, and paint thinners). Household single-use batteries, fluorescent bulbs, and mercury-containing items round out the bulk of the top-20 inquiries.

HHW programs today range from an occasional collection event to "full-service" programs with collection facilities serving 30,000 or more households per year. These may include large educational campaigns, product stewardship efforts, and other elements as well.

Table 2.3. The Top 20 Searched HHW Materials in the Earth 911 System

Searches	Service
66,125	Used Motor Oil
38,439	Paint Disposal
20,117	Single-Use Batteries
17,007	Paint Recycling
16,319	Fluorescent Bulbs
12,868	Paint Donation/Exchange
9,095	Mercury-Containing Items
7,575	Car Batteries
5,384	Antifreeze
5,380	Used Tires
4,239	Gasoline and Unwanted Fuels
3,988	Used Oil Filters
2,966	Paint Thinners
2,830	Propane Tank Recycling
2,820	Household Cleaners
2,225	Unwanted or Outdated Medications
1,818	Fire Extinguisher
1,515	Pesticides
1,446	Transmission Fluid
1,439	Brake Fluid

Source: Ann Reichman, Earth 911, personal communication, 26 Apr. 2007.

Collection services include the following:

- Fixed or permanent sites—facilities that collect HHW at a designated location, either a stand-alone facility or one connected with an MSW transfer station or landfill;
- Mobile collections (King County, WA's Wastemobile might be the largest and longest-running mobile service, begun in 1989 and serving 20,000 customers in 2006);
- Satellite depots (simpler drop-off sites in outlying areas, connected to a central sorting/processing center);
- Events (monthly, quarterly, annual, satellite to fixed facilities);
- Curbside (not common, often restricted to certain wastes such as motor oil or batteries);
- Door-to-door (Toronto's "toxics taxi" is a long-running example; other such services are usually limited to homebound individuals or offered by appointment or for rare or unusual instances);
- Selected drop sites (depots) for certain wastes: paints, oil, batteries – e.g., California's "ABOP" (antifreeze, batteries, oil, paint) sites.

Many HHW collections provide a reuse ("drop-and-swap") option for the less hazardous leftovers that are still useable, such as unopened cans of motor oil, latex paint, non-corrosive cleaning supplies, fertilizers, and many other still useful products. These types of services reduce costs by eliminating disposal. Screening criteria usually prohibit reuse of most pesticides and other more hazardous materials.

Take-back of selected wastes at retail sites is another major service option, as noted in the Earth 911 data above. Major examples include automobile parts or service outlets that accept used motor oil from do-it-yourself oil changers. Many retail electronics stores accept rechargeable batteries via the RBRC program. Some retail chains are beginning to experiment with take-back of computers, monitors, and other consumer electronics ("e-wastes").

Many public education programs today advertise collection service specifics and usually attempt to encourage people to buy or use less, to seek out alternative products that contain less hazardous ingredients, or to try simple home recipes. Campaigns appear to be light on evaluation.

Toxicity reduction efforts have been reserved to some of the larger programs that have sought voluntary reformulations of problematic products, promotion of safer alternative products, or state legislation mandating changes. Earlier efforts on mercury in batteries and lamps, for example, have shown dramatic, positive results. Today's efforts focus on remaining mercury-containing products, e-wastes, paints, and more exotic constituents such as brominated flame retardants. Legislative remedies at the state level are rising to address many of these product or chemical issues. National dialogues are underway, often guided by the Product Stewardship Institute, for paints, thermostats, fluorescent lamps, and other product categories in hopes of creating more product stewardship approaches across the country.

As early as 1985, Galvin advocated an "ideal program" outline that included HHW collection as only one of numerous elements.[94] Other elements included consensus recommendations on disposal; a "wizard" to answer questions (such as a phone hotline); a waste exchange to promote reuse options; close cooperation with waste handling contractors; promotion of safer alternative products; public education to raise awareness; and a multi-stakeholder committee in whatever region the program serves to promote communication among government agencies, businesses, and citizen interests. Duxbury stressed throughout the 1990s the need to set goals and measure progress, to think more broadly about what results were desired, to look beyond simply "having a program" to goals such as toxicity reduction, maximizing participation and the amount of HHW collected, and reducing the future generation of HHW through behavior change and other source-reduction efforts.[95] In 1995, Duxbury produced a classic editorial, "A 'Best' HHW Program?"[96] that contained such timely and pertinent advice that we reproduce its key points here:*

A "Best in the Country" HHW Program would:

- Develop a comprehensive program with goals for HHW and CESQG collection, education, and toxicity reduction;
- Be innovative and experimental;
- Identify products with hazardous constituents; develop collection, waste management, education, and reduction plan[s] for each category;
- Maximize participation in the collection program;
- Observe the waste management hierarchy: maximize reuse and recycling;
- Identify effective ways to bring about behavioral change;
- Establish collection, education, and reduction priorities based on products and local problems;
- Develop baseline data on attitudes, sales, amount of HHW in MSW and wastewater, and collection information on amounts and types of HHW by product type;
- Evaluate progress toward goals;
- Involve other public agencies (fire, solid waste, sewer, health, schools, water, etc.) and private firms; and
- Establish a dedicated funding source.

Where to Go from Here?

Even as the provision of "core" services for HHW collection and public outreach expands in numbers and geographic coverage, programs to address HHW continue to evolve. Today,

---

*Duxbury's article went on to recommend specific components for *collection* (*e.g.,* establish a permanent program with a fixed facility and other collection mechanisms for specific wastes and outlying areas; clean out stored HHW from 10% of new households per year over a ten year period; reuse and recycle 70% of the HHW turned in); for *education* (*e.g.,* define baseline awareness level; design a program aimed at behavior change; track changes); for *toxicity reduction* (*e.g.,* set specific priorities; achieve measurable reductions in sales and in amount of HHW in solid waste and wastewater over a ten year period); and for *CESQGs* (*e.g.,* establish a program complementary to HHW efforts; include identification, education, inspection, compliance, and waste reduction; ensure that collection services are available, supplementing private-sector services where needed). (Dana Duxbury, "A 'Best' HHW Program?" *Household Hazardous Waste Management News*, no. 24 (March 1995), 1–2.)

the types of consumer products considered to contain hazardous chemicals has increased to include a wide variety of electronics, plastics, building materials such as thermostats, lamps, carpeting and furniture, detergents and pharmaceuticals, to name but a few. HHW is no longer simply paint, old pesticide, and used motor oil. HHW program planners are beginning to wonder if institutionalizing HHW collection (often along with filling potholes and providing other essential services of local government) is really the best answer, especially when local tax- or rate-payers pick up the whole, expensive tab. Pressure is mounting on two parallel and related tracks: the further reduction in toxicity of product contents and the development of product stewardship systems, in both cases either by manufacturer initiative or through state legislation. Instead of strictly addressing waste management in HHW programs, greater focus is being placed on hazardous chemical exposure and environmental health, especially children's environmental health.

The chapter author hopes that this quick synopsis of 27-plus years of HHW history can serve both as a chronicle of the movement and an informative look at progress and trends. The future is ripe for some major turning points ahead, as products get greener, product stewardship systems pick up more of the wastes from the responsibility of local governments, and policies promote a healthier, safer, less hazardous world. We look forward to being able to say, "Household hazardous waste – that was *so* last century."

Appendix 2-A

Synopsis of the First 22 Annual Conferences on HHW in the U.S.

1. First Conference, Nov. 1986, Arlington, Va. Focused solely on HHW; Definition of HHW, arguments; Why is HHW a problem; Focus on single-day collection events: early examples, set-up, health & safety, contracting, publicity. Dana Duxbury, ed., *Summary of the First National Conference on Household Hazardous Waste Collection Programs, November 18–20, 1986, Arlington, Virginia* (Medford, Mass.: Tufts University Center for Environmental Management, 1987); available via National Technical Information Service #PB89-179-501.
2. Second Conference, Nov. 1987, San Diego, Calif. Title changed from "HHW Collection Programs" to "HHW Management"; Continued debate about HHW and the problem, including representatives of product manufacturers; International perspectives; Continued focus on collection programs and how to set them up; Beginning discussion of other management options; Beginning to call out "special wastes" such as batteries, oil, paint. Dana Duxbury, ed., *Summary of the Second National Conference on Household Hazardous Waste Management, November 2–4, 1987, San Diego, California* (Medford, Mass.: Tufts University Center for Environmental Management, 1988); available via NTIS #PB89-179–519.
3. Third Conference, Nov. 1988, Boston, Mass. More debate with product manufacturers; Continued focus on collection programs, and the increasing variety of examples and options, including emergence of a few "permanent" programs to replace the one-day events; Continued focus on batteries, oil, paint. Dana Duxbury, ed., *Summary of the Third National Conference on Household Hazardous Waste*

Management, November 2–4, 1988, Boston, Massachusetts (Medford, Mass.: Tufts University Center for Environmental Management, 1989).

4. Fourth Conference, Nov. 1989, Orlando, Fla. First discussion of toxicity and source reduction; Continued focus on "how-to" for collection programs, with ever-increasing sophistication based on experience; Greater focus on the need for and examples of permanent services; First mention of fluorescent lamps as a mercury concern; Continued focus on batteries, oil, paint; First mention of CESQGs. Dana Duxbury, ed., *Proceedings of the Fourth National Conference on Household Hazardous Waste Management, November 6–8, 1989, Orlando, Florida* (Andover, Mass.: Dana Duxbury and Associates, 1990); available via NTIS #PB90-163-189.

5. Fifth Conference, Nov. 1990, San Francisco, Calif. Source reduction is major theme; First sessions on product evaluation, life-cycle analyses, green labeling; First mention of "behavioral change" as part of education programs; Much focus on "how-to" for collection programs, with many case studies; Many sessions on education; "heavy metals" sessions mainly focused on mercury in batteries; Full sessions also on paints and pesticides. Dana Duxbury, ed., *Proceedings of the Fifth National Conference on Household Hazardous Waste Management, November 5–7, 1990, San Francisco, California* (Andover, Mass.: Dana Duxbury and Associates, 1991); available via NTIS #PB91-206-607.

6. Sixth Conference, Dec. 1991, Seattle, Wash. Achievement of at least one HHW event in all 50 states; Continued presentations on collection options, details, experiences, "how-to"; Increased examples of "fixed" facilities and their design; First full session devoted to fluorescent lamps; First full session on cleaning products and problematic ingredients; Major emphasis on toxicity and volume reduction; Discussion of "green" products and consumer marketing; Announcement of PRBA, the assoc. that served as forerunner of the Rechargeable Battery Recycling Corporation; Multiple sessions on batteries, paint; First full session on CESQGs. Dana Duxbury, ed., *Proceedings of the Sixth National Conference on Household Hazardous Waste Management, December 3–7, 1991, Seattle, Washington* (Andover, Mass.: Dana Duxbury and Associates, 1992); available via NTIS #PB92-169-390.

7. Seventh Conference, Dec. 1992, Minneapolis, Minn. Source reduction a major theme of keynote remarks; Greater focus on recycling and waste management related to HHW collection services; Four full sessions on CESQGs; Four full sessions on source reduction; First mention of behavior change and social marketing; First mention of sustainable development; First mention of finding and sharing information electronically "on-line." Dana Duxbury, ed., *Proceedings of the Seventh National Conference on Household Hazardous Waste Management, December 8–12, 1992, Minneapolis, Minnesota* (Andover, Mass.: Dana Duxbury and Associates, 1993); available via NTIS #PB93-170-116.

8. Eighth Conference, Nov. 1993, Burlington, Vt. Opening remarks by Gov. Howard Dean; Discussion of the proposed universal waste rule; Heavy focus on recycling paint, and on getting mercury out of batteries and fluorescent lamps; First mention of consumer electronics; Continued major focus on source and toxicity reduction concepts; CESQG waste management gets nearly as much attention as HHW; formation of NAHMMA. Dana Duxbury, ed., *Proceedings of the Seventh National Conference on Household Hazardous Waste Management, November 6–10, 1993,*

Burlington, Vermont (Andover, Mass.: Dana Duxbury and Associates, 1994); available via NTIS #PB94-181-047.

9. Ninth Conference, Nov. 1994, Austin, Tex. Continued source reduction theme; Discussions of how to apply the universal waste rule, and if it should apply to fluorescent lamps; First use of the term product stewardship; First mention of emergency collection in flood disasters; Announcement of formation of RBRC to collect rechargeable batteries; Focus on program evaluation; CESQG issues fully integrated into conference. International City/County Management Association, *Proceedings of the Ninth Annual Household Hazardous Waste Management Conference, Austin, Texas, November 17–19, 1994* (Washington, D.C.: ICMA, 1994).

10. Tenth Conference, Dec. 1995, Philadelphia, Penn. Title changed from "HHW Management" to include "Household, Small Business, and Universal Waste"; Much discussion about applying the universal waste rule; First full sessions on behavior change theory, as opposed to general education; First mention of cathode ray tubes as an HHW/universal waste; Pros and cons of reuse/swap programs; More on disaster response regarding HHW collection; Focus on paint product stewardship in British Columbia; Continued refinements of "how-to" collection service management, contracts, etc. International City/County Management Association, *Proceedings of the Tenth Annual Hazardous Materials Management Conference on Household, Small Business and Universal Waste, December 3–6, 1995, Philadelphia, Pennsylvania* (Washington, D.C.: ICMA, 1995).

11. Eleventh Conference, Nov. 1996, St. Petersburg, Fla. Focus on setting performance goals and priorities as programs mature, have to manage costs; Discussions on building partnerships, advanced management strategies, behavior change, universal wastes; continued focus on mercury and paint. International City/County Management Association, *Proceedings of the Eleventh Annual Hazardous Materials Management Conference on Household, Small Business and Universal Wastes: Building Sustainable Partnerships, November 6–9, 1996, St. Petersburg, Florida* (Washington, D.C.: ICMA, 1996).

12. Twelfth Conference, Nov. 1997, San Diego, Calif. Themes included product stewardship/extended producer responsibility and sustainability; Continued sessions on batteries, paint, pesticides, oil, behavior change, CESQGs, universal wastes. Solid Waste Association of North America and North American Hazardous Materials Management Association, *Proceedings of the 1997 Hazardous Materials Management Conference on Household, Small Business, and Universal Wastes, San Diego, California, November 16–21, 1997* (Silver Spring, Md.: SWANA, in conjunction with NAHMMA, 1997).

13. Thirteenth Conference, Nov. 1998, Kansas City, Mo. Keynote focus on children's environmental health; First mention of environmental justice related to HHW; Full sessions on agricultural pesticide "clean sweep" programs and container recycling programs; First full session on consumer electronics; Continued sessions on mercury policy, paint, behavior change, reuse, and evaluation. Solid Waste Association of North America and North American Hazardous Materials Management Association, *Proceedings from 1998 Hazardous Materials Management Conference on Household, Small Business and Universal Waste, Kansas City, Missouri, Novem-*

ber13–18,1998 (Silver Spring, Md.: SWANA, in conjunction with NAHMMA, 1998).

14. Fourteenth Conference, Nov. 1999, Tucson, Ariz. Key theme of product steward-ship and extended producer responsibility; First use of terms clean (and cleaner) production, industrial ecology, precautionary principle, chemicals' policy; Con-tinued mention of environmental justice and outreach to English-as-Second-Lan-guage populations; Continued sessions on ag pesticide and container collections, consumer electronics, behavior change, paints and mercury. Solid Waste Associa-tion of North America and North American Hazardous Materials Management Association, *Proceedings from the 1999 SWANA/NAHMMA Hazardous Materials Management Conference, November 14–19, 1999, Tucson, Arizona* (Silver Spring, Md.: SWANA, in conjunction with NAHMMA, 1999).

15. Fifteenth Conference, Nov. 2000, Boston, Mass. Key theme of product reformula-tion, greener or less toxic products, and environmentally preferable purchasing; Continued focus on product stewardship and EPR; References throughout to sus-tainability, green marketing, green product design; Extended sessions on electron-ics, mercury; First focus on school laboratory chemicals; Continued sessions on CESQGs, pesticides and IPM, paint, and media communications. Solid Waste Association of North America and North American Hazardous Materials Manage-ment Association, *Proceedings from the 2000 Hazardous Materials Management Conference on Household, Small Business and Universal Waste, Boston, Massa-chusetts, November 12–17, 2000* (Silver Spring, Md.: SWANA, in conjunction with NAHMMA, 2000).

16. Sixteenth Conference, Sept. 2001, Portland, Oreg. Product stewardship is main theme; Sessions on "stewardship 101," electronics, manufacturer take-back, and green electronics procurement; Parity of CESQG with HHW sessions; Much dis-cussion about improving public education, waste-reduction efforts; training on community-based social marketing. North American Hazardous Materials Man-agement Association, *Sixteenth Annual Hazardous Materials Management Confer-ence on Household and Small Business Waste, September 4–8, 2001, Portland, Oregon* (Conference agenda, NAHMMA).

17. Seventeenth Conference, Sept. 2002, Dallas, Tex. Opening keynote on precaution-ary principle; Product stewardship a main theme again; Major focus on electronic wastes; Mercury also a focus, but hardly a mention of batteries, instead fluorescent lamps and other sources get most attention; Ongoing sessions on HHW programs, including planning and case studies. North American Hazardous Materials Man-agement Association, *Seventeenth Annual Hazardous Materials Management Con-ference on Household and Small Business Waste, September 3–7, 2002, Dallas, Texas* (Conference agenda, NAHMMA).

18. Eighteenth Conference, Oct. 2003, Kansas City, Mo. Building partnerships is key theme; Session on persistent, bioaccumulative, toxic chemicals (PBTs); Bromi-nated flame retardants mentioned for first time; Sessions on regional and com-bined HHW/CESQG programs; E-waste updates; First mention of pharmaceuti-cals. North American Hazardous Materials Management Association, *Eighteenth Annual Hazardous Materials Management Conference on Household and Small*

Business Waste, Exploring New Vistas, October 6–10, 2003, Kansas City, Missouri (Conference agenda, NAHMMA).

19. Nineteenth Conference, Dec. 2004, Miami Beach, Fla. Postponed three months by Hurricane Frances; Major focus on electronic wastes, mercury reduction, and product stewardship approaches; Parity of CESQG and HHW discussions; Innovative programs in Florida; First full session on pharmaceuticals (formation of "pharmwaste" listserv); Full session devoted to CCA-treated wood. North American Hazardous Materials Management Association, *Nineteenth Annual Hazardous Materials Management Conference on Household and Small Business Waste, December 6–10, 2004, Miami Beach, Florida* (Conference agenda, NAHMMA; individual presentations available at Florida DEP's website).

20. Twentieth Conference, Oct. 2005, Tacoma, Wash. Environmental health is a key focus; Full sessions on health and the environment, environmental justice, precaution; Numerous sessions on details of product stewardship: models, third-party organizations, financing; First full session devoted to PBDEs; Case studies of HHW collections; Full session on program evaluation; Also E-wastes, paint, pharmaceuticals, pesticides, behavior change. North American Hazardous Materials Management Association, *Twentieth Annual Hazardous Materials Management Conference on Household and Small Business Waste, September 18–23, 2005, Tacoma, Washington* (NAHMMA: compact disk of all individual presentations).

21. Twenty-First Conference, Nov. 2006, Bloomington, Minn. Opening keynote on green chemistry and chemical policy; European REACH initiative; HHW in natural disasters such as hurricanes and floods; E-wastes, thermostats, mercury-reduction (including Clancy, the mercury-detecting dog), pharmaceuticals; Product stewardship theme; Future planning, what have we learned, how do we make significant strides forward. North American Hazardous Materials Management Association, *Twenty-first Annual North American Hazardous Materials Management Conference on Household and Small Business Waste, October 23–27, 2006, Bloomington, Minnesota* (Conference agenda, NAHMMA; compact disk of all individual presentations).

22. Twenty-Second Conference, Oct. 2007, San Diego, Calif. Still pending as this manuscript goes to press. Agenda included a focus on chemicals policy and green chemistry initiatives; high-hazard wastes (*e.g.,* explosives); E-wastes, pharmaceuticals, universal wastes; social marketing; and product stewardship/take-it-back partnerships. North American Hazardous Materials Management Association, "Draft Agenda for 22nd Annual NAHMMA Conference: 'Solutions within R.E.A.C.H.: Programs and Policies for a Less Toxic World'," www.nahmma.org (2 Aug. 2007).

Appendix 2-B.
Key People in the HHW Chronology

Many people have contributed to the growth of HHW programs over the past 27 years, as chronicled in Chapter 2. Most go unnamed in the text, except for a few of the earliest pioneers. The author of Chapter 2 wishes to highlight at least a few of the key people whose names turned up as the history was being written, with apologies to the many, many people who we miss. For the most part, the following individuals are people who were involved beyond their immediate program or company, who influenced the field at the national level. Primarily, these names were culled from the agendas of the national conferences, and are arranged first by state or company, then in roughly chronological order based on the first year in which they spoke at a national conference.

Pre-1986 dates represent first significant activity related to HHW, as found in available records. Dates listed from 1986 to 2006 represent first appearance as a speaker at the national conferences or other key forum; it is presumed that direct HHW activity at the local program or company level preceded the date at which each individual rose to national involvement or prominence.

The early, pre-conference years: 1980–1985

1. Alaska: *Jim Sweeney, Glen Miller* and *David Wigglesworth* (1983).
2. California: *Gina Purin* (1981); *Peter Burnes* (1983); *Joan Dotson, Chris Walker, Diane Takvorian, Jan Bluemer,* and *Steve Van Stockum* (1984); *Judy Orttung* (1985).
3. Connecticut: *Glen Goldsmith* (1984).
4. Florida: *Frank Walper* (1983); *Jan Kleman* (1984).
5. Kentucky: *Keith Brock* (1982).
6. Maine: *Rob Denny* (1981).
7. Massachusetts: *Dana Duxbury* (1981); *George Smith* (1982); *David Blackmar* and *Chris Curtis* (1984); *Kate Gage* (1985).
8. Minnesota: *Susan Ridgley* (1985).
9. New Mexico: *Donna Lacombe* (1985).
10. North Carolina: *Bill McClelland* (1980).
11. Oregon: *Len Malmquist* (1982).
12. Washington: *Dave Galvin* (1979); *Wally Swofford* (1980); *Susan Ridgley* (1981); *Rick Pierce* (1982); *Dave Bader* (1982).
13. Wisconsin: *Ken Satyshur* and *Jill Schmidt* (1984).
14. U.S. Environmental Protection Agency, Washington, D.C.: *Michael Flynn* (1985);

Government and community groups: 1986–1990

1. Alabama: *Janet Graham* (1989).
2. Alaska: *Glen Akins* (1988) and *Bill Kryger* (1990).
3. Arizona: *Doug Wilson* (1989).
4. California: *Diane Christensen, Linda Pratt, Emy Chan Meiorin,* and *Bill Merry* (1987); *Rob Arner* (1988); *Judy Frantz* (1989); *Fernando Berton, Karen Feeney,* and *Bill Quan* (1990).
5. Connecticut: *Leslie Lewis* and *Joanne Foster* (1986).
6. Florida: *Jeane White* (1989).
7. Kansas: *Kathleen Warren* (1990).

8. Massachusetts: *Nancy Wrenn* (1989).
9. Michigan: *Robert Ceru* (1987); *Chuck Cubbage* and *Cynthia Fridgen* (1989).
10. Minnesota: *Susan Ridgley* (1986); *Ned Brooks* (1987); *Nancy Misra* and *George Kinney* (1989); *Liz Gelbmann* (1990).
11. Missouri: *Sondra Goodman* and *Marie Steinwachs* (1988); *Sarah Dewey* (1990).
12. Nebraska: *Shirley Niemeyer* (1990).
13. New York: *Sharon Rehder* and *David Kleckner* (1989); *Rob Arner* (1990).
14. Vermont: *Michael Bender* (1989).
15. Washington: *Mike Aarhaus* and *Jim Sachet* (1986); *Richard Conlin* (1987); *Bill Green* (1988); *Philip Dickey* (1989); *Shirli Axelrod* and *Jack Wolfin* (1990).
16. U.S. Environmental Protection Agency, Washington, D.C.: *Gerry Dorian* (1986); *Allen Maples* (1987); *Tracy Bone* and *Kathy Margolis* (1989).
17. Ontario, Canada: *Claudia Marsales* (1989).
18. Vienna, Austria: *Gerhard Vogel* (1987).

Government and community groups: 1991–1995

1. Arizona: *Chris Warner* and *Bill Rathje* (1991).
2. California: *Isao Kobashi, Brian Johnson,* and *Paula Kehoe* (1992); *Lesli Daniel* (1995).
3. Colorado: *Brian Rimar* (1991).
4. Florida: *Rob Madden* (1993); *Deborah Rose* (1994); *Cleaette Fritz* (1995).
5. Maryland: *Aron Trombka* (1993).
6. Massachusetts: *Carolyn Dann* (1991); *Barry Connell* (1993); *Lynn Rubinstein* (1994); *Scott Cassel* and *Michael Frishman* (1995).
7. Minnesota: *Leslie Goldsmith* (1991); *Anne Thorson* (later *Kleinschmidt*) and *Cheryl Lofrano-Zaske* (1992); *John Gilkeson* and *Leslie Wilson* (1994).
8. New Hampshire: *Amy Dyer Cabaniss* (1994).
9. New Jersey: *Mike Winka* (1992).
10. New York: *Ann Lemley* (1994).
11. Oregon: *Maggie Conley* (1991); *Jim Quinn* (1993).
12. Pennsylvania: *Rachel Rosenzweig* (1991).
13. South Carolina: *Pam Bergstrand* (1995).
14. Texas: *Ingrid Dierlam* (later *Dierlam-McDonald*) (1992).
15. Vermont: *Jennifer Holliday* and *Andrea Cohen* (1991); *Steve Parker* (1994).
16. Virginia: *Rob Arner* (1994).
17. Washington: *Annie Bringloe, Sally Toteff,* and *Susan Ridgley* (1991); *Annette Frahm* and *Ray Carveth* (1993); *David Nightingale* and *Laurel Tomchick* (1994); *Lauren Cole* and *Gail Gensler* (1995).
18. Wisconsin: *Roger Springman* (1994).
19. U.S. Environmental Protection Agency, Washington, D.C.: *Terry Grogan, Charlotte Mooney,* and *Jim Darr* (1991); *Eugene Lee* (1994); *Kristina Meson* (1995).
20. British Columbia, Canada: *Ron Unger* and *Paul Iverson* (1995).

Government and community groups: 1996–2000

1. Arizona: *Frank Bonillas* (1999); *David Tavares* (2000).
2. California: *Gerri Silva* and *Maria Trapalis-Baird* (1996); *Debbie Raphael* (1997); *Shirley Willd-Wagner* (2000).
3. Connecticut: *Tom Metzner* and *Amy Dyer Cabaniss* (1996).
4. Florida: *Jack Price* and *Lois Rose* (1996); *Raoul Clarke* (1998).
5. Indiana: *Stephanie Biehn* (1997).
6. Michigan: *Tom Dewhirst* (1998).
7. Minnesota: *Joe Spitzmueller* (1996); *Sally Patrick* and *Emily Moore* (1997); *Heidi Ringhofer* (1999); *Jennifer Volkman* (2000).
8. Missouri: *Bill Lewry* (1998).
9. New Hampshire: *Alan Borner* and *Jennifer Smalley-Kaufman* (1996).
10. Oregon: *Rick Volpel* (1997); *Abby Boudouris* (1998).
11. Pennsylvania: *Phil Pitzer* (1999).
12. Texas: *Jack Ranney* (2000).
13. Utah: *Carol Werner* (2000).
14. Vermont: *Lynn Rubinstein* (1999); *Sami Izzo* (2000).
15. Washington: *Jim Hanna* (1996); *Monica Hairston* (1997); *Dave Waddell* (1998); *Michael Davis* and *Joe Hoffman* (1999).
16. U.S. Environmental Protection Agency, Washington, D.C.: *Sue Nogas* and *Amy Breedlove* (1997); *Nancy Fitz* (1998); *Marilyn Goode* (1999).
17. Ottawa, Canada: *Trish Johnson-Cover* (1999).

Government and community groups: 2001–2006

1. Arizona: *Anne Reichman* (2004).
2. California: *Matt McCarron* and *Rich Berman* (2002); *Ionie Wallace* and *Ann Blake* (2003); *Rob Darcy* (2005).
3. Colorado: *Hilary Collins* (2003).
4. Florida: *Irene Gleason* (2002); *Laurie Tenace* (2003); *Bill Hinkley, Glen Perrigan,* and *Al Gomez* (2004).
5. Iowa: *Becky Wehrman* (2001); *Elyn Holton-Dean* (2005).
6. Kansas: *John Shidler* (2001); *Kolin Anglin* (2003).
7. Massachusetts: *Joy Kirschenbaum* (2001).
8. Minnesota: *Garth Hickle* and *Teresa Gilbertson* (2001).
9. Missouri: *Laura Yates* (2002); *Lara Isch* (2004).
10. Oregon: *Lisa Heigh* and *Kevin Masterson* (2001).
11. Texas: *John Porter* (2002); *Cheryl Burton-Fentress* (2006).
12. Washington: *Sego Jackson* and *Ken Armstrong* (2001); *Deanna Seaman* (later *Carveth*) (2003); *Jim Neely* (2004); *Liz Tenant* (2005); *Ryan Kellogg* (2006).

Product manufacturers: 1986–2006

1. Chemical Specialties Manufacturers Association (CSMA): *Robert Etter* from S.C. Johnson (1987); *Soonya McDavid* (1990); *Robert Pauline* (1994); *Douglas Fratz* (1997); an affiliate group, the Household Products Disposal Council: *Gary Moore* (1986), later called the Household and Institutional Product Information Council: *Janet Kreizman* (1997); CSMA changed its name in 2000 to the Consumer Specialty Products Association.
2. National Paints and Coatings Association: *Robert Nelson* (1987); *Robert Foreman* (1988); *Barbara Walz* (1990); *Matthew Dustin* (1991); *Soonya McDavid* (1994); *Kristina Cook* and *Stacy Lisette* (1995); *David Lloyd* (1997).
3. Soap and Detergent Association: *Richard Sedlack* (late 1980s); *Jane Meyer* (1994).
4. Association of Petroleum Re-refiners: *George Booth* (1989).
5. American Petroleum Institute: *Chuck Krambuhl* (1991); *Craig Campbell* (1992); *Brad Jones* (1995).
6. Portable Rechargeable Battery Association: *David Thompson* (1991); *Norman England* (1992); Rechargeable Battery Recycling Corporation: *Jeff Bagby* (1995); *Ralph Millard* (1997); *Kim Kelly* (1999); *Cheryl Lofrano-Zaske* (2000); *Sean Burchill* (2001).
7. National Electrical Manufacturers Association: *Ric Erdheim* (2001).

Individual Companies:

1. Drackett: *Donald Lofty* (1987).
2. Rayovac: *Raymond Balfour* (1987).
3. Jarvie Paint: *Curt Bailey* (1989).
4. Eveready: *Terry Telzrow* (1990); *Michael Babiak* (2001).
5. Black & Decker: *William Hill* (1990).
6. Major Paint: *Arnold Hoffman* (1990); *Hubert Kim* (1991).
7. Church & Dwight: *Bryan Thomlison* (1991).
8. Dow: *Christine Baldridge* (1991); *John Wood* (1995).
9. Duracell: *Keel Kelly* (1991); *David Barrett* (1997).
10. Panasonic: *David Thompson* (1991); *Richard King* (1995); *Mark Sharp* (2001).
11. Proctor & Gamble: *Robert Vashon* (1991); *Patrick Hayes* (1995).
12. Clorox: *Jim McCabe* (1992); *Terry Bedell* (1994).
13. Green Paint: *Scott Herbert* (1992).
14. Glidden Paint: *David Maurer* (1992).
15. Benjamin Moore: *Carl Minchew* (1994).
16. G.E. Lighting: *Beverly Grimm* (1992).
17. S.C. Johnson: *John Owens* (1994); *Chip Brewer* (1997).
18. Philips Lighting: *Paul Walitsky* (1994).
19. Honeywell: *Nancy Onkka* (1994); *Steve Keefe* (1999).
20. Reckitt & Coleman: *Steve Hinden*, *Eileen Moyer* (1995); *Bill Lafield*, *Jan Wengler* (1997).

21. Solaris: *Kevin Cannon* (1995).
22. Rochester-Midland: *Steve Ashkin* (1995).
23. Seventh Generation: *Steve Ashkin* (1999).
24. Sony: *Doug Smith* (2000).
25. Hewlett Packard: *Renee St. Dennis* (2001).

Southern States' Resource Guide (1996–2000):

1. Household and Institutional Product Information Council: *Janet Kreizman, Terry Bedell, Jan Wengler, Patrick Hayes*.
2. National Paints and Coatings Association: *Kris Cook*.
3. Soap and Detergent Association: *Jane Meyer*.

Hazardous waste contractors: 1980–2006

1. Advanced Environmental Technology Corporation (AETC), in East and Midwest: (1985); which merged with Chemical Waste Management to form Advanced Environmental Technical Services (AETS): *Eric Laut* (1995).
2. Amazon Environmental, in California: *John and Lorraine Segala* (1999).
3. American Environmental and Safety Specialists, in California: (1982).
4. Aptus, in Minnesota: (1988); later acquired by Rollins.
5. BKK Corp. in California: (1983).
6. Browning-Ferris Industries, in California and Southwest: (1990).
7. Burlington Environmental, in Washington: *Jack Wolfin* (1992); *Tim Ritchie* (1994); later acquired by Philip.
8. Care Environmental in New Jersey and the Southeast: (early 2000s).
9. Chemical Pollution Control, in New York: (1986).
10. Chemical Processors, Inc., in Washington: *Ron West* (1980); *Roger Nelson* (1982); *Glen Dillman* (1986); later acquired by Burlington.
11. Chemical Waste Management, throughout East and Midwest: (early 1980s); in California: *Steve Drew* (1988); *Tonie Santos* (1989); in Illinois: *Eric Laut* (1990).
12. Clean Harbors, Inc., in New England: (1983); across East Coast: *Patrick O'Toole* (1993); *Richard Flaherty* (2000); national: *Kelby Neal* (2006).
13. CECOS-BFI in Texas: (1988).
14. Crosby & Overton on the West Coast: (1988).
15. Curbside, Inc. (a Safety-Kleen subsidary) in Arizona: *Patrick Anderson, William Anderson* (2000).
16. Drug & Lab Disposal, in Michigan: (1984).
17. Dow Chemical Co., in Midland, Mich. (early, company-sponsored collections): *Ted Ilgenfritz & Ryan Delcambre* (1984).
18. EQ, in Florida: *Curt DeBrunner* (2004).
19. GSX, in South Carolina and East Coast: *Danny Stubbs* (1984); *Liz Morgan* (later *McCormick*) (1986); became Laidlaw in 1988.

20. Heritage Environmental, in Indiana and Washington: *Joel Hall* (1994); *Barry Legg* (1999); *David Blair* (2003).
21. Laidlaw Environmental Services, in the East Coast: *Liz McCormick* (1988); *LeeAnn Merashoff* (1991); *Richard Thornton* (1994); *Brenda Murphy* (1995).
22. McDonald and Watson, in New England: (1985).
23. MSE Environmental, in California and the Midwest: *Gil Cretney* (1993); *Frank Doerfler, Jr.* (1995); *Janice Oldemeyer* (2000); *Cheryl Burton-Fentress* (2003); became part of Teris in 2004.
24. N.E.I. Resource Services, in Minnesota: (1985).
25. Norcal Solid Waste Systems, Inc., in California: *Larry Sweetser* and *Gina Purin* (1989); *Deanna Seaman* (1992); *Susan Patane* (2000).
26. Northeast Solvents, in Massachusetts: *LeeAnn Merashoff* (1987).
27. Northwest EnviroService, in Washington and Alaska: *Larry Wilkinson*, *Bill Kryger* (1984); *Thomas Poliquin* (1992).
28. Onyx Environmental, in the Midwest: *Eric Laut* (1999); in California: Jim Hanna (2000); became part of Veolia in 2006.
29. Philip Environmental Services, in British Columbia: *Ron Unger* (1995); in California: *Janice Oldermeyer* (1995); *Kirsten Liske* (1998); *Sue Bruning* (2000); in Missouri: *Greg Hicks* (1996); in Washington: *Mike O'Donnell* (2005).
30. Radiac Research, in New England and Northeast: (1984).
31. Rifer Environmental, in Washington: *Wayne Rifer* (2001).
32. Rollins Environmental Services, in Delaware: (1988).
33. Safety-Kleen, in Midwest: (1991).
34. Safety Specialists, in California: *Michael Borden* (1984).
35. Sanitary Fill Co., in California: *Larry Sweetser* (1985); *Cedar Kehoe* (1989); *Tom Watkins* (1991); *Brad Drda* (1992); became part of Norcal in 1989.
36. SCA Chemical Services, Inc., in Massachusetts, Florida, and East Coast (1982); became part of GSX in 1983.
37. Teris, in West and national: (2004).
38. Veolia, in the Midwest and national: *Eric Laut* (2006).

About the Author

Dave Galvin is program manager for King County Water & Land Resources Division's office of the Local Hazardous Waste Management Program, a regional partnership addressing HHW and well as CESQG hazardous materials in the metropolitan Seattle area.

Notes

1. Rachel Carson, *Silent Spring* (Boston: Houghton-Mifflin 1962), 174.
2. Elizabeth Bennett and David Galvin, *Household Toxicants and Water Quality* (Seattle, Wash.: Municipality of Metropolitan Seattle [Metro], May 1980).
3. The author would like to point out a seminal publication, largely forgotten, that appeared in 1978: Albert Fritsch, ed., *The Household Pollutants Guide* (Garden City, NY: Anchor Books, 1978).

This small paperback, from the Center for Science in the Public Interest, focused exclusively on toxic and otherwise hazardous *products* in the home and did not address disposal at all, yet serves as a milestone, way ahead of its time. It was the first nationally available publication on hazardous household products, prescient in many ways regarding health concerns from such products as aerosols, building materials, mercury, vinyl chloride, and flame retardants.

4. Susan Ridgley and David Galvin, *Summary Report of the Household Hazardous Waste Disposal Project* (Seattle: Metro, 1982); Susan Ridgley, *Toxicants in Consumer Products* (Seattle: Metro, 1982); David Galvin and Leonard Guss, *Public Opinions and Actions* (Seattle: Metro, 1982); Claire Dyckman and Lolly Smith-Greathouse, *SLEUTH: Strategies and Lessons to Eliminate Unused Toxicants: Help! – Educational Activities on the Disposal of Household Hazardous Waste* (Seattle: Metro, 1982); Susan Ridgley and Judy Fey, *Directory for Household Hazardous Waste Disposal in Seattle-King County* (Seattle: Metro, 1982).

5. Gina Purin, *Household Hazardous Waste: Solving the Disposal Dilemma* (Sacramento, Calif.: Golden Empire Health Planning Center, 1984).

6. Gina Purin, Judy Orttung, Steven Van Stockum, and Janet Page, *Alternatives to Landfilling Household Toxics* (Sacramento: Golden Empire Health Planning Center, 1987).

7. Rachel Laderman, Carol Sarnat, Gary Moore, Edward Stanek, Robert Tuthill, and Cleve Willis, *Toward a Comprehensive Program for Management of Household Hazardous Wastes in Massachusetts* (Amherst, Mass.: University of Massachusetts, Environmental Institute, 1985).

8. Early agricultural pesticide collection history was provided in personal communications from Rob Denny, Bill McClelland, and Joe Hoffman, pioneers in this field; Joe Hoffman, personal communications, 8 June 2007 and 14 June 2007. See also U.S. EPA, *State of the States Report: Pesticide Storage, Disposal & Transport* (EPA/734-R-92-012) (Washington, D.C.: U.S. EPA, September 1992).

9. Dana Duxbury, "The National Listing of Household Hazardous Waste Collection Programs – 1993," in *Proceedings of the Eighth National Conference on Household Hazardous Waste Management, November 6–10, 1993, Burlington, Vermont*, ed. Dana Duxbury (Andover, Mass.: Dana Duxbury and Associates, 1994), Appendix VI; the chart contained in this appendix (reproduced as Table 2.1) is the latest available summary of the National Listing database, which is now lost.

10. Laderman *et al., Toward a Comprehensive Program*, 259–61.

11. Dana Duxbury, "History of Household Hazardous Waste," in *Summary of the First National Conference on Household Hazardous Waste Collection Programs, November 12–20, 1986, Arlington, Virginia*, ed. Dana Duxbury (Medford, Mass.: Tufts University Center for Environmental Management, 1986), 2–3B.

12. Purin, *Household Hazardous Waste: Solving the Disposal Dilemma*, 32–33.

13. Galvin and Guss, *Public Opinions and Actions*, 31–61.

14. Laderman *et al., Toward a Comprehensive Program*, 46–47, 217; Purin, *Household Hazardous Waste: Solving the Disposal Dilemma*, 17–18.

15. League of Women Voters, *Household Hazardous Waste Collection Project – How-To-Kit* (Lexington, Mass.: LWV, 1983).

16. Dana Duxbury, ed., *Summary of the First National Conference on Household Hazardous Waste Collection Programs, November 18–20, 1986, Arlington, Virginia* (Medford, Mass.: Tufts University Center for Environmental Management, 1987), 2–3, 18, 48.

17. Gina Purin, *Sacramento County's Household Poison Project Summary Report* (Sacramento: Golden Empire Health Systems Agency, 1983).

18. Duxbury, "History," 3A–3B; Duxbury, "The National Listing," 618; Dana Duxbury, "A 97 Percent Increase since 1995!," *Household Hazardous Waste Management News*, no. 35 (August 1998), 1,8.

19. Dade County Grand Jury, *Report of the Grand Jury on Hazardous Waste* (Miami: Circuit Court of the Eleventh Judicial Circuit of Florida in and for the County of Dade, November 9, 1983).

20. Duxbury, "History," 3A–3B; Duxbury, "The National Listing," 618; Duxbury, "A 97 Percent Increase," 1,8. Duxbury's tallies of HHW-related projects and programs evolved over the years that she and her colleagues kept the National Listing. Modifications were made regularly as new information was added to the database, resulting in regular changes to the annual summary charts reported in the national conferences. The overall trends are clear. The National Listing database is now lost, preventing attempts to clarify some of the earliest programs for this history.

21. "'White Hat' Hazwaste Programs Target Homeowners, Small Shops," *Waste Age* (May, 1984): 80–86.

22. "Programs to Collect Household Hazwastes Experience a Boom," *Waste Age* (August, 1985): 65–71.

23. Lee Thomas, *Memorandum: Household Hazardous Waste Collection Days* (Washington, D.C.: U.S. EPA, 7 June 1984).

24. Marcia Williams, "EPA Perspective on Household Hazardous Waste," in *Summary of the First National Conference on Household Hazardous Waste Collection Programs, November 12–20, 1986, Arlington, Virginia*, ed. Dana Duxbury (Medford, Mass.: Tufts University Center for Environmental Management, 1986), 1.

25. U.S. EPA, *A Survey of Household Hazardous Wastes and Related Collection Programs* (EPA/530-SW-86-038) (Washington, D.C.: U.S. Environmental Protection Agency, 1986).

26. Winston Porter, *Clarification of Issues Pertaining to Household Hazardous Waste Collection Programs* (OSWER Policy Directive No. 9574.00-1) (Washington, D.C.: U.S. Environmental Protection Agency, 1988).

27. U.S. EPA, *Household Hazardous Waste Management: A Manual for One-Day Community Collection Programs* (EPA/530-R-92-026) (Washington, D.C.: U.S. Environmental Protection Agency, 1993).

28. *Summary of Proceedings for the April 15–16 [1985] 'Great Lakes Regional Household Hazardous Waste Disposal Conference: Coordinating Local Collection Days"* (Ann Arbor, Mich.: Ecology Center of Ann Arbor, 1985).

29. Dana Duxbury, ed., *Summary of the First National Conference on Household Hazardous Waste Collection Programs, November 18–20, 1986, Arlington, Virginia* (Medford, Mass.: Tufts University Center for Environmental Management, 1986).

30. The North American Hazardous Materials Management Association has many of the annual conference proceedings available to members via its website (www.nahmma.org) and, as this book goes to press, intends to complete the scans of all previous proceedings so as to offer access to a complete set of conference proceedings and/or presentations.

31. Dana Duxbury, "Household Hazardous Waste Management Program Directions," in *Proceedings of the Sixth National Conference on Household Hazardous Waste Management, December 3–7, 1991, Seattle, Washington*, ed. Dana Duxbury (Andover, Mass.: Dana Duxbury and Associates, 1992), 8–12.

32. Douglas C. Wilson, *The Implications of Behavioral Aspects on the Production and Discard of Household Hazardous Wastes*, University of Arizona M.A. Thesis (Ann Arbor, Mich.: University Microfilms International, 1985).

33. William L. Rathje, Douglas C. Wilson, V.W. Lambou, and R.C. Herndon, *Characterization of Hazardous Household Wastes in Marin County, California, and New Orleans, Louisiana* (Las Vegas, Nev.: U.S. EPA, 1987).

34. William Rathje and Cullen Murphy, *Rubbish!, The Archaeology of Garbage* (New York: HarperCollins, 1992).

35. Charles P. Cubbage and Amy L. Potter, "National Survey of State Programs for Unusable Agricultural Pesticide Collections – 1999 Update," in *Proceedings from the 1999 SWANA/NAHMMA Hazardous Materials Management Conference, November 14–19, 1999, Tucson, Arizona* (Silver Spring, Md.: SWANA, in conjunction with NAHMMA, 1999), 111–122.

36. "Unwanted Pesticides: Farm and Home," *Household Hazardous Waste Management News* no. 4 (Winter, 1990): 3, 8.

37. The Pesticide Stewardship Alliance, www.tpsalliance.org/index.html (12 May 2007).

38. See, for example, descriptions of the comprehensive British Columbia program, www.env. gov.bc.ca/epd/epdpa/ips/index.html (25 July 2007).

39. U.S. EPA, *Consumer Labeling Initiative*, www.epa.gov/oppt/labeling/ (25 July 2007).

40. U.S. EPA, *Consumer Labeling Initiative* website.

41. *U.S. EPA's Read the Label First Campaign*, www.epa.gov/oppt/labeling/pubs/articles.htm (12 May 2007).

42. Christoph Scharff und Gerhard Vogel, eds., *Waste Minimization, Household Hazardous Waste Management, International Experiences – Conference Proceedings, 2nd Vienna Conference on Waste Management, May 13–17, 1991* (Vienna, Austria: International Solid Waste Association, 1991).

43. *Waste Watch Center* flier (Andover, Mass.: WWC, c. 1990).

44. *Household Hazardous Waste Management News*, no. 31 (February, 1997).

45. Gregory Lie, "Hennepin County: Comprehensive Waste Management," *Household Hazardous Waste Management News*, no. 10 (August, 1991), 3, 7.

46. Robert Etter, "The Chemical Specialties Manufacturers Association's Views on Household Hazardous Waste Management," in *Summary of the Second National Conference on Household Hazardous Waste Management, November 2–4, 1987, San Diego, California*, ed. Dana Duxbury (Medford, Mass.: Tufts University Center for Environmental Management, 1988), 13–14.

47. Allen Maples, "Defining Household Hazardous Waste," in *Summary of the Second National Conference on Household Hazardous Waste Management, November 2–4, 1987, San Diego, California*, ed. Dana Duxbury (Medford, Mass.: Tufts University Center for Environmental Management, 1988), 11–12.

48. Christopher Cathcart, "Know the Facts Before You Green Your Clean," www.cspa.org/ontherecord/ (18 May 2007).

49. "The Six Point Program for Leftover Paint," www.paint.org/con_info/sixpoint.cfm (18 May 2007).

50. "SDA Unveils CleaningProductFacts.com," www.cleaning101.com/newsroom/04-06-07 .cfm (26 May 2007); see also www.cleaningproductfacts.com .

51. Association of Bay Area Governments, *Disposal of Hazardous Waste by Small Quantity Generators: Magnitude of the Problem* (Oakland, Calif.: ABAG, 1985).

52. *Toxic Substances in Your Home* brochure (Seattle: Municipality of Metropolitan Seattle [Metro], 1979).

53. *Beginning at Home: Tackling Household Hazardous Wastes*, 18-minute video (Boston: League of Women Voters of Massachusetts, 1986).

54. Jack Lord, *Hazardous Wastes from Homes* (Santa Monica, Calif.: Enterprise for Education, 1986).

55. EHMI, *Household Hazardous Waste Wheel®* (Durham, NH: Environmental Hazards Management Institute, 1987).

56. Sondra Goodman, "Integrated HHWM Education Program," in *Summary of the Third National Conference on Household Hazardous Waste Management, November 2–4, 1988, Boston, Massachusetts*, ed. Dana Duxbury (Medford, Mass.: Tufts University Center for Environmental Management, 1989), 99–100.

84 Dave Galvin

57. *The World Is Full of Toxic Waste – Your Home Shouldn't Be* (San Diego: Environmental Health Coalition, 1984).

58. Michael Bender and Michael Frishman, "An Assessment of Consumer Information and Household Hazardous Materials Shelf Labeling Programs in Iowa and Vermont," in *Proceedings of the Tenth Annual Hazardous Materials Management Conference on Household, Small Business and Universal Waste, December 3–6, 1995, Philadelphia, Pennsylvania* (Washington, D.C.: International City/County Management Assoc., 1995).

59. Michael Dennis, "Changing Public Behaviors with Information: Lessons from Social Psychology and Evaluation Research," in *Proceedings of the Eighth National Conference on Household Hazardous Waste Management, November 6–10, 1993, Burlington, Vermont*, ed. Dana Duxbury (Andover, Mass.: Dana Duxbury and Associates, 1994), 56–64.

60. Annette Frahm, Dave Galvin, Gail Gensler, Gail Savina, and Anne Moser, *Changing Behavior: Insights and Applications* (Seattle, Wash.: Local Hazardous Waste Management Program in King County, 1995).

61. Douglas McKenzie-Mohr and William Smith, *Fostering Sustainable Behavior: An Introduction to Community-Based Social Marketing* (Gabriola Island, B.C.: New Society Publishers, 1999).

62. Philip Dickey, *Buy Smart, Buy Safe* (Seattle: Washington Toxics Coalition, 1994).

63. Philip Dickey, *Grow Smart, Grow Safe* (Seattle: Local Hazardous Waste Management Program in King County, 1998).

64. Philip Dickey, *Safer Alternatives for the Home and Garden* (Seattle: Washington Toxics Coalition, 2006).

65. Waste Watch Center, *Cleaning Products Summit Meeting, March 30–31, 1995* (Andover, Mass.: Waste Watch Center, 1995).

66. Philip Dickey, Dana Duxbury, David Galvin, Brian Johnson, and Arthur Weissmann, *Concerns with Household Cleaning Products – A White Paper* (Seattle: Washington Toxics Coalition, 1995).

67. "CA EPA 'Safer Substitutes Policy' 11/12/96," *Household Hazardous Waste Management News*, no. 31 (February 1997), 8.

68. Calif. Peer Review Project, *Alternatives to Household Chemicals* (Santa Barbara, Calif.: Santa Barbara County, May 1999).

69. Southern States Waste Management Coalition, *Resource Guide: Household Product Waste Management, A Resource Guide for Local Solid Waste Officials and Governments on Managing Household Product Waste and Household Hazardous Waste* (Norcross, Georgia: Southern States Energy Board, 1999), 1.

70. Southern States Waste Management Coalition, *Resource Guide*.

71. D. P. Weston, R. W. Holmes, J. You, and M. J. Lydy, "Aquatic Toxicity Due to Residential Use of Pyrethroid Insecticides," *Environmental Science and Technology* 39, no. 24 (December 2005): 9778–9784.

72. Philip Dickey, Washington Toxics Coalition, personal communication (16 June 2007).

73. Franklin Assoc., *Characteristics of Products Containing Lead and Cadmium in Municipal Solid Waste in the United States, 1970 to 2000* (Washington, D.C.: U.S. EPA, 1989).

74. U.S. EPA, *Municipal Solid Waste in the United States – 2005 Facts and Figures* (Washington, D.C.: EPA, 2006).

75. Franklin Assoc., *Characteristics of Products*.

76. U.S. EPA, "The 'Battery Act'," *Enforcement Alert* 5, no. 2 (March 2002).

77. U.S. EPA, *Characterization of Products Containing Mercury in Municipal Solid Waste in the United States, 1970 – 2000* (EPA/530-R-92-013) (Washington, D.C.: U.S. EPA, April, 1992); David Barrett and Mike Babiak, "Recycling Dry Cell Batteries," *Household Hazardous Waste Management News*, no. 24 (March, 1995), 7–8.

78. "Kem-Tone Wall Finish," *National Historic Chemical Landmarks*, acswebcontent.acs.org/landmarks/landmarks/kem/kem_paint.html (27 May 2007).

79. "A Brief History of Milk Paint," www.milkpaint.com/about_history.html (27 May 2007).

80. "A Primer on the Paint and Coatings Industry," *Issue Backgrounder* 15, no. 1 (National Paints and Coatings Association, February 2007), www.paint.org/ind_issue/ib_2–07.pdf (27 May 2007).

81. "Clean Air and the Paint and Coatings Industry," *Issue Backgrounder* 10, no. 2 (National Paints and Coatings Association, March 2002), www.paint.org/ind_issue/ib_march02.pdf (27 May 2007).

82. "PSI Paint Project – National Dialogue," Product Stewardship Institute, www.productstewardship.us (27 May 2007).

83. Jeffrey Victor, "What's in a Fluorescent Lamp," in *Proceedings of the Sixth National Conference on Household Hazardous Waste Management, December 3–7, 1991, Seattle, Washington*, ed. Dana Duxbury (Andover, Mass.: Dana Duxbury and Associates, 1992), 186–8.

84. Janet Graham, "Used Oil: The DIY Dilemma," *Household Hazardous Waste Management News*, no. 3 (Fall, 1989), 3,8.

85. Brad Jones, "Used Oil?," *Household Hazardous Waste Management News*, no. 28 (February, 1996), 2.

86. Earth-911, "The Importance of Used Motor Oil Recycling," www.earth911.org (15 May 2007).

87. Philip Dickey, Washington Toxics Coalition, personal communication (16 June 2007).

88. R. D. Swisher, *Surfactant Biodegradation* (New York: Marcel Dekker, 1987), 1–2.

89. Swisher, *Surfactant Biodegradation*, 714–725.

90. Sylvia S. Talmage, *Environmental and Human Safety of Major Surfactants: Alcohol Ethoxylates and Alkylphenol Ethoxylates* (Boca Raton, Fla.: Lewis Publishers, 1994), 263–275.

91. Susan Jobling, David Sheahan, Julia A. Osborne, Peter Matthiessen, and John P. Sumpter, "Inhibition of Testicular Growth in Rainbow Trout (*Oncorhynchus mykiss*) Exposed to Estrogenic Alkyphenolic Chemicals," *Environmental Toxicology and Chemistry* 15, no.2 (July 1995): 194–202.

92. Philip Dickey, *Troubling Bubbles* (Seattle: Washington Toxics Coalition, 1997).

93. U.S. EPA, "Key Characteristics of Laundry Detergent Ingredients," www.epa.gov/dfe/pubs/laundry/techfact/keychar.htm (23 May 2007).

94. David Galvin, "Creating Awareness of Household Hazardous Waste Problems," in *Summary of Proceedings for the April 15–16 [1985] "Great Lakes Regional Household Hazardous Waste Disposal Conference: Coordinating Local Collection Days"* (Ann Arbor, Mich.: Ecology Center of Ann Arbor, 1985).

95. Dana Duxbury, "Goals for the Institutionalized Program," *Household Hazardous Waste Management News*, no. 6 (Summer, 1990), 1, 8; Dana Duxbury, "Reducing Toxics," *Household Hazardous Waste Management News*, no. 11 (November, 1991), 1,3; Dana Duxbury, "The Future?" *Household Hazardous Waste Management News*, no. 21 (June, 1994), 1, 7; Dana Duxbury, "HHW Take-Back," *Household Hazardous Waste Management News*, no. 22 (September, 1994), 1,6–7; Dana Duxbury, "'HHW' Today," *Household Hazardous Waste Management News*, no. 25 (June, 1995), 1, 7–8; Dana Duxbury, "A New Paradigm," *Household Hazardous Waste Management News*, no. 30 (October, 1996), 1–2; Dana Duxbury, "Goals," *Household Hazardous Waste Management News*, no. 38 (August, 1999), 1, 8.

96. Dana Duxbury, "A 'Best' HHW Program?" *Household Hazardous Waste Management News*, no. 24 (March, 1995), 1–2.

CHAPTER 3

The Mechanics of HHW
Collection and Management

Sue Bruning

Mike O'Donnell

Operating HHW Collection Programs

The process of hosting a household hazardous waste collection event has changed little in the past 25 years with the exception of more permanent HHW facilities replacing single day collections. The focus of current HHW collection efforts ranges from targeted collection of used motor oil in rural areas to full-service, multi-million dollar HHW collection facilities with full-time staff and staggering budgets. Starting small will help a public agency to obtain a better understanding of the logistical mechanics and most important, to learn the financial implications of undertaking household hazardous waste collection.

HHW Program Costs

Projecting the costs of hosting an HHW collection in a community new to the process is not simple. There are many factors influencing cost, the most important being the types of material collected and the extent and effectiveness of program promotion. Most HHW program managers limit advertising by focusing on a target segment of the population and specifying few material categories, or using a single media source. Blanketing a community with TV, radio and newspaper advertisements can be overly effective in increasing collection participation resulting in large participation and cost overruns. Predicting turnout is difficult for communities that have never hosted a collection and larger-than-expected participation is common.

Accepting additional types of material can also increase participation and costs. Simply collecting motor oil and antifreeze is an easy and cost effective means of removing the wastes, however, it does not recognize or include the most hazardous products that homeowners keep in basements and garages. Collecting high hazard materials including solvents, pesticides, and pool chemicals necessitates contracting with companies that are certified to handle, transport, and dispose of the material.

Every HHW program manager should exercise discretion in determining which items to exclude from HHW collection. Limiting the types of wastes managed through an HHW program is essential for cost control. For instance, a program may add used motor oil, propane tanks, and rechargeable batteries to the list of unacceptable items because there are other convenient opportunities for recycling within the community. Latex paint is sometimes refused from HHW collection programs because local regulations allow it to be solidified (by drying out in the open air or mixing with kitty litter or sawdust) and placed in the trash. Although latex paint is readily recycled, the low risk for landfill disposal combined with the expense of recycling often leads local agencies to focus resources on other, more difficult-to-manage wastes.

Convenient programs have greater participation rates and often, higher expense. A once-a-year (*i.e.,* single-day) temporary event typically services 2–4% of households within a 15 mile radius of the advertised location. A fixed or permanent facility may draw occasional visitors from a larger population radius, though the convenience of the service (*i.e.,* greater number of collection opportunities) will draw new and repeat customers. Contrary to logical thought, HHW volume collected from established HHW facilities does not diminish over time.

Types of Collection Programs

Antifreeze, Batteries, Oil, Paint (ABOP)

ABOP collections focus on the four categories representing the largest percentage of HHW that can be easily collected, while avoiding high hazard and high expense categories of HHW.

- Antifreeze – Antifreeze from Do-It-Yourself auto mechanics is common at HHW programs. Antifreeze is a health hazard due to the toxicity of ethylene glycol, and it is readily recycled. Programs generally pay for the recycling service.
- Batteries – Automotive batteries contain sulfuric acid and lead. Both are hazardous, but the acid can be rendered harmless through neutralization and lead is readily recycled. Collected batteries can be sold to local recyclers due to the value of scrap lead.
- Oil – Most HHW programs can be paid for used motor oil that is not contaminated with solvents, water, antifreeze, or other materials. Two options exist for managing used oil; it can be reprocessed as a fuel substitute in industrial applications or recycled into new oil through certified recyclers. Contaminated oil must be managed through fuel blending at RCRA permitted cement kilns or destructively incinerated.
- Paint – Paint and paint-related products (such as paint thinner and stains) represent up to 65% of the total volume of material received at a full service HHW collection.

Both latex and oil-based paints have numerous management options available for processing.

Though latex is not accepted at many HHW programs due to its low hazard, management options include reuse through on-site give-away programs, recycling into paint, beneficial reuse through incorporating latex into cement products, and solidification for landfill. Each of these options incurs cost. Because latex paint is inherently non-hazardous, many communities are not accepting it, to reduce overall disposal costs for the HHW program.

Solvent-based, paint-related materials can be managed through recycling or fuel blending. Recycling is not a common management method, though several programs exist in Canada. Fuel blending is the most preferred disposal method due to the high British Thermal Unit (BTU) value of the consolidated products. BTU is a measurement of heat value or energy content and paint-related materials are a valuable fuel substitute for RCRA permitted cement kilns.

Temporary HHW Collection Programs

Communities considering public HHW collection programs generally start with temporary weekend event services. These single-day events are typically held in a large parking lot centrally located in the community. Advertising, public education, and traffic control are performed by the agency, while a hazardous waste management contractor is responsible for all aspects of on-site operations including site set-up, operations, site tear-down, hazmat transportation, and disposal. Costs are directly related to the amount of advertising and participation but range from approximately $50 per car for large events to $125 per car for small rural collections (2007 figures). Large events quickly benefit from economies of scale in that they better utilize labor, equipment, supplies, and transportation resources, lowering per unit costs.

Mobile HHW Collection Programs

Similar to temporary HHW collections, mobile programs are often held in large parking lots centrally located in a community. A mobile program can obviously move, being situated in various locations throughout a jurisdiction. This operation model is best suited where large distances or heavy traffic separates the population. Mobile service is an option when establishing multiple fixed facilities is cost-prohibitive.

Mobile events may be single-day or multi-day events. Additional labor and supply costs are required to move equipment and personnel, but mobile events provide comprehensive geographical coverage. As with temporary events, advertising, public education, and traffic control is usually provided by the coordinating agency while the hazardous waste management contractor is responsible for all aspects of on-site operations including site set-up, operations, site tear-down, hazmat, transportation and disposal. Costs are directly related to the amount of advertising and participation, but range from $70 to $110 per vehicle (2007 figures).

Permanent HHW Collection Programs

Choosing to site a permanent HHW collection program has positive and negative consequences. The most compelling reasons to build a permanent HHW facility are the improved
public access to a disposal site rather than once- or twice-a-year temporary or mobile service. The primary down side to permanent facility is the long-term financial commitment to
funding the program. Long-term liability considerations, worker exposure, and low capture
rate may temper supporting this model.

When programs transition from mobile or temporary collections to a fixed facility, a
number of operational factors change immediately. Labor and project management are the
first impacted. While coordinating an annual HHW collection can be a small component
of an employee's job responsibility, managing a large HHW facility requires dedicated
staff with responsibility. Whether an agency dedicates an employee to the task or subcon-
tracts, labor costs will become a significant component of the operating budget. Properly
allocating labor resources can benefit from analyzing the community to determine operating hours that most effectively service the population. Many rural areas are serviced well
by a very small fixed facility that is open once or twice a month. Programs serving more
populated communities should determine operating hours on population density within a
15 mile radius of the facility. Annually, most permanent facilities will service from 2 to 5%
of the households in the area, although some have participation rates upward of 10%.

Disposal volumes at permanent facilities do not tend to decrease over time. The Pacific
Northwest is home to many facilities that have been operational for up to 15 years. Generally speaking, captured material volumes increase 5–10% annually for the region. Cost for
operating a fixed facility will range from $50 to $90 per vehicle. The factors impacting cost
are participation, labor utilization, types of waste collected, and management method for
final waste disposal. Volume discounts will lower costs.

CESQG Collections

Conditionally Exempt Small Quantity Generator (CESQG) collections are increasingly
being held in communities, often the day before a temporary HHW. Though regulations
vary from state to state, CESQG businesses are those that generate less than 220 lbs. of
hazardous waste or 2.2 lbs of extremely hazardous waste per month. As a CESQG, the
business shares the same RCRA exemption as HHW thereby eliminating burdensome hazardous waste coding and annual reporting requirements. It is in the best interest of the
public agency or other HHW program provider to include CESQG collection as part of
a comprehensive HHW program. Extending the same contracted HHW disposal rates to
small businesses will encourage their participation and remove hazardous materials that
may otherwise be disposed improperly. Assuming the businesses pay directly for their disposal, the costs to the organizer are limited to the contractor labor costs.

Use of Contract Labor

Managing HHW requires using hazardous waste management contractors in some capacity, though some components of a collection program can be managed by a public agency.

For a medium-to-large permanent HHW collection program requiring full-time employees, staffing can be the most expensive component of the program. For this reason, most permanent HHW programs hire in-house labor to administer and service their collection program. Weighing the benefits of in-house or subcontracted labor is an exercise in risk vs. benefit.

Employees handling hazardous materials require specialized training, and medical monitoring, and are at risk of disability due to hazardous material exposure or physical strain. In-house labor is generally less expensive although the burden of long term worker liability falls on the public agency.

Subcontract labor is generally more expensive per hour but is often competitive with government staff rates when compared with the true government labor costs including benefits. For new programs, regional subcontract labor markets must be evaluated to properly assess these costs. A Request for Proposal (RFP) is generally required because HHW collection costs commonly exceed procurement spending thresholds, necessitating a bid process to find a suitable contractor.

Problem Wastes

While most of the incoming HHW is routine and relatively low-risk, program managers must always be prepared to respond to special wastes that present potentially dangerous situations. As presented, among the most common household hazardous waste items accepted at collections are paint, pesticides, cleaners, aerosols, motor oil, and antifreeze. There are a few types of wastes that all programs deem unacceptable to manage and they generally include, radioactive, biological, and explosive wastes. Some common items, considered unacceptable materials for most HHW programs, are listed below.

1. Radioactive Wastes
     Smoke detectors
2. Biological Wastes
     Specimens
     Human or animal waste
     Sharps
3. Explosive Wastes
     Fireworks
     Flares (marine)
     Dynamite
     Ammunition
4. Business Wastes
5. Other Wastes to Consider
     Appliances
     Asbestos
     Compressed gas cylinders
     Fire extinguishers
     Electronic waste

Pharmaceuticals (controlled substances)
PCB-containing items
Railroad ties or other treated wood
Tires

Items considered to be unacceptable may be very dangerous to handle. Even a bumpy ride to the HHW collection event poses a significant threat for some shock-sensitive materials such as a jar of crystallized picric acid. It simply is not worth the risk of potential harm to residents or collection program staff. In addition to the potential threat of harmful exposures or other accidents, some unacceptable materials are extremely expensive to properly package, transport, and dispose. Depending on the exact compound and volume of waste, transportation and disposal of radioactive waste, for example, can cost tens of thousands of dollars for just a few grams of material.

Household hazardous waste is exempt from handling and disposal regulations under the federal Resource Conservation and Recovery Act (RCRA). However other laws do not include an HHW exemption and have a major impact on the way HHW is managed. For example, the Department of Transportation (DOT), the Occupational Safety and Health Administration (OSHA), and the Toxic Substances Control Act (TSCA) all have purview over the way HHW is transported, handled, and disposed. Moreover, some states have implemented additional regulations for the management of HHW. When planning an HHW collection event or creating a new program, the best approach is to first contact your state environmental regulatory agency to determine what regulations apply to your type of collection program.

Many of the items deemed unacceptable require special equipment or special employee training and certification to manage. The HHW collection facilities are not equipped to manage these waste streams and the employees do not have the proper training and certification.

The Operations, Health, and Safety Plan for an HHW program details which types of waste are unacceptable. Accepting explosives or radioactive items endangers site workers and event participants. These items should not be accepted or stored at an HHW facility. The plan also includes specific procedures for handling such items should they be inadvertently accepted or for the sake of public safety if it cannot be returned to the resident. A hazardous waste management contractor who is specially trained and licensed to handle the material should be called. Most often, this is the most expensive way to manage the waste but may be the only way to properly and safely dispose of the material. The rule in HHW management is to "expect the unexpected." Often, program managers make prior arrangements with the local police department and bomb squad who can handle explosive items such as ammunition or crystallized picric acid. A bomb box may be constructed for the on-site detonation of certain items, but such activity should always occur under the direct supervision of the bomb squad. Finally, program managers should turn to one of the many HHW networks to consult with colleagues. Chances are someone else has already dealt with this type of problem and will either have a solution or recommend additional resources. Also, if the information is available, contact the product manufacturer. In the case of cylinders, the manufacturers may take back the cylinder at no or low cost or have information on the proper end of life management for the product.

Collection Preparation, Planning, Transportation, and Disposal Logistics

It takes a highly trained staff to receive, sort, package, and label HHW as well as specially licensed transporters and disposal facilities to properly manage HHW. Regardless of the type of HHW services provided at collections, the following considerations apply. Certain types of programs, like door-to-door collection of HHW, may have additional unique concerns.

Operations, Health, and Safety Plan

The program specific Operations, Health, and Safety Plan includes very detailed information on how operations are to be conducted for each component of the HHW program. In addition, the plan describes the hazards associated with specific operations, precautions that are to be implemented to protect employees and participants against those hazards, contingency and emergency procedures, site diagrams, and copies of applicable permits. It is the responsibility of the HHW program manager to research local and state regulations to determine if there are specific elements required for the Operations, Health, and Safety Plan.

A copy of the plan is submitted to the local emergency coordinators (police or fire departments) for review and approval prior to operations. It is best to submit the plan at least thirty days prior to opening a collection facility or holding a collection event to ensure a thorough review and allow time for changes to the plan based on recommendations by the coordinators. State or local regulations may also require that the plan be filed with a regulatory agency.

Training

A comprehensive HHW program includes a training curriculum that has been specially designed to provide HHW employees with the knowledge and tools to operate HHW and other hazardous waste management activities safely and in full compliance with state and federal regulations. The training curriculum should be designed for all levels of employees who are involved with HHW, and cover safe and legal operations for all components of the HHW program. The curriculum must be reviewed annually by management and updated continually to ensure that employees stay aware of changes in the regulatory environment. A sample training matrix is provided in Table 3.1. The matrix details required training courses for each level of employee.

The training records for all employees should be kept on file at the HHW facility or administrative office and made available for review by inspectors during operating hours. If labor is outsourced for HHW operations, it is the program manager's responsibility to ensure that subcontracted employees provide adequate training documentation.

Table 3.1. HHW Training Matrix

Type of Training	Site Supervisor	Chemist	Technician
OSHA HAZWOPER			
40 Hour initial	X	X	
24 Hour initial			X
8 Hour annual refresher	X	X	X
First Aid / CPR	X	X	
Hazard Identification	X	X	
Forklift	X	X	
DOT	X	X	
Respiratory Fit	X	X	
Medical Surveillance	X	X	

Emergency and Contingency Planning

As previously mentioned, the event Operations, Health, and Safety Plan contains a contingency plan which details proper procedures for spills or other potential releases, medical emergencies, inclement weather, and other out of the ordinary events. Prior to the collection event, the plan is submitted to local emergency coordinators such as the police and fire departments. It is best to meet with these agencies before the event as well.

Emergency information is clearly marked and stored at the site's command center. Emergency information includes a copy of the Operations, Health, and Safety Plan, a map to the nearest hospital, phone numbers for emergency coordinators and other responders, and safety references such as the DOT guide book and chemical dictionary.

Site Lay-out

A scale drawing of the event site or permanent facility is an important part of the Operations, Health, and Safety Plan. The drawing should include at least all of the following:

- Ingress and egress of traffic
- Unloading zone
- Hot zone
- Decontamination zone
- Break area
- Restrooms, if applicable
- Safety equipment (air horn, fire extinguisher, etc)
- Spill kit
- First aid supplies
- Waste storage areas
- Lab pack area
- Waste packaging area, including bulking area

- Trash bins
- Vehicle staging for outgoing waste load
- Emergency evacuation route
- Traffic control personnel
- Supply storage
- Office
- Other significant site features

The site map should be updated for each temporary collection event or annually for a permanent HHW facility.

Mobilization and Site Set-Up

Mobilization is the process of preparing the location for the HHW collection event. In the case of a permanent facility, mobilization is minimal; workers don their personal protective equipment, prepare containers for packaging waste, ensure supplies are well stocked and the safety equipment is working. The mobilization for a temporary collection event is much more extensive. Often the mobilization crew starts from scratch in a parking lot or public works yard. All of the necessary supplies and equipment are first loaded onto a large truck and transported to the collection site. Then the crew lays down visqueen or other type of poly plastic sheeting, erects a canopy for protection from the elements, and continues to set up the site according to the site map and operations, health, and safety plan. Nearby storm drains are covered and sealed. All safety and emergency equipment is tested to ensure that it is working properly. Traffic cones are used to create the traffic lanes. Directional signs are posted on major thoroughfares. In some cases, portable toilets and sinks, forklifts and roll-off bins for (non-hazardous) trash are delivered to the site. Often the mobilization for a temporary event occurs on the day prior to the collection event because of the time it takes for complete mobilization. It typically takes 4 – 8 hours for complete mobilization and set-up of a temporary collection site.

It is best if the collection site is prepared to accept participants at least thirty minutes prior to the published start time. Inevitably, residents line up early and starting an event just thirty minutes early can alleviate a backlog of cars and reduce stress levels for both the participants and the workers. HHW operations have been streamlined over the years and with this improvement came short line waits, generally 5–10 minutes, for residents.

Traffic Flow

The best traffic flow patterns incorporate the following guidelines:

- Use existing routes if possible
- Never cross the flow of traffic
- The entrance should be separate from the exit
- Stop residents for survey or greeting before they reach the hot zone
- Lanes should be wide enough to accommodate large trucks and trailers

- Create a contingency lane for large or leaking loads to pull out of the main traffic flow
- Allow enough queue space, including a second line, so that traffic does not back up onto major roadways

For large single-day collection events, provide an adequate number of traffic control personnel to direct participants through the queue safely. Traffic control personnel stationed at the entrance should be able to verbally communicate with the Site Supervisor or Traffic Supervisor to ensure a safe, even flow of traffic into the collection event. Another important area for traffic control personnel is any point where lanes merge or where participants enter the unloading area. The unloading area can be one of the most dangerous areas at the collection event because participants become engrossed in the operations around them or become confused by the traffic cones. The unloading area should have one traffic control person for every two unloading positions. For example, three traffic control personnel should be stationed in an unloading area consisting of two lanes of traffic with three unloading positions in each lane.

Safety Meeting

Prior to the start of the collection event, the Site Supervisor will invite all levels of on-site staff to attend the site safety meeting. Attendance of the meeting is mandatory. The primary purpose of the meeting is to familiarize event staff with the collection site, operations, and the appropriate safety precautions to be taken to protect staff, participants, and the environment. Topics covered in the safety meeting include each staff member's role in the collection event, location of safety equipment, identification of the emergency response coordinators, contingency plans, evacuation route, waste packaging guidelines, list of unacceptable materials, chemical and physical hazards associated with the day's activities, personal protective equipment requirements, and safety precautions.

Personal Protective Equipment

Personal protective equipment (PPE) is the first line of defense in protecting employees from exposure to hazardous waste. PPE includes protective clothing and footwear, respiratory protection, and eye and hearing protection. The Operations, Health, and Safety Plan details the specific PPE required for each level of employee at the collection event. Typically, staff is required to wear a Tyvek suit or work uniform, steel toed boots, safety glasses with side shields, and puncture resistant gloves with an inner liner. Additional respiratory protection may be required for employees performing hazardous characterization ("hazcat") testing or bulking certain materials.

Greeting and Surveys

Many HHW programs station participant greeters at the event entrance. Residents enjoy a friendly face to greet them as they enter the collection site or to wish them well as they exit; after all, this is a social event as well. The employees assigned to these tasks should therefore be friendly, easily approachable, and have some type of distinguishing outerwear such as a traffic vest, company shirt, or jacket. These greeters may request survey data from participants. Greeters and survey administrators should not wear the same personal protective equipment as the hot zone personnel. Appropriate personal protective equipment for these employees includes sun/weather protection and traffic vests and they should stay out of the collection area where the hazardous materials are being handled.

Administering surveys or providing public information/education and outreach materials is best done either before the participant reaches the unloading area or just before the participant is leaving the collection site. Surveys or other distractions should be avoided while waste is being unloaded from participants' vehicles.

Screening the Waste

Prior to entering the unloading area, each participant's waste is screened in the vehicle for unacceptable material, excessively large loads, and leaking materials. This is also the best time to instruct all passengers to remain inside their vehicle, and extinguish cigarettes, and explain the unloading zone procedures. If any unacceptable items are identified, the screener should immediately tell the participant and notify the Site Supervisor. The Site Supervisor then makes the decision to accept the material or provides instructions on proper disposal options for the resident. If a participant arrives with an excessively large load, over 200 pounds of waste, the individual should be directed to the contingency lane where the Site Supervisor may ask a few questions to determine the nature of the waste and the reason for the large load. If it is highly probable that the waste was generated by a business, the load may be rejected and the participant will be referred to a specially designed small business program (Conditionally Exempt Small Quantity Generator) or notified when CESQG wastes will be accepted at the site if this is the case, or given a list of local hazardous waste contractors. A large load can of course be a cost burden on the program.

Unloading Waste

As the participant is directed into the unloading position, staff should instruct the participant to turn off the vehicle engine and release the trunk or unlock the doors to allow access to the waste. The participant should also remain inside the vehicle at all times, for safety and liability reasons. Often, this rule must be verbally reinforced.

If staff detects any damage to the vehicle as a result from loading or transporting the waste, the driver should be notified immediately before any waste is removed from the vehicle. In this case, the participant should be directed to the contingency lane so that subsequent vehicles are not held up during the investigation. This Site Supervisor should be notified and can assist with the proper clean-up of any spills. Any vehicle damage should be noted and a site incident report completed and kept on file. If possible, damage should be documented with a photograph if appropriate.

The waste should be removed from the vehicle and placed onto a cart. If the staff finds an unlabeled container, the participant should immediately be asked for material identification and, if known, the staff can properly label the container. If the participant does not know the material, the technician must attempt to obtain as much information about the material as possible and then place it on the unknown table for prompt hazard categorization.

To reduce the risk of injury due to load lifting, only the top level of a two shelf cart should be used. Heavy items should always be placed on the cart and wheeled to the appropriate packaging area. The cart with waste should then be wheeled to the hot zone where the waste is sorted and packaged.

Should a participant request the return of a box, bag, or other container, it may be best to move the vehicle to the contingency lane to wait for the return of the container. Gasoline containers should only be returned when site operations allow for bulking of flammable liquids.

Sorting the Waste

Once the waste is moved into the hot zone, it is sorted by hazard class and packaged for transportation and disposal. The first step in sorting waste is to identify the product ingredients by reading the label. When participants bring labeled containers to the collection event, trained chemists and technicians verify that the label and waste match through a visual determination. All non-original containers (*i.e.,* food containers and others) and contents are visually inspected to verify content. If a visual conclusion cannot be made, it is assumed to be unknown until a trained chemist confirms the hazard class of the waste. Unlabeled containers are taken to the lab pack area where hazardous characterization tests (hazcatting) will be performed by a chemist. Once the product is conclusively identified it can be lab packed accordingly, for proper storage and transportation.

Segregating the Waste

Packaging of the waste is the most important task during the collection event. Only highly trained and experienced chemists and technicians should package the waste. The consequences of improperly identified and packaged waste can be grave.

Wastes are categorized by hazard class using information provided by the label on the container. Initially, HHW should be segregated by the general classification of the waste (such as paint, pesticide, cleaner). See Table 3.2. The ingredient with the highest hazard and/or concentration determines the hazard class. All labels are read carefully and trained technicians pay close attention to the ingredients.

Table 3.2. HHW General Waste Categories

Hazard Class	Description
2.1	Aerosols
2.1	Propane cylinders
2.2	Fire extinguishers
3	Flammable liquids
3	Oil-based paint
4.1	Flammable solids
4.2	Air reactive (spontaneously combustible)
4.3	Water reactive (dangerous when wet)
5.1	Oxidizing, acid
5.1	Oxidizing, alkaline
5.1	Oxidizing, neutral
5.2	Organic peroxide
6.1	Toxic
8	Corrosive, acidic
8	Corrosive, alkaline
8	Mercury
9	Asbestos
9	PCB ballasts
9	PCB containing materials
None	Antifreeze
None	Car batteries
None	Fluorescent light tubes
None	Latex paint
None	Motor oil
None	Oil filters
None	Electronic waste
None	Sharps
None	Household batteries (alkaline and rechargeable)

Packaging the Material

Wastes are packaged into a variety of containers in one of three methods: bulk, loosepack, or lab pack. Typical container types include poly, steel, or fiber drums in 5 gallon, 15 gallon, 30 gallon, or 55 gallon sizes. Other containers include cubic yard or cubic meter boxes, 200–300 gallon totes, 40-yard roll-off bins, and aboveground storage tanks typically used only for motor oil. When bulking a material, individual containers of the same type of material are consolidated or poured into a single container. For example, cans of latex paint, if accepted at collections (they are low hazard) are poured into a 55-gallon drum. Loosepack refers to the packaging of small containers of the same type of material into a larger container. For example, aerosol cans are packaged into a 55-gallon drum. The packaging of material should only be performed by trained chemists or technicians. In this packaging method, items of the same hazard class are carefully packaged into a drum in layers. The space between containers and between the layers is filled with an absorbent material such as vermiculite or dry-sorb (*i.e.,* kitty litter).

Labeling the Waste

All containers of waste should be properly labeled at all times. The specific type of label required depends on type of material and any additional state or local labeling requirements. All HHW must meet the Department of Transportation (DOT) labeling requirements. Typically, each label includes the following information:

- Generator's name, address, and identification number
- Proper shipping name of material per DOT regulations
- Date of first accumulation

Additional hazard class labels may be required depending on the type of material. Directional (up arrow) labels may be required depending on the packaging method.

Manifesting and Paperwork

Once the waste is collected, identified, and properly packaged, the containers are loaded onto the transport vehicle. Although HHW is exempt from the federal Resource Conservation and Recovery Act (RCRA), it is not exempt from the Department of Transportation regulations on the safe transport of hazardous waste. Thus, HHW must be shipped on a hazardous waste manifest or on a bill of lading. The person completing the shipping papers must have extensive training in the proper labeling and shipping of hazardous waste per DOT regulations. The type of paperwork used (manifest or bill of lading) is determined by the type of waste. Universal wastes (such as fluorescent light tubes and batteries) and non-hazardous wastes (such as latex paint and motor oil) may be shipped on a bill of lading. Hazardous waste must be shipped on a uniform hazardous waste manifest. Refer to DOT regulations for more information.

Depending on the type of waste shipped and the waste management facility that receives the waste, the load may also require a land disposal restriction (LDR) form. The EPA LDR program is designed to ensure that land disposed hazardous waste does not pose a threat to human health or the environment. Land disposal includes landfill, injection well, or other land-based disposal method.

Transportation to Disposal Facilities

Prior to the HHW collection event, the program manager will have established an agreement or contract with a fully permitted and licensed hazardous waste management facility or recycling facility. Hazardous waste facilities are referred to as TSDFs – Transportation,

Storage, and Disposal Facilities. There are different types of TSDFs that may receive and handle the waste.

Primary versus Secondary Facility

The primary receiving facility is the first facility that receives the waste. It is listed on the hazardous waste manifest as the Designated Facility. When the waste is received by the primary TSDF, it may be sent through the appropriate disposal technology (such as waste-water treatment, incineration, or fuel blending) or it may be consolidated with other waste and shipped to a secondary facility for final disposal.

Some receiving facilities are permitted ten-day transfer stations. These types of facilities are not permitted to store waste longer than ten days. In this case, the facility will receive small shipments of waste from a number of different generators. The containers are sorted by the final disposal destination. When the facility has accumulated enough drums to send to a single final disposal facility (or the drums have reached their ten-day storage limit) those drums are loaded onto one large truck and transported for disposal.

Demobilization

Once the collection event is concluded and closed to the public, event staff will finish packaging all waste on site. In the case of a temporary collection event, all waste is transported off site following demobilization on the last day of the event. All supplies, materials, and equipment are removed from the site unless prior arrangements are made. All litter is removed and the site returned to its pre-event condition.

With permanent HHW facilities, waste may be stored in separated compartments designated by compatibility of materials for a future shipment date. However, all containers of waste at the facility must have proper labeling and must be securely sealed for storage. Supplies, materials, and equipment are neatly stored. All paperwork is filed. In some cases, a daily inspection is conducted once the site is completely demobilized. The inspection includes a waste inventory which details the types and volumes of waste stored on-site. The inspection logs and waste inventories are kept on site with other important paperwork including copies of shipping documents and certificates of disposal.

Post-Event Considerations

In the weeks following a temporary collection event, or events at permanent facilities, it is very important to follow through on post-event considerations.

First, any data collected through participant surveys should be loaded into a database used for tracking and analyzing data. By tracking and analyzing certain data points, a program manager can monitor disposal trends, such as changes in total volume of waste, number of participants, average volume per participant, collection costs, and even the effectiveness of publicity or education and outreach methods. Many programs also track participant demographics such as age, gender, ethnicity, income, own/rent housing, and education level, to generally gauge the composition of their population.

To verify disposal of the HHW that is collected, a program manager can request a certificate of disposal or a certificate of destruction. It typically takes at least a week and often longer for the waste load to reach the final disposal facility. The primary receiving facility can provide the generator with a certificate of disposal as evidence that the waste was received by the facility and has been routed for proper disposal. If the primary receiving facility sends the waste to a secondary receiving facility, the certificate of disposal or other receiving report will cross reference the original incoming manifest with any outgoing manifests containing that waste. For example, ABC Disposal provides a certificate of disposal showing that it received a full load of HHW from Metropolitan City on March 1, 2006, on manifest number 123456. ABC Disposal consolidated the waste into two outbound shipments: latex paint was shipped to XYZ Recycling on manifest 987654 on March 15, 2006, and the rest of the waste was shipped to Sun Incineration on manifest 564782 on April 1, 2007. For further documentation of proper waste management, the generator may also request a certificate of destruction or certificate of final disposal. These certificates are generated by the end disposal facility regardless of how many facilities previously handled the waste. It can take up to one year for some wastes to undergo final disposal; tracking of the certificates of destruction can be a time-consuming task.

It is a good practice to have regular meetings with the parties responsible for the success of the HHW program. This includes program managers, collection staff, and contractors. Volunteers, while very important to programs, need not attend these meetings. During these meetings, each party offers feedback on what appears to be working or any current challenges related to program operations. Safety incidents should be reviewed to determine the root cause of the problem and procedures implemented to reduce future occurrences. It is also a good idea to share participant feedback, both positive and negative. All of this will improve streamlining of the program and foster an environment where continuous improvement is planned.

Waste Management Methods—
A Hierarchy of Disposal

There are a number of disposal technologies available, each with unique advantages and disadvantages. The purpose of HHW collection programs is to reduce the volume of HHW entering the municipal solid waste system or being improperly disposed in other ways. Many program managers choose to follow the waste management hierarchy in an effort to increase recycling, reduce overall disposal, and conserve resources. (See Figure 3.1.) The waste management hierarchy places the highest emphasis on source reduction, *i.e.,* the reduction of HHW through purchases of less hazardous alternatives, conservative purchasing policies, and complete and proper use of products. Following reduction and reuse, waste should be recycled when feasible, such as bringing used motor oil to a quick-lube or other facility (note: the individual should identify a recycling station before changing the oil). Next, preference is given to treatment and then incineration. Waste is sent to landfill only when no other technology is available.

Table 3.3 lists some common HHW streams and the disposal methods widely available for each waste stream.

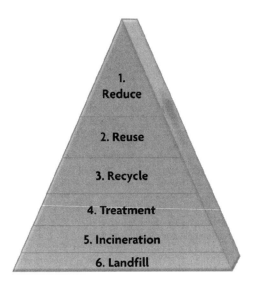

Figure 3.1. Waste Management Hierarchy

Reuse

Many products can be diverted from disposal by reuse. This is accomplished by material exchange or material reuse programs. These may be offered on-site at a collection. Some states have established formal networks designed to help business find markets for non-hazardous materials they have traditionally discarded. HHW programs across the country have successfully incorporated material reuse programs into their routine operations. The program works by identifying incoming HHW items that meet stringent reuse criteria. The items are set aside in the reuse area or "shop." Residents may then shop at the reuse shop and take the products at no charge. Often, residents are required to sign a liability waiver to ensure that the product will be utilized for its originally intended use. The waiver also provides a layer of legal protection to the agency sponsoring the reuse program. The material reuse program guidelines, including product criteria and liability waiver, should be incorporated into the Operations, Health, and Safety Plan.

Recycle

Recycling of material has become much more common as Americans' environmental consciousness has risen. There are different forms of recycling. Often, a particular product is refined or cleaned and returned to its original use. Examples of this type of recycling include motor oil and latex paint. Another form of recycling will reduce a product to its component parts that can then be used in new products. For example, fluorescent light tubes are broken down into glass, aluminum, and mercury-containing phosphor powder. Each component is then recycled and used to make other products. HHW items that are

Table 3.3. Common Disposal Methods

Waste Stream	Available Disposal Method				
	Recycle	Alternative Fuel	Treatment	Incineration	Landfill
Aerosols	X			X	X
Propane cylinders	X			X	X
Fire extinguisher	X			X	X
Flammable liquids		X		X	X
Oil-based paint		X		X	X
Flammable solids				X	X
Air reactive (spontaneously combustible)				X	X
Water reactive (dangerous when wet)				X	X
Oxidizing, acid			X	X	X
Oxidizing, alkaline			X	X	X
Oxidizing, neutral			X	X	X
Organic peroxide				X	
Toxic				X	X
Corrosive, acidic			X	X	X
Corrosive, alkaline			X	X	X
Mercury	X				X
Asbestos					X
PCB ballasts	X			X	X
PCB-containing materials	X			X	X
Antifreeze	X			X	X
Car batteries	X				X
Fluorescent light tubes	X				X
Latex paint	X			X	X
Motor oil	X			X	X
Oil filters	X			X	X
Electronic waste	X				X
Sharps				X	X
Household batteries (alkaline and rechargeable)	X			X	X

commonly recycled include latex paint, propane cylinders, rechargeable batteries, mercury, antifreeze, motor oil, and oil filters.

Alternative Fuel or Fuel Blending

Fuels blending or alternative fuel management is the process of combining high BTU-value materials, such as oil-based paint, solvents, and gasoline to use as an energy source alternative to fuel cement kilns. Using this waste-derived fuel reduces the kiln's consumption of traditional fossil fuels such as coal and oil. HHW items commonly fuel blended include oil-based paint and flammable liquids.

Treatment

Treatment is widely available for corrosive and oxidizing wastes. There are a variety of specific treatment methods available such as chemical oxidation and reduction, neutralization, metal precipitation, flocculation, filtration, and carbon adsorption. Generally speaking, the hazardous characteristic is removed through a chemical process (acids and bases are neutralized) and the waste is then discharged through the wastewater discharge or is sent to a hazardous waste landfill. HHW items commonly sent for treatment include cleaners and pool chemicals.

Destructive Incineration

Destructive Incineration, or thermal incineration, heats the hazardous waste to extremely high temperatures (over 1,800–2,200°F), which converts the solid and liquid wastes into gases. The inorganic materials, such as metals, drop out during the process as residual ash. The gases pass through air pollution control devices that further remove particulates and other pollutants to regulatory standards. The ash residue is treated to meet regulatory specifications and is then sent to a hazardous waste landfill. HHW items commonly incinerated include pesticides and organic peroxides.

Landfill

Landfill technology has changed greatly over time, especially with respect to hazardous waste disposal. Hazardous waste landfills are required to meet stringent federal and state standards regarding their location, design, construction, operation, and final closure. Prior to reaching a hazardous waste landfill, many wastes have undergone treatment such as stabilization or neutralization. Of all the disposal methods, landfill is often the least expensive option. HHW items commonly sent to landfill include alkaline batteries and asbestos.

HHW program managers do not always choose the highest level disposal technology. There are many factors involved in this complex decision. One very compelling factor is price. The higher level technologies are often more expensive. It can cost nearly three times more to recycle alkaline batteries than it costs to send them to a hazardous waste landfill. As shown in Table 3.3, the most preferred technologies are not available for some waste streams. Asbestos, for example, can only be managed through landfilling. As with most industries, the technology is constantly changing and improving. It is important for a program manager to routinely search for new and better disposal options.

Summary

In this chapter we have provided an overview of HHW collection and management. It is not all-inclusive. Therefore, it is necessary to refer to appropriate local, state, and federal rules and regulations for adequate information. Also, consult with certified chemical waste handlers and other relevant parties.

About the Authors

Sue Bruning is the Director of Product Line Management, Household Hazardous Waste Services for Clean Harbors Environmental Services. Clean Harbors is North America's leading provider of environmental and hazardous waste management services.

Mike O'Donnell is the Pacific Northwest HHW Business Manager for Philip Services Corporation (PSC), a fully integrated environmental company servicing the needs of private and public entities across the United States.

CHAPTER 4

HHW Collection Facilities

David Nightingale
Bill Lewry

The Trend toward Collection Facilities

The trend toward communities building permanent HHW collection facilities stems from the common experience with HHW collection events. Most communities in the U.S. that have initiated collection of their citizens' HHW have done so by holding one-day HHW collection events. These go by different names depending on the local preference; single days, Tox-Away-Day, Toxic Round-Ups, HHW Amnesty Days, and many others. Regardless of the name, they all function essentially the same way: municipal staff find a convenient parking lot in the community and hire a contractor to bring in equipment and supplies to operate an HHW collection day/weekend or week. Twenty-four hours later, the site returns to its normal use and the event leaves no trace.

While these collection events are very popular with the public and elected officials, they are costly and provide a very time-limited opportunity for homeowners to properly manage their HHW. These events do not serve the citizens when they move to another community. Moving day is when most homeowners discover their paint and stain may not go in the moving truck. Mobile collection events do not serve residents who must move and properly manage their HHW, causing them to leave it behind in the garage behind the water heater for the new resident. There are also significant set-up and breakdown costs associated with collection events. Because of these factors, most communities that start down the path of regular HHW collection convert from collection events to permanent HHW facilities.

Many in the HHW profession believe that on the cost-basis of per pound or per customer, a permanent collection facility is less expensive than collection events. Kansas City, Missouri, for example, operates both collection types and they base their operations at a fixed [permanent] collection station (developed from geographical necessity). They report 2005–2006 costs of $0.51/lb for the fixed facility and $0.72/lb for mobile events. The reasons for the lower permanent facility costs include:

- No set-up and breakdown costs
- Time and ability to more precisely characterize and package waste

- Ability to store waste and thus have the choice of the best vendor pricing for individual waste streams
- Ability to maximize local reuse of good products to avoid shipping and disposal costs
- Ability to store truckload size shipments for most or all shipments
- Ability to store low-volume wastes (such as inorganic mercury compounds and organic peroxides) for a longer period to gather a larger volume, which reduces shipping and disposal costs

A national survey of well-established HHW collection facilities was conducted for Portland (Oregon) Metro in 2005. Of the 25 programs fully completing the survey, only one reported not having at least one permanent collection facility, and that one has since built multiple facilities.[1] Municipalities are tending to base their HHW collection strategies on a permanent collection facility or facilities.

Washington state shows a typical progression of communities transitioning from collection events to permanent collection facilities. Figure 4.1 shows that in the early 1990s, more and more local communities were experimenting with collection events. The peak of collection events occurred in the mid-1990s and then declined as permanent fixed collection facilities replaced collection events.[2] Currently there are approximately 54 HHW collection facilities serving the 39 counties in the state and only a few dozen collection events per year are held statewide. The vast majority of HHW is collected at permanent facilities in Washington state and over 95% of the population has access to one or more permanent collection facilities within their county.

Progression from HHW Collection Events to Facilities in Washington State

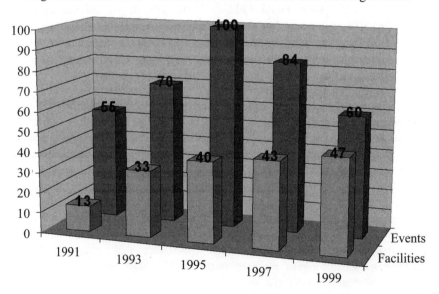

Figure 4.1. 1991–1999 Collection events compared with permanent HHW facilities in Washington state.

HHW collection facilities are often co-located with solid waste facilities although some collection systems rely on non-waste related locations such as fire departments and municipal yards. Meeting the local requirements for land use and zoning restrictions can be significant. Neighborhoods and businesses often challenge facility sites as they are typically perceived as dangerous to the community as opposed to an asset. These challenges can be handled with a good public involvement plan and inviting the community to participate in facility siting.

Characteristics to consider when siting a new facility include:

- Good customer access via paved road
- Adequate vehicle queuing space
- Room to expand if needed in the future (likely)
- Adequate turning radii for supply and shipping trucks (estimate 53 feet semi) that is separate from customer queuing lanes
- Proximity to schools, daycare facilities, and nursing homes (further is better)
- Proximity to typical customer destinations (closer is better)
- Similar business types as neighbors to the facility
- Utilities already on or very near building site
- Possible reuse of existing buildings
- Existing zoning
- Proximity to emergency services
- Operational aspects other than HHW being considered (such as a recycling buy-back center, recycled latex paint store, etc.)

Development of HHW Collection Facilities

HHW collection facilities have been successfully built at former parking garages, in business parks, fire stations, wastewater treatment plants, solid waste facilities, motor pool yards, and other commercial and industrial sites.

Once a facility location is determined, the biggest hurdles are typically meeting all of the building and fire code requirements. A competent, committed design team who can take the concept for a facility from idea to a standing building that is ready to operate is essential to this process. The construction code requirements are found in the current, locally adopted version of the International Construction Codes. The International Codes include:

- International Building Code
- International Fire Code
- International Mechanical Code
- International Electrical Code, and
- Others such as plumbing, grading, etc.

The system of International Codes is complex, interdependent, and extensive. The design team needs to include a professional who is comfortable using these codes. Further, the nature and quantity of HHW typically stored and processed at HHW collection facilities typically leads to requirements for "High-Hazard," 'H,' occupancy ratings for at least part of the building.

HHW that is processed and stored on-site typically results in the need for secondary containment, excellent ventilation (local and area), backup power for critical electrical systems, explosion-proof wiring and fixtures in certain areas, fire suppression systems, and other special features and construction methods. Other than the International Codes, there are some other resources that can help to determine appropriate requirements from the National Fire Protection Association (NFPA), and others:

- NFPA 497, Recommended Practice for the Classification of Flammable Liquids, Gases, or Vapors and Hazardous (Classified) Locations for Electrical Installations in Chemical Process Areas; NFPA (http://www.nfpa.org)
- NFPA 70, National Electrical Code; NFPA
- NFPA 30, Flammable Liquids; NFPA
- Industrial Ventilation—A Manual of Recommended Practice; American Conference of Governmental Industrial Hygienists (ACGIH) (http://www.acgih.org/store/)
- HHW and CESQG Collection Facility Operations, Design, and Resource Manual; Special Waste Associates (http://www.specialwasteassoc.com – in press)

It should be the goal for HHW facilities to remain exempt from full hazardous waste regulation when possible to reduce the administrative burden, but it is recommended that all facilities be practically operated and managed as if they were RCRA-regulated Treatment, Storage, and Disposal Facilities (TSDF) in order to promote employee and process safety.

Pre-Design Details

- Plan to design for the future. Before commencing design work for a new facility, or expansion of an existing site, consider volume, waste streams, and processing possibilities in the foreseeable future.
- In some cases, depending upon the location and demographics, it could be feasible to use commercially available prefabricated buildings, and simply expand the number of units as future need arises. This approach works well and is fiscally conservative but creates a cluttered look once there are more than three of these at a site. Care should be taken when using this approach, however. Of overriding concern will be the availability of political and fiscal capital in future years to readily accomplish the needed expansion goals, and ensuring the site is sufficiently large to accommodate them. These prefabricated units function particularly well in situations where the operation plan calls for minimal waste processing and lower waste volumes common to a satellite collection location or a less urban community. They are usually built of steel and of limited interior height and do not accommodate the large size of typical paint can crushers nor provide the needed spot ventilation for such operations.
- Design the operation around the processes and practices that are most likely to be used, with as much adaptability as feasible. One can never ask often enough, "What

if?" For instance, how does the program intend to manage latex paint? Will staff bulk it, blend it, and recycle it to the community? If so, the design must incorporate processing space.

- Have a manufacturing engineer or process engineer review the plans; a small front-end investment could provide significant long-term savings. These professionals will review for material flow, space constraints, ergonomics, and space requirements for various waste management processes.
- Consider the levels of training when designing a facility. If training will not be provided to accommodate a specific material stream, it may not make sense to accommodate that material stream. A good example here is dismantling electronics for reusable parts. If the program does not intend to train staff to manage electronics this way, then find another site for electronics management.
- Consider the needs of staff, clients, and material safety in the receiving area. Ideally, all receiving areas should be covered. This helps alleviate comfort issues and provides protection from direct sunlight and rain, both of which can make incoming materials less stable. Covered receiving areas are essential when dealing with DOT Class 4 or Dangerous When Wet materials. The debate continues over the idea of having inside receiving locations where the client vehicle is driven into the building—this is becoming a greater concern as recent studies are showing significant half life of small particulate matter in the lungs (such as generated from car exhaust), and the potential for damage created by the same. A sign requesting that clients shut off their vehicle engines is often a simple long-term safety investment. An example of an above referenced study can be found at: http://www.nih.gov/news/pr/dec2005/niehs-22.htm. In addition, in most climates drop-off area canopies need to provide a significant overhang beyond the spill containment area often designed into the drive-through area. This is needed to avoid collection of blown rain in the spill control structure. The amount of overhang will depend on local weather conditions. The amount of overhang will be greater the higher the typical winds and the higher the eaves height of the canopy. Sometimes it is possible to put an end wall parallel to the building at the end of the canopy to block prevailing winds from that direction. All of these methods also provide more shade on hot days.
- Facility security beyond gates and alarm systems is a newer aspect of the design process. New rules promulgated by the Department of Homeland Security (DHS) require various types of waste be reported and secured differently than older facilities. Each facility needs a DOT Security plan as well. The DHS rules impact facilities differently depending on the type of security selected—third party remote monitoring, on-site guards, commissioned public safety staff, or a passive system consisting of perimeter fences, signs, and cameras and recording equipment with remote alarms.
- Will the facility use electrical or air power to operate equipment in the facility? Electrical requires the installation of explosion proof plugs/sockets in all appropriate areas, at as much as $700 per matched pair, while air power has the drawback of ongoing compressor maintenance, but the plug socket arrangement is intrinsically safe and costs only around $10. An additional aspect to the benefit of air power is that an explosion proof, one horsepower motor for air is typically two to three hundred dollars, while a similarly rated electrical motor can be around ten times that.

- Stand-by power—If you are installing stand-by power, you will have an on-site generator. It is best to choose one that is properly sized for the load required by the electrical code and plan for additional capacity to accommodate any anticipated future expansion needs. Generators are expensive and it is inadvisable to replace them during their working life, especially if you can anticipate your future needs with good planning.

The Design Process

Early in the design process, before hiring an engineering or architectural firm, local staff should lay out conceptual elements of the desired facility. Become informed and identify preferences by visiting other facilities and talking with their managers. Select the building features and operating procedures that will work well for the community and make a list. Then spend some time sketching what needs to go where and why including material flow and location of processes like bulking flammables and blending latex paint. Material handling processes should accommodate the following:

1. Universal Waste Rule
2. HHW vs. Conditionally exempt small quantity generator (CESQG) collection operations (ability to track and manage small business waste and collect a fee)
3. Latex paint acceptance or denial; recycling
4. Oil-based (Alkyd) Paint and Flammable Liquids bulking or lack of bulking
5. Lead-Acid Battery storage
6. Combustible Liquids (used oil, oil filters)
7. Antifreeze
8. Fluorescent Lamps
9. Electronic Wastes
10. Acids (various kinds)
11. Bases
12. Oxidizers
13. Organic Peroxides
14. Reactives (and dangerous when wet)
15. Explosives (classification, characteristics, black powder)

This homework will allow for more effective communication with the design professionals so that they understand what is needed and why. Surprisingly, even national design firms have few if any design professionals who have worked on more than a few HHW facility designs. Seek out a design professional who has designed more than a handful of HHW collection facilities. An additional good source for guidance is the chemical waste/disposal contractor who will be a potential partner in the facility. Hazardous waste management organizations may be willing to give advice on certain structural and procedural requirements as well as needs a typical organization may have that will influence facility design.

Doing the design homework and being a strong voice in the design process are critical because HHW facilities are unlike any other type of solid waste handling facility. The intensity and complexity of HHW management is higher than any other component of solid waste. Consequently, to be efficient and safe, more thought is required to carefully design the workspace and the relationship between the various steps in collecting and managing HHW.

The basic steps for managing HHW are:

1. Waste acceptance
2. Sorting
3. Packaging or processing
4. Storage
5. Shipment

It is necessary to be well informed to communicate the specifics of the operations to the design team. For example, there should be adequate space for all containers (in process of being filled, empties in storage, and full in storage), supplies, aisles for carts or forklifts, and customer separation from all of the operations except waste acceptance.

Some additional basic parameters include:

- Efficient flow of material—handle each item as few times as possible
- Design for ergonomics (reduce strain on workers by low-stress workstations and use of machines instead of muscle power—use counterbalances and pulleys)
- Ventilation and noise engineering controls (refer to OSHA guidelines and rules)
- Separate customer service area and shipping bays to allow normal operations and shipping to occur simultaneously
- Maintain any waste exchange areas so they are remote from waste operational areas and ensure they are designed to function as a waste exchange area
- Ensure dual exit routes from principle locations
- Design in alarms and fume hoods

Facility Design Summary

Key parameters are to document operational choices, space planning, site constraints/ needs, infrastructure and equipment needs, fire and building code, and budget matching. It is important to:

- Determine waste types and amounts per household based on local mobile collection event experience or nearby communities; figure out how to store the representative 100 drums and the DOT compatible classes of waste
- Decide if the facility will have a waste exchange
- Specify what operational choices have been made
- Focus on space planning for the various processes
- Identify site constraints/needs (wetlands, access, zoning, neighbors, etc.)
- Determine infrastructure needs (water, sewer, power, etc.)
- Identify equipment options and needs
- Do budget matching
- Have example diagrams

Justification Process

Most organizations get one opportunity to sell the program to the economic and political decision makers. Planning and complete documentation of all decisions are critical to explaining the proposed facility design and budget.

Operating Efficiencies: Often efficiency = operating cost savings = safer workplaces

- Workflow patterns, straight-line vs. round about
- Capital expense vs. employee stress, comfort, and accidents
- Labor intensive costs vs. automation costs (capital expense vs. operating cost)
- Maintenance Costs
- Typical Operating Expenses
- Waste Exchanges

Functional Facility Design Exercise

First consider what materials will be accepted at the facility—explosives, ammunition, radioactives, and medical waste are often excluded materials. It is easiest to screen materials by DOT hazard class rather than EPA waste designations because facilities pack and ship waste by DOT class. The EPA classifications do not help segregate waste into the proper shipping drums. All or some of these materials may be accepted.

Class 1 – Explosives*
Class 2 – Gases
Class 3 – Flammable liquids (and combustible liquids in the US)
Class 4 – Flammable solids, spontaneously combustible, and dangerous when wet
        materials
Class 5 – Oxidizers and organic peroxides
Class 6 – Toxic materials and infectious substances*
Class 7 – Radioactive materials*
Class 8 – Corrosive materials
Class 9 – Miscellaneous dangerous goods*

Even a few grams of explosive materials can be dangerous if it becomes unstable or managed improperly. NASA uses a lot of common, as well as less common, explosive material in the space program. Consequently, they have developed a safety guide that provides some good information and guidance on the handling and storage of explosive materials. See http://www.hq.nasa.gov/office/codeq/doctree/1740_12.pdf

---

*Often chemical waste contractors will not accept radioactive or infectious substances or some dangerous goods. Some explosives may not be accepted. Ammunition and similar products may be referred to their police or fire department for disposing these materials. While not the norm, some HHW and CESQG collection programs accept limited amounts of explosive materials. In some areas there are mobile units that slowly burn small caliber ammunition, common road flares, and fireworks in batches. Private specialty disposal companies as well as some law enforcement agencies operate these units. Check with your local or state air quality authority before considering use of such services in your area.

Most of the major DOT hazardous materials Classes are subdivided into Divisions. For instance in Class 1, Explosives, there are Divisions 1.1, 1.2, 1.3, etc. With the exception of subclass 8, the other subclasses (with a few exotic exceptions) can be commingled in a single storage area unless the containers are compromised. Check with a licensed chemical waste contractor if you have questions.

It is necessary to provide operations space for miscellaneous equipment and storage, such as traffic cones and portable signage. It is a good idea to purchase and install one of the commercially available floor plan drafting or architectural packages for layout ideas and space need calculations. These preliminary conceptual drawings can be very helpful to the design team in understanding what is needed and provide a jump start to the design process.

This is also the time to begin working closely with an industrial, process, or manufacturing engineer. The dollars spent here will greatly impact the final product and can enhance or reduce the reputation of the guiding staff.

Footprint of the Facility

The typical footprint of a facility will depend upon many factors. An example is provided for the Kansas City, Missouri, operations. Please note that there are significant differences in the dynamics produced by both geographical locations and rural/urban demographics. Facility needs and requirements will vary by community.

For a population base of 100,000 households, there may be an average of 5% resident participation [Lewry survey, 2003, KCMO participation], giving a vehicle throughput of around 5,000 per year. Average volume could vary between 60lb. and 150lb. With 135 lbs. per vehicle [KCMO annual report 2006], there is an estimated throughput of 675,000 lbs./year. Estimate that as the program matures, usage will increase (by up to 100%), but weights will likely decrease (by up to 30%). It should be noted that to "design for tomorrow," a good estimate in this scenario is 1,000,000 lbs. of material per year.

A typical tractor-trailer only holds 40,000 lbs. of material (drummed/loose packed) so about 25 tractor trailer shipments/year may be needed. Thus, tractor-trailer access will be needed rather than access for a smaller box truck. Estimating a storage capacity of 3 times the floor space of a tractor-trailer, around 1,300 square feet of storage space may be needed, based upon drum size. Not all items are contained in drums and for loose-packed and cubic yard boxes, an additional 1/3 is optimally added, bringing the square footage to around 1,700. A 100% loading is then initiated to allow for walls, inspection, and aisle space, bringing the total storage area to around 3,400 square feet. Next, a dock is needed for shipping/receiving, ideally with some type of load leveling or dock plate system. This must allow maneuvering and staging room, typically a 600 square feet minimum. Total storage/dock area combined is now 4,000 square feet for this example, or about 1 square foot per 250 lbs. of annual throughput. Due to sociopolitical, geographic, and demographic limitations, and other specific needs, these serve only as guidelines. Significantly smaller and much larger HHW collection facilities have been built across the U.S. Some recent facilities have exceeded 10,000 square feet.

In Kansas City, Missouri, processing area requirements are typically around 75% of storage area requirements. This can increase or decrease dramatically depending upon operational throughput and seasonal adjustments. This is close to 1 square foot per 200 lbs. of throughput, or 3,000 square feet in this example, approximately the size of the Kansas City facility. A good estimate for a moderately sized facility is one square foot of operational area for every 200 lbs. of anticipated annual throughput.

Tool storage and miscellaneous equipment storage are often overlooked, but for items as varied as yard tools and forklifts, process materials and operational supplies, it would be appropriate to allow 15% of the operational area or about 450 square feet (the approximate size of a double car garage).

Decontamination areas, restrooms, lunch rooms, control (HVAC, heaters, compressors, and extraction fans, etc.) and offices typically require an additional 1,500 square feet and up to 250 more for a "swap shop" for usable material exchange.

Total anticipated square footage for a 1,000,000-pound facility therefore could be about 9,200 square feet, ideally on a single level (though mezzanine type operations have also been shown to function well).

Storage Options

The storage of items on open shelving should be avoided if possible. In some facilities, cabinets are used for initial temporary storage, as it has been found through experience that there are many benefits to this system such as financial and employee comfort. The financial benefit becomes obvious when it is considered that for a larger facility, six air changes per hour are required in order to keep the air "clean," and in areas of the country with extreme climactic changes this can create significant utility bills sometimes running into several thousand dollars per month. An exhaust fan installed in the main operations area with an auto damper for use in case of spills can accomplish this effectively when coupled to individual exhausts taken from each cabinet. It is much more cost efficient and environmentally friendly to change the air six times in ten or twelve cabinets than in an entire facility. If this route is taken, it is beneficial to tie in automatic air monitoring to the air exchange system. Employee exposure is also significantly reduced.

The employee comfort issue is significant as there will be many chemicals off-gassing from the collected material in the operations area. These trace amounts of chemicals will be breathed by the staff, potentially leading to chemical sensitivities over extended timeframes.

Carbon Footprint

The design stage is the best time to consider the carbon footprint of the facility, which should be as close to zero as possible. When considering the carbon footprint, it is useful to examine all aspects of the site design. Requiring participants to drive additional miles to the facility location will increase the carbon footprint, not to mention potentially decrease the participation rate. Consider renewable energy options. Solar power could be used for water heating, or perhaps there are other options to purchase "green power." Determine if it is feasible to install an underground heat pump system for heating and cooling assistance. As energy costs continue to soar, the paybacks from these options will continue to increase.

If the area of land is large enough, green space with tree plantings will provide beauty and shade in addition to sequestering carbon. One community planted an orchard around its facility; providing an additional employee and volunteer benefit. A very effective and energy saving method of construction involved "day lighting" which is typically accomplished by using translucent panels or skylights, which can double as "blowout panels."

In designing and operating a permanent facility, it is important to think practically yet creatively, and with a mind toward employee, contractor, and participant ease, safety, and satisfaction—both in the present and in the future.

About the Authors

David Nightingale has been assisting localities and states in the development of HHW programs since 1987. During this time he has visited over 100 HHW collection facilities in North America while working for public and private sector employers. He currently serves on the North American Hazardous Materials Management Association (NAHMMA) Board of Directors. He has provided training for HHW operations health and safety as well as workshops for HHW facility design and is a part-time consultant and author for Special Waste Associates.

Bill Lewry, a divisional manager with Kansas City, Missouri, has qualified as a CET, REP, CHMM, and holds certification from the ASSE. His research focus in recent years has been in enhancing employee health and safety in the waste handling arena through a combination of education, design, and process improvement, while promoting sustainability in governmental operations. He also currently serves on the LEPC, SWMD, state rulemaking committees and as a Board member of NAHMMA.

Notes

1. Comparison of Household Hazardous Waste Programs, Metro Solid Waste and Recycling Department, Portland OR, Cascadia Consulting Group, Fall 2005.

2. Nightingale, D., and Ellis, E., *Moderate Risk Waste Collection System Report*, WA Dept. of Ecology, Publication #00-07-041, December 2000, Olympia, WA, p. 6.

CHAPTER 5

Creative Collection and Management Options

Sue Bruning

Traditionally, household hazardous waste (HHW) has successfully been collected in the U.S. through single-day collection programs begun in the early 1980s. Permanent HHW facilities sprang up not long after. By 1997, there were more than 3,000 HHW single-day and permanent facility collection events throughout the United States.[1] Disasters precipitate further HHW collection. According to the U.S. Environmental Protection Agency (EPA), over one million pounds of HHW was collected in the aftermath of hurricanes Rita and Katrina in 2005.[2] While it is difficult to estimate exactly how much HHW is in our homes, garages, and storage areas, we do know that on average, less than 10% of American households participate in HHW collection programs.[3] While traditional government-sponsored collection programs emphasize the waste management hierarchy of reduce, reuse, recycle, treatment, incinerate, landfill (in the order of most to least preferred), budgetary restrictions and other limited resources often steer waste disposal efforts to the less expensive lower hierarchy methods. In order to address these challenges, HHW programs across the country are implementing creative collection and waste management practices.

Shortcomings of Traditional HHW Collection and Management

Limited Access

The popularity of HHW programs is increasing; at least one HHW program exists in each of the fifty United States. However, there are still many communities with no collections or inconsistent offerings. Even if an HHW program exists, certain populations such as the elderly, disabled, or homebound have difficulty or cannot access the services. Non-English-speaking populations are also underserved due to cultural barriers and untargeted, often ineffective education and outreach materials. They are not getting the message or they are not able to interpret it.

Convenience

In order to maximize participation, the HHW collection opportunity must be convenient for the public. Long distances to drop-off sites and limited and few days of operation are barriers to convenience and subsequently, participation. Residents are less likely to travel long distances to drop off their waste. Collections offered once or twice a year mean that residents must store materials and be available on the selected day. Commonly, single-day collections are held only in the spring and fall. Fewer drop-off days means that more people participate on the day(s), necessitating a longer wait for participants to deposit materials. Even with more frequently held collections at permanent HHW facilities, very few communities offer collection opportunities on a daily basis. The hours of collection are also limited to 4–8 hours per day. Convenience means proximity to multiple collection opportunities with user-friendly hours of operation. Even greater convenience comes in the form of curbside collection as opposed to drop-off. Americans love one-stop shopping and now seem to prefer no-stop shopping, *i.e.,* services at home rather than elsewhere. The increase and success of residential curbside recycling is evidence of this phenomenon. According to a recent study commissioned by Metro Solid Waste and Recycling Department (Portland, OR), seven of the 25 communities (28%) surveyed provide door-to-door collection service for HHW.[4] Through a benchmark report released in January 2007 by Ken Wells of the Sonoma County Waste Management Agency in Sonoma County, California, the agency determined that door-to-door collection of HHW was an important, albeit expensive, component of its comprehensive HHW program that serves seniors, disabled residents, and conditionally exempt small-quantity generators.[5]

A New Concept

A component of municipal solid waste, household hazardous waste is a relatively new idea in our society. The HHW industry has only been active since the 1980s and the idea of HHW and collection opportunities did not become widespread until the late 1990s. In many parts of the country, Americans are unaware that certain hazardous items from the home should not be placed in the trash. It is going to take many more years of public education, outreach, and improvements in the HHW collection industry, to increase overall awareness and participation rates from the meager 5 to 10% we see today.

Limited Outreach and Advertisement

Many HHW program managers face a dilemma when it comes to program advertising. First, advertising can be expensive, consuming a large portion of the overall operating budget. Second, successful outreach and advertising can significantly increase event participation.

Therein lies the dilemma. The program resources must be able to support the increased waste volumes resulting from the advertising campaign. Can a program be too successful? Perhaps it can because participation costs money—the more people, the more the direct costs. Still, materials need to be diverted from the municipal solid waste stream to avoid other potential direct and indirect costs, such as pollution.

Creative Collection Opportunities

In an effort to increase program participation and waste diversion, the industry has implemented some innovative approaches to stretch valuable resources and maximize available opportunities for local communities. These solutions break down many barriers to participation discussed in the previous section and often lead to stronger, more sustainable HHW programs.

Multi-Jurisdictional Programs

Local governments are getting creative by joining forces to pool resources, such as funding and staff time and talent. For example, three San Francisco Bay area water pollution control agencies—Bay Area Pollution Prevention Group, Bay Area Storm Water Management Agencies Association, and Bay Area Dischargers Association—have joined together to raise public awareness of how wastewater and storm water pollution occur and what can be done to prevent it. One quantifiable success from the effort is a ban on copper sulfate, once used to kill the roots of trees and plants that commonly penetrate household pipes and drains. The ban was the result of a public education campaign on the negative effects the copper was having on the Bay ecosystem. As a result of that campaign there has been a measurable reduction of copper in the San Francisco Bay area.[6]

The result of interagency cooperation is a more powerful, single message with consistent branding for environmentally responsible behavior. Consider an educational campaign that promotes the use of the local HHW collection program. The interest to the wastewater treatment agency is keeping pharmaceuticals and other hazardous materials that cannot be rendered harmless in treatment, from going down the toilets and drains. The storm water agency uses the campaign to help prevent motor oil and other wastes from entering storm water drains and contaminating marine or fresh water sources. The pollution prevention agency promotes the use of less toxic alternatives. Finally, the solid waste agency works to protect groundwater from contamination and preserve precious limited landfill space by diverting HHW from landfill disposal. The multi-agency message becomes more powerful, serving as an impetus for enhanced public education for behavioral change.

The HHW industry is also experiencing some consolidation in the form of regionalization of local HHW programs. There are many examples of joint power authorities, regional solid waste associations, and other cooperatives that join cities, counties and states. Such regional programs can support one or more large permanent HHW collection facilities, whereas the individual cities might only be able to host one day of collection per year. "In Kansas, Pottawatomie, Riley, Marshall, and Morris counties decided to work together to collect HHW under the umbrella of the Big Lakes Regional Council. Governed by a board made up of three elected officials from each participating county, the Regional Council assesses fees on participating counties and is eligible for grants. The organization determined that it would be less expensive, through economies of scale, to perform the HHW tasks as a single entity."[7]

Purchasing Cooperatives

Government procurement often requires a formal bid process in order for agencies to secure a contract for HHW management or related services. The task can be daunting for many agencies. Purchasing cooperatives are designed to reduce the procurement burden while at the same time ensure competitive market rates and service flexibility for their members. Regional cooperatives allow only neighboring counties, cities, towns, or villages to assume the specific pricing, terms, and conditions of a contract. Statewide co-ops allow any jurisdiction within the state to assume the contract specifications. Moreover, a number of state co-ops open their contracts to other states. The process of assuming pricing, terms, and conditions of another agency's contract is often referred to as "piggybacking." Piggybacking requires a written letter of agreement between the participating public agencies and the service provider. The states of Washington, Oregon, and Tennessee are a few of the states that offer contract piggybacking for HHW services.

In addition to reducing the procurement burden, purchasing cooperatives also help smaller agencies manage their liability. The purchasing cooperative often has additional legal and risk management resources available for drafting and reviewing the procurement documents, insurance requirements, and contract language. The co-ops often assist with regulatory reporting and data analysis for trend monitoring.

Targeted Waste Streams

Small collection events targeting a single type of waste such as pharmaceuticals, or a general class of material such as universal waste, may be an effective means of increasing public awareness on a certain disposal issue. However, pound for pound and dollar for dollar, it often results in a poor return on investment. The San Francisco Bay Area's Safe Medicine Disposal Days underscores this point. In May 2006, the Bay Area Pollution Prevention Group (BAPPG) held a series of 39 collection events for residential pharmaceutical waste. Approximately 1,500 residents (0.02% of the population) from a service area of 7,000,000 residents participated. The program collected 3,634 pounds of pharmaceutical waste. While this diversion of waste is of course beneficial, the BAPPG states in its post-event report, "This is an inefficient way to have residents properly dispose of meds: San Francisco's total cost (advertising and staff time): $87,000—$175 per person served—$450 per pound disposed."[8] Compare that cost with a recent survey of twenty-five HHW programs across the state. The median costs of the programs surveyed was $0.67 per pound and $55 per participant.[9]

On a more positive note, the BAPPG also found that the media's attention helped build the case supporting wastewater agencies that are trying to develop a long-term solution for a potential problem in the future. Since the 2006 pilot program, many local agencies have gone on to develop pharmaceutical collection programs within their communities.

Collect It Curbside

Convenience is a key factor in increasing HHW program participation. The recent availability of curbside service for used motor oil and oil filters in some areas has had a dramatic effect on reducing the occurrence of improper disposal of these items. These curbside programs often require special containers for the materials and pick-ups are often in conjunction with the regular trash or recycling curbside service. In addition, communities may offer curbside collection of universal waste items (such as batteries and fluorescent lights) and consumer electronic waste. All of these HHW items are low-hazard posing minimal risk in curbside collection. The benefit of curbside collection is twofold. It offers increased convenience for residents and it reduces the volume of HHW to be managed through temporary collection events or permanent collection centers.

Multiple Program Components

The early HHW programs were inadequate in meeting the needs of some population segments. For disabled, homebound, and elderly residents, loading HHW into a vehicle and transporting it to a collection is not an option. For residents physically able to participate in a collection event, scheduling conflicts for the year's one-day event can prevent participation. One way to address these obstacles is the implementation of multiple program components.

The permanent collection facility infrastructure is improving as more and more communities replace temporary collection events with year-round permanent collection centers. There are some communities, especially in rural areas, where a permanent facility is not feasible due to limitations such as funding and convenient access to the population. Regional programs that service both rural and urban areas have found it beneficial to maintain mobile collection events in addition to the permanent facility. Adding a door-to-door collection component addresses the needs of the disabled, homebound, and elderly, and increases the convenience factor for over-scheduled households who find it difficult to make time for an HHW drop-off. In a 2005 survey of twenty-five HHW programs across the U.S., twenty programs (80% of respondents) had implemented some combination of permanent collection centers, mobile events, and door-to-door collection.[10]

Adding multiple collection program components can become expensive. The HHW Program Manager must understand the demographics of the service area to determine the most effective use of resources and the best mix of services to offer. Participant co-pay is one way to help offset the higher cost of door-to-door collection; it is assessed on individual program usage.

Location, Location, Location

The number one rule in many industries is to consider "location, location, location." In service areas with high rates of self-haul for municipal solid waste or recyclables, placing an HHW collection center within the boundaries of, or next to, a solid waste transfer station or recycling center makes sense. Simplifying drop-off procedures will increase participation rates. If it is not feasible to place a full-scale HHW collection center at these locations, adding limited HHW service can provide some benefit. For example, a self-serve oil and oil filter drop-off or a designated area for universal wastes may be added to existing recycling centers or transfer stations with special permitting.

Multi-Site Collection Events

In a large geographic service area, communities should consider hosting multiple collection events throughout the region and on the same day. Multiple location collections increase the convenience for residents by reducing travel distance to a collection site. It also enables maximization of advertising dollars. For example, an agency would only incur costs for design and placement of one advertisement that could be placed in multiple media across the region, also providing consistency in message and branding. The County of Fresno, California, has long held single-day collections in multiple cities on the same day. The main collection site services the Fresno/Clovis metropolitan area. Additional sites rotate throughout the east and west sections of the county. These collection events are held once in the spring and once in the fall. This program is available to a service population of more than 800,000 residents across 6,000 square miles.

Mail-Back Programs

Certain HHW items may be disposed through mail-back programs. A mail-back program provides the agency or the resident with a disposal container and a postage-paid shipping container. The HHW is placed in the container according to the specific shipping instructions and mailed to a final disposal facility. Mail-back programs are currently available for syringe needles ("sharps"), rechargeable batteries, cellular phones, ink cartridges, toner, mercury-containing thermostats, and some electronic waste. For some waste streams such as sharps, mail-back programs can be more expensive on a per-pound basis than the traditional collection methods of disposal at an HHW facility or medical facility. However, programs such as the collection of rechargeable batteries and cellular phones by the Rechargeable Battery Recycling Corporation (RBRC), are free to the consumer. Due to the rising concerns of pharmaceutical waste polluting our waterways through septic system disposal, some agencies are pursuing mail-back programs for used pharmaceuticals.

Product Exchange Programs

Product exchange programs are used to encourage residents to bring in a specific hazardous product in exchange for a less hazardous alternative at no cost. The concept of "free" exchange is an attractant that increases participation.

Exchange programs are common in the U.S. for mercury-containing thermometers, for example. Residents bring in their mercury thermometers and receive non-mercury replacements at no cost to them. Often, these exchanges are funded by state environmental departments or through state or federal grants. Other materials that are suitable for exchanging include:

- Single use batteries for rechargeables;
- Used motor oil for a reusable drain pan or funnel; and
- Old propane tanks (pre-1998) for OPD-equipped tanks.*

Private Industry and Community Partnerships

Whether their interest is community goodwill or the result of a Supplemental Environmental Project (SEP) to reduce enforcement penalties, private sector companies have a vested interest in providing HHW services for their communities. The public-private partnership is a win-win situation: the community receives a valuable service and the private industry partner benefits from:

- Increased foot traffic (especially important to retailers);
- Increased community awareness; and
- Improved community relations.

Full Funding

Private industry can assist communities with funding. Full funding of a one-day collection event is the most advantageous to the local community. This includes event advertising and outreach, and waste collection, transportation, and disposal. The private industry partner may be able to leverage its existing hazardous waste disposal agreements or utilize its in-house capabilities for many aspects of a collection event. Often, the collection event will be held in conjunction with a community celebration such as an Earth Day event or anniversary of incorporation of the city or town.

Partial Funding

The private industry partner may choose to make a flat monetary contribution to the local agency to assist with the financial obligations of a collection event. It is best to approach the potential partner with a total cost estimate for the event. Financial assistance can be provided as a partial payment of the total event cost, a flat contribution per event participant, a flat dollar amount, or payment for specific services such as disposal. Reaching an understanding between partners in advance of the collection event is important in event planning. It will affect many decisions such as the level of advertising and considerations that may affect the amount of waste accepted from each participant and the types of items to be collected at the event.

---

*On April 1, 2002, a National Fire Protection Association (NFPA) safety code went into effect that prohibits the refilling of propane tanks that are not equipped with overfill protection devices (OPD). It is estimated that over 40 million propane tanks without OPDs are currently in circulation.[11] Many of these tanks, when deemed acceptable material, are brought to HHW programs for proper disposal.

In-Kind Services

In-kind services such as graphic design and printing for outreach material, volunteer staffing for traffic control, participant greeting, educational material dissemination, and selected waste handling activities (assuming that personnel are properly trained) such as unloading participant vehicles and bulking of paint or motor oil can have a significant impact on reducing overall event costs. If volunteer staffing is used, it is essential that the stakeholders closely coordinate pre-event planning. If using an HHW contractor, the Site Supervisor should meet with the private industry partner during pre-event planning to discuss the level of volunteer involvement, the abilities and experience of volunteers, and the specific roles and expectations of volunteers.

The private partner may also offer to provide in-kind donations such as waste containers, event supplies, equipment, or meals for the staff on collection day(s). The following list includes common equipment, supplies, and materials utilized for HHW collection activities.

1. Waste Packaging
        Banding materials
        Cubic yard boxes, lids and liners
        DOT-approved drums (all sizes)
        Drum crayons
        Drum liners
        Duct tape
        Overpack drum (85 gallon)
        Paint bulking equipment (Optional)
        Pallets
        Polyethylene bags
        Shrink wrap
        Ultrasorb
        Vermiculite
2. Hazard Class Identification
        Chor D Tect Kit
        Coliwasa tube
        Disposable containers
        Field Unknown ID Kit
        Geiger Counter
        Glassware, pipettes, test tubes
        Oxidizer test paper
        Peroxide test paper
        pH test paper
        Propane with torch tip
        Sample jars
        Sharps containers
3. Spill Control and Emergency Response
        Absorbent pigs, socks, and pads
        Bloodborne pathogen kits

Cellular phone
Emergency air horn
Emergency eyewash
Emergency shower
Fire extinguisher
Industrial first-aid kits
Mercury spill kit
Neutralization solutions
Shovels, brooms, dustpans

4. Personal Protective Equipment and Safety
Chemical-resistant gloves (nitrile and butyl)
Disposable face shields
Dust/mist masks
Face shield replacements
Plastic apron
Poly-coated Tyvek suits
Rain suits
Respirator cartridges and wipes
Respirators (full-face and half-face)
Safety glasses and wrap-around goggles
Steel toe boots with metatarsal guards
Sunscreen
Traffic vests
Tyvek disposable coveralls
Windsocks
Work gloves (cotton)

5. Paperwork
Bills of lading
CESQG & SQG's forms (optional)
DOT-approved drum labels
Drum inventory sheets
Hazardous waste manifests
Hazardous waste markings
Hazardous waste placards
Land disposal restriction forms
Participant survey forms (optional)

6. Miscellaneous Equipment and Administrative Supplies
Assorted hand tools
Barricade tape, cones, and flags
Canopy for hot zone and break areas
Chemical resistant carts
Copier and copier supplies
Drum dolly and grabber
Equipment van
Extension cords
Fax

Forklift (optional)
Name badges
Office supplies
Paint can openers
Pallet jack
Phone
Portable restroom facilities
Potable water
Spray adhesive
Spray paint
Tables (6–8 foot) and chairs
Tables for waste sorting
Tractor/Trailer
Traffic barricades, delineators, cones
Trash cans
7. Reference Library
40 CFR
49 CFR
Chemical Dictionary
Local/State Regulatory Guide
US DOT Emergency Response Guide

Event Location

A temporary HHW collection event requires space. Parking lots are ideal locations for single-day collection events. Allowing a collection event to be held in the business' parking lot is a valuable contribution that requires minimal resources from the partner. Ideally, the event is held on a day that will not interfere with routine business operations. If the event occurs during regular business hours, special accommodations can be made for the employees to utilize the collection event before or after it is open to the general public. For example, if the collection event were to be open to the public from 8:00 am to 1:00 pm, the partner's employees could utilize the event from 7:00 – 8:00 am or 2:00 – 3:00 pm. This system reduces the amount of time employees have to wait to dispose of their HHW.

Extended Producer Responsibility and Take-Back Programs

As the number of consumer products meeting the definition of household hazardous waste increases, local government is becoming more burdened with the cost of proper HHW disposal. Sights are set on extended producer responsibility and this growing product stewardship movement. According to the Product Stewardship Institute, product stewardship is "a principle that directs all participants involved in the life cycle of a product to take shared responsibility for the impacts to human health and the natural environment that result from the production, use, and end-of-life management of the product."[12]

Product stewardship programs are rising across the United States. The California Take-It-Back Partnership is "a collaboration of state government, city and county government, businesses, non-profit agencies and non-governmental organizations to provide free, local and convenient ways for California residents to recycle everyday household wastes such as batteries, fluorescent lamps and electronic devices that can no longer be disposed of in the trash."[13] The Take It Back Network[14] (available in certain communities in the state of Washington) is a partnership among government agencies, retailers, repair shops, charitable organizations, and recyclers that provides consumers with options for recycling certain wastes—and their hazardous components—in a safe and cost effective manner. Currently, the Take It Back Network accepts electronic products and fluorescent light bulbs. The U.S. EPA's Plug-In To eCycling is "a voluntary partnership between EPA and consumer electronics manufacturers and retailers to offer consumers more opportunities to donate or recycle – to "eCycle" – their used electronics."[15]

Creative Management Options

Reaching a larger portion of the population is half the battle. It is also important to focus efforts on sustainable waste management methods. Creative approaches to reducing the cost of waste management without compromising the waste management hierarchy include consolidation of waste, material exchange programs, product reuse, on-site management, recycling of non-waste materials, and revenue generating programs.

Maximum Consolidation

Consolidation of waste results in a significant cost savings. Consolidation is achieved through the packaging method and the selected shipping container. All HHW must be packaged according to Department of Transportation (DOT) regulations and specific requirements of the primary receiving facility.

Reducing the number of shipping classes reduces the total number of containers shipped and allows for use of larger containers. For example, liquid and solid acids can be packaged together into a fifty-five gallon drum as opposed to shipping one twenty gallon container of corrosive liquid and one twenty gallon container of corrosive solid.

A well-designed permanent collection facility includes adequate storage capacity. Storing containers until they are full (up to the permissible 90 days) reduces disposal costs, especially when transportation and disposal rates are based on the number of containers shipped. Adequate storage capacity also accommodates large shipping containers such as fifty-five gallon drums, cubic yard boxes, totes, pallets, and roll-offs. HHW should only be shipped in containers smaller than a 55-gallon drum when the receiving facility requires it or to ensure regulatory compliance.

Federal regulations allow for the co-mingling of HHW and CESQG wastes. It is the responsibility of the HHW Program Manager to determine if this practice is allowed under state and local regulations. This method of consolidation also ensures maximum efficiency in transportation and disposal. In addition, this practice simplifies manifesting, packaging, and labeling of waste, as well as reducing the number of containers shipped and thus the total overall operating costs.

Bulking of HHW is another consolidation packing method; many of the HHW streams are suitable for bulking. Bulking of waste may be done manually or with the use of mechanical crushing units that are currently available for paint cans, aerosol cans, oil filters, and fluorescent light tubes. However, the bulking of certain materials such as flammable liquids, pesticides, and corrosive liquids is more dangerous than bulking the lower hazard materials such as antifreeze, motor oil, and latex paint. It is the responsibility of the HHW Program Manager to ensure that all employees involved in the bulking process have adequate training and certification and are equipped with the appropriate level of personal protective equipment. In addition, certain engineering controls may be required regarding ventilation, fire suppression, and electrical systems. The primary benefit of bulking is disposal cost savings. Bulking reduces the number of drums generated that results in lower transportation and disposal costs. On average, approximately one fifty-five gallon drum of bulked paint will be generated from two cubic yard boxes of loose packed paint. This reduction can result in thousands of dollars in savings for a large HHW program. Savings in disposal must be weighed against the capital expenditure and increased labor to conduct the bulking activity.

A central processing facility (CPF) allows further waste consolidation for those HHW programs that involve multiple collection sites or combine temporary collection events with permanent facility collections. In this system, waste is collected at satellite facilities or temporary collection events and transported directly to the program's central processing facility. The CPF receives the HHW and consolidates the waste into larger containers or bulks the material. This approach has been very successful for the County of San Bernardino, California. San Bernardino is the largest county in the 48 contiguous states.[16] It operates 15 permanent collection facilities throughout the county. The HHW is transported from the individual satellite sites to the County's CPF where it is further consolidated. The HHW is then transported from the CPF to the disposal facility by a licensed contractor.

Material Reuse Programs

In the waste management hierarchy, reduction is most preferred. One way to reduce the amount of household hazardous waste is by determining that an item is not yet waste, but rather a usable material. This is accomplished through Material Reuse Programs (MRPs) also known as Stop and Shops or Stop and Swap. MRPs are common components of HHW programs across the country. The purpose of the MRP is to divert incoming products from the waste stream that meet certain specifications, instead offering these to the public at no charge. The benefits are numerous. There are no handling or disposal costs associated with the items distributed through the MRP so that total disposal cost for the program is reduced. The MRP attracts residents to the HHW program.

In an MRP, there are risk management issues to consider. Any person accepting material from the MRP should sign a liability waiver. The liability waiver is written to protect the agency that sponsors the MRP. Certain precautions should be taken to ensure that participants intend to use the product(s) according to its original purpose or design. An agency may consider implementing certain volume restrictions on items that could be used for unlawful or illicit purposes such as creating graffiti, huffing, or cooking methamphetamines.

Product Reuse

The second priority of the waste management hierarchy is reuse. Reuse is available for many HHW streams including consumer electronic waste and latex paint. Some electronic waste management companies will refurbish computer equipment for distribution or sale. When selecting an electronic collection service provider, it is important to understand how the material is processed, how the material is managed if it cannot be refurbished, and who the end users and downstream markets will be. Latex paint from HHW programs is often reused for local graffiti abatement programs. Preparing latex for graffiti abatement requires minimal processing. The paint is sorted by color, usually into three categories: white, light colors, and dark colors. Some screening or filtering is required to remove any heels, chunks, or foreign objects. The paint is then stirred and poured into five gallon buckets for distribution.

On-Site Management

Certain HHW streams may be managed right at the permanent collection center depending on the capabilities of the facility as well as state and local regulations. On-site management is often done for latex paint. Some programs solidify latex paint and send it to the local municipal solid waste landfill. Others may process the paint for use in graffiti abatement.

Lewis County in Washington operates the Haz-o-Hut at the Solid Waste Central Transfer Station in Centralia, Washington. This unique program processes barbeque propane tanks on site. Any propane remaining in the tanks is evacuated and used to fuel the program's forklift. The brass valves are removed and recycled. The empty tanks are also recycled as scrap metal.

Non-Waste Item Recycling

Along with the household hazardous waste, other non-waste items associated with the collection activities are suitable for recycling. A significant amount of HHW arrives in cardboard boxes and paper grocery bags. These items are easily segregated and recycled. A significant portion of "trash" generated from HHW collection activities is a result of the bulking of paint, motor oil, and antifreeze. It may require a little research but often, the empty bottles and cans can be recycled.

Revenue Generating Waste

A few waste streams can actually generate revenue for an HHW programs. Payments are dependent upon a number of complex factors including current market conditions for the commodity and regulatory requirements. Revenue generating waste streams include motor oil, electronic waste, freon, and automotive batteries. In addition, programs such as Portland, Oregon, operate a latex paint recycling program that generates revenue from the sale of its recycled latex paint product.

About the Author

Sue Bruning is the Director of Product Line Management, Household Hazardous Waste Services for Clean Harbors Environmental Services. Clean Harbors is North America's leading provider of environmental and hazardous waste management services.

Notes

1. U.S. Environmental Protection Agency, "Household Hazardous Waste Facts and Figures," http://www.epa.gov/msw/hhw.htm#Figures (17 Jan. 2007)

2. U.S. Environmental Protection Agency, "EPA Announces an Estimated One Million Pounds of Household Hazardous Waste Collected," 31 Oct 2005, http://yosemite.epa.gov/opa/admpress.nsf/d9bf8d9315e942578525701c005e573c/38e67e7742b06f83852570ab0058a66c!OpenDocument (17 Jan. 2007)

3. U.S. Environmental Protection Agency, "Household Hazardous Waste Management: A Manual for One-Day Community Collection Programs," US EPA Document # EPA530-R-92-026. August 1993, http://www.epa.gov/epaoswer/non-hw/househld/hhw/Sec05.pdf (17 Jan. 2007)

4. Cascadia Consulting Group, "Comparison of Household Hazardous Waste Programs," Fall 2005.

5. Edmonds, Bruce J., and Chace Anderson. "HHW Programs: From One-Day Events to Integrated Strategies," Elements 2008, *MSW Management* vol. 17, no. 3, p 44–54.

6. U.S. Water News Online, "Bay Area Agencies Sponsor Stormwater and Wastewater Pollution Prevention Campaign" March 1997, http://www.uswaternews.com/archives/arcquality/7bayare3.html *(15 June 2007)*

7. Edmonds, Bruce J., and Chace Anderson. "HHW Programs: From One-Day Events to Integrated Strategies," Elements 2008, *MSW Management* vol. 17, no. 3, p 44–54.

8. Bay Area Pollution Prevention Group, "Report on the San Francisco Bay Area's Safe Medicine Disposal Days," August 2006, http://www.baywise.info (27 March 2007)

9. Cascadia Consulting Group, "Comparison of Household Hazardous Waste Programs," Fall 2005.

10. Cascadia Consulting Group, "Comparison of Household Hazardous Waste Programs," Fall 2005.

11. http://www.mcmua.com/HazardousWaste/FAQ_Propane.htm (27 March 2007)

12. http://www.productstewardship.us/displaycommon.cfm?an=1&subarticlenbr=55 (15 June 2007)

13. CA Take it Back: http://www.dtsc.ca.gov/TIB/index.cfm (27 March 2007)

14. Take It Back Network (PNW): http://www.takeitbacknetwork.org (27 March 2007)

15. Plug Into E-Cycling: http://www.epa.gov/epaoswer/osw/conserve/plugin/index.htm (27 March 2007)

16. http://www.sbcounty.gov/da/welcome.asp (15 June 2007)

CHAPTER 6

Community-Based Social Marketing and Behavior Change

P. Wesley Schultz*

Jennifer J. Tabanico

In recent years, many public and private organizations have implemented programs and outreach campaigns designed to promote environmentally responsible behaviors. These programs have addressed a range of behaviors including recycling, energy conservation, household hazardous waste disposal, litter reduction, green buying, utilization of public transportation, and ride sharing, to name a few. These programs are typically created to address an identified problem or meet an adopted policy or mandate. Yet, without exception, the success of these programs hinges on community participation. That is, success requires behavior change on the part of residents. Too often, at some point in the program (or sometimes from the outset), participation wanes.

In an effort to bolster the program and motivate behavior on the part of residents, program managers take action in two primary ways: (1) change the program, or (2) market the existing program with the hope of increasing participation. Most programs begin with the latter (usually because it is cheaper). They develop a series of messages—either in-house or with the help of an ad agency—intended to "raise awareness" and "educate" the community about the program and the problem it addresses. These approaches tend to be primarily information based, with the goal of "getting the message out." Such messages are not unique to HHW programs. Indeed, corporate, government, and non-governmental entities worldwide spend billions of dollars developing media campaigns in an attempt to increase knowledge or raise awareness about engaging in a particular behavior. The assumption is that if people are educated about a particular behavior (such as the location of a community HHW collection center), or if they knew about the magnitude of the problem (*e.g.*, pollution from improper disposal), they would act. We assume that "if people only knew, they would surely do the right thing." Unfortunately, behavioral science suggests that this assumption is flawed. Although information-based campaigns can positively increase awareness and

*Address inquiries to Wesley Schultz, Department of Psychology, California State University, San Marcos, CA, 92096. wschultz@csusm.edu.

attitudes about a specific behavior or problem, they are largely ineffective at creating lasting changes in behavior.[1] While our focus in this chapter is on environmental behaviors,
the ineffectiveness of information-based messages at changing behavior has repeatedly
emerged from a variety of applied research domains.[2]

Despite the research showing the ineffectiveness of these traditional information-
based approaches, they continue to be widely implemented. Fortunately, there are more
effective alternatives. For more than 100 years, psychological research has uncovered
a range of basic principles about motivation and behavior, and from this research have
emerged several techniques that can be easily implemented. While these techniques have
been widely known in the academic literature for many years, researchers and policymakers in applied fields have only recently begun to incorporate them into their programs
targeting behavior change.

The strength of using social psychological principles of behavior change is that they
take into account both personal and situational variables. Decades of research in social psychology have provided an arsenal of tools for changing behavior, and a number of useful
theoretical models.[3] In the current chapter, we present Community-Based Social Marketing as a broad approach that can be used to promote behavior change across a variety of
settings. After introducing the basic framework, we illustrate with three program examples
targeting the proper disposal of used motor oil. Finally, we discuss several important considerations for practitioners interested in following this approach.

Overview of Community-Based Social Marketing

Community-Based Social Marketing stands in stark contrast to the traditional information-
intensive approach still so widely utilized by applied organizations. CBSM is unique in that
it packages basic principles of social psychology with applied research methods in a way
that provides a usable framework for practitioners working to promote behavior change.
While CBSM has been used primarily in the context of pro-environmental behavior, it is
easily applicable to a range of other behaviors. Community-Based Social Marketing uses
a four-step process to foster sustainable behavior change.[4] These four steps are: (1) identifying the barriers to a targeted behavior, (2) using behavior change tools to overcome the
barriers, (3) piloting the selected tools using empirical research methodology and a control
group, and (4) evaluating the project once it has been widely implemented. Below we
briefly elaborate on each step.

Step 1: Identifying Barriers

The CBSM approach recognizes that barriers to engaging in environmental behaviors vary
depending on the population, context, and behavior of interest, and that multiple barriers
can exist simultaneously for each behavior. These barriers can be either internal to the
individual (*i.e.,* motivation) or external to the individual (*i.e.,* structural elements of the
program). The first step in the CBSM approach is to identify the barriers for the target
behavior through reviews of existing literature, focus groups, and surveys.

The fundamental element of the barrier identification process is to focus on people who *don't* already engage in the target behavior. If the goal of the program is to collect waste pesticides at a HHW collection facility, it is important to identify the barriers perceived by people who *don't* already use the facility. Doing surveys or interviews with individuals at the facility will provide interesting data—but it is dangerous to assume that the findings will generalize to the broader population. Indeed, the fact that they showed up at the collection facility when others did not, makes them qualitatively different. Uncovering barriers is a hallmark feature of the CBSM approach, and an essential first step in creating an effective outreach campaign or improving an existing program. But it means going outside the office, beyond the individuals who are already utilizing the program, and getting information about the target audience—people who *don't* use the program.

Step 2: Tools of Behavior Change

The second step in the CBSM approach is to select a behavior change tool that addresses the identified barriers, and to use these tools to develop intervention and program materials that will overcome these barriers and change behavior. The first question that needs to be answered is whether the reasons for not participating in the program are internal or external to the individual. External barriers are aspects of the program itself that decrease the likelihood that an individual will participate. They are sometimes referred to as "structural barriers." For example, limited days and hours of operation, travel distance to an HHW collection, difficulty of the behavior, and inconsistent collection methods are structural elements of the program that may operate as barriers to participation. Internal barriers reside within the individual and include psychological variables like motivations, perceptions, beliefs, or attitudes. Examples of internal barriers include unfavorable attitudes toward the program, lack of knowledge about the program or how to use it, seeing the behavior as unimportant, or perceptions that few others use the program. The greatest strength of CBSM as an alternative to information campaigns is that it draws heavily on the social science research literature, particularly the social psychological literature, to identify tools for overcoming internal barriers. These tools may include providing normative information, using commitment and consistency, and using the norm of reciprocity. Later in this chapter we provide a more detailed summary of behavior change tools.

Steps 3 and 4: Piloting and Evaluating the Strategy

Once the behavior change program has been designed, the third step is to pilot the intervention strategy. Based on the CBSM approach, the program should be piloted with a small portion of the community using an intervention and a control group. If the pilot is not successful, the strategy should be refined and then piloted again. If the pilot is successful at changing behavior, the strategy can be implemented more broadly. Once the successfully piloted program is in place within the community, the fourth step of CBSM requires that the program be carefully evaluated by comparing baseline measures of behavior to behavior at several points following the intervention. Wherever possible, the large-scale evaluation should also include a control group.

Advantages of Community-Based Social Marketing

The CBSM approach is rapidly gaining acceptance in a variety of governmental and non-governmental organizations (see www.cbsm.com for hundreds of notable examples). The strengths of the CBSM approach are fourfold. First, the decisions made at each step of the program development process, from design to implementation, are based on empirical data. This is a substantial improvement over intuition or historical precedence, and it offers a solid foundation for developing an effective program. Second, the program is pilot tested on a small scale *before* large-scale implementation. This can be a cost-saving mechanism that allows the development team to try out different approaches until they are confident that their approach will work. The third strength of the CBSM approach is program evaluation. Ongoing evaluation ensures that at the conclusion of the program, there are data to substantiate the effectiveness (or lack thereof) of the program. These data can be invaluable in informing subsequent outreach campaigns, changing or proposing new local policies, or demonstrating compliance efforts with political mandates (*e.g.,* diversion rates).

The fourth strength of the CBSM approach is a focus on behavior. In recent years, many applied areas of research have focused more on *intention* or *attitude* as outcomes, rather than behavioral outcomes. In part, this shift was one of efficiency—studying behavior requires a time lag in measurement, whereas attitudes can be assessed as an immediate outcome. That is, behavior change typically occurs at a later time and in a different context from the intervention, adding an additional layer of difficulty to the evaluation process. Attitudes are an easy proxy. However, there is evidence that attitudes or intentions can change without a corresponding change in behavior, and it appears that attitudes are more malleable to outreach messages than is behavior. Note that this finding does not imply that changing attitudes will not lead to a change in behavior, only that the linkage is imperfect and inconsistent. In other words, behavior change resulting from an intervention can be mediated by changes in attitudes or intention, but focusing on these as the primary outcomes does not substitute for measurements of behavior.

Applications of Community-Based Social Marketing

The Community-Based Social Marketing approach has been successfully used to change a wide range of environmentally responsible behaviors including energy conservation, reduction of CO_2 emissions, water conservation, recycling, and use of public transportation.[5] CBSM methods have also been used to address activities contributing to poor air quality such as improper automobile maintenance and engine idling. One environmental issue that has gained considerable attention in recent years is the problem with greenhouse gas emissions (particularly CO_2). While a number of behaviors contribute to this problem, the CBSM approach involves targeting a specific behavior that can be changed at a community level. For example, the *Turn It Off* project used CBSM to encourage motorists to avoid idling their engines while waiting in their vehicles.[6] After identifying barriers and motivations related to the specific behavior, the researchers designed marketing materials utilizing psychological tools of behavior change to remove the perceived barriers. The materials consisted of various combinations of prompts, public commitments, and information about the benefits of turning off their motors. The frequency and duration of engine idling was measured at baseline, during the intervention, and at follow-up. Results showed that while informational signs alone were not effective, the combination of public commitment and signs reduced the frequency of idling by 32% and the duration of idling by 73%.[7]

In our own work, we successfully used the CBSM approach to increase proper tire maintenance among California motorists in an effort to reduce the number of waste tires generated.[8] By surveying a random sample of California motorists, our research team identified improper tire inflation as the primary behavior linked with increased tire wear (compared with alignment, balancing, rotation, or checking tread). Indeed, our survey showed that 59% of vehicles on the roadways in California had at least one tire that was over- or under-inflated by 5 PSI, and 64% of respondents reported not checking their tire pressure within the past month (the interval recommended by tire manufacturers). Based on the barrier survey findings, we then proceeded to develop, implement, and evaluate an intervention promoting proper tire inflation. The intervention had both a structural component (we provided motorists with a free tire pressure gauge) and a motivational one (*e.g.*, advertising the safety of properly inflated tires). In a pilot intervention conducted with local gas stations, we were able to produce a 46% increase in the number of motorists who reported checking their tire pressure in the past month, and a 17% decrease in the number of vehicles with one or more improperly inflated tire. In contrast to traditional marketing campaigns that were already in place (*e.g.*, local billboards and radio advertisements), the *community-based* approach ensured that the strategies were designed to target specific barriers and motivations as well as a specific behavior.

These examples illustrate the potential of the CBSM approach for promoting behavior change. In the next section, we focus on a specific behavior—used motor oil disposal—and describe three pilot interventions that were developed and tested in diverse regions of California.

The Problem of Waste Motor Oil

The 20th century saw a transformation of the American landscape, brought about by the automobile. Automobile manufacturing revolutionized economic and industrial practices; the availability of cars altered the lifestyles of working Americans; and consumption and pollution resulting from combustion engines directly affected every person in the country. In 2004, 92% of households in the United States had a vehicle available to them for regular use, and personal vehicles were used for over 97% of all trips of fewer than 300 miles. The U.S. Department of Transportation estimates that in 2004, there were 243 million cars on U.S. roadways, and the average household had nearly two vehicles. In 2001, Americans drove a total of 2,287,000,000,000 (trillion) miles, and the average motorist drove an estimated 16,000 miles per year.[9]

Because cars are primarily powered by combustion engines, lubrication of moving parts is essential. In order to promote engine longevity and performance, automobile manufacturers recommend changing a vehicle's motor oil at specified intervals, ranging from 3,000 to 15,000 miles. In practice, the average motorist changes his or her motor oil every 4,200 miles.[10] That's approximately four oil changes per vehicle, per year. The average oil change uses 1.25 gallons. This results in more than 1.1 billion gallons of motor oil sold each year. [11]

Used motor oil poses a number of threats to the environment. Used motor oil is insoluble and can contain heavy metals and toxic chemicals, which can directly harm living organisms.[12] In the environment, motor oil pools on the surface of ponds and lakes, blocking sunlight, impairing photosynthesis, and destroying natural habitats. Motor oil contaminates drinking water and can render fertile soil unusable for agriculture. Alarmingly, the U.S. Environmental Protection Agency estimates that 200 million gallons of used motor oil are improperly disposed by consumers each year.[13] It is the leading contaminant in the nation's waterways, and banned in landfills nationwide.[14]

California, like many states across the country, tracks the volume of motor oil sold and recovered. In 2005 (the most recent data available), 153.5 million gallons of lubricating oil were sold in the state. Of this, 91.3 million gallons were collected for recycling or disposal—a 59% capture rate. The remaining 41% of the oil sold was either stored, burned off, spilled, or improperly disposed.[15] While the federal government has not classified waste motor oil as hazardous, it is so classified in three states (California, Massachusetts, and Rhode Island), and nationwide it is handled like other household hazardous wastes (*e.g.,* pesticides, cleaners) at HHW collection sites. Used motor oil has many alternative uses and can easily be recycled. It can be re-refined into oil or other lubricants; it can be reprocessed into fuel oil or diesel oil; and it can be burned for industrial processes or heating. Collecting the oil requires a collection infrastructure, and more important, it requires behavior on the part of the motorists.

The majority of the used oil that is collected comes through automotive service stations or dealers. While a large majority of motorists utilize a professional mechanic or service shop for their cars' oil changes, a substantial percentage of motorists choose to change their own oil. Nationally, an estimated 40% of motorists are do-it-yourself (DIY) oil changers.[16] However, this figure varies dramatically by state, area, and demographics. In California, surveys suggest that 19% of the population change their own oil, and DIY oil changing is more common among men, older individuals, those with lower income, lower education, and more in rural settings.[17] Many states report an oil capture rate in excess of 95% for oil changed at service stations or by professionals. But the capture rate for DIY oil is substantially lower—generally only 30–40%.[18]

Nationally, there are a number of different collection systems for DIY oil. The most common is to integrate oil collection with stand-alone waste collection facilities. However, the low rate of participation for such stand-alone centers results in very little oil collected.[19] Some states have partnered with automotive retailers to provide a collection mechanism at the point of purchase. Other collection sites include mechanics and local shops, unstaffed storage facilities (particularly for rural areas), transfer stations, and curbside collection programs. To support these programs, many states have followed the Petroleum Institute's Model Bill that attaches a fee of 2–4 cents per quart of oil sold. The funds are used to support local programs, research, and marketing. Despite efforts to build an oil collection infrastructure, however, many programs have remarkably low rates of participation.

Once a used oil collection program is established, how do we motivate DIYers to participate? More specifically, how can we move beyond the informational brochure or billboard and utilize CBSM techniques to promote proper oil disposal among DIYers? In the following section, we summarize three strategies that were pilot tested in California.

For each program, we describe the CBSM process through the first three steps (identifying barriers, developing interventions, and pilot testing with a control group). Combined, the results suggest that DIYers can be motivated to participate in collection programs, and that CBSM provides a useful toolkit for practitioners working on these programs.

Curbing Improper Oil Disposal in Napa County

This first CBSM program example comes from a DIY program we designed and piloted in Napa County, California. Napa County is a small rural county north of the San Francisco Bay Area. The county has a population of approximately 125,000, with most individuals clustered into four city areas. Census data show that the county is mostly white in racial background (80%), with a median household income of $52,000.[20] The oil collection program in Napa County includes 20 collection centers, as well as a curbside oil collection program offered to single family households in the four more densely populated areas.

The current project focused on the existing curbside collection program that served 5,400 single-family households (about 20% of the county's population). To utilize the curbside collection program, residents needed to call the hauler to join the program and receive a free oil-recycling container. The program also required that residents call to request a pickup, and then place the oil at the curb on collection day. Using the 19% DIY rate, we estimated that there were 1,026 potential users of the curbside program generating an estimated 8,593 gallons of oil each year. Yet, only 339 DIYers were enrolled in the program. Furthermore, in the year prior to our intervention, only 600 gallons of oil were collected through the curbside program.

After assembling the background data, we conducted a telephone survey with a small sample of Napa County residents to identify the barriers to oil recycling. Using a Random Digit Dialing technique, we contacted 509 residents in Napa County. Of these, 95 (19%) were do-it-yourself oil changers, and 56 were homeowners who lived in the regions served by the curbside collection program. The most frequently cited disposal method for used oil was a county-maintained HHW collection facility (45%), followed by a retail collection center (33%). Curbside collection was listed by 11% of respondents. The admitted improper disposal rate was 5%.[21]

Our survey identified two key motivational (internal) barriers to utilizing the curbside collection program. The first was a lack of knowledge. Only 45% of residents served by the curbside program knew about its existence, and of those who knew about the program, only 8% could describe the program in any detail. The respondents who knew about the program had favorable attitudes about curbside collection and believed that it was easy to use. The second uncovered barrier was a perception that most other residents did not use the program. That is, there was a social norm against utilizing the curbside collection program.

In an effort to increase utilization of the program, we created and distributed two motivational pieces about the program through postal mail. Note that there are a number of other avenues we could have pursued with our intervention, including a potential structural intervention to make collection easier (*e.g.,* remove the need to call and request a pickup). Based on the available data and the feedback from the hauler regarding costs associated with a structural change, we opted to focus on the motivational side of the equation.

Additionally, we chose to use direct mail as our message medium. Alternatively, we could have developed point-of-purchase pieces, or inserts in the waste management or utility bill. Both of these would have provided viable channels for distributing our message since they would reach the full audience (including residents who do not already use or know about the program). However, point-of-purchase or billing inserts were a bit too broad, and potentially could have reached many residents who were not served by the collection program. Conversely, distributing flyers at a community HHW event, or at the county collection centers, would have been unlikely to reach our target audience—those who were not already engaging in the desired behavior. Direct mail provided us with an affordable, broad-based distribution channel for reaching all households in our target area.

The first direct-mail piece was a trifold, color brochure with information about the program and testimonials from local residents about the ease and benefits of using the curbside program (along with pictures and quotes from local residents). The brochure was randomly included with either a mail-in response card or telephone number for residents to join the program. By using a call-in number versus a mail-in response card, we intended to evaluate the possible external barrier of making a phone call to join the program. A second direct-mail piece was sent a week following the first, and reinforced the basic normative message.[22] Importantly, the marketing materials were designed specifically to target the identified barriers (lack of knowledge, low social norm) and were embedded within the target community (e.g., testimonials from local residents, local contact information). It also highlighted a specific target behavior—join the program.

The brochures were distributed using a delayed treatment control group. That is, two of the four populated areas received the mailing first, and then three months later the remaining two areas received the mailing. This allowed for a comparison of the response to the brochure against an untreated control condition. We want to underscore the importance of using a control group to evaluate the impact of outreach materials. Had we distributed the marketing materials to all four communities simultaneously, we would not be able to rule out other variables as the primary cause of behavior change. While our delayed treatment methodology lacks random assignment to condition (the fundamental element of an experiment), it provides an excellent method for ruling out variables such as season or timing as causal factors. The primary outcome measures were the number of responses to join the program, and the amount of oil collected in the months following the mailing.

Results of the pilot program were encouraging. In the first treatment condition (phone-in to sign up), there was a 22% increase in the size of the program; in the second treatment condition (mail-in sign up) there was a 45% increase in the size of the program. During the same period, the two control communities showed no change in the size of the program. When the intervention was distributed four months later to the delayed treatment communities, we again saw a corresponding increase in the size of the program (see Figure 1). Additional data ware obtained showing the number of oil pickups each month. During the two months following the intervention, there was a 248% increase in the amount of oil collected through the curbside program. The control condition showed no change during this period. Interestingly, longer-term, follow-up data one year later showed a return to baseline levels in the amount of oil collected. While the size of the program was still substantially larger than it was initially, the volume of oil collected had returned to baseline levels. This final point suggests the need for ongoing intervention materials, or a more permanent change to the structure of the program.

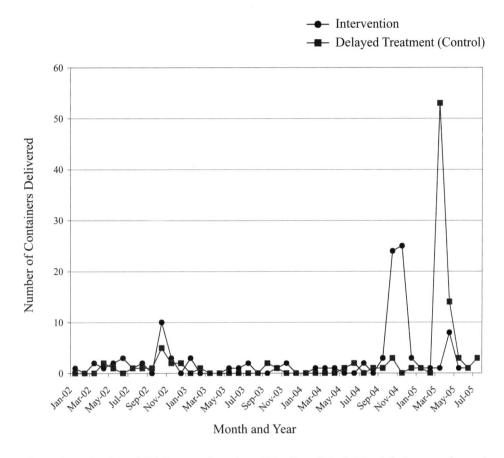

Figure 6.1. Number of Oil Storage Containers Distributed Each Month in Intervention and Control Communities in Napa County.

An Oily Situation in Los Angeles

Our second CBSM example takes place in Los Angeles, California. Los Angeles is a large and ethnically diverse region, with a population of approximately 10 million. Demographics show that 74% of residents are white, 10% black, 13% Asian, and 47% are of Hispanic or Latino origin (regardless of race). Using statewide averages, we estimated that there were 1.9 million do-it-yourself oil changers in LA County, generating nearly 10 million gallons of waste motor oil per year. The used oil recycling program in Los Angeles consists of over 600 certified oil collection centers and weekly special collection events. These certified collection centers will only accept used oil if it is stored in a proper container.

Through a series of focus groups, county officials had identified lack of a proper storage container as an important barrier to proper disposal. Because of the existing data, we did not conduct any additional barrier surveys and we proceeded to develop a structural intervention focused on distributing proper containers to DIYers in LA County. To test the efficacy of this approach, we partnered with local retail sites to distribute free, 15-quart oil containers to customers who purchased DIY supplies. The containers were distributed to customers as an incentive to return to the respective site and recycle their used oil. In addition to the container distribution, our research team created and pilot tested an alternative motivational message to accompany the container. The final message—"take the last step"—was affixed to half of the free oil containers. The sticker was in both English and Spanish ("Tome el último paso"). The other half of the containers was affixed with the standard state-sponsored sticker, containing the 1-800-CLEANUP phone number for the nearest collection center.

To evaluate the impact of the free motor oil containers, we identified eight matched pairs of Kragen Auto Parts stores throughout the county (16 stores total). The stores were matched based on the volume of oil collected, the primary language of the customers, and the growth in oil volume over the past four years. One member of each matched pair was randomly selected to receive the intervention, and the other served as a control. Four of the intervention stores received the free container with the standard sticker, and four received the free containers with the "Last Step" sticker.

In all, we distributed approximately 3,000 free oil storage containers. Containers were distributed during the first quarter of 2004 and the impact was tracked in the quarterly volume of oil collected at each store for a year following the intervention. Results showed that the "Take the Last Step" sticker produced the largest increase in the amount of oil recycled during the intervention. The average "Last Step" store collected 1,624 gallons of oil (SD = 513), compared to their matched control stores of 1,331 (SD = 382). This corresponds to a 22% increase in the amount of oil collected. The standard sticker (*Mean* = 1,009) also produced an increase in the amount of oil recycled, compared to the matched controls (*Mean* = 955), but the increase of 6% was not statistically significant.

The oil collection data were also analyzed by comparing changes to historical trends. In the four years preceding our CBSM intervention, there had been a slow but steady quarterly increase in the volume of oil collected through the certified centers (*Beta* = .89; *slope* = 33). For the four stores that received the standard sticker, the observed value did not deviate from the 95% confidence interval around the score predicted by the prior four years. That is, the amount of oil collected was not more than would have been predicted given the historical trend. But for the stores that received the "Last Step" message, the observed value (M = 1,624) was significantly larger than the 95% confidence interval around the predicted value of 1,296. That is, it was substantially larger than what would have been expected from the existing trend. Taken together, the results show that the free oil container combined with an added motivational element ("Take the Last Step") produced a substantial increase in the amount of oil collected.

The Slippery Slopes of Rural Madera County

Our third CBSM pilot took place in Madera County, California. According to the U.S. Census, Madera has a population of 142,788. The population is mostly white (89%), and nearly half of the population is of Hispanic or Latino origin (48%). [23] The county is rural, with a Census estimate of 57 persons per square mile. For comparison, California state has

217 persons per square mile; Los Angeles County has 2,344 per square mile; Napa County has 165 per square mile.

Used oil recycling in Madera County is managed through eight certified collection centers and sporadic special oil collection events. Based on population and statewide DIY rates, we estimated that 264,681 gallons of oil were generated by DIYers each year. But in the year prior to our intervention, only 38,596 gallons were collected through the eight certified centers (~15%).

Prior to the initiation of our CBSM pilot, Madera County had done little outreach to the DIY community, and there were no existing data from which to identify the barriers. As a starting point for our project, we conducted random digit dialing interviews with a sample of 502 Madera County residents. Of these, 125 were DIYers, resulting in a 25% county-wide DIY rate. As is typical for DIY surveys, the overwhelming majority of respondents were male (88%). Other demographics were comparable with county census figures, including ethnicity, income, age, and homeownership. The most common method reported for disposing of used motor oil was a retail collection site (49%), followed by a non-retail collection site (19%). The rate of admitted improper disposal was 10%.

The survey uncovered two clear barriers to proper disposal in Madera County. The first was inconvenience, including limited hours of operation, too few collection centers, and distance to the collection center. The second identified barrier was lack of motivation. While respondents had a favorable attitude toward oil recycling, they perceived it to be relatively difficult, and future intentions to use a collection center were generally low. Based on these findings, we developed a two-pronged intervention approach. The first was a structural intervention, designed to increase the number of collection facilities across the county. In particular, our aim was to recruit new retail collection centers in the rural areas of the county (at the time of our work, all eight collection facilities were in the more densely populated areas). The second prong of our intervention was to increase motivation on the part of DIYers by invoking a commitment to utilize the center.

Our first intervention—to increase the network of certified collection centers in the county—failed. At the start of the project, there were eight certified centers, located primarily in the more heavily populated areas of the county. By using GIS mapping software, we identified populations that were underserved by the existing network and we targeted retail outlets in those locations. Then, by canvassing the targeted communities, we identified 46 potential new collection centers. With the assistance of county staff, we contacted each site and offered to complete all paperwork required to become a certified collection center, and to pay all costs associated with their collection center status (including purchasing and installing storage tanks, hauling, and advertising). Of these 46 identified stores, 12 were willing to meet with our team and receive more information about the certification process. Unfortunately, following the initial meeting, none of the stores opted to proceed with certification. The reasons listed by each were classified into five categories:

- Liability issues surrounding spillage or leaking tanks
- Not enough room for the storage tank
- People leaving oil outside the store during non-business hours
  (so-called orphan oil)
- The financial costs of maintaining the program—staff costs for paperwork
- Too much unwanted contact with the government

These findings might be useful for future efforts to expand certified oil collection centers in rural areas. While recruitment efforts in rural areas might ultimately prove successful, we believe that other collection alternatives should be considered.

Our second intervention aimed to increase utilization of the existing collection centers. Based on prior research showing the potential for personal commitments to alter behavior, DIYers were approached at the point-of-purchase and asked to make a pledge to recycle their used oil and filters.[24] The pledge was verbal, and was reinforced with a sticker that read: "No matter what I drive, I pledge to recycle my used oil and filters." The person signed the pledge, and we affixed the pledge sticker to a funnel that we gave to them as a reminder of their stated commitment. The approach was developed to be simple so that it could be easily adopted more widely across the county.

To test the efficacy of the pledge intervention, we pilot tested it with a sample of 94 customers from Napa Auto Parts as they exited the store. Customers were randomly assigned to one of three experimental conditions: (a) information about where to recycle used oil, (b) information plus a free funnel with a standard recycling sticker (with the 1-800-CLEANUP phone number), or (c) information plus the funnel with the personal pledge sticker affixed. They were then asked a series of questions about their past behavior and future intentions to take their oil to the collection center. Participants were contacted again four weeks following the intervention and asked a series of questions about their recent behavior.

Results from the initial survey revealed a high rate of improper disposal. Nearly 20% of DIYers admitted to improper disposal over the past year, and only 53% reported using a collection center. When asked if, "the next time I change the oil on my car, I will recycle my used oil and filter" (with responses from 1 = strongly disagree to 5 = strongly agree), we found marginal differences across the three conditions. As expected, the information-only condition had the lowest intention, followed by the funnel-only condition. The commitment intervention showed the highest score. Of the 94 initial participants, 42 responded to our one-month follow-up. When asked about the "last time you changed the oil in your car," more participants in the commitment (37%) and funnel-only condition (40%) reported taking it to a collection center than did participants in the information-only condition (22%). In addition, more participants in the control condition reported improper disposal (6%), compared with participants in the commitment (0%) and funnel-only conditions (0%). The remaining oil was reported as "stored."

Practical Considerations

From the description and examples above, it is evident that Community-Based Social Marketing offers a promising alternative to traditional information-based outreach campaigns. But when faced with developing and implementing a CBSM campaign, the practitioner will quickly be faced with a number of important decisions. In the following section, we offer some clarification and practical considerations.

1. Be Specific

Social marketing campaigns are almost always linked with a problem. For example, too many toxics in the waste stream; bacteria from pet excrement in local waterways; fertilizer run-off; illegal dumping of waste tires; high carbon emissions from motorists; and so on. The campaign is clearly intended to change behavior, but which behavior? First, it is essential to choose a behavior that is linked with the desired outcome. For example, if our goal is to decrease residential energy consumption, asking residents to "turn out the lights" when they leave a room is unlikely to move us toward our goal. Light bulb use is simply not a large enough percentage of residential energy consumption. We would be better off focusing on a larger one-time behavior such as turning down the temperature on the water heater, or adding extra attic insulation (but not both in the same message).

In addition to choosing a behavior that is associated with the desired outcome, it is essential to focus on a single specific behavior. Oftentimes, agencies use a marketing campaign as an opportunity to plug several different (hopefully related) programs and behaviors. For example, "keep your tires properly maintained and combine errands into one trip," "shift into clean: recycle oil and repair leaks," or "put waste in its place: dispose of used batteries and electronic waste." While such confounded messages are seemingly efficient by stretching advertising dollars to cover multiple programs, they are much less likely to change behavior than a more focused message.

Broad messages intended to spur residents to conserve energy are also unlikely to be effective (*e.g.,* "flex your power"). Focusing on a single behavior is essential for creating an effective behavior change campaign. Telling local residents to "put waste in its place," "help keep our waters clean," or "conserve energy at home" are too vague, and do not give a specific action. What *exactly* do you want people to do? Be as specific as possible—what, where, when? For example, "Take your used motor oil to Kragen Auto Parts on Saturday to be recycled." Similarly, in our work we have found that focusing on what to do tends to be more effective than focusing on what *not* to do. First, telling people what not to do violates the specificity principle described in the preceding paragraph. It fails to give them a specific concrete action to perform. Second, telling people what not to do actually primes the behavior. That is, it gets people thinking about the undesirable behavior. Psychological research on priming has shown that the mere mention of a behavior or topic can increase the frequency of associated actions.[25]

2. Defining a Barrier

Simply stated, a barrier is anything that decreases the likelihood that an individual will engage in the desired behavior. As we discussed earlier in the chapter, barriers can be internal or external to the individual. Effective social marketing interventions target a specific barrier, and sometimes both an internal and an external barrier simultaneously. That is, the intervention involves a change to the program (structural) combined with an educational outreach piece (motivation). The LA intervention described earlier provides a good example of this two-pronged approach. The free oil containers were a structural intervention and the "last step" message was motivational.

3. Identifying Barriers

Identifying barriers to the target behavior is a hallmark of the CBSM approach. Begin by reviewing existing data. Most programs regularly collect information about the number of participants, types of materials, feedback from residents, and so forth. Sometimes there is already sufficient data on hand to identify the key barriers. But it is important to move beyond the office and program staff and even the HHW collection participants. That is, the data used to identify the barriers must come from members of the target audience. And in this regard, not all data are equally useful.

There are some types of data that should *not* be used in determining the barriers to a target behavior. These include: calls to a "hotline" or 1-800-telephone number, the number of hits or comments submitted through a program website, conversations with participants at a collection event or other program-sponsored activity, and feedback from program staff about the problems with the program. While these sources of data can provide a starting point, they cannot be taken as representative of the target population. They are samples of convenience—people who are fundamentally different from your target population of non-participants. And remember that the goal of the program is to reach people who *don't* already do the behavior. Identifying the barriers for these people often requires a survey.

4. Barrier Surveys

Surveys provide an excellent method for obtaining information about the target population, including people who do not currently utilize the program. Surveys can be conducted by postal mail, telephone, or in person. For a variety of reasons, we recommend against the use of email or Internet as a survey mode.[26] The goal of the survey is to solicit data from a broad and representative sample of the target population. They can be conducted by staff within the organization or contracted to a research firm or local university.

The three most prominent methods used to collect survey data are postal mail, telephone, and in-person interviews. Each of these methods can provide high-quality data, and determining which to use should be based on the topic, target population, and budget.

Mail surveys

This medium provides a cost-effective way to reach a large population. In our work, costs run about $10 per complete, so obtaining a sample of 1,000 would cost about $10,000. Response rates vary considerably, but using the Tailored Design Method, we have consistently obtained response rates in excess of 50%.[27] The biggest limitation with a mail survey is that the final sample size cannot be guaranteed. Indeed, your organization might spend $10,000 and get only fifty returned surveys. Another limitation is language. If the target population is ethnically diverse, with a large percentage speaking a language other than English, they will not be able to respond to the survey. Sending the questionnaire in two languages is a cumbersome but viable method (we routinely send English and Spanish to selected areas, based on Census block group data), but more than two languages is problematic.

Telephone surveys

Telephone surveys provide an efficient mode through which to reach a large audience. Using a Random Digit Dialing method it is possible to reach a diverse sample of residents, and having a multi-lingual survey team can allow responses from a range of groups with limited English proficiency or literacy. With telephone surveys, it is easy to set a target sample size (*e.g.,* 1000) and to continue making calls until the sample is reached. Given these advantages, telephone surveys have been the method of choice for professional survey teams for the past 30 years. Although changing technologies (*e.g.,* cell phones, internet, answering machines, "do not call" lists) have introduced some problems, telephone surveys continue to be widely used. In our experience, costs run between $30 and $40 per complete.[28]

In-person interviews

While telephone and mail surveys are useful for reaching a broad audience, in-person interviews provide an excellent mode for obtaining in-depth data or reaching a narrowly defined population. One form of in-person interview—the intercept survey—is particularly useful in CBSM work. Intercept surveys are conducted out in the community (*e.g.,* at a retail location). In our work, we have used intercept surveys to reach do-it-yourself (DIY) oil changers by surveying customers at auto parts stores. Intercept surveys are more expensive than the other modes discussed above, with costs ranging from $50 or more per complete.

Web-based survey

As mentioned earlier, we are not advocates of web-based surveys for obtaining representative samples. However, many professional survey organizations have moved to web-based data collection. These organizations often maintain a large panel of ready survey-takers, and they sample from their panel for various surveys. While the costs for such surveys are generally low ($5–$10 per complete), their representativeness is highly suspect. In addition, although segmentation is generally possible (*e.g.,* surveying only DIYers, or homeowners), it is usually not possible to get residents in a specific city or region.

In addition to mode of data collection, there are several other important considerations in conducting the barrier survey. First is sample size. Most professional survey firms (*e.g.,* Gallup, CNN) aim for a sample size of 1,000. This number provides a high level of confidence in estimating characteristics of the population ($\pm 3\%$)—for example, the percentage of DIYers in the state. A sample size of 1,000 also affords a reasonable number of splits—that is, segmenting of the population. But the number 1,000 is not sacrosanct. Indeed, if the survey is intended to find female, Latina, DIYers, completing 1,000 random surveys with the general population would not be enough. But for most purposes, we find that a smaller sample size is sufficient. In most cases we are interested in finding the reasons that people give for not engaging in the target behavior, and their perceptions and knowledge about the program. In cases like this, where our interests are in descriptive and correlational results, a random sample of 100 is sufficient.[29]

In addition to the survey mode and sampling method, question wording and survey structure are fundamental to a good barrier survey. There are many good sources for instruction on writing survey items.[30] Our advice is to keep it simple. Clearly worded questions that directly measure the variables of interest are best. Keep the survey short (no longer than 10 minutes to complete), and write the questions so that they are understandable at a fifth grade comprehension level. Include both open-ended and closed-ended response formats. Open-ended items allow respondents to answer in their own words—for example, "Would you please describe the single most important reason why you do not recycle your used motor oil?" In contrast, closed-ended items provide for quantitative responses. For example, "Using a scale from 0 (not at all) to 10 (definitely), how much is *not knowing where to take it* a barrier that prevents you from taking your used motor oil to a collection center?"

A final point about barrier surveys pertains to interpretation. Survey data are based exclusively on self-report, and are thereby subject to the many limitations inherent in these types of responses. Indeed, psychological research is clear in showing a variety of insidious errors that undermine the accuracy of an individual's explanations for his/her behavior.[31] Thus, asking people why they do (or do not) engage in a specific behavior can lead to erroneous targets of intervention. For example, in a 2002 survey of California residents, we asked respondents to rate a series of reasons for conserving energy in their homes.[32] Not surprisingly, the highest rated "reason for conserving energy" was environmental protection, followed by benefits to society, saving money, and lastly, because other people are doing it. Yet, when we conducted a field experiment to test motivational messages targeting each of these "reasons," only the message "other people are doing it" was actually motivational. The lesson: people are generally bad judges of what motivates them to engage in a behavior.[33]

One solution, which we have adopted in our work, is to look beyond the simple percentages and descriptive statistics (*i.e.,* means, frequencies, standard deviation). Correlations can be particularly useful in this regard, and can help to identify variables that are related to the target behavior. Correlations provide information about the strength and direction of the relationship between two variables. The direction of these relationships can be either positive or negative. Positive correlations exist when high scores on one variable are associated with high scores on another variable (*i.e.,* increases in knowledge about the location of an HHW facility are associated with increases in reported use of the facility). Negative correlations exist when high scores on one variable are associated with *low* scores on a second variable. For example, when high ratings of perceived barriers are associated with low ratings of self-reported behavior. In our work, we have often looked at correlations between self-reported perceptions of barriers and self-reported behavior. Barriers that correlate strongly (and negatively) with the behavior are those that are excellent targets for intervention (regardless of the mean scores or percentages). One word of caution when making these interpretations is to remember that correlations do not indicate causation. For example, a positive correlation between knowledge and behavior only indicates that these variables are related, and we cannot assume that increased knowledge will *cause* an increase in the desired behavior.

Tools of Behavior Change

Throughout this chapter, we have maintained that psychological research offers a wealth of principles and techniques that can be used to motivate behavior change. While a thorough review of these techniques is beyond the scope of this chapter, we highlight seven principles in the space below.[34]

Reciprocity

One of the most fundamental human social tendencies is the obligation to repay what another person provides for us. Social scientists have found this rule to exist across cultures, and it appears that reciprocity is an adaptive mechanism that allows cultures and societies to function. This norm of reciprocity is extremely powerful, and applies even when the favor is not invited. Reciprocating reduces the uncomfortable feeling of indebtedness, and often the person will agree to a larger request as repayment for a small favor. In social marketing, reciprocity is most often invoked with give-aways or incentives (*e.g.,* free compact fluorescent light bulb, free oil container, inserting a $1 bill with a mail survey).

Commitment and Consistency

Individuals have a basic desire to remain consistent in their thoughts and actions. To maintain consistency, we will often change our beliefs or attitudes to match our behaviors. Similarly, we will alter subsequent behaviors to be consistent with our earlier actions. This principle can be invoked by obtaining an initial commitment (either verbal or written) to engage in the target behavior. It can also be invoked by asking residents to take a small first step (put a small sticker in their window) and then follow with a larger request. Similarly, stickers or other media that commit the person to a course of action (*e.g.,* "I recycle") can be effective motivational elements.

Liking

People are much more likely to comply with a request from someone they know or like. Some of the factors that contribute to our liking for another person include similarity, praise or compliments, familiarity, or physical appearance. Requests to participate in a program are much more effective when they come from a familiar or liked source (*e.g.,* a friend, a neighbor, even a clerk at a neighborhood store).

Authority

Messages that come from an expert or perceived authority on a topic can be particularly influential. Status as an authority can come from titles, appearances, or affiliations. This principle is invoked when an organization uses a famous or credible spokesperson (*e.g.,* a NASCAR driver promoting proper oil disposal, or the actor Tim Allen promoting proper disposal of tools and batteries).

Social Proof

Humans are social animals, and as a result we use the behavior of others as a guide for our own actions. Seeing other people doing something (such as utilizing a program), or even just having the perception that other people are doing it, legitimizes the behavior and increases its frequency. Similarly, deviating from a norm can prompt feelings of pressure to conform. This principle can be invoked through advertising (*e.g.,* testimonials from local residents who use the program) or by making a behavior public (*e.g.,* visible curbside recycling bins).

Scarcity

One of the basic tenets of economics is that limited supply and high demand lead to increased value. That is, as the availability of an item decreases and the demand increases, our desire to obtain the item increases. In advertising and marketing, this is often invoked through "limited time," "while supplies last" events, or promotions given away to the first few customers.

Norm of Responsibility

A final principle that can lead to persuasion is the norm of responsibility. In general, we feel obligated to help those who are in need, especially individuals who cannot help themselves (like children or the elderly). As such, when a niece or nephew calls and asks if we would be willing to listen to their new sales pitch (and give them tips to improve), we are likely to agree (and in the end, purchase the product that they are pitching). This approach is often used by environmental programs that market their products through schoolchildren. Class sessions on recycling, litter, or household hazardous waste can include elements advocating the desired behavior that are taken home by children and given to parents.

Each of the seven principles just described can be easily incorporated into a social marketing campaign. As we have stated throughout this chapter, we recommend maintaining a specific focus and using just one principle at a time.

Identifying the Target Audience

One mistake that is often made in outreach campaigns is a tendency to focus on people who already engage in the target behavior. That is, finding individuals who already participate in the program and asking these people the reasons for their actions. Using these motivations as targets for interventions is based on faulty logic and can lead to ineffective campaigns and programs. Given that the target population generally consists of individuals who do not engage in the desired behavior, it is best to identify the behavioral barriers for them. Indeed, these barriers might be quite different from those identified in a broader sample or in a sample of people who already perform the behavior. We strongly advocate for the use of representative samples or targeted samples of nonperformers. Unfortunately, this point is often omitted in the barrier phase of CBSM work.[35]

A Personal Touch

Research in psychology, communication, and marketing has repeatedly shown that person-to-person communication can be considerably more influential than passive media messages.[36] Indeed, this is one of the distinguishing elements of the *community-based* approach to social marketing. Unlike traditional forms of marketing, *community-based* social marketing emphasizes personal contact, and tailoring the outreach materials to a specific community and target population. The more narrowly defined the community, the more precise and focused the outreach materials and campaign can be. But there is a tension between *reach* and *impact*. Reach refers to the number of people who receive the message. Personal communication tends to have a narrow reach—the outreach team can only talk with a limited number of people. Impact refers to the change in behavior produced by the outreach campaign. The ideal is to design a campaign with high reach *and* impact. Unfortunately, such campaigns are rare.

A conceptual drawing of the relationship of impact and reach is shown in Figure 2. As shown, personal contact increases the amount of behavior change that results from a persuasive message (*i.e.,* its impact). One-on-one personal contact generates the highest amount of behavior change, followed by group discussions, personalized feedback, indirect contact like direct mail, and finally mass media messages (radio, television, and billboard). In the HHW arena, one innovative approach that utilizes one-on-one contact with high reach involves partnering with local retailers. At the point of purchase, clerks or floor staff can educate customers about disposal of different products. For example: "That's a good product, but make sure that you don't throw it in the trash. Because of all the dangerous chemicals, you need to take it to the collection center at ____. Here's a map and collection hours. It's free to use the center." Or consider the sales associate at a local auto parts store who tells a customer buying motor oil, "Hey, make sure to bring your used oil back here to be recycled. I've got a free storage container, if you need one."

Here we have suggested that one-on-one personal communications tend to produce the largest changes in behavior, and we have provided a conceptual example of how this could be implemented in a retail establishment. It's important to note here that such an approach *can* be effective, provided the management and staff at the retail establishment agree to participate. This cooperation often turns out to be difficult to obtain, and floor staff tend to take liberties with the wording or protocol that can undermine its effectiveness. While we believe that retail partnerships can be an effective means for making one-on-one personal contact, such relationships need to be carefully cultivated, and it's important to tailor the messages to the clientele and business model of the establishment.

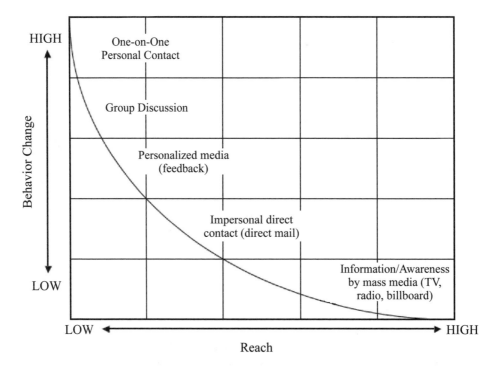

Figure 6.2. A Conceptual Drawing of the Inverse Relationship Between Reach and Impact.

One Size Fits All?

It is tempting to look for ideas in neighboring areas to find current "best practices" for program design and outreach. Indeed, using similar messaging or branding can help to reinforce the message, and using a consistent set of graphics, logos, or messaging across a county, region, or state can stretch advertising dollars and reduce the likelihood that messages will compete against each other. Despite the potential advantages, there are some pitfalls with this approach.

Recall that a distinguishing feature of Community-Based Social Marketing is its emphasis on local programs, local barriers, and context-specific interventions. If the "community" is too large, we lose the local context. But how large can we go? How do we define community? Is a community a neighborhood, census tract, city, county, state? And how many people comprise a community? While there is no clear answer to these questions, the critical element is similarity. That is, a "community" shares many important demographic characteristics, and (most important) they share a similar set of barriers to the target behavior. We recommend using data to drive intervention decisions. If a neighboring area has created an effective collection program, use data to determine its applicability to your area prior to implementing. Are the target populations similar in demographics? Who uses the program? What barriers does the new program address, and do these barriers exist in your community? Again, consistent with the theme of this chapter: use data to inform your program and outreach.

Conclusions

Every HHW program in the country relies on human behavior. In order to succeed, residents must use the collection system to dispose of their waste. Unfortunately, most programs, and subsequent outreach efforts to improve these programs, are based on faulty assumptions about human behavior. We often assume that lack of behavior results from lack of knowledge. We assume that "if people only knew about the program, surely they would use it." If this were true, then effective outreach materials would simply need to educate residents about the program. As a result, we have thousands of print, radio, and display advertisements nationwide that are intended to inform residents about the program or sometimes to "raise awareness" about the seriousness of the issue.

Unfortunately, the assumption that lack of action results from lack of knowledge often turns out to be false. While lack of knowledge can be a barrier to action, it is not sufficient by itself to motivate behavior. Because of this, many existing outreach efforts fail to motivate behavior change. Community-Based Social Marketing provides an alternative to information-based messages. The CBSM approach uses data from the target population to inform program and outreach material development. CBSM works by focusing on a specific behavior, surveying the target population to establish a base rate and barriers to the behavior, developing an intervention or making structural changes that directly address the barriers, and collecting data to evaluate the efforts to promote behavior change. The approach has been successfully used in many areas including HHW collection, and it offers a promising alternative for practitioners looking for an effective way to improve the success of their programs.

About the Authors

Jennifer Tabanico is a full-time researcher at California State University, San Marcos, where she currently oversees funded projects from the U.S. Department of Justice and the California Integrated Waste Management Board.

Wesley Schultz is Professor of Psychology at California State University, San Marcos. His research activities in recent years have focused on the social and behavioral dimensions of sustainability, and on utilizing psychological principles to develop more effective environmental programs.

Acknowledgments

The work summarized in this chapter was supported by a contract from the California Integrated Waste Management Board.

We want to acknowledge the important contributions to this project by Dana Stokes, contract manager with the CIWMB. Also our county collaborators, Amy Garden (Napa County), Melinda Barrett (Los Angeles County), and Jim Shields (Madera County). Our colleagues at the Social and Behavioral Research Institute, Allen Risley, Lori Large, and Chuck Flacks. Finally, the university students who helped with data collection, field intervention, and community outreach: Matt Dorlaque, Azar Khazian, and Leilani Lumaban.

Notes

1. P. Wesley Schultz, "Knowledge, Education, and Household Recycling: Examining the Knowledge-Deficit Model of Behavior Change," in *New Tools for Environmental Protection: Education, Information, and Voluntary Measures,* ed. Thomas Dietz and Paul C. Stern (Washington, DC: National Academy Press, 2002), 67–82.

2. Most notable among these research domains are health-related behaviors. See for example, Peter D. Jacobson, *et al., Combating Teen Smoking: Research and Policy Strategies* (Ann Arbor, Mich.: University of Michigan Press, 2001) on smoking prevention; Cassia Lewis, *et al.,* "Asthma Education Increases Knowledge of Rural Parents and Children with Asthma and Affects Parents' Reports of their Child's Asthma Symptoms," *Journal of Allergy and Clinical Immunology* 115, no. 2 (February 2005): 132, on asthma maintenance; Carlos D. Sanchez, *et al.,* "Diabetes-Related Knowledge, Atherosclerotic Risk Factor Control, and Outcomes in Acute Coronary Syndromes," *American Journal of Cardiology* 95, no. 11 (June 2005): 1290–94, on diabetes; Andrew Baum and & Lorenzo Cohen, "Successful Behavioral Interventions to Prevent Cancer: The Example of Skin Cancer," *Annual Review of Public Health* 19, no. 1 (1998): 319–33 on sun protection behaviors; Jeffrey D. Fisher and William A. Fisher, "Changing AIDS-Risk Behavior," *Psychological Bulletin* 111, no. 3 (May 1992): 455–74, on AIDS protective behavior; Matthew O. Howard *et al.,* "Substance Abuse," in *Handbook of Preventive Interventions for Adults,* ed. Catherine N. Dulmus and Lisa A. Rapp-Paglicci (Hoboken, N.J.: Wiley and Sons, 2005), 92–124, on substance use; and John S. Baer *et al.,* "An Experimental Test of Three Methods of Alcohol Risk Reduction with Young Adults," *Journal of Consulting and Clinical Psychology* 60, no. 6 (December 1992): 974–79, on binge drinking among college students.

3. See for example Albert Bandura, *Social Learning Theory* (Englewood Cliffs, N.J.: Prentice-Hall, 1977); Robert B. Cialdini, Raymond R. Reno, and Carl A. Kallgren, "A Focus Theory of Normative Conduct: Recycling the Concept of Norms to Reduce Littering in Public Places," *Journal of Personality and Social Psychology* 58, no. 6 (June 1990): 1015–26; and Leon Festinger, *A Theory of Cognitive Dissonance* (Stanford, Calif.: Stanford University Press, 1957).

4. Doug McKenzie-Mohr and William Smith, *Fostering Sustainable Behavior: An Introduction to Community-Based Social Marketing* (Gabriola Island, B.C.: New Society Publishers, 1999); Doug McKenzie-Mohr, "Promoting Sustainable Behavior: An Introduction to Community-Based Social Marketing," *Journal of Social Issues* 56, no. 3 (Fall 2000): 543–54; Doug McKenzie-Mohr, "The Next Revolution: Sustainability," in *Psychology of Sustainable Development*, ed. Peter Schmuck and P. Wesley Schultz (Boston: Kluwer, 2002), 19–36; see also Stuart Oskamp and P. Wesley Schultz, "Using Psychological Science to Achieve Ecological Sustainability," in *Applied Psychology: New Frontiers and Rewarding Careers*, ed. Stewart Donaldson, Dale Berger, and Kathy Pezdek (Mahwah, N.J.: Erlbaum, 2006), 81–106.

5. McKenzie-Mohr, "Promoting Sustainable Behavior," 543–54.

6. McKenzie-Mohr Associates and Lura Consulting, "Turn It Off: Reducing Vehicle Engine Idling," *Community Based Social Marketing,* 2001, www.cbsm.com/Reports/IdlingReport.pdf. (15 Jan. 2007).

7. McKenzie-Mohr, "Turn It Off."

8. P. Wesley Schultz, *Community-Based Social Marketing Pilot to Increase Proper Tire Maintenance* (Sacramento: California Integrated Waste Management Board, 2005).

9. Data compiled from Energy Information Administration, "Household Vehicles Energy Use: Latest Data and Trends," *U.S. Department of Energy*, 2005, http://www.eia.doe.gov/emeu/rtecs/nhts_survey/2001/tablefiles/0464(2005).pdf (20 Feb. 2007); U.S. Department of Transportation, "National Household Travel Survey 2001," *Bureau of Transportation Statistics*, 2003, http://www.bts.gov/publications/highlights_of_the_2001_national_household_travel_survey (20 Feb. 2007); and U.S.

Department of Transportation, "National Transportation Statistics 2006." *Bureau of Transportation Statistics*, 2006, http://www.bts.gov/publications/national_transportation_statistics (20 Feb. 2007).

10. California Integrated Waste Management Board, "Used Oil Source Reduction Study: Busting the 3,000 Mile Myth," Report produced under contract by the Social and Behavioral Research Institute, Sacramento, Calif., 2007.

11. American Petroleum Institute, "More on Recycling Motor Oil," 2006, http://www.api.org/ehs/performance/recycling/morerecycling.cfm (28 Feb. 2007).

12. U.S. Environmental Protection Agency, "Used Oil Management Program," 2007, http://www.epa.gov/epaoswer/hazwaste/usedoil (12 May 2007).

13. U.S. Environmental Protection Agency, "Municipal Solid Waste: Oil," 2003, http://www.epa.gov/msw/oil.htm (12 May 2007).

14. California Integrated Waste Management Board, *California's Used Oil Recycling Program* (Sacramento, Calif.: CIWMB Publication # 332-97-015, March 2002).

15. California Integrated Waste Management Board, "Used Oil Recycling Rate Annual Report: 2005," 2007, http://www.ciwmb.ca.gov/usedoil/rateinfo (12 May 2007).

16. North Carolina Department of Environment and Natural Resources, "Oil-Related: Used Oil Commodity Profile," 1998, http://www.p2pays.org/ref/02/0162212.pdf (28 Feb. 2007).

17. Rufus Browning, "To the Greatest Extent Possible: Do-It-Yourselfers and the Recovery of Used Oil and Filters," *California Integrated Waste Management Board* 2005, http://www.ciwmb.ca.gov/Publications/UsedOil/61105008.pdf (5 Mar. 2007); Rufus Browning and Holley Shafer, "DIYers and Used Oil Disposal," *California Integrated Waste Management Board* 2002, http://www.ciwmb.ca.gov/Publications/UsedOil/61101009.pdf (30 Mar. 2007); and California Integrated Waste Management Board, "Community Based Social Marketing Pilot To Increase Do-It-Yourself Oil Recycling Rates," *California Integrated Waste Management Board* 2006, http://www.ciwmb.ca.gov/Publications/default.asp?pubid=1168 (11 May 2007).

18. Rufus Browning, "DIYers – Who Are the Best Targets?" (presentation at the Used Oil and Household Hazardous Waste Conference, San Diego, Calif., April, 2005), www.ciwmb.ca.gov/hhw/events/AnnualConf/2005/April28/Session4/DIYers/DIYTarget.pdf (8 April 2007).

19. California Integrated Waste Management Board, *Household Universal Waste Generation in California* (Sacramento, Calif.: CWIMB Publication # 520-02-004, August 2002); U.S. Environmental Protection Agency, "Household Hazardous Waste," 2006, http://www.epa.gov/msw/hhw.htm (20 Mar. 2007).

20. United States Census Bureau, "State and County Quickfacts," *American Fact Finder* 2005, http://quickfacts.census.gov/qfd/states (10 Mar. 2006).

21. Estimating improper disposal rates is challenging since many respondents are reluctant to admit to the socially undesirable (and illegal, in some cases) behavior. The percentage reported in this paper is admitted improper disposal—that is, the percentage of respondents who reported throwing used oil in the trash, pouring it down a drain, pouring it on the ground, or an alternative use (*e.g.,* weed abatement, treating cow hooves, lubrication for sawing wood). A 2002 report by researchers at San Francisco State University found that 8% of a statewide sample admitted improper disposal; an additional 11% could not name a disposal facility or location (suspected improper disposers). Thus, the figure reported here probably underestimates (substantially) the improper disposal rate.

22. Details about these messages are available in the final technical report for this project. It is available on-line at: http://www.ciwmb.ca.gov/Publications/default.asp?pubid=1168.

23. United States Census Bureau, "State and County Quickfacts."

24. See, for example, Iser G. DeLeon and R. Wayne Fuqua, "The Effects of Public Commitment and Group Feedback on Curbside Recycling," *Environment and Behavior* 27, no. 2 (March 1995): 233–50; Michael S. Pallak and John J. Sullivan, "The Effect of Commitment, Threat, and Restoration of Freedom on Attitude Change and Action-Taking," *Personality and Social Psychology Bulletin* 5, no. 3 (July 1979): 307–10; and Glenn E. Shippee and W. Larry Gregory, "Public Commitment

and Energy Conservation," *American Journal of Community Psychology* 10, no. 1 (February 1982): 81–93.

25. See, for example, Henk Aarts and Ap Dijksterhuis, "The Silence of the Library: Environment, Situational Norm, and Social Behavior," *Journal of Personality and Social Psychology* 81, no. 1 (January 2003): 18–28; and also John A. Bargh and Tanya L. Chartrand, "The Unbearable Automaticity of Being," *American Psychologist* 54, no. 7 (July 1999): 462–79; and John A. Bargh *et al.,* "The Automated Will: Nonconscious Activation and Pursuit of Behavioral Goals," *Journal of Personality and Social Psychology* 81, no. 6 (December 2001): 1014–27.

26. While e-mail and Web surveys are tempting to use because of the low cost, they are unlikely to generate a representative sample. First, not every household has e-mail or Internet connectivity, so the sample is already biased against lower-income households. Second, response rates for Web surveys are notoriously low (in the 1% to 5%) range. While low response rates do not necessarily produce biased samples, there is reason to suspect that people who respond care more about the topic (and are more likely to already do the behavior) than non-responders. If problems of access and low response rate can be overcome, Internet and e-mail *might* provide a useable medium. But in our experience, these should be avoided.

27. Don A. Dillman, *Mail and Internet Surveys: The Tailored Design Method*, 2d ed. (New York: Wiley, 2002).

28. Of course, costs are affected by a number of factors, including length of the survey, required screening items (*e.g.,* limiting the survey to homeowners, or commuters), number of languages, and sample size.

29. Our sample size of 100 is based on a statistical power analysis of the correlation coefficient. A sample of 85 will provide sufficient statistical power to detect ($p < .05$) a medium effect ($r = .30$) with power of .80. Note also our emphasis here on *random sample*. Focusing on a smaller sample should allow the practitioner to dedicate more energy (and resources) on the method by which the sample is obtained. Every effort should be taken to obtain an unbiased, representative sample of the target population. For more on statistical power analysis see Jacob Cohen, *Statistical Power Analysis for the Behavioral Sciences*, 2d ed. (Hillsdale, N.J.: Erlbaum, 1988).

30. For more on writing survey items see Dillman, *Mail and Internet Surveys;* Arlene Fink, ed. *The Survey Kit*, 2d ed. (Thousand Oaks, Calif.: Sage, 2002); and Stuart Oskamp and P. Wesley Schultz, *Attitudes and Opinions*, 3d ed. (Mahwah, N.J.: Erlbaum, 2005).

31. See for example Robert B. Cialdini, "Basic Social Influence Is Underestimated," *Psychological Inquiry* 16, no. 4 (2005), 158–61; Thomas Gilovich, Dale Griffin, and Daniel Kahneman, eds., *Heuristics and Biases: The Psychology of Intuitive Judgment* (New York: Cambridge University Press, 2002); Amos Tversky and Daniel Kahneman, "Advances in Prospect Theory: Cumulative Representation of Uncertainty," in *Preference, Belief, and Similarity: Selected Writings by Amos Tversky*, ed. Eldar Shafir (Cambridge, Mass.: MIT Press, 2004), 673–702; and also Jacquie D. Vorauer and Dale T. Miller, "Failure to Recognize the Effect of Implicit Social Influence on the Presentation of Self," *Journal of Personality and Social Psychology* 73, no. 2 (August 1997): 281–95.

32. Jessica M. Nolan, "Home Energy Conservation as a Social Dilemma: Exploring the Role of Social Uncertainty" (Master's thesis, California State University San Marcos, 2004).

33. Cialdini, "Basic Social Influence Is Underestimated," 158–61; Richard E. Nisbett and Timothy D.Wilson, "Telling More Than We Can Know: Verbal Report on Mental Processes," *Psychological Review* 84, no. 3 (March 1977): 231–59.

34. Interested readers are directed to more complete treatments by Robert B. Cialdini, *Influence: Science and Practice*, 4th ed. (Boston: Allyn and Bacon, 2001); Robert Levine, *The Power of Persuasion: How We're Bought and Sold* (Hoboken, N.J.: Wiley, 2006); and McKenzie-Mohr and Smith, *Fostering Sustainable Behavior.*

35. Throughout this chapter, we have argued that practitioners should focus their efforts on identifying and targeting people who don't already utilize the program. However, these efforts should

not alienate the existing users, and changes should generally be made to complement the existing program.

36. See for example Paul R. Abramson, John H. Aldrich, and David W. Rohde, *Change and Continuity in the 2000 and 2002 Elections* (Washington D.C.: CQ Press, 2003); Samuel J. Eldersveld and Richard W. Dodge, "Personal Contact or Mail Propaganda? An Experiment in Voting and Attitude Change," in *Public Opinion and Propaganda,* ed. Daniel Katz, Dorwin Cartwright, Samuel J. Eldersveld, and Alfred McClung Lee (New York: Dryden Press, 1954); Daniel Katz and Paul F. Lazarsfeld, *Personal Influence: The Part Played by People in the Flow of Mass Communication* (Glencoe, Ill.: Free Press, 1955); and also Paul F. Lazarsfeld, Bernard Berelson, and Hazel Gaudet, *The People's Choice*, 2d ed. (New York: Columbia University Press, 1948).

CHAPTER 7

Product Stewardship: Shared Responsibility for Managing HHW

Scott Cassel

Ending the Industry Unfunded Mandate

Product stewardship is a movement that seeks to change the way products are designed and how waste is managed and financed. It is a paradigm shift and a massive reorganization of relationships among those who make, supply, sell, import, transport, use, and manage products. It is about the need for manufacturers, retailers, consumers, and others to step up to take greater responsibility for the products they make, sell, and buy. It is about a product's transition from glory to garbage. Product stewardship seeks to provide that product with a new beginning or a safe ending.

Manufacturers produce billions of products each year, many only slightly updating a similar version that was sold the year before. We crave new, advanced, exciting, different, and more powerful items that make our lives easier, more productive, or just plain fun.

Retailers connect product manufacturers and importers to product users. They have mastered the art of distribution, as have many manufacturers and businesses selling over the Internet. They can pour out requisite quantities of stuff to satiate the thirst of a massive metropolis or reach remote residents in the countryside. Unaware of product impacts, consumers buy and use up products that have become more and more complex. And when the party ends—when those ever-so-desirable products lose their luster—they are tossed into the garbage, the recycling bin, or down the drain. Local governments are left to ponder how to manage it. They pick up where a product's life ends.

As corporate America designs and sells the next cool thing to meet or create customer demand, local governments are figuring out how to deal with the things that came before and are now cast aside. They must determine how they are to be collected; where they should be stored and consolidated; whether they can be reduced, reused, or recycled; and how to pay for it all. The special term used by many local governments for this predicament is an "industry unfunded mandate." Just as local governments must be provided funding from their state if they are mandated to perform a public function, many local governments now demand new strategies and systems to fund the end-of-life management of used products. By providing these services, government has subsidized part of industry's cost of doing business, which is no different from materials supply, production, assembly, shipping, and marketing. If these end-of-life management costs were included in a company's business decision, some products might never have been designed.

Waste Management at the Local Level

The way that waste is managed has changed over time. Long ago, local officials labored to avoid disease by removing horse manure from streets and finding a place on the outskirts of town for other discarded wastes. When these piles became too great, local government was expected to better manage the problem. They constructed space for landfill disposal and later built incinerators. Over time, as our society began to understand that "waste" meant inefficiency and environmental impacts, these garbage mavens were asked to become experts on waste reduction, reuse, and recycling. With each change, our public works officials took on more responsibility. They were well situated to become the front lines of the product stewardship movement.

The turning point came as government officials began to understand that some of the products purchased by consumers contained the same hazardous materials as those found in the industrial facilities they permitted. Retailers made it easy for us to bring these hazardous products directly into our homes. While the public outcry for recycling bottles, cans, and paper could be satisfied by providing a bin to fill with scrap, the public demand to manage household hazardous waste (HHW) required more. Product toxicity was flourishing, and government lacked the funding or the systems to protect the public health.

Hazardous products "tipped" the solid waste management scale. They brought to light the impossible task of local government to serve as a backstop for whatever consumers disposed. Local officials were being counted on to properly manage all types of hazardous products that could pollute our air, water, or land, such as paint, motor oil, automobile batteries, and solvents. They needed to collect more and more products, which were being manufactured and consumed at a faster and faster pace. No longer was it acceptable to collect HHW from a small percentage of the population with a goal to do better. Local officials needed to increase HHW collections and find the money to support it. They could not rely on satisfying this need by increasing taxes or raising trash fees owing to citizen opposition to taxes and big government programs. They needed a paradigm shift in how waste was managed and financed, and they wanted to ensure a more sustainable future. They turned toward product stewardship.

What Is Product Stewardship?

Product stewardship is an approach in which manufacturers, importers, retailers, government officials, consumers, and others share responsibility for reducing negative impacts to human health and the natural environment that result from the production, use, and end-of-life management of a product. While each stakeholder has a unique role to play, those with the greatest ability to reduce a product's impact over its entire life cycle (*i.e.,* manufacturers and retailers) are viewed as having the greatest degree of responsibility. Only manufacturers have the knowledge about the hazardous materials contained in a product and have the power to reduce the hazard at its source.

Product stewardship systems seek to apportion responsibility for providing program information, logistics of end-of-life product management, and funding. These systems shift the cost of end-of-life management of products from the public sector to manufacturers (and in some cases, retailers) and by extension, to the consumer. By shifting costs, policymakers create the funding base needed to sustain end-of-life management programs that reduce public risk and create environmental benefits. In addition, shifting costs from the public to the private sector often creates efficiencies in operations that lower overall system costs.

Product stewardship can include actions taken by an individual manufacturer, importer, retailer, government agency, or any other actor in the product supply chain. It can include a manufacturer changing the design of a product so that it consumes less energy in its use; incorporates recycled content; uses less material or more recyclable material; or substitutes toxic materials with less-toxic or non-toxic materials. It can include a retailer taking back a product it sells at its store and paying for its recycling. Product stewardship could also include government passage of a law that requires manufacturers to eliminate the use of certain hazardous substances or to set up systems for collecting and recycling their equivalent share of the products they put on the market. Government could also develop an agency policy to procure products made with non-toxic ingredients. However, since the intent of product stewardship is to reduce lifecycle impacts, it has become associated with broad agreements that share management responsibility among a large group of actors connected by complex business relationships.

The concept of requiring manufacturers to take responsibility for the end-of-life management of their products was imported from overseas. In Europe and elsewhere, including Canada, the terms "producer responsibility" and "extended producer responsibility" (EPR) began to be used to extend the producer's[1] obligation for reducing environmental impacts beyond the traditional manufacturing facility boundary to encompass products when they reach the end of their useful life.

In Europe, EPR was designed to provide incentives to producers to improve the environmental performance of their products and to involve them in the collection and recycling of products at the end of their life. The original intent of EPR systems was to encourage design changes that make products less wasteful, less toxic, and more reusable and recyclable. In an idealized EPR system, the cost of managing a product at the end of its life is included in the product purchase price in a way that is invisible to the consumer, similar to the costs of production and marketing. However, many EPR systems today, particularly those in Canada, include end-of-life product management fees that are visible to consumers. In either case, it is expected that product users, rather than all taxpayers, will pay for the end-of-life management services.

The common denominator of true EPR systems is that they provide a financial incentive to manufacturers to design environmentally superior products by internalizing end-of-life product management costs into the purchase price of products. In addition, manufacturers play a significant role in end-of-life management of their products even while the responsibility is shared among key stakeholders. EPR in Europe often includes retailer take-back of end-of-life products and local government collection of end-of-life products from their citizens.

The term "product stewardship" was originally used by industry to describe the responsibility that companies assumed for managing facility operations—air and water emissions, waste management, worker safety, and other controls that, for the most part, take place within the confines of the manufacturing plant or on facility grounds. Product stewardship became the term of choice in the United States because it was simpler to understand and emphasized shared responsibility for reducing product impacts. Since "producer" was not in the term, it was also perceived as easier to engage industry in dialogue.

Product stewardship implies a broader set of systems in which the end-of-life management cost of a product is reflected in its purchase price, and is inclusive of the narrower EPR systems. Policymakers currently debate whether product stewardship systems that allow for visible fees can meet product stewardship goals even if the funds are managed by an industry-run stewardship organization. Some believe that visible fees collected by a government agency are only a funding mechanism and should not be called product stewardship because there is no industry involvement in establishing and managing the fees, and therefore little incentive to reduce costs. They also question whether citizens and politicians will accept a visible product fee that is often perceived as a tax, especially if such fees have been mismanaged by government in the past. Product stewardship expands beyond end-of-life product management to also include impacts across a product's entire lifecycle. For example, product stewardship can include efforts that seek to reduce impacts from mining bauxite for aluminum as a component of a beverage container recycling program.

Product stewardship and EPR can still mean different things to different people, and we are in the midst of rapid changes in understanding what these terms mean and how they can be implemented. It is very possible that definitions presented here will change or blur over time so that product stewardship and EPR mean virtually the same thing, or that EPR comes to be understood as the best example of a product stewardship approach. There are a myriad of EPR and product stewardship systems operating around the world, and each system must be evaluated on its own merits. What is most important is that we seek changes in underlying roles and responsibilities along the product supply chain so that we reach the goal of product sustainability.

One thing is certain—all product stewardship systems represent a paradigm shift in how consumer products are designed and managed at end-of-life, and that each system must be negotiated among a different set of stakeholders under a different set of conditions. Each new program builds on the experiences of those before it, and the results of these negotiations have become the new waste management systems of today.

Product Stewardship and Corporate Social Responsibility

Product stewardship is part of the wider corporate social responsibility (CSR) movement, that seeks to extend a company's responsibility beyond its statutory obligations. CSR emphasizes the interplay between economic, environmental, and social criteria (the "triple bottom line"),[2] and seeks corporate changes that align with sustainability principles. The movement attempts to set standards to which companies should adhere if they are to be considered good corporate citizens and then sets up a process for accountability. CSR efforts promote change through positive press, corporate competition, and shareholder resolutions. They can also include industry-driven efforts through the establishment of environmental management systems, sustainability reporting, goal-setting, and other self-accountability measures.

Product stewardship, on the other hand, more narrowly focuses on the products that are manufactured and sold by corporations in an industry sector, but then takes a broad life-cycle approach within that purview. While product stewardship addresses an entire industry sector (*i.e.,* consumer electronics, paint, thermostats, or carpet), CSR efforts are often company specific, and address a full range of company activities. Although the main focus of the product stewardship movement has been environmental, it has begun to incorporate broader societal impacts. For example, the export of scrap electronics to third world countries has heightened awareness of the significant environmental and worker health issues pertaining to metals extraction from scrap material using harmful recycling practices.[3] As more attention is paid to impacts related to production, end-of-life management, and other product lifecycle stages, product stewardship will likely expand in focus to cover additional social concerns.

Another difference between the two approaches is that product stewardship uses governmental regulatory power to leverage industry action. In product stewardship, while responsibility weighs heavily on manufacturers, government is still a key player involved in many aspects of program development, including planning, goal setting, oversight, monitoring progress, and enforcing laws that maintain a level playing field across an industry sector. CSR efforts are usually accomplished by industry with prodding from non-governmental organizations; government plays a more limited role. The lines cross between these two approaches to corporate change when companies, on their own, take significant steps to reduce emissions, change product design (*e.g.,* lightweight packaging), or meet voluntary standards in ways that address stewardship of the products they make or sell. The ultimate goal of both approaches is to change corporate culture so that environmental and social considerations are institutionalized and become as much a part of corporate decision making as profit-and-loss statements.

Goals of a Product Stewardship Approach

Product stewardship, in its broadest sense, seeks sustainable ways for products to be responsibly designed, manufactured, distributed, used, and managed after use to conserve resources and protect the environment and human health. In addition to this broad goal, product stewardship systems seek more specifically to accomplish the following: (1) internalize external costs into the product purchase price, (2) promote product design changes, (3) cover the costs of product collection, transportation, and end-of-life management, (4) diversify end-of-life management options, and (5) drive cost efficiencies in product end-of-life management.

Internalize Product Externalities

At its most basic level, product stewardship seeks to eliminate negative, external environmental and social costs imposed along the entire product lifecycle. These costs include, for example, mercury contamination of our nation's fish. The disposal of mercury-containing products, such as thermometers, thermostats, and fluorescent lamps is one of the sources of mercury released to our environment and contributes about one-third of mercury releases to air in the United States.[4] Mercury in many of our nation's waterways has resulted in the need to restrict the amount and types of fish we eat. External costs also include pharmaceutical wastes and pesticides that pollute waterways and are suspected of causing male fish to take on female characteristics including egg production. And they include the cost to manage biosolids contaminated by hazardous materials, run-off from mining operations, water pollution from improperly disposed used oil and paint, and car exhaust from the transport of HHW materials to collection sites.

Product stewardship systems seek to incorporate the real product lifecycle costs into the product purchase price, and thus prevent future environmental and social costs. The cost to avoid lifecycle impacts should be no different from the costs to manufacture, transport, or market that product. By including this cost in the purchase price, the product user pays the price rather than all taxpayers, many of whom do not use the product. Internalizing costs to protect against external product impacts will raise societal awareness and shared responsibility. We may, in fact, discover that it costs more to dispose of some products than companies are charging customers for the privilege of using them.

Product Design Changes

Many product stewardship systems seek to reduce future environmental impacts by removing hazardous materials from product design and making them easier to reuse, recycle, or dispose when the consumer no longer wants them. For example, by requiring a manufacturer to remove hazardous materials from batteries and to make them as clean as a piece of steel, the hazard from heavy metals is removed. This is the highest form of product stewardship. European Union discussions led to a law phasing out the use of specific hazardous materials in electronic products. This law, the Restriction on Hazardous Substances Directive (discussed later), demonstrated that companies could begin to move down the path of sustainability.[5]

Making manufacturers responsible for the end-of-life management of their products theoretically provides them with a direct financial incentive to design products that are environmentally superior in order to minimize future management costs for which they are now responsible. By requiring a manufacturer to collect unwanted televisions or computers, and paying for their reuse or recycling, manufacturers are more likely to design future product models to make the product more easily reusable or recyclable.

However, in Europe the next phase of the debate has started. Some argue that product design will only be achieved under an "individual responsibility" model[6] since environmentally innovative companies with the best product designs will benefit most through lowest end-of-life management costs. These advocates believe that "collective responsibility" provides no incentive to a company to improve environmental product performance since all companies pay the same per unit cost to manage end-of-life products regardless of how environmentally superior their product design may be (see discussion of individual versus collective systems).

Others believe that product design will best be influenced by bans on specific hazardous materials, mandates to use a minimum percent of recycled content, or procurement preferences for products meeting specified sustainability criteria. Studies to date have not conclusively shown the effect of product stewardship policies on product design improvements.[7] However, all agree that products need to be designed with fewer toxics and need to be more sustainable, and that this might take a combination of approaches to achieve. Some manufacturers have suggested that a reward for businesses that remove toxics and make cleaner products is to exempt them from collection responsibility.

One key to any sustainable waste management strategy is to minimize product toxicity so that scrap materials can more easily be turned into a raw material resource for the manufacture of new products. Products that are sustainably designed will retain all or most of their value at end-of-life. For example, current electronic waste has a greater concentration of metals than mined rocks. Mining scrap electronic materials from well-designed products is the future of sustainable waste management and needs to be built into the design of new products. The concept of using scrap materials to manufacture new products in a closed loop system is known as "cradle-to-cradle" product management.[8]

Cost Coverage

One of the key aspects of product sustainability is the need for a funding source to ensure that HHW is properly managed at end-of-life. Product stewardship systems therefore seek to cover the costs of collection, transportation, and end-of-life management of HHW products, most of which have a "negative value" where end-of-life management costs are greater than the value of the scrap material.

Currently, most programs that manage HHW are run by government and paid for through taxes, utility rates, or end-of-life fees. Product stewardship systems seek to shift the costs currently paid by all taxpayers through government-run programs onto product users, and to eliminate end-of-life recycling or disposal charges. If people are forced to pay to recycle a product, government officials find that they often will dump it illegally, bury it in their garbage, or store it.

End-of-life fees work for the small percentage of the population who understands the environmental ramifications of disposing of HHW, when other free options are available and the fee provides added convenience, or as a way to jumpstart a collection infrastructure. One goal of product stewardship programs, therefore, is to make the end-of-life program appear "free" for those whose behavior we seek to change, even though the full cost is embedded in the product price. While there are several ways in which end-of-life management costs are folded into the purchase price of a product, funding under a product stewardship system ultimately comes from the consumer, whether or not it is financed through producer responsibility or broader product stewardship systems.

As shown in Europe and Japan, when producers become financially liable for elements of managing products at the end-of-life, they ask for full control of the operation. In Europe, the compromise achieved is that each party finances those process steps under its control. For example, household collection is financed by municipalities; retailer collection is financed by retailers; and producers finance product design, recycling, and disposal.[9]

Diversify End-of-Life Management Options

Once manufacturers, importers, and retailers agree that they have a role to play in end-of-life product management, they often believe that existing government programs can successfully handle the increase in HHW products that would need to be collected to make an environmental difference. While most governments agree that their infrastructure (*i.e.,* collection facilities and associated management and operations staff) should be a key piece to a product stewardship solution, many cannot handle an increase in volume even if their costs were covered. Most facilities collect HHW from an estimated 5 to 10% of the population. While some permanent facilities may have planned to eventually collect 80 percent of all HHW products, many sites are wedged into existing solid waste transfer stations or landfills. These facilities do not have the space to handle significantly increased volumes of HHW and greater drop-off traffic.

Many product stewardship systems, therefore, provide "collection payment incentives" for all entities, public and private, that wish to collect target products. This mechanism creates an incentive for existing HHW sites and new market entrants to expand opportunities for citizens to drop off their HHW, thereby diversifying the HHW collection infrastructure. For example, in 2007 the California Integrated Waste Management Board paid 20 cents per pound for electronic equipment collected by registered collectors. These payments have resulted in an increase in the private collection infrastructure (at non-profits, retailers, and other non-municipal locations), reducing the traditional management burden on government. Other product stewardship systems mandate the retail collection of particular HHW items to achieve this same result. A diversified system is a healthy framework for sustainable management of HHW.

Cost Efficiencies

If you were seeking the most cost effective product stewardship approach, would you hire a government agency or a private company? While there are a surprising number of savvy government officials with entrepreneurial attitudes, many observers of product stewardship systems (from government and the private sector) agree that the private sector is best positioned to deliver the most cost-effective product stewardship programs. Hence, many product stewardship systems authorize or enable producers or other responsible entities to discharge their obligations directly and individually or collectively through a non-profit producer responsibility organization that manages stewardship responsibilities on behalf of member manufacturers and/or retailers.

Responsible companies, when acting on their own or through collectives that they influence, have strong incentive to minimize additional costs imposed on themselves or their customers for end-of-life management, and drive system efficiencies in ways that government-run programs are less capable of achieving. With government assigned to planning, goal setting, enforcement, and oversight, manufacturers are free to innovate in ways that the private sector does best—seeking lower costs and new methods to achieve the desired goals. However, as experienced in Europe, producer responsibility organizations that achieve market domination can also be run inefficiently once competition for efficient services is eliminated. European and Japanese programs have also shown that municipalities can play an important role by providing collection services of varying convenience to residents at the prices they are willing to pay. This dynamic adds another level of system efficiency.

Key Elements of a Product Stewardship System

Product stewardship and EPR systems have been implemented in a variety of ways around the world. However, several elements are central to all systems—product scope, performance goals, fair competition, individual and collective responsibility, and sustainable financing.

Addressing the Problem: Product Scope

The scope of the product stewardship system is an important first consideration, and one that should be commensurate with the problem. For example, U.S. electronics collection programs initially targeted the most toxic components of computers and televisions, namely cathode ray tubes—the heavy, leaded picture tubes in computer monitors and television sets that protect us from harmful radiation. Over time U.S. electronics laws began to include all computer and television components, including related equipment such as printers, scanners, keyboards, speakers, VCRs, and DVD players (collectively called "peripherals"). European laws, from the start, covered all electronic and electrical products with a plug and a cord, which also addressed other environmental impacts (*i.e.,* chlorofluorocarbons in air conditioners and refrigerators). To establish vibrant recycling industries, Europe, as well as Japan, increased the supply of scrap materials by including a wide scope of products in their product stewardship laws.

Although most electronic products do not contain obvious amounts of lead, many do contain other heavy metals (*i.e.,* cadmium, mercury, nickel), toxic materials (*i.e.,* brominated flame retardants), and other compounds that government officials believe should not be disposed or even used. By taking a full lifecycle approach, what is considered "the problem" has broadened. With this expanded viewing lens, the disposal of most products represents wasted energy and natural resources, as well as lost jobs and economic value since potentially recyclable material is discarded.

Product stewardship systems are careful to scope the category of products to be covered so that the development of the system is manageable. Too wide of an initial scope may result in the inclusion of too many stakeholders during legislative negotiations and delay program implementation on the highest priority items. In addition, some programs phase in the infrastructure over time, starting slowly to accommodate the increased supply of materials from collections and ensuring that sufficient funds are available to manage the program effectively. Phasing in the scope over time is often a prudent measure. Once the initial system is set, it is often easier to increase products in the system over time, as long as those additional products are considered during the outset of the program. This more cautious approach provides greater assurance that program support can be built steadily over time, decreasing the risk of losing political support if problems occur.

Accountability through Performance Goals

Most stakeholders agree on the need for strict accountability in meeting program goals. However, they differ in how to measure program progress and success. Deciding when a program is a success can be controversial. Stakeholders often differ over how quickly results should be obtained, and how much progress can be achieved over a given period of time. Environmental groups and an increasing number of government agencies have begun to advocate achieving a "zero waste" goal to get the most use from materials and minimize inefficiencies and environmental impact. This full lifecycle approach includes getting as close as possible to 100 percent recycling, especially for HHW that are perceived as having greater health and environmental impacts than other non-hazardous solid wastes.

HHW programs in the United States traditionally collect a low rate of material. Goals are now being set for what it will take to make a significant environmental difference. Taking toxics out of the waste stream is understood to be of prime importance, and a greater priority than recycling bottles, cans, and newspapers. Increasingly, HHW collection goals are set at over 80 percent to reflect what is perceived as achievable and necessary from an environmental perspective. The recycling rate of lead-acid automobile batteries, for example, has already achieved a 98 percent recycling rate in the United States.[10] This high rate is spurred by the value derived from the recycled lead, which is greater than the cost of collection and recycling, thus creating a strong financial incentive. Other stakeholders, however, still view zero waste goals (or high collection and recycling goals) as unattainable for most HHW and argue against setting goals that they feel cannot be achieved.

There is also disagreement over who should be responsible for achieving high collection, reuse, and recycling goals, no matter how they are measured. Many stakeholders believe that responsibility for meeting the goals should be shared, and that all stakeholders have a role to play. Some, however, believe that manufacturers ultimately should be responsible for program performance since they have the ability to increase program funding to pay for greater education, more convenient and abundant collection opportunities (along with retailers), incentives, and other program variables. They believe that, while consumers have a strong responsibility to manage HHW properly, manufacturers and retailers are responsible for providing the systems to enable the public to act responsibly.

Manufacturers, conversely, argue against being held responsible for meeting program goals that rely on consumer action for success. They emphasize that they cannot force consumers to make use of collection programs no matter how convenient they are, and believe that the key variable is whether consumers have developed a "separation culture," which may be independent of the degree of outreach, convenience, incentives, or funding provided to gain consumer attention and motivate action. Some manufacturers argue that, in some cases, no amount of funding will achieve the goal, and that it is better to initiate a program early and start developing cultural change rather than spend time haggling over targets that might take many years to reach. Ultimately, they question whether the economic, social, and environmental value of HHW collection, reuse, and recycling outweighs the cost.

Another factor is the consequences of failure if established goals are not met. For example, some programs might only include motivational goals with no punitive measures if they believe that responsibility is shared equally among stakeholders. Others might require manufacturers or other entities to provide additional education, collection sites, or incentives if program goals are not achieved on time. Still other programs might impose financial penalties on manufacturers if goals are not met, as is the case with Minnesota's electronics recycling law. Another penalty for not meeting a performance goal could be increased government intervention. If a performance goal is not met, for example, industry might lose program autonomy and flexibility as government becomes more prescriptive in its oversight. One illustration of this loss of flexibility might include a requirement on manufacturers and/or retailers to submit detailed program plans for agency approval.

Each product stewardship program must resolve competing interests among divergent stakeholders as well as the timeframe for increasing responsibility in relation to progress made. Programs in Europe and Japan, for example, rely on municipalities to influence consumer end-of-life behavior and often require that municipalities collect products. In addition, they often increase consumer convenience by requiring that retailers collect products, with manufacturers being responsible for recycling and transportation from collection sites. How this issue unfolds in the United States and other countries will be central to the development of the product stewardship field.

There are two main ways that quantitative goals are set, each with a different degree of accountability: (1) amount of material collected, reused, or recycled; and (2) a rate (expressed as a percentage) based on both the amount of material collected, reused, or recycled and another variable (*i.e.,* amount sold, amount available for collection, etc.).

Amount of Material Collected, Reused, or Recycled

This approach involves setting goals based on the volume or weight of the product or hazardous material collected, reused, or recycled from the target population (*i.e.,* pounds of electronic scrap, number of mercury thermostats, pounds of mercury recovered from the mercury thermostats). Goals for subsequent years could be set to increase material collected as compared to the prior year or to the base year. The benefit of this approach is that goals are set on actual amounts, providing a degree of certainty. However, a downside to this approach is that there is no context from which to evaluate the amount collected, reused, or recycled.

For example, a program can triple its annual collection rate of rechargeable batteries, from 1,000 to 3,000 pounds of material. However, if the number of rechargeable batteries that residents are disposing is 100,000 pounds per year, the program would only be collecting 3 percent of the amount that needs to be collected, with the rest being disposed. While the yearly increase is a significant improvement over the previous year, it might not be considered successful depending on program expectations.

Evaluating a program based on the amount of material collected is a good way to begin a program when attention should be focused on putting a system in place. These data can then be used to set more accountable program goals over time. Programs operated voluntarily by companies usually report progress in this manner. Electronics companies, the Rechargeable Battery Recycling Corporation (RBRC), and the Thermostat Recycling Corporation (TRC) all issue reports on progress made based on pounds of material collected. In addition, Maryland's electronics law, which became effective in 2005, requires manufacturers to report the total weight and number of computer equipment devices collected, recycled, refurbished, and reused.[11]

A variation of the approach that relies on actual amounts of material collected is to peg goals to the best performing programs in a given jurisdiction (*i.e.,* state, regional, or national). For example, goals for a national paint stewardship program might compare all state programs to the state that collects the most leftover paint per capita. A goal for each state might be to reach the level of recycling of that high-performing state in a given number of years. As the best performer increases its collection rate, other programs must stretch their goals to keep up with the best program. This variation broadens the horizon for what are considered the best performing programs and stretches the performance of other programs.

Percentage-Based Goals

 Early programs in Europe and Canada, and others in the United States, calculate performance goals based on the amount of material collected as a percentage of what is generated. For example, if 100,000 tons of electronic equipment are generated annually, and 10,000 tons of equipment are recycled and 90,000 tons were disposed, this would represent a 10 percent recycling rate.

Performance goals specifying the percentage of electronics to be recycled appear in the Minnesota electronics recycling law passed in 2007. Under this law, manufacturers must meet annual targets for collection and recycling of specific electronic products equal to 60 percent (by weight) of sales to households/consumers in Year 1 and 80 percent in Year 2.[12] Maine also established recycling rate goals for mercury thermostats in its 2006 law that are equivalent to at least 70 percent by January 1, 2009, and 90 percent by January 1, 2010 (two and three years following program implementation).[13] These high rates were chosen from environmental conviction rather than replicating existing experiences.

Europe's electronics recycling law (discussed below) sets a target of a minimum of 4 kilograms (8.82 pounds) per inhabitant, which is equal to approximately 25 percent of products sold. This minimum standard has allowed countries to establish different methods of achieving progress with maximum flexibility. While some countries (*i.e.,* Ireland) achieve almost 11 kilograms (24¼ pounds) per resident, others still achieve only the minimal target of 4 kilograms without being out of compliance.[14]

Manufacturers often oppose percentage-based goals owing to concern about being held accountable for not meeting aggressive targets and financial implications for underachievement. Instead of debating a performance rate (*i.e.,* whether 25 percent or 75 percent) and the consequences for not meeting the rate, many companies have chosen to criticize the methodology behind establishing percentage goals by claiming a lack of accuracy.

By contrast, most government agencies and environmental groups believe that percentage-based performance goals are a foundation for any environmental planning, and that companies themselves rely on such projections for their own measure of company performance. Government agencies are well versed in measuring recycling results based on the percentage of material collected as compared to the amount generated. In the 1990s, most state agencies challenged themselves, as well as local jurisdictions within their states, to meet ever-increasing recycling rates. In addition, the U.S. EPA has a long-standing goal, recently updated, to recycle 35 percent of municipal solid waste. While some might debate whether this is the correct national recycling goal, the point is that the agency has chosen to use a recycling *percent* rather than a recycling *amount* as the way to measure program performance. The agency uses the recycling percent goal as guidance to its staff in providing grant funds; grant proposals are judged to a large extent on whether they will help the agency achieve its recycling goal.

The major benefit of this approach is that it provides a more meaningful measure of how well a program is doing in its bid to collect, reuse, or recycle. A downside is that this method requires the development of a methodology for estimating the amount of material that is generated or available for collection, reuse, or recycling. Since this amount might become the basis for determining a manufacturer's legal obligation, it needs to be as accurate as possible. For example, while we know how many mercury thermostats are collected nationally through data collected by TRC, we can only estimate today the number of mercury thermostats that are being replaced each year. Since no one requires homeowners and heating and cooling contractors to keep track of the number of thermostats they replace, we can only estimate that number through manufacturer sales data, an estimate of the frequency of thermostat replacement, and other variables. To solve the issue of accuracy pertaining to a producer's obligation under the European Waste Electrical and Electronic Equipment Directive (WEEE Directive), the legislation requires producers to report the amount of electronic appliances they sell into the market. After these "WEEE Registries" are established, which will take several years, they will be used to establish performance goals based on a percentage of products sold into the market.

Next Steps in Performance Goals

Decisions about the type of performance goal (based on amount or a rate), the actual goal (low or high), who is responsible for achieving the goal (manufacturers or shared), and the ramifications of not meeting the targets will continue to be critical to product stewardship programs. Developing clear definitions that are harmonized among nations will be a first critical step to clarify program intent. It will also serve to increase program efficiency so that manufacturers and retailers do not need to translate among various programs in which they operate.

To the extent that these products originate from the manufacturer and are distributed by retailers, it is likely that public sentiment will hold manufacturers and retailers mainly responsible for providing consumers with adequate education, convenient and abundant collection opportunities, and/or incentives to motivate behavior. When these conditions are provided, the emphasis on responsibility for meeting performance goals is likely to shift to consumers, who are ultimately the ones needed to act in an environmentally responsible manner. Existing programs and their varied approaches to performance measures will guide the development of subsequent evaluation methods for incorporation in future product stewardship programs.

Fair Competition: Leveling the Playing Field

No company wants to step out ahead of the competition if doing so will put it at a competitive disadvantage. Why should they? All companies should compete on a "level playing field." Therefore, product stewardship systems must be fair to all companies and not disrupt market dynamics. Voluntary systems, consequently, often contend with the problem of "free riders," those companies that benefit from a program without having to contribute financially. Since there are no regulatory or statutory requirements that a company must adhere to in a voluntary agreement, some companies might not do so, thereby giving non-compliant companies an advantage. Some companies do the "right thing" by setting up take-back opportunities or paying for such programs, while other companies that are not part of the solution and do not make any financial contribution still have systems available to manage their end-of-life products.

Voluntary agreements might be possible when there is a strong trade association that has the power to speak on behalf of the entire industry, although anti-trust concerns must certainly be satisfied. While companies are allowed to convene and develop a mechanism for assessing fees for recycling and other purposes, anti-trust laws forbid them from colluding on the price they will charge consumers to recover their costs.

Most stewardship systems therefore rely on legislation and/or regulation that legally require the participation of all manufacturers (and perhaps retailers) across the industry, and provide government with the authority to enforce against those companies that are non-compliant. TRC's four member companies, for example, represent only about 50 percent of the market for thermostat sales.[15] Over the past decade, TRC paid for the collection and recycling of all brands of mercury thermostats brought into the program, with non-member companies bearing no financial responsibility for their products. As government attention focused on the lack of TRC program performance and the need to increase the number of thermostats recycled, TRC began to seek a legislative remedy that would require all manufacturers to become contributing members of the TRC program or set up their own equivalent recycling system.

Individual and Collective Responsibility

A major tenet of producer responsibility systems is that government should provide incentives to manufacturers to design environmentally superior products. One major objective of stewardship systems is to minimize environmental impact by removing product hazards or by collecting and properly managing end-of-life products. Companies that have adopted an EPR strategy as part of their business model, such as Hewlett Packard, Dell, Apple, and other members of the European Recycling Platform[16] argue that "individual responsibility" is the best way to provide producers with incentive to redesign products. These companies believe that once a company is responsible for its own products, they can calculate the financial benefit of a new design feature. For example, if removing mercury from thermostats reduces a company's recycling cost per unit, the company that invests in non-mercury technology has a financial incentive only if it receives the benefit of its investment directly. If a company with a mercury thermostat pays the same recycling cost as the premium-brand company that develops a non-mercury thermostat, there will be little incentive for that design change.

One difficulty with an individual responsibility approach is the need to identify the brand of product collected. Research by the European Recycling Platform, a stewardship organization, seeks to solve that problem by using a "Return Share Model" as an interim step to full individual responsibility. This model recognizes that products lasting longer owing to better design require fewer resources to deliver service to the consumer. This value can be measured in the number of scrap products by brand returned by the consumer for recycling, or a brand's "return share." This approach requires statistical sampling methods that are under development. Electronics laws in Washington and Maine use a return share model.

Dell was the first electronics manufacturer in the U.S. to offer a free recycling option to all consumers for its brand of products. Sending a United Parcel Service (UPS) driver to a resident's dwelling ensured that the company only received back Dell products. Other manufacturers also offer direct take-back programs, some with costs and others without. However, the consumer interest in these programs has not been very high. Apparently, many consumers find it more convenient to bring that Dell product to a special electronics scrap collection event, a retailer, or an HHW collection center that accepts consumer electronics, since Dell also requires residents to provide their own box and to package up the equipment. At HHW facilities, these products would likely be mixed with other companies' electronics, diluting the design change benefit. The Return Share Model seeks to solve that problem by calculating the volume of each producer brand returned.

While some advocate for an individual responsibility approach to promote product design changes, others find cost efficiencies in joining with other companies in jointly managed systems. These collective systems are managed by a non-profit corporation through any one of many possible governance structures. Most often, these organizations are heavily represented by manufacturers, but sometimes they include retailers and other stakeholders. The organizations are known as producer responsibility organizations (PROs), stewardship organizations, and third party organizations (TPOs). Although pure collective systems result in efficiencies through their joint management framework, they will not promote environmental design changes as readily as individual responsibility systems. Others argue for collective systems to manage historic[17] wastes to spread out the cost of retroactive liability among all manufacturers since a company cannot change the design of old products but only new ones. These people believe that individual responsibility should be pursued only when historic products are largely removed from the waste stream.

The key for product stewardship is to extract from these systems the best of both worlds—incentives for individual companies to make design changes while taking advantage of collective cost savings. While some believe that there is a conflict between individual and collective responsibility, the European Recycling Platform has demonstrated that the principle of individual responsibility can be realized in conjunction with a collective responsibility framework.[18] Most product stewardship systems allow companies to choose whether they want to satisfy program requirements individually or collectively. The potential benefits of the various systems in operation around the world are the subject of evaluation, as they are too new for definitive results. As we move forward on product stewardship, one challenge for policymakers will be to develop systems that allow companies to directly benefit from the design changes in which they invest.

Sustainable Financing

Currently, most end-of-life management costs for HHW in the United States (*i.e.,* collection, reuse, recycling, disposal) are largely borne by state and local agencies through government programs, and are paid for through taxes. Other ways of funding programs are through end-of-life fees charged to consumers when they return a product for recycling or disposal, or through solid waste utility rates. There are two basic types of product stewardship financing systems that seek to cover end-of-life product management costs by incorporating these costs into the purchase price of a new product: (1) Advanced Recycling Fees and (2) Cost Internalization (or "producer responsibility").

Europe and Japan have developed systems that share financial responsibility. In those countries, producers usually are financially responsible for the portion of the process on which they have influence, namely transportation and recycling of scrap products. Municipalities and retailers often pay for the collection of products at municipal depots or at retail, parts of the process on which they have most influence.

Advanced Recycling Fee

An advanced recycling fee (ARF) is a separate charge placed on a new product and paid by a consumer at retail to cover the cost of the product's eventual end-of-life management. An ARF is paid in advance so that when a consumer is ready to recycle the product, a "free" system is available for its collection, transportation, and management. Buying a product and paying an ARF is like buying that product's recycling service in advance. In reality, the ARF paid on a current product pays for the recycling of a product bought years before. One advantage of ARF systems is that the fund created can immediately cover the costs of recycling these past products.

An ARF can be either visible or invisible to the consumer. In the U.S., many state governments have placed visible ARFs on products such as tires, motor oil, and lead acid batteries. California's 2003 electronics scrap recycling law, the first electronics product stewardship system in the U.S., is also based on a visible ARF. Some Canadian ARFs, however, are invisible to the consumer.

Funds collected in ARF systems can go into a government-managed fund or an industry-managed fund (handled through a producer responsibility organization). While most ARFs in the United States are paid into government funds, ARFs in Canada are most often paid into an industry fund and managed by a stewardship organization. A key disadvantage of government-managed funds is the possibility of state legislatures seizing these dedicated funds for other funding purposes. Another downside is the need for additional government staff to manage the fund collection, grant distribution, contractor services, and other operational functions.

Those supporting industry-managed funds believe that these functions can be provided more cost effectively when managed by the private sector. Some in Europe, however, believe that ARFs that pay into a single organization—whether public or private—provide little incentive to improve efficiency since central funds act as monopolies. These proponents believe that the most efficient systems are ones that provide competition among private organizations, which would exclude an ARF.

Cost Internalization

A second type of financing system involves manufacturers and importers that internalize end-of-life management costs into the cost of doing business so that they are invisible to the consumer, even though the costs may be passed on to the consumer. These are called "producer responsibility" systems. By internalizing end-of-life management costs, manufacturers and importers have direct management ability to increase efficiency, improve service, and cut costs. The ability to control management decisions is the biggest advantage for a producer responsibility system compared to an ARF, which does not become part of a company's profit and loss statement and therefore does not result in company actions toward greater efficiency.

The two most common voluntary industry-wide programs in the U.S. are run by RBRC and TRC. Both of these programs were developed by manufacturers to fund collection and recycling programs that are free to consumers, who can bring their batteries and thermostats to participating public and private collection sites. These products do not have to be sorted by brand since the program accepts all manufacturer brands. Manufacturers' costs to collect and recycle the batteries and thermostats, and to publicize the programs, are included in the purchase price of the products. The entire program is paid for by funds derived from manufacturers that pay according to a formula based on market share and established by RBRC and TRC. Most scrap electronics recycling laws recently enacted in the U.S. are following the producer responsibility model, including those in Maine, Washington, Minnesota, Texas, Oregon, Connecticut, and North Carolina.

In most European countries, the WEEE Directive is implemented through cost internalization, which fosters competition among several stewardship organizations in one country. For example, the establishment of four stewardship organizations in Austria in 2005 has reduced the take-back cost from 75 cents per kilogram of electronic product placed on the market to 8 cents per kilogram within a six-month period.[19]

Deposits

Deposit systems create an extra incentive for residents to bring their used product in for collection. Under such a system, consumers pay an extra charge, similar to an ARF, at the time the product is purchased at retail. However, unlike an ARF, if the consumer returns the used product, they will receive a return deposit, or a portion of the deposit. Deposits have been effective at increasing the rate of recycling, although they add significant costs and complexity to the program since part of the revenue must be paid back to consumers who return their products. Examples of deposit-related systems include state laws on beverage containers, and some state laws on automobile batteries, pesticide containers, and used motor oil.

End-of-Life Fees

End-of-life fees are charged by some government agencies and private entities at the point where a product is collected for recycling or disposal. They are used to obtain program revenue to collect used products. Government officials usually view these fees as inadequate long-term solutions because they charge residents for "doing the right thing" and often result in illegal disposal. Given a mandatory fee for collection, many consumers dispose of products in the garbage, a vacant lot, or the woods rather than taking the product to a collection location. Fees are best used to jump-start programs, as a supplement to a product stewardship system, or to gain experience on a pilot project basis. In 2007, Staples became the first retailer to announce that it would take back computers, for an end-of-life fee, in all of its stores nationally.[20] This program is viewed as a supplement to, but not a substitute for, a funding system that will collect and recycle electronics equipment without an extra fee from residents.

Changing Behavior through Stakeholder Engagement

Product stewardship represents a fundamental shift in how products are managed and who pays. For this shift to occur, corporations and small businesses must change their behavior and embrace new responsibilities. Most often this dynamic is akin to the repositioning of a large vessel in a harbor. It occurs slowly, steadily, and with caution.

There are three basic approaches to changing corporate behavior: (1) mandates, (2) voluntary initiatives, and (3) negotiated agreements. The environmental movement in the U.S. has progressed along this path, starting with strong "command and control," unilateral regulations, and moving to voluntary schemes to achieve corporate environmental improvements that go beyond regulatory compliance.

With its expanded focus beyond plant emissions to the entire product lifecycle, product stewardship requires a new approach that includes all entities that play a role in the lifecycle chain. No longer does government solely rule with a unilateral, regulatory fist, nor does it plead for voluntary actions. Product stewardship combines voluntary and regulatory approaches into a collaborative, negotiated process that seeks shared responsibility among key stakeholders.

For example, manufacturers are often called on to incorporate the end-of-life management costs into their product's purchase price, set up producer responsibility organizations to manage collection and recycling programs, and become engaged in all aspects of reducing impacts across their product's lifecycle. Retailers are asked to carry environmentally superior products, take back products in their stores, collect fees under ARF systems, and educate consumers about product choice and recycling options. Governments are expected to enact laws and regulations, set goals, enforce against non-compliant companies and citizens, and at times plan and initiate programs. And consumers ultimately need to buy environmental products and manage them safely at the end-of-life.

These collaborations are based on the premise that voluntary agreements are quicker and less costly to implement, but are often motivated by the fear of having to abide by a patchwork of state and local laws that will add cost and complexity. While the engagement of stakeholders under product stewardship appears to be voluntary, progress must satisfy the interests of all key stakeholders. Each party has the option of taking legislative or regulatory action if negotiations do not proceed quickly enough toward meeting joint goals set forth at the beginning of negotiations.

Shared responsibility has taken on different meanings in Europe, Canada, and the United States. In Europe, it is common for municipalities and retailers to pay for collection of products, whereas in the United States it is less common for municipalities and retailers to accept these roles within the context of newly developed product stewardship systems. However, in Canada, while municipalities often pay for collection, retailers do not collect. The concept of shared responsibility is currently highly fluid, as programs mature and as stakeholders seek common global definitions and systems. Each product negotiation, therefore, will result in a new alignment of resource sharing as all stakeholders seek to reach common product stewardship goals.

Facilitated, multi-stakeholder dialogues offer industry a way to reduce their environmental impact in a meaningful way. The meeting with stakeholders can occur in an objective forum that is devoid of the eleventh-hour posturing that pervades legislative wrangling. For each product sector, there is a different set of stakeholders. For example, those with the greatest stake in reducing impacts from leftover paint are the virgin paint manufacturers, recycled paint manufacturers, retailers selling paint, government agencies (local, state, and federal), painting contractors, homeowners, waste management companies, and outlets for reused paint (*i.e.,* Habitat for Humanity). Key stakeholders concerned about mercury thermostats are thermostat manufacturers, retailers, heating and cooling contractors and wholesalers, government agencies, environmental groups, and homeowners.

As government agencies engage in discussions with manufacturers and retailers about product responsibility, the traditional role that they play in waste management is also being re-negotiated. Transformation on all sides takes place as discussions follow a predictable trajectory. Most companies initially resist the massive change inherent in internalizing end-of-life costs into the product price. They push for more government programs, then "concede" and promote end-of-life fees. Slowly, on their own terms and with greater understanding through probing questions, they begin to accept greater responsibility. At the same time, as companies begin to engage meaningfully, governments loosen their prescriptive posture and allow companies greater flexibility to meet performance goals.

Product stewardship has thus become associated in the U.S. with the active negotiation of stakeholder roles through a collaborative dialogue process. In Europe, these are called consultations. By agreeing to participate in a facilitated process, each stakeholder agrees to seek fair and justifiable ways to reduce product impacts. Each stakeholder has a unique role to play. Each one has critical information that other stakeholders do not have, and it takes the molding of input from these experts to develop the best product stewardship solutions.

Manufacturers, for example, have the best knowledge about production costs, the function of materials incorporated into the products, market dynamics, and product performance. Retailers are the closest to consumers, knowing how and why they purchase items, how they can be motivated to purchase products, and transportation and distribution mechanisms. Government agencies are expert at understanding the logistics and costs of collection, the markets for recycled materials, and ways to reduce environmental impacts. And environmental and consumer groups know which products and systems factor in health and safety considerations, identify the need for change, and push for new ways of thinking. A stakeholder group's best ideas are incorporated into jointly developed agreements. By involving all parties early and often in the process, each stakeholder will be more committed to implementing the agreements.

A key to the success of stakeholder approaches is that the process must focus on a limited industry sector to make the dialogue manageable. If too many interests are included, it is more difficult to address them all within a given dialogue. For example, fewer manufacturers would be involved in a dialogue that focused solely on household paint than if the dialogue also addressed paint for industrial and marine applications. Another product example, packaging, could involve manufacturers and recyclers of glass, plastic, paper, metal, and other materials. More voices mean greater complexity in developing solutions to satisfy interests, increasing cost, and the timeframe for reducing impacts.

Product stewardship involves a delicate dance. If government forces progress too quickly, it can create an industry backlash. But if companies proceed too slowly, government might pursue the traditional, unilateral, prescriptive legislative path. If progress is consistent and meaningful, the result can be measurable environmental improvements about which all stakeholders can feel a sense of achievement. Many times, product dialogues also result in personal changes in individual stakeholders, as relationships strengthen over time, even among traditional adversaries.

The Paint Product Stewardship Initiative (PPSI) is one such stakeholder dialogue. Starting in 2003, the non-profit Product Stewardship Institute has facilitated a national dialogue aimed at reducing the generation of leftover paint, increasing reuse and recycling opportunities, and improving methods of marketing recycled paint. Following extensive research that included interviews with over 35 key stakeholders, the PPSI brought together participants from over 60 companies, industry associations, and government agencies. The discussions and collaboration resulted in an April 2005 Memorandum of Understanding (MOU) to conduct 11 projects. Dialogue participants jointly contributed $880,000[21] to complete nine of those projects[22] that will help develop a nationally coordinated leftover paint management system. In 2007, the National Paint and Coatings Association Board of Directors issued a Resolution that committed the paint industry to take responsibility for managing leftover paint. The Resolution formed the basis for a second MOU that includes a demonstration project in one state and a plan for rolling out a national system for the management of leftover paint in other states.

What Motivates Industry to Make
Product Stewardship Changes

There are five fundamental reasons that manufacturers, retailers, and other industry stakeholders are motivated to make changes that reduce the health and environmental impacts of their products: (1) to gain competitive advantage, (2) reduce business risk (including threat of legislation), (3) create/maintain an image of sustainability, (4) corporate ownership control, and (5) company leadership.

Competitive Advantage

Implementing product stewardship initiatives usually will not result in initial financial savings or profits for a company. However, in some instances it might give a company an edge over its competitors. Small retailers, with closer ties to their communities and an emphasis on service, have begun to take back products such as thermostats and fluorescent lamps in their stores. Product take-back is considered an added service for customers and can counter lower prices offered at large retailers. Even big retail chains, however, can find a competitive advantage in taking greater responsibility. In 2007, after a five-state pilot project and a two-year permanent program, Staples, Inc., began to collect all brands of computer equipment in its stores nationwide. While they currently charge an end-of-life fee, the service is free in states with electronics laws that provide payments to collection locations.

If all companies in an industry have end-of-life responsibilities, companies might see relative savings compared to the competition if they get involved early, develop government partnerships, and gain experience through early leadership. When HP, Sony, Electrolux, and Braun established the European Recycling Platform in Europe in 2002, their objective was to gain a competitive advantage by smart and effective management of their take-back obligation. Over 900 other companies have since joined the ERP end-of-life management scheme.

Reduce Business Risk

Corporations seek certainty, which creates stability and efficiency, resulting in greater confidence in the company and an ability to attract financing, good staff, and satisfied customers. Attempts to "rock the boat" and create uncertain business conditions will often be met by resistance. One of the great motivators in changing company behavior has been the threat or issuance of product stewardship legislation.

According to Bette Fishbein, an early proponent of producer responsibility, "Battery legislation in states such as New Jersey and Minnesota was a driving force behind the RBRC program ... It is far more efficient to have a single national program to collect and recycle Ni-Cds rather than different requirements and programs in different states. But without legislation at the state level, it is doubtful that a national program to recycle Ni-Cds would have been implemented. Conflicting state laws on labeling and mandatory collection actually led the battery industry to encourage federal legislation ... The RBRC take-back system enabled industry to comply with the mandatory take-back requirements already legislated in some states and to pre-empt legislation in other states."[23] Although the federal battery legislation does not require take-back, it did assist the industry in setting up its voluntary collection program.

The more legislation that is proposed on a product, the more interest there is likely to be in a product stewardship solution. However, companies need to perceive legislative activity as fair (*i.e.,* that it will impact competitors equally and provide sufficient freedom and flexibility to implement the legislation). For example, to prepare for passage of Europe's WEEE Directive, the four founding companies in the European Recycling Platform viewed the manufacturer take-back obligation as a business opportunity, not a burden, and sought ways to minimize the impact on their markets. Having the same conditions imposed on all companies was viewed as a positive aspect of the legislation. Once they knew the basic details of the WEEE legislation, their objective was to turn the obligation into a business strategy.[24]

For this reason, many companies and trade associations have been willing to meet in national dialogues to develop one basic approach that is agreed upon by all key stakeholders. Many have been willing to take responsibility for recycling their products at end-of-life in exchange for the certainty of one law, regulation, or program that must be met by all companies in that industry sector. However, if multiple bills seek different outcomes, companies might decide to fight all legislation to maintain the status quo.

Create/Maintain an Image of Sustainability

No company wants bad press. Most strive to be good neighbors in the community and want to be perceived as a company that cares about reducing its social and environmental impacts. Those that are most successful in creating a solid image of sustainability are able to back their claims with real examples. They continually strive to connect to their customers by conducting research and developing technologies that keep them ahead of others. But a company does not have to be a leader to stay out of trouble, nor be perceived as a "green" company. A positive image will often keep regulatory officials from coming down hard if there is room for flexibility and discretion.

Failure to keep up with social norms of what is expected, particularly if one is perceived as a leader, puts the company at risk of being singled out for bad press and appearing on an environmental group's hit list. Environmental groups are expert at exploiting a company's aversion to being held up as a "bad actor." For example, battered by the environmental group ForestEthics for selling wood products from endangered forests, Staples responded. The company created a new position—Vice President for Environmental Affairs—with broad latitude on environmental initiatives. The person who filled that position created the Staples computer take-back program, among other company take-back initiatives. The Greenpeace Guide to Greener Electronics ranks the best and worst companies according to a range of environmental criteria, and receives extensive press attention. Another of the ForestEthics efforts, its Dirty Secret Campaign, embarrassed Victoria's Secret into talks that led to an agreement to reduce the impact of the company's catalog production on Canada's Great Boreal Forest. These tactics, while risky and not mainstream, have often kept companies engaged in finding product stewardship solutions.

Corporate Ownership Control

Companies often move toward sustainability more slowly than some people would like. In such cases, several organizations have refined a new tool called shareholder resolutions that seek shareholder support to wrest control over company decisions. These resolutions seek to force a company's leadership to take certain actions that they have been unwilling to do on their own. Many of these organizations are faith-based, and seek changes that are not only environmental, but also social. One non faith-based organization, As You Sow Foundation, develops resolutions against leading electronics manufacturers to urge them to develop take-back systems and take greater corporate responsibility for electronics scrap. To date, while an increasing number of resolutions have been floated over the past few years, they have served more to draw attention to the issue and embarrass the company than actually voting to force change. However, as the public becomes better versed on the goals of producer responsibility efforts, these resolutions are likely to gain greater support.

Company Leadership

Almost every industry has its leaders and laggards, and the leaders play a key role in moving that company, and often the entire industry, forward. Charismatic champions often drive companies, leading with experience and ability, personal confidence to take a risk, and company support owing to staff respect and high performance. Leadership companies are role models for other companies. They become the one to watch, the one to emulate, or the one to outperform, and their practices are used by government to prod other companies to move in the same direction. At times, company leadership programs form the basis for industry standards that formalize the aspiration of what others seek to achieve. One notable leader of the corporate social responsibility movement, Interface, established its "Mission Zero" goal to eliminate any negative environmental impact by 2020, which has refocused other companies on the social imperative to move aggressively toward sustainability.

Several organizations work with companies to seek change by linking environmental and social performance to long-term business value. One such organization, Ceres, is a coalition of investor, environmental, and public interest organizations seeking to advance corporate responsibility through stakeholder engagement, public disclosure, and performance improvements. It established the Global Reporting Initiative (GRI) in 1997 "...with the mission of developing globally applicable guidelines for reporting on the economic, environmental, and social performance of corporations, governments and non-governmental organizations (NGOs)."[25] GRI seeks to set a standard for leading companies to follow, setting a strong pace for others.

Company leadership can also be translated into business advantage directly through the procurement of products that are environmentally preferable. The Electronic Product Environmental Assessment Tool (EPEAT) "... help[s] purchasers in the public and private sectors evaluate, compare and select desktop computers, notebooks and monitors based on their environmental attributes. EPEAT also provides a clear and consistent set of performance criteria for the design of products, and provides an opportunity for manufacturers to secure market recognition for efforts to reduce the environmental impact of its products."[26] Industry was a strong member of the team that created EPEAT.

Other multi-stakeholder, industry-driven product sustainability standards are starting to penetrate the marketplace for carpet, textiles, and office furniture, largely in response to the "green building movement." This is new territory for all stakeholders (governments, manufacturers, retailers, NGOs, and consumers), especially as it relates to the criteria to be considered in such standards, where to set the bars, and how the standards should be tightened over time. These standards are a starting point for a long journey toward better practices in a much broader economic system that itself is far from sustainable. These efforts, however, are starting to draw attention from other industries interested in also starting a voyage toward sustainability. It will be important for government, NGOs, and others to engage deeply in these efforts to help them gain and sustain credibility.

In addition, individual companies have initiated their own efforts to green their supply chains and educate consumers. Wal-Mart is a prominent example because it is the largest retailer in the country and one of the largest companies in the world. Its actions potentially have enormous impact on the marketplace. Wal-Mart has developed a packaging scorecard that will "... allow Wal-Mart buyers to have all the information about packaging alternatives or more sustainable packaging materials in one place, allowing them to make better

purchasing decisions." [27] Wal-Mart will grade suppliers and make buying decisions aimed
to help the company save money by reducing excess packaging and to spur developments
in more sustainable packaging design. Wal-Mart is also looking at ways that it can recover
packaging to help close the loop by incorporating these materials back into its products.

Home Depot has developed an Eco Options label program that it hopes will help consumers in identifying products that have "... less of an impact on the environment than
competing products." [28] Whole Foods has also introduced its Whole Trade Guarantee that
"... ensures environmentally responsible practices, more money for producers and farmers,
and better working conditions and higher wages for workers." [29] All of these efforts represent the rising consciousness of the retail sector in an attempt to meet growing consumer
demand for environmentally sustainable products. It also offers an opportunity for governments and NGOs to work with this powerful sector to further drive the product stewardship
movement.

In Europe, the four founding companies of the European Recycling Platform invented
a new way of running a WEEE take-back program. They took a high risk by challenging
the conservative industry position of a one-system monopoly and lowered costs by managing take-back systems using business principles and competition, which will benefit industry, government, and consumers. [30]

What Motivates the Public to Take Greater Environmental Responsibility

Product stewardship is based on the premise that companies need to provide better products and services so that consumers can make better choices that move our society toward
a more sustainable future. There is only so much a resident can do if there are barriers to
action, such as if there is only one annual HHW collection event and it operates when the
person is on vacation. Similarly, we cannot expect consumers to buy "greener" products
when none exist that are comparable in price, quality, and/or availability. The public relies
on government and industry to provide them with information on the problem and on convenient opportunities to "do the right thing." This reliance on government and industry is
the reason why product stewardship began its focus on businesses.

Manufacturers, importers, and retailers need to provide better options. Without those
options, we cannot expect consumers to do anything more than small, individual acts that,
no matter how innovative, will not be enough to change personal and societal norms. The
solutions provided need to be basic enough so that the vast majority of the public can
take meaningful action. These actions have been sorely lacking in the management of
HHW since hazardous products were first recognized as a problem. Product stewardship
can greatly contribute to positively changing that scenario. However, it is the consumer's
responsibility to ultimately use the new services, buy the "greener" products, and return the
end-of-life products to the appropriate collection systems.

While there are many variables affecting motivation, three of the basic ways to help
motivate citizens to make better environmental decisions are: (1) Information, (2) Convenient Actions, and (3) Incentives and Disincentives.

Information

The consumer needs to be educated on the problem created by the product they consume, and what they can do to contribute to solving that problem. They need to know where to take leftover paint and mercury thermostats, and where to buy recycled paint and a non-mercury thermostat. But beyond the basics, consumers must come to understand the life-cycle impacts of consumer products and the importance of their role in each context.

In some cases, this will be easy. A growing number of people know that they should limit the amount of fish they eat owing to its mercury content. Fewer people know the sources of mercury, including which household products contribute to that problem and which fish have the lowest mercury content. But how many people know about the life-cycle impacts from mining titanium dioxide, a key ingredient in latex paint? Armed with information, people will have the best reasons to take advantage of the best choices companies and governments give them. This information needs to be meaningful, easy to understand, and something with which the public can identify. As multiple product stewardship solutions develop, it has become increasingly important to simplify information to the public through a single website and toll-free telephone number and other coordinated information.

In product stewardship negotiations, few companies argue with the need to provide information to the public. The debate, however, centers on how to provide that information, its cost, and who pays. Ultimately, success in reducing lifecycle product impacts will translate into progress toward developing a sustainable culture. To achieve this goal, each of us needs to understand that waste is a resource that has a value in the creation of future products.

Convenient Actions

While a lack of knowledge can be a barrier to action, knowledge in and of itself is not enough to motivate behavior. Once residents are provided with information about how to manage HHW and how to avoid future hazardous products, they need an easy way to take action. A product becomes a stewardship issue because of the lack of infrastructure for its collection, transportation, and processing. Multiple collection options add convenience for residents. However, convenience has a price.

Studies from the United Kingdom and France indicate that the separate collection of products increases transportation emissions and can be counter-productive to reducing greenhouse gases. Each region will need to optimize collection strategies with the involvement of municipal, retail, and other collection entities. Consumer convenience should also be balanced by the responsibility of the consumer to take action. While it might be most convenient for all residents to have their HHW picked up door-to-door by appointment, this would also negate most environmental benefits.

Product stewardship negotiations focus on how many collection options are needed based on the size of the population or the geographical extent. For urban dwellers, a municipal or retail option might suffice, while rural residents might require a mail-back program or an extensive system based on mobile collections or "milk-run" operations to reduce costs through consolidation. Some urban areas are even experimenting with curbside collection of motor oil and leftover paint to provide added convenience and lower costs by attaching collection equipment to trucks already on the road collecting other recyclable materials.

Incentives and Disincentives

Education and convenient opportunities are part of the foundation needed to get residents to act. But, if people are not self-motivated to protect health, safety, and the environment and manage their HHW, we need to do more than educate them about the problem and provide them with a convenient way to manage the product. Often, residents need incentives and disincentives to motivate them to participate, such as a reward for taking the desired action or a penalty for *not* taking action. Like most policies, a mixture of approaches may be needed, even if the incentives are targeted for one set of actors and penalties toward another. For example, Maine's thermostat program requires wholesalers and contractors to collect mercury thermostats, with penalties for non-compliance, while also providing a $5 per thermostat incentive for each mercury thermostat returned by a homeowner or contractor.

Financial Incentives

Financial incentives are perhaps one of the best methods for changing consumer behavior, although the cost of these measures must be considered. One example is a deposit on beverage containers, which doubles the rate of recycling containers with a deposit as compared to other containers without a deposit. In Massachusetts, when enacted in 1981,[31] the 5-cent deposit initially resulted in recycling rates for deposit containers of over 80 percent. However, as the value of a nickel in present-day dollars decreased, the recycling rate dropped to under 70 percent. Another incentive program, called "Pay as You Throw," requires residents to pay for garbage disposal (paying a per bag or barrel fee) but allowing them to recycle for "free" (*i.e.,* where recycling costs are built into the price of the bag or barrel fee). These incentive programs yield some of the highest recycling rates in the country.

Many product stewardship financial incentives include a cash "bounty" or a store coupon paid to a resident or business if they return an item. The 2006 national voluntary agreement on auto switches includes a cash bounty for those returning mercury auto switches. Maine's 2006 thermostat law requires manufacturers to pay homeowners and contractors a $5 incentive payment for returning a mercury thermostat. In addition, some states have retail automobile battery return programs, in which retailers charge a $5 or $10 "core charge" upon purchase of a new automobile battery, but rebate that money if the consumer brings in a used automobile battery at the time of purchase or within 30 days of the purchase. Finally, some retailers and manufacturers offer a coupon good toward a future purchase if an item is returned for recycling. For example, HP offers a coupon off the purchase of a new hardware product on the HP Home & Home Office Store for consumers that recycle their computer hardware through HP's recycling service.[32] These programs all provide incentives for consumers to return end-of-life products.

A healthy recycling market can remove the need for a financial incentive and motivate action that benefits the environment. In Europe, scrap metal dealers experienced a revival in 2007 owing to a sharp increase in scrap metal prices. This phenomenon created a high demand for metallic waste products such as washing machines and dishwashers collected under the WEEE Directive. In the United States, consistently high demand for scrap lead has contributed to the high rate of lead-acid automobile battery recycling. If a waste product has value, there will be great interest in recovering the product. If a financial subsidy can stimulate recycling markets so that value can be maintained in the long term, we will have moved another step closer to sustainability in that product sector. This value can also be designed into the product so that end markets are planned for the recycled material prior to it being manufactured. However, if no value can be derived for the end product, financial incentives may be needed over a much longer period of time to motivate consumer action.

Financial Disincentives

While not nearly as popular politically, waste bans and other disincentives can prod residents to take action. Bans on the disposal of electronic scrap are a key component of product stewardship legislation, but should only be implemented if a robust recycling infrastructure is first in place. Banning disposal but offering no available alternative will only frustrate residents and create political problems. Disposal bans send a clear signal to the public that a product should be handled in a special manner. Owing to the difficulty in enforcing against households and small businesses, these measures mostly play an educational role.

The Origin of Product Stewardship and EPR Systems

Early Efforts

Companies have long sought ways to reduce the costs of production, which in turn have sometimes reduced environmental impacts. For example, once single-use soda bottles replaced refillable bottles, they were made lighter and with fewer materials. While this reduced production costs, it also reduced energy and material use, transportation burdens, and other environmental impacts. As product manufacturers sought new ways to save money through product design innovations, environmental groups and government agencies stepped up to force additional changes to alleviate growing environmental and litter problems.

Pollution prevention, toxics use reduction, and similar programs placed their emphasis on decreasing the amount of toxics (*i.e.,* hazardous materials) used in the manufacture of products. These programs sought to change company practices by showing that up-front investments in new technologies could save money over time while also reducing pollution. For example, 3M Company's employee-based Pollution Prevention Pays (3P) program, initiated in 1975, is widely recognized as one of the earliest successful attempts at preventing pollution while saving the company money.[33]

Product stewardship, by contrast, focuses on toxics used in the products themselves. Consumer products deliver toxic materials into our homes through effective product distribution networks. These products are presumed to be safe to use, but if improperly handled, stored, or disposed, there is the potential for risk. While pollution prevention managers met with company engineers to reduce toxics at the plant, solid waste managers met with company facility managers and citizens to recycle non-hazardous wastes. It would take public outrage over litter to force manufacturers to manage their products at the end-of-life.

U.S. Beverage Container Laws

The first product stewardship laws in the Unites States pertained to the collection of beverage containers. In 1971, Oregon became the first state in the nation to pass a "bottle bill." Today, there are 11 states with beverage container laws,[34] with Hawaii's law passing in 2002. These laws grew out of concern over roadside litter. Later bottle bills introduced in other states promoted resource conservation and recycling goals. However, with the exception of Hawaii, none of these bills gained legislative traction and were ultimately defeated by strong industry lobbyists. Before the passage of Hawaii's law, the last new bottle redemption law enacted was in California in 1986.

Beverage container laws typically require bottlers to pay a handling fee for the collection of the container, and require retailers to take back containers of the type they sell. In some states, this requirement spawned the creation of redemption centers to provide the collection service. Thus, the bottle bill became one of the earliest experiments in shared responsibility. It provided consumers with an incentive to recycle, funded through a deposit derived from consumers themselves. It required manufacturers to pay a handling fee to those collecting their product at the end-of-life. It required retailers to take back products they sold. And government was required to monitor the program, enforce against non-compliant retailers and manufacturers, and combat fraud from bottles purchased in non-bottle bill states.

Since their introduction, bottle bills and subsequent beverage container laws have been contentious. There is no doubt that these programs produce greater results than any other program that collects and recycles beverage containers. In states with these laws, the recycling rate of containers on which the deposit is paid is over double the rate for containers that carry no deposit. According to a report by the Sound Resource Management Group of Washington, 191 containers per capita are recycled in states without bottle bills, while states with bottle bills recycle 490 containers per capita.[35] However, bottlers and retailers claim that program costs do not justify their results. This stalemate accounts for the passage of only one state law in the past 20 years.

Beverage container laws were followed by state and national legislative and voluntary initiatives aimed at requiring, or encouraging, manufacturers to meet recycling targets, develop markets for collected materials, or use a specified percentage of recycled content in their products. The major targets of these efforts were traditional non-hazardous products and materials, such as newsprint, plastic, glass, and telephone directories.[36] These efforts attempted to make manufacturers take greater responsibility for the environmental impacts of their products, even though many times these actions would not be financially advantageous to the companies. These initiatives did not, however, take a comprehensive approach to the life cycle impacts created by these products. Instead, they focused on a part of the problem and often included an array of industry sectors in one piece of legislation. This strategy, no doubt, contributed to industry's success in blocking much of these efforts.

Recent comprehensive voluntary initiatives also have not been successful in developing solutions to the declining recycling rate of beverage containers.

Product Stewardship and Hazardous Products in the U.S.—Tires, Motor Oil, and Automobile Batteries

In the early 1990s, there was a profound shift in focus toward "special wastes" (*i.e.,* products that presented a management problem for local public works officials). Tire piles in some locations burned out of control for days, precipitating public alarm that led to laws creating funds for the cleanup of old piles and ensuring that new ones did not form. Used motor oil recycling laws sprouted from public concern over oil slicks in the ocean and inland waterways, and laws on automobile batteries were enacted to ensure that these lead-acid products would not be abandoned in vacant lots or in the woods. These laws fostered the creation of companies to collect and process the scrap products. They also spurred the creation of end markets that would use processed materials in the construction of roads, playgrounds, and other products from scrap tires, re-refined oil from used motor oil, and smelted lead and recycled plastic products from automobile battery casings.

The laws that addressed environmental problems resulting from these products were initiated by the manufacturers of tires, motor oil, and automobile batteries. These companies, through their associations, developed, promoted, and encouraged government to pass legislation that required consumers to pay visible "advanced recycling fees" that were collected at retail and deposited into a state-managed fund. These government grant programs provided funds for public and private collection centers, and covered the cost of handling, transporting, and recycling the products.

While these laws reduced much of the immediate environmental risk from HHW products, they relied heavily on government staff, retailers, and consumers, but not on manufacturers. According to the Product Policy Institute,

> the American Petroleum Institute (API) promoted model legislation for used oil that utilizes state monies or consumer fees to finance state funds that are used to operate used oil collection facilities. Seventeen states have laws based on the API model. Similarly, the Rubber Manufacturers Association was instrumental in getting 35 states to pass scrap tire legislation in which fees, collected from consumers by tire dealers in most cases, fund government managed tire management programs.[37] Finally, the Battery Council International (BCI) successfully promoted legislation for collecting lead-acid batteries used in cars and trucks. Unlike regulations for used oil and scrap tires, lead-acid battery laws, which have been passed in 37 states, require retailers to take back used batteries and require consumers to pay a "core charge," which is a deposit paid by any person who purchases a new battery without returning a used battery at the same time.[38] A common feature of the take-back programs for all three products is the absence of significant producer responsibility, either physical or financial, assigned to brand-owners.[39]

German/European Packaging Ordinance[40]

The 1991 "German Packaging Ordinance"[41] laid the groundwork for the worldwide EPR revolution. By all measures, this initiative unleashed a tidal wave of opinion, one side supporting its waste reduction incentive for producers, and the other side opposing its strong regulatory approach and complex implementation.

With its enactment, the concept of producer responsibility took hold in Europe. The German government passed legislation that required a deposit on certain non-refillable containers and also required retailers to take back the packaging from consumers. The legislation places direct responsibility for meeting specific waste reduction targets for product packaging on those who place a packaged product onto the market (manufacturers or importers, who are called "producers"). However, the ordinance provided an exemption if producers could meet collection and recycling targets through an alternative privately financed plan. Producers could either develop and implement take-back schemes for their product packaging or join a certified national waste management scheme.

The industry-proposed system that allowed for its exemption was called the Green Dot program, and to originally operate this program, industry created the Duales System Deutschland GmbH (DSD) company. DSD subcontracted the collection service to waste management companies and municipalities. At the start of the program in Germany, DSD was the only certified compliance scheme.

The role of a compliance scheme such as DSD is to oversee the collection, sorting, and recycling of packaging waste with the support of municipal waste management partners and waste management/recycling companies. Until 1996, DSD owned the Green Dot trademark, the licensing of which finances the waste management system. In order to rule out packaging-political trade barriers in Europe from the start, DSD founded the Packaging Recovery Organization Europe (PRO EUROPE) in 1995. The primary task of PRO EUROPE is to award the Green Dot trademark to national collection and recovery systems within the European Union (EU), the European Economic Area, and the candidate countries in accordance with uniform rules and regulations.

In the late 1990s, many producers, municipalities, and waste management companies in Germany became dissatisfied with the service and attitude of DSD because it was perceived to be acting as a monopoly. Following lawsuits against DSD, Europe and Germany forced open the packaging take-back market to competition resulting in at least three compliance schemes entering the German packaging market. With the acquisition of DSD by the financial investor KKR in 2003, DSD lost the license for the Green Dot, which is now used in all of Europe as a symbol that stands for the take-back of packaging material.

Since 1999, when the monopoly was cracked, packaging take-back costs have lowered as a result of competition among packaging compliance schemes. DSD is no longer the preferred supplier owing to its pricing structure. Companies that have a contract with DSD to collect packaging waste pay a fee for the service based on each unit sold. Other compliance schemes, such as VfW and Interseroh, instead calculate their packaging take-back service fee based on the volume of material returned.

A key lesson learned from the development of the German packaging scheme is that competition among compliance schemes optimizes efficiency and improves service better than any other management practice. This result was also achieved in the United Kingdom where over 27 packaging compliance schemes compete with each other for customers, service, and price. Producers often initiate these compliance schemes, but so do other companies including those involved in logistics and waste management. The United Kingdom has one of the lowest packaging take-back costs. However, many other European Member

States still use single packaging schemes, although the trend in more countries is to copy the German and British experiences.

European Electronics Waste Management – WEEE and RoHS[42]

A decade later, in 2003 after a long consultation process, the European Community enacted the Waste Electrical and Electronic Equipment Directive (WEEE Directive), which requires electronics manufacturers selling in Europe to be responsible for recycling all electronics that depend on electricity (*i.e.,* those with a plug, battery, or switch). There are 10 WEEE categories, including large household appliances, refrigerating appliances, small domestic appliances, consumer electronics, information technology and telecommunications, toys, tools, sports equipment, medical devices, monitoring and control instruments, and automatic dispensers.[43] The WEEE Directive, and its accompanying Restriction on Hazardous Substances (RoHS) Directive, which bans certain hazardous materials from the production of electronics, swept EPR into the United States.

These laws significantly affected how electronic products worldwide were designed and managed at the end-of-life. Any manufacturer that wishes to sell in the 27 member states of the European Union must comply with these directives. The WEEE and RoHS Directives operate under the principle of shared producer responsibility whereby producers are responsible for product design including the elimination of certain hazardous substances. Producers are also responsible for setting up take-back schemes, which are contracted out for the pickup and transport of materials from designated collection points to recycling facilities.

The WEEE Directive requires each individual producer (manufacturer or importer) to meet its obligation by joining a collective scheme or by establishing an individual scheme. The Directive requires that producers share responsibility for the cost of managing "historic"[44] end-of-life electronic waste from private households[45] prior to August 13, 2005, according to the actual market share of each producer per type of equipment. To do so, all Member States have implemented National WEEE Registries to which each producer must report on the amount of appliances sold (by weight). The Registry calculates each producer's market share per type of equipment, which becomes that producer's take-back obligation. The producer is required to report its collection volume to assess compliance. In some countries, individual producers conduct the registration and reporting tasks, while compliance organizations provide these services for the producers in other countries.

Besides the responsibility for managing historic waste, the WEEE Directive also imposes individual producer responsibility that requires a company to takeback its own products sold after August 13, 2005, and to provide a financial guarantee for this responsibility. The WEEE Directive provides flexibility in complying with this responsibility either by joining a collective scheme or through a company-specific scheme. By September 2006, only 12 of the 25 Member States had adequately transposed the Directive to distinguish between collective and individual systems. "Of these 12, only Germany, Italy, and Sweden have mandated an individual financial guarantee for new electrical and electronic equipment placed on the market (regardless of the compliance scheme they have joined)."[46] All Member States have adopted national legislation to implement the WEEE Directive. In Austria and Ireland, for example, execution started on August 13, 2005. Italy will be the last country to begin enforcement by January 1, 2008. To inform consumers not to discard appliances into the trash, products since August 2005 must be labeled with a crossed-out-dustbin.

Until 2011, producers are allowed to charge their customers (retailers or wholesalers) a visible fee to recover end-of-life management costs, and retailers are allowed to pass this visible fee onto consumers. However, in most countries the visible fees have disappeared, as the administration has been more costly than the benefits. As of August 2007, only four countries maintained a mandatory visible fee, while in all other countries the producer's take-back costs are internalized into the product price.

Retailers and municipalities must provide collection sites for the return of WEEE at their own expense and with no cost to the consumer. They must also provide educational information for the consumer provided by the producer. However, in most countries the producer compliance schemes contribute to the retailer and municipal efforts. For example, in Germany, producers provide free collection containers to retailers and municipalities, and pick them up from the collection points.

The implementation of the WEEE Directive has sparked the setup of multiple take-back compliance schemes. In almost all countries, several schemes compete with each other, which has significantly reduced the take-back cost, as seen particularly in Austria. These compliance schemes are either established by producers or by companies involved in logistics or waste management. In Europe, a new market for take-back compliance services has recently been developed, spurred by the creation of the European Recycling Platform that stimulated competition and opposed single monopoly stewardship organizations.

The companion RoHS Directive restricts the use of six hazardous substances in electrical and electronic products that are covered by the WEEE Directive. The RoHS Directive was adopted in February 2003, and took effect on July 1, 2006. As of that date, new electrical and electronic products that contain more than the agreed levels of lead, cadmium, mercury, hexavalent chromium (or chromium VI), and polybrominated biphenyl (PBB) and polybrominated diphenyl ether (PBDE) flame retardants are banned from sale in the European Union.[47] Similar directives have been introduced in other parts of the world. In the U.S. for example, the California Electronic Waste Recycling Act (enacted in 2003) references the RoHS Directive, as does China's equivalent electronics waste management law.[48]

Canadian Product Stewardship

As European producer responsibility systems were evolving, similar waste management dynamics began to unfold in Canada. Faced with dwindling funding and an increase in waste generation, the provinces began to place responsibility on producers to find end-of-life solutions for their products. In 1994, British Columbia, Canada's furthest western province, enacted the country's first producer responsibility legislation, which addressed paint. The province continues to have some of the most progressive product stewardship systems in Canada. Other provinces eventually adapted these systems to develop their own provincial brand of product stewardship.

Canada now has four national stewardship programs—for used cell phones/rechargeable batteries, domestic beer-related packaging, ozone-depleting substances, and obsolete, unusable, or banned pesticides and pesticide containers. It also has numerous provincial programs on the following items: medications; tires; motor oil, containers, and filters; electronics; paint, stains, and varnishes; lead acid batteries; solvents/flammable liquids, gasoline, and pesticides; and beverage containers. By 2007, there were nearly 50 product stewardship programs throughout Canada.

Canadian product stewardship systems include a wide range of programs that Duncan Bury, Environment Canada, divides into five categories based on the degree of producer responsibility: (1) Government, (2) Quasi-Government—delegated agency, (3) Shared Responsibility—industry and municipalities, (4) Industry "Light," and (5) Industry "Premium."[49]

The Government model involves a tax collected from the consumer at the point of purchase. The tax may go into the general fund and be subject to government budgeting pressures with no guarantee that it will all be appropriated to the recycling and management of those products.

The Quasi-Government model involves delegating the program to a quasi-government agency that manages the program through inclusion of a variety of stakeholders. Industry (including manufacturers, importers, and retailers) will play an advisory role only and have no direct responsibility for program funding or operation. ARFs are either set by government regulation or by the quasi-government agency and are dedicated to end-of-life management, although changing and setting fees can be difficult. Commonly, there is no municipal role even though municipalities can offer their collection systems for a fee paid by the agency. There is also no connection between producers and end-of-life management of their products. Therefore, this model is considered as a weak or non-existent producer responsibility system. An example is the Alberta Recycling Management Authority (AMRA) Alberta electronics recycling program.

Under Canada's Shared Responsibility model, industry and municipalities share operational and funding responsibilities. Industry can be apportioned part of the total system cost of a stewardship/recycling program or part of the operational system. For example, taxpayer dollars might pay for half the system costs, while industry funds the remaining portion. A second example is where municipalities pay for collection, while producers cover transportation and end-of-life management. An example of this model is the Ontario "Blue Box" multi-material recycling program that is operated by municipalities but with 50 percent of its funding provided by Stewardship Ontario, the stewardship organization representing the packaging and printed paper industry. A similar multi-material recycling program model has recently been launched in Quebec with Eco-Enterprise, the industry stewardship organization for that program.

The Shared Responsibility model is often used to share and offset costs of existing programs and avoids replacing one system with another. Since municipalities commonly fund and operate collection facilities under this model, public perception is that municipalities are still 100 percent responsible. In reality, system responsibility is proportionate to the degree of influence for that entity. The large data requirements to establish legitimate costs make this model burdensome, along with the need for trust to be established between partners that must divide responsibilities and costs.

In the Industry Light model, industry is given a legal mandate to operate a producer responsibility program and has control over the funding mechanism, recycling, and promotion. Industry's ability to negotiate program costs and efficiencies may be limited by mandated sole source contracts and other government interventions. These prescriptive elements might delay start-up of the program and compromise producer flexibility. Government retains control over some key issues, such as goal setting, planning, and enforcement. Unless constrained by a government directive, municipalities are able to negotiate industry access to municipal collection systems. An example of this model is the Saskatchewan Waste Electronic Equipment Program (SWEEP) that was directed by the province to negotiate exclusively with SARCAN for the operation of the collection system. This directive reduced competition among end-of-life service providers and did not allow industry the flexibility that likely would have resulted in lower costs.

In the Industry Premium model (or full producer responsibility), industry has full responsibility to fund and operate the program from collection through end-of-life management. Industry sets fees, determines the collection mechanism, promotes the program, and contracts for recycling and other services. Government's role is to provide high-level policy direction, set objectives, and enforce against non-compliance. Under this model, industry decides whether it wants to negotiate with municipalities for their collection services. This model requires performance goals and reporting to ensure that government objectives are being met. Examples of this model are the British Columbia product stewardship programs for paint, pesticides, oil, flammable liquids, solvents, beverage containers, pharmaceuticals, tires, and electronics. The British Columbia electronics program sought bids from multiple collection and recycling service providers, and such competition should lead to reduced service costs.

Both the Industry Light and Industry Premium models could include systems that contain a fee, whether visible or invisible, as long as there is significant industry responsibility. However, Canadian systems are striving to move toward product stewardship systems that include the costs of end-of-life management in the product price in the same way as manufacture, distribution, and advertising. Canadian systems are also striving to enhance the premium model by supplemental legislative and regulatory approaches that drive design, much like the WEEE and RoHS directives work together to achieve end-of-life management and design changes. Canadian approaches seek the use of several system tools to develop a full product stewardship program.

Importing EPR to the U.S.

The WEEE and RoHS directives became standards for the type of producer responsibility systems that were sought in the United States many years before their actual enactment dates. While the WEEE Directive addressed the end-of-life management of products, RoHS focused on product design and the elimination of hazardous materials. While these directives changed the way manufacturers designed their products worldwide, they did not automatically result in the transfer and acceptance of producer responsibility in the United States. Product stewardship was a new concept for all stakeholders, requiring a steep learning curve, along with a translation into the U.S. cultural and economic context. In addition, manufacturer executives from the United States often did not have the in-depth knowledge of producer responsibility systems that their European counterparts possessed, even if the same companies were operating under the European systems.

For a market-based U.S. economy that is home to Milton Friedman and is the birthplace of capitalism, the European systems appeared to put too much power in the hands of government at the expense of corporations. In Europe, the EU and its member countries have strong political support from citizens. The governments led with a matured view of waste management fueled by restrictions on disposal space, and disposal costs that soared sooner than rates in other countries. By contrast, in the United States, the federal government has traditionally left waste management decisions to state and local government, many of which have large land masses available for landfills, with correspondingly lower disposal costs. The wide-open American frontier mindset, coupled with a reluctance to interfere with corporate operations and profits, delayed the acceptance of a system that put unprecedented responsibility for waste management on product manufacturers and retailers. Time was needed for these concepts to be embraced by the U.S. public.

The Center for Clean Products and Clean Technologies at the University of Tennessee hosted the country's first academic symposium on EPR in November 1994. In cooperation with U.S. EPA, this initiative sought to extract from the European context EPR policies for implementation in the U.S.[50] In 1995, the President's Council on Sustainable Development adopted "extended product responsibility" as "a voluntary system that ensures responsibility for the environmental effects throughout a product's life cycle by all those involved in the life cycle."[51]

In 1994, the Organization for Economic Cooperation and Development (OECD) started a multi-year research program on Extended Producer Responsibility that culminated in a Guidance Manual for governments (OECD 2001) that acknowledged that responsibilities under EPR are inherently shared by retailers, distributors, and consumers. However, the first guiding principle of EPR policies and programs was "to provide producers with incentives to incorporate changes upstream at the design phase in order to be more environmentally sound."[52]

While federal officials and academics from the United States debated EPR concepts, state and local solid waste officials in the United States were forging their own paths toward product stewardship. In the late 1990s, faced with decreasing waste management budgets, increasing waste, reduced recycling, and an increase in toxic products, state and local officials unknowingly began to trace the steps of their Canadian and European colleagues. They targeted hazardous products, and at the top of the list were heavy metals such as mercury and cadmium. As states began to initiate legislation that would place product end-of-life responsibility on producers, industry began to respond.

Voluntary Industry EPR Program – Rechargeable Batteries

In 1995, the Portable Rechargeable Battery Association established the Rechargeable Battery Recycling Corporation (RBRC) to manage a program for the recovery and recycling of nickel-cadmium (Ni-Cd) batteries. RBRC is a non-profit corporation composed solely of battery manufacturers. Its voluntary take-back program, which began in 1996 under the name *Charge Up to Recycle!*®, was the first national, industry-wide producer responsibility program to be implemented in the United States. Around this time, the U.S EPA estimated that Ni-Cd batteries comprised less than 0.1% of municipal solid waste in the U.S. by weight but accounted for 75% of its cadmium content.[53]

RBRC's effort was prompted by eight state laws with take-back requirements for rechargeable batteries, growing interest in Europe to ban cadmium from rechargeable batteries, and the passage of comprehensive legislation in Minnesota and New Jersey. "Both states require that rechargeable batteries be easily removable from products, be labeled as to content and proper disposal, and be banned from the municipal waste stream. In addition, they require manufacturers to take rechargeable batteries back at their own expense for recycling or proper disposal."[54]

The RBRC program was expanded to include Canada in 1997, and further broadened in scope to include all small rechargeable batteries in 2001, including Ni-Cd, Nickel Metal Hydride (Ni-MH), Lithium Ion (Li-ion), and Small Sealed Lead-Acid (SSLA). In 2004, RBRC enlarged the collection program to include used cell phones, thereby changing the program name to *Call2Recycle*™.

RBRC funds the program by licensing the right to use the organization's chasing arrows recycling logo on products and packaging. Manufacturers contribute funds to RBRC based on their market share. These funds are used to conduct an education campaign and to establish collection sites at retail outlets, municipal locations, and commercial establishments.[55] The program is free for the consumer and for collection sites, which use special prepaid shipping containers provided by RBRC.

To ensure that the RBRC recycling program became the national model, the battery industry sought federal legislation that facilitated its national rollout. The Mercury-Containing and Rechargeable Battery Management Act ("The Battery Act") became law on May 13, 1996. "This legislation reduce[d] barriers to the battery collection and recycling system and avoid[ed] the need to deal with inconsistent legislation in different states."[56] Although the federal Universal Waste Rule (UWR)[57] was in effect at this time, each state needed to adopt the UWR, making implementation of the RBRC cumbersome. The Battery Act established national, uniform labeling requirements for Ni-Cd and certain SSLA rechargeable batteries, and mandates that they be "easily removable" from consumer products. The Act also made the UWR immediately effective in all states, rather than having to wait for them to adopt it one by one. While the RBRC program is voluntary for retailers, both California and New York City passed laws requiring retailers to collect and recycle rechargeable batteries. The batteries are recycled at a metals recovery facility in Pennsylvania. The metals, such as nickel and cadmium, are recovered; the nickel is used to make stainless steel and the cadmium is used to make new batteries.

The RBRC program was an important step for industry in the U.S. since battery manufacturers took full responsibility for their products at end-of-life. The program has also illustrated serious shortcomings of voluntary programs that have no mandated performance goals or reporting requirements and therefore lack accountability.[58] The RBRC system provides an extensive network of collection opportunities for residents to bring spent rechargeable batteries for recycling. At the same time, RBRC provides public education and brands the program with the face of "Al the Tool Man" from the television show, *Home Improvement*. However, a 2004 survey conducted by INFORM, Inc. on the RBRC program found that many stores listed as drop-off sites did not know about the program. Others did not exist at the address given, and few consumers were aware of the program.[59]

While the number of batteries collected each year increases, there is no evidence that the program in North America has succeeded in capturing anywhere near a majority of batteries that need to be collected. In fact, a 2007 Canadian study[60] reported that the recycling rate in the RBRC-run collection program for all secondary (rechargeable) batteries generated in Canada in 2005 was 5.6 percent.

Making Mercury Products a Priority

In the early 1990s, when the public became more aware of the hazardous products in stores and in their homes, HHW managers had not yet begun to differentiate risks posed by the multitude of toxic products on the market, which became a critical distinction as budgets for HHW programs began to shrink. At the outset, programs typically encouraged residents to collect all products. Since most collections were one-day events, funding decisions were made based on the number of cars and not on the contents of products brought by residents. If a car was turned away, there was no way of knowing if it contained a jar of elemental mercury, latex paint, or an empty bottle of hydrogen peroxide.

One of the first states to prioritize waste streams was California, which set up "ABOPs," which were collection sites that focused on antifreeze, batteries (lead acid), oil, and paint. Another early advocate for HHW product prioritization was Massachusetts. In the state's first comprehensive plan for managing hazardous household products in 1996,[61] Massachusetts set a policy of phasing in the collection of priority waste streams into three categories: high volume materials, universal waste materials, and low volume materials. High volume materials included automotive products (used oil, oil filters, antifreeze, auto batteries, and gasoline), leftover paint products, and household batteries (Ni-Cds and button cells). Universal waste materials included certain mercury batteries, thermostats, and pesticides,[62] and low volume materials included solvent-based glues, metal cleaners, toxic art supplies, chemistry sets, photographic chemicals, and other HHW that pose environmental and health risks in relatively small quantities.

With the release of a seminal document in 1996 by state officials, *Mercury in Massachusetts: An Evaluation of Sources, Emissions, Impacts, and Controls*,[63] mercury products became a top priority for the state, including thermometers, thermostats, fluorescent lamps, and household batteries (which, at the time, was the leading source of mercury from products). In-state mercury releases were estimated to contribute 41 percent of total mercury releases from the air to land and water in the state. Mercury-containing products burned in municipal waste combustors were estimated to contribute the largest share of the in-state mercury releases. These mercury emissions entered already stressed water bodies. With over 70 percent of its solid waste being combusted,[64] and with fish advisories issued on a significant number of state water bodies owing to mercury pollution, Massachusetts set out to remove mercury from the waste stream.

NEWMOA Mercury Products Legislation

Massachusetts was not alone in its focus on mercury products. States in the Northeast and Midwest (Great Lakes Region), supported by the Mercury Policy Project, Clean Water Action, and other environmental groups, began to lead a national effort to remove mercury products from the waste stream. In 1998, the Conference of New England Governors and Eastern Canadian Premiers (the "Conference") developed a Mercury Action Plan to reduce mercury pollution in the region. To assist the New England states and the Eastern Canadian provinces in implementing the Action Plan, the conference asked the Northeast Waste Management Officials Association (NEWMOA) to develop model legislation that would synthesize approaches and provide a comprehensive and consistent framework for managing mercury-containing wastes.

Starting in 1999, the states in the Northeast and other parts of the country actively began to use NEWMOA Mercury Education and Reduction Model Legislation to pursue enactment of legislation focused on reducing mercury in products and wastes. The legislation is based on producer responsibility and includes restrictions on the sale of certain mercury-added products, phase-outs and exemptions, labeling, a disposal ban, and a manufacturer collection requirement that reads (in part): "The cost for the collection system must be borne by the manufacturer or manufacturers of mercury-added products. Manufacturers may include the cost of the collection system in the price of the product and may not assess a separate fee for the use of the collection system."[65, 66]

In 1998, Massachusetts went one step further by limiting the amount of mercury emissions from solid waste combustion facilities and imposing a requirement that all solid waste combustion facilities remove mercury-containing products prior to combustion. This regulation,[67] one of the first in the nation, forced companies to set up product take-back systems for the collection and recycling of mercury-containing HHW that, for years, went into the household garbage. As a result of this regulation, the state's subsequent mercury products law (modeled after the NEWMOA model bill), and the closing of several solid waste incinerators, the state was able to show a significant reduction in mercury pollution in 2007 in its water bodies, particularly in the northeastern part of the state.[68]

Voluntary Industry EPR Program—Thermostats

In response to rising concerns over mercury and the threat of legislation in multiple states, a second voluntary industry-wide take-back program was launched. To increase the collection and recycling of retired mercury thermostats, the three largest mercury thermostat manufacturers—Honeywell, General Electric, and White-Rodgers—established a non-profit entity in 1998 called the Thermostat Recycling Corporation (TRC). A typical mercury thermostat contains 3 grams of mercury that can be released into the environment if the thermostat is broken or improperly disposed.[69] The program began in nine states at its inception and became a national program (excluding Alaska and Hawaii) in 2001. The number of thermostats and the amount of mercury collected and recycled annually has increased over time as the program has expanded and taken root.[70]

The TRC program was preceded by a take-back system that Honeywell had established in Minnesota after the state legislature enacted a law in 1992 prohibiting the disposal of mercury thermostats, assigning responsibility for compliance to contractors removing thermostats from households, and requiring manufacturers to provide education and incentives to encourage recycling. Honeywell established several take-back programs to serve a variety of customers. A wholesaler-based, reverse distribution system for heating and cooling contractors was initiated in 1993; a homeowner mail-back program began in 1994; and collections from HHW centers began in 1995. The Honeywell mail-back program was never expanded nationally and was subsequently terminated by the company in 1999 based on cost.[71]

TRC used Honeywell's experience, along with market research, to design a program to serve the heating and cooling wholesaler/contractor distribution chain, which distributes and installs 75 percent of all thermostats.[72] TRC believed that this supply chain could retrieve the greatest number of thermostats. Homeowners, who replace thermostats with units purchased at retail stores, account for approximately 25 percent of thermostats installed. TRC did not provide options for homeowner collection until later in the program, and discontinued all Honeywell-initiated programs except the wholesaler-based reverse distribution system.

In 2004, following concerns about the TRC program performance expressed by state and local governments and a critical report published by NEWMOA,[73] the Product Stewardship Institute began a national dialogue to increase the recycling of mercury thermostats and explore ways to reduce the continued production of mercury thermostats.[74] After conducting extensive interviews with TRC, thermostat manufacturers, and other key stakeholders, PSI developed a Background Summary Report that highlighted the problems, key issues, and potential solutions to managing mercury thermostats. PSI convened two stakeholder meetings in July and October 2004, after which the multi-stakeholder group reached agreement on seven priority initiatives.

Dialogue participants, including Honeywell and TRC, agreed to expand the TRC program to wholesaler chain stores; begin collecting thermostats at contractor locations; begin collecting at HHW facilities nationwide (following a pilot project); and test a financial incentive on contractor recycling behavior in two states. In conjunction with PSI, they also created a comprehensive model thermostat program to provide states with a menu of legislative options from which to choose. As of 2007, 10 states restricted the sale of mercury thermostats,[75] and several followed Maine's lead and introduced legislation in 2007 to maximize the recovery of mercury thermostats following replacement. The two biggest legislative issues that remain to be resolved include performance goals and financial incentives for households and contractors.

National Carpet Recycling Agreement

As states in the Northeast and Midwest targeted mercury products, another Midwest initiative sought to capitalize on existing product stewardship efforts by several carpet manufacturers. In 1999, the Midwestern Workgroup on Carpet Recycling, spearheaded by the states of Minnesota, Iowa, and Wisconsin, with involvement from the U.S. EPA, began a multi-stakeholder dialogue. The regional effort grew into a national initiative over the two-year dialogue. The resulting National Carpet Recycling Agreement was signed on January 8, 2002, by a consortium of industry representatives, including carpet and fiber manufacturers, the Carpet and Rug Institute, state and local government agencies, nongovernmental organizations, and the U.S. EPA.[76]

The agreement set a nationwide goal of 40 percent diversion of carpet from landfills by 2012, including a 15 percent increase in recycling. The agreement outlines the roles and responsibilities for the Carpet America Recovery Effort (CARE), an industry-led, third party organization that assists in the development of a carpet collection and recycling infrastructure, and identifies viable markets for post-consumer carpet. CARE publishes an annual report outlining the results of its efforts. By helping to promote markets for secondary carpet fiber, CARE is seeking to divert carpet from landfills and incinerators into value-added products and to build the collection infrastructure to eventually support carpet-to-carpet recycling.[77]

National Electronics Product Stewardship Initiative (NEPSI)

In 2000, the Product Stewardship Institute identified electronics as the nation's top product in need of an end-of-life management strategy following its survey of state officials. State and local government agencies were concerned about the hazardous components of computers and televisions, the rapid obsolescence of these products, and the significant volume they represent in the waste stream. PSI coined the term National Electronics Product Stewardship Initiative (NEPSI) and began to coordinate state and local agency interests in a product stewardship solution.

The creation of NEPSI caught the attention of electronics manufacturers and others, and in early 2001, the U.S. EPA spearheaded the country's first national dialogue on electronics management. The dialogue included 45 representatives, with about a third each from government, industry, and other stakeholder interests. During the three years of meetings, the Electronic Industries Alliance (EIA) represented manufacturers, while PSI coordinated participation and comment from over 20 state agencies and numerous local governments. The Silicon Valley Toxics Coalition played a significant role representing environmental interests. The meetings were facilitated by the Center for Clean Products and Clean Technologies at the University of Tennessee.

Although the NEPSI dialogue did not result in a national agreement, it was a significant turning point in the United States. Since it was the first large multi-stakeholder product dialogue, it attracted national attention and a large commitment of resources. NEPSI also became the first dialogue, along with the national carpet discussions, in which industry consciously committed to take a product stewardship approach. This transformation took several years to evolve and was heightened in response to state legislative pressure that started to increase as the bid for a national negotiated solution started to wane.

As a result of the increased national attention, companies began to compete on voluntary take-back initiatives. These systems became significant transitional solutions offered by companies to meet the growing expectation for producer responsibility. HP, Dell, and a coalition of ARF supporters led by Panasonic, Sony, Sharp, and Philips were the first to offer free periodic collections of scrap electronics. By 2006, a number of electronics companies offered some type of end-of-life collection program for their products, with some providing money-back coupons on the sale of new equipment. In that year, Dell became the first company in the United States to collect its own end-of-life equipment for free from consumers. In August 2007, Sony followed with a collection program in conjunction with Waste Management to collect Sony products for free at specific locations, while other companies still charged the consumer for take-back service.

In 2004, stakeholders negotiated a formal resolution facilitated by EIA, PSI, and the University of Tennessee. The resolution outlined a scope of products to be covered by federal legislation and a hybrid financing system that would start with an ARF to cover historic and orphan products but transition to producer responsibility at a later date based on a series of criteria to be determined. The resolution put a halt on further discussions until manufacturers could come back with a viable system to which they all agreed.

The next time that a national proposal was floated by a coalition of manufacturers was 2007. By then, NEPSI had disbanded and states focused on passing their own legislation. The manufacturer ARF coalition that was formed during the NEPSI discussions successfully passed the first electronics end-of-life management law in the country, the CA ARF. Following this development, multi-stakeholder coalitions formed in each state to challenge ARFs and push for producer responsibility. HP developed model state legislation and worked with influential environmental groups, including the Silicon Valley Toxics Coalition, Computer TakeBack Campaign, Washington Citizens for Resource Conservation, and the Natural Resources Council of Maine, as well as charities, retailers, and governments, to pass electronics legislation.

In 2005, Maine became the first state to pass a law based on producer responsibility. Since local governments assumed the collection responsibility, it was called "partial producer responsibility" in the U.S. Maryland passed the third electronics law, which was partly funded by a manufacturer registration fee. When Washington became the fourth state with an electronics recycling law, it signaled a clear national trend toward full producer responsibility. By 2007, nine states passed electronics recycling laws, with only the first one being an ARF, while the rest are some version of producer responsibility. Two, however, only cover computers and not televisions.[78]

The NEPSI process laid the foundation for each of these state laws, as most of the participants learned about the positions and interests of manufacturers, retailers, recyclers, and other stakeholders through the many NEPSI meetings. Every aspect of the electronics end-of-life management issue was discussed during these meetings, including the scope of products to be covered, reuse and recycling infrastructure, financial payments to provide incentives for collection, financing system options, environmentally sound processing standards, performance goals, creation of a stewardship organization, and federal preemption of state laws.

As a result of the numerous NEPSI interactions, strong relationships formed among stakeholders that led to important spin-off projects and initiatives outside the process. For example, NEPSI inspired the development of EPEAT and other procurement related initiatives. In addition, Northwest Product Stewardship Council member agencies that participated in the NEPSI process launched the Take it Back Network, composed of small retailers and other businesses that provided collection service and demonstrated the convenience and practicality of retail take-back.

To help fill a void by an absence of retailer participation in NEPSI, U.S. EPA initiated a series of key retail pilot projects with Staples, Office Depot, and Good Guys that lay the foundation for retail participation in electronics collections.[79] These projects were part of EPA's wider Plug-In To eCycling program, which is a partnership between EPA and consumer electronics manufacturers and retailers to offer consumers more opportunities to donate or recycle their used electronics.[80] In 2007, Staples became the first retailer to provide significant electronic recycling services at all of its stores nationwide after having worked with PSI and the Take it Back Network to pilot the program. Finally, the National Center for Electronics Recycling was formed to help fulfill information needs identified by

NEPSI participants. These examples are only a sample of the many activities that built on the knowledge and relationships developed through NEPSI.

This first national product stewardship dialogue has become a reference point for new initiatives on other product categories, as well as a background for continued work on national electronics legislation. While states without electronics legislation continue to push for their own state laws, many groups continue to seek federal legislation that will bring electronics end-of-life management systems to all states in the country. In addition, many that participated in NEPSI have provided key leadership and experience to other emerging stewardship initiatives.

The Growth of U.S. Product Stewardship Organizations

Northwest Product Stewardship Council

Following a decade of striking out on their own, and in the footsteps of the regional mercury products efforts, states began to mobilize for the specific purpose of establishing multi-state product stewardship agreements. "In 1998, aware of a growing international interest in and implementation of EPR, a small committed group of solid waste professionals from government agencies in the greater Seattle area began meeting to learn more about this policy tool, and how it might be used domestically." This group of professionals chose to call themselves the Northwest Product Stewardship Council (NWPSC) because "product stewardship" encompassed both product and producer responsibility, and was easier for the public to understand.[81] The U.S. EPA provided key support for the council.

The group got a significant early boost when the Seattle City Council adopted a new solid waste plan called "On the Path to Sustainability," "… which adopt[ed] zero waste as a guiding principle, and product stewardship as one of the programs for achieving future goals." Such visible policy support in conjunction with growing participation from other local governments in Washington and Oregon justified staff and funding for product stewardship, which was critical to the growth and coordination of the regional effort.[82] The NWPSC's initial focus was on the purchase of computer (and related) equipment with environmental attributes, and the development of purchasing guidelines for procurement officials. These efforts pushed for design changes through market dynamics.

In April 2000, the council held the country's first regional product stewardship conference, which attracted nearly 200 attendees from government, business, and non-profit organizations. The goal of the conference was to "… expand awareness of product stewardship and develop a structure in which ongoing dialogue and action could continue."[83] In addition to computers, the council targeted televisions, tires, medical industry waste, apparel, and retail grocers as other priority products and sectors. By 2007, the NWPSC refocused its priorities on the following projects: electronics, pharmaceuticals, beverage containers, mercury products, paint, and tires.[84] The council maintains a loose-knit structure that allows it the flexibility to pool resources to fund product-focused projects. It is also increasingly involved in policy development, and was a critical player in developing and passing Washington state's product stewardship-based electronics recycling law. The council has become a model for other state and regional councils around the United States. One of its core strengths is its ability to conduct important pilot projects and initiatives with broad-based regional support that can be replicated in other U.S. regions. The council also coordinates the regional input from multiple agencies in national dialogues, which allows state and local officials to participate in numerous activities without over-burdening any single entity.

North American Hazardous Materials Management Association

As the Northwest regional effort was blossoming, a 1999 conference of the North American Hazardous Materials Management Association (NAHMMA) hosted several speakers from the U.S., Canada, and Europe on the topic of EPR. Founded in 1993, NAHMMA grew to 500 members in 2007, and is dedicated to pollution prevention and reducing the toxicity of municipal waste streams. The conference highlighted the efforts of British Columbia's impressive product stewardship programs.

The introduction of these product stewardship ideas to NAHMMA conference participants caught hold of a large group of U.S. state and local HHW managers who were struggling with collection rates of an estimated 3 to 5% on even highly hazardous products. These officials were ripe for a new solution that would solve their dilemma of limited government funds while faced with increasing public demand for HHW services.

One state official from Massachusetts responsible for HHW management realized that state and local officials around the country, acting independently, could not command the attention of industry. However, a group of government officials acting together would have greater leverage in convincing manufacturers and retailers to take greater responsibility for the lifecycle impacts of their products. State and regional efforts were essential, but so was a national network that would link not only government officials across the nation but all those working toward the goal of sustainability and better product management—from industry, environmental groups, academia, and other sectors.

Product Stewardship Institute, Inc.

In December 2000, the Product Stewardship Institute (PSI), a national non-profit membership-based organization, was founded to serve as the collective voice of state and local governments across the country on product stewardship issues. As a kick-off to its creation, PSI coordinated the country's first national forum for government officials to discuss product stewardship policies and programs. Over 100 government officials from 20 states attended the two-day national Product Stewardship Forum. Prior to the forum, PSI surveyed state officials across the country to determine their five top waste management priorities for which a product stewardship approach was recommended. These five products—electronics, paint, mercury-containing products, pesticides, and tires—became the focus of the forum agenda. PSI has since worked on the following additional product sectors: mercury thermostats, fluorescent lighting, paint, pharmaceuticals, radioactive devices, gas cylinders, pesticides, tires, beverage containers, and phone books.[85]

PSI's mission is to "… pursue initiatives to ensure that all those involved in the lifecycle of a product share responsibility for reducing its health and environmental impacts."[86] PSI has a Board of Directors composed of state and local government officials and an Adjunct Council composed of businesses, environmental groups, and other organizations.

PSI's five-point *Principles of Product Stewardship* serves as a guiding compass for the organization and its members. These *Principles* were developed in 2001 by a consensus of government officials and were synthesized from policy efforts of the NWPSC, Minnesota, Oregon, U.S. EPA, and international EPR agencies and organizations. The five principles include: (1) shared responsibility, (2) internalizing a product's lifecycle cost into the purchase price, (3) providing incentives for manufacturers to make cleaner products and follow sustainable management practices, (4) flexibility to achieve goal-oriented results, and (5) specific roles for industry, government, and consumers. PSI's *Principles of Product Stewardship* became a simple but effective way to spread the concept of product stewardship, as many influential organizations and agencies adopted these *Principles* in whole or in part and, in turn, spread the word further to their members.[87]

PSI brings priority waste management issues to the attention of manufacturers and retailers, and seeks collaborative solutions through a mediated series of meetings. PSI has developed a four-phased model for engaging stakeholders, involving research, dialogue, implementing agreements, and evaluating outcomes.[88] Through the PSI dialogue process, stakeholders agree on the basic problem before determining the dialogue focus and goals. PSI facilitates discussions on issues that lead to prioritized strategies on which agreements are based. Stakeholders jointly implement and evaluate most dialogue projects.

By August 2007, PSI membership included 40 states and 46 local governments, representing over 80 percent of the U.S. population.[89] This broad-based support ensures that product stewardship and its message of fiscal and environmental relief are well understood by those who establish our nation's environmental laws and policies. PSI has developed a multi-stakeholder network of government, industry, and environmental representatives, and fosters communication with these groups through an annual forum, conference calls on a myriad of timely issues, and other means.

State and Regional Councils

As product stewardship spread throughout the country, manufacturers and retailers began to engage with other stakeholders, seeking the elusive balance between their responsibility to shareholders and their societal responsibility to eliminate the lifecycle impacts caused by their products. For most, it was a quick lesson in options to reduce waste, reduce the use of hazardous materials in product manufacture, take back their products, and change the way that recycling programs were financed. The time became ripe for state and local governments to push for a stronger EPR model, one that directly involved manufacturers and provided them with financial incentives to change the design of their products.

In 2003, the Product Policy Institute (PPI) was founded to "advance sustainable production and consumption and good governance." PPI is a not-for-profit research and communication organization that believes that government should set and enforce sustainable industry performance standards that are based on producer responsibility, a polluter pays approach, and precaution.[90] Working with local governments in California, PPI assisted in the formation of the California Product Stewardship Council (CPSC) in 2006, which was modeled after the NWPSC and the British Columbia Product Stewardship Council. CPSC galvanized local government support for producer responsibility, and prepared these agencies to influence state, regional, and national policy, at times in conjunction with PSI and other organizations. By 2007, other regions of the country began to mobilize support for their own regional product stewardship councils, including the Midwest and Northeast.

Topics in Product Stewardship and HHW

Framework Legislation

Initial product stewardship efforts involved a product-by-product approach. Stakeholder groups were formed for each product topic (*i.e.,* mercury thermostats, paint, or electronics), and focused on developing a system for managing each product separately. Some of the program elements developed to manage these products are similar for most products, although other elements are unique to a product and its particular set of stakeholders. The next generation of product stewardship systems will seek ways to take advantage of similarities among products to create efficiencies, and to identify those elements that require a product-specific approach.

British Columbia passed a framework Recycling Regulation in 2004 that includes nine product categories, including HHW.[91] The Recycling Regulation was enacted under the authority of the Environmental Management Act and provides a framework for EPR, including core requirements applying to all programs and schedules for the implementation of each product category covered by the regulation. The governing political party (cabinet) can add product categories without new legislation. The new regulation unifies and coordinates key elements (*i.e.,* funding, level of producer accountability, performance measures, etc.) that were previously included in separate regulations for each product category. Having a framework regulation makes it easier to add new product categories, and it creates a level playing field between programs as all producers are operating under the same rules.

The Canadian province of Manitoba also drafted a series of stewardship regulations in January 2006 that identified the need for a common strategy for managing all HHW, along with electronics, tires, and packaging/printed paper.[92] Green Manitoba, an agency of the provincial government, is scheduled to finalize the regulations by September 2007. Manitoba's authority comes from its Waste Reduction and Prevention (WRAP) Act that enables the Minister of Conservation to enact regulations by Order in Council. It requires the development of an annual WRAP Strategy Report and provides for the designation of products or materials for waste reduction responsibilities. A variety of economic instruments and producer responsibility requirements can be established under the Act, including product levies, dedicated funds, deposits, and return-to-retail requirements.[93]

State and local agencies in the U.S. have also recognized the need to develop framework legislation, with the Northwest Product Stewardship Council governments and the state of California taking a lead. The advantage of a broad framework is that a state legislature can approve an overall approach to product stewardship that will not require repeated trips to the legislature. Instead, adding product categories and program details could be left to administrative agencies. Such an approach will save time for all parties, which will translate into greater environmental protection at lower cost.

Mercury Stockpiling – Eliminating the Toxic Product Loop

As scientists and engineers find substitutes for toxic materials in products, our society will begin to reduce the mining and generation of these materials, use up what we have, and stockpile the remainder. However, hazardous materials removed from end-of-life products may still become ingredients in new products. It is ineffective to spend large sums of money to divert hazardous products from the waste stream if the toxic material is being used in a new product and sent back into commerce. To reverse this trend, congressional legislation has been introduced to develop a permanent repository in the U.S. for the stockpiling of mercury and to ban the export of mercury from the U.S., including mercury-containing products collected in HHW programs.[94] Mercury is mined worldwide, increasing the amounts entering the market. Mercury is also reintroduced into the market through municipal programs that collect mercury thermostats, fluorescent lamps, auto switches, dental amalgam, and other products. Companies that recycle these products distill the mercury and sell it on the global market. Other hazardous household products might also require a similar stockpiling approach, including rechargeable batteries (nickel, cadmium, other metals) and automobile batteries (lead).

Institutionalizing Change in Agencies and Corporations

Product stewardship is a new concept. It requires all of us to think differently. Instead of government agencies issuing unilateral legislation or regulations for response and comment, product stewardship is best implemented as a collaborative strategy. It is a new way of doing business, and it requires that stakeholders have faith in a process that will result in the best policies, regulations, laws, or programs. Any break in communication can undermine the initiative.

For product stewardship to be fully integrated throughout a company or agency, it needs support from those at the top, as well as from those who will implement the initiatives, and everyone in between. Sudden changes in staffing, especially those in high-level decision-making positions, can prove to be detrimental to product stewardship efforts. Since collaborative approaches are based on relationships, it is important that, when people change positions or leave a company or agency, new staff pick up where others leave off. These sudden changes in company or agency positions have been a significant barrier to multi-stakeholder negotiations, which often involve incremental progress over several years. These changes have, at times, led to distrust, reversing years of progress. The situation can often be avoided by a policy or declaration from a company's board of directors or CEO, a Memorandum of Understanding (MOU) by a multi-stakeholder dialogue group, or from an agency's top environmental official.

The states of Minnesota and Oregon were the first to develop agency-wide policies in the U.S. that defined product stewardship and set out a plan for managing waste streams in a new way. Minnesota attempted to codify this approach in legislation, which was eventually defeated, although it remains as a guiding principle for agency staff. In 2007, the California Integrated Waste Management Board (CIWMB) became the first state agency to take a strong producer responsibility approach by issuing a policy (Strategic Directive 5) that directs staff to pursue strategies that will require manufacturers to develop systems for the take-back of their products at the end of their life. The directive reads, in part, "It is a core value of the CIWMB that producers assume the responsibility for the safe steward-ship of their materials in order to promote environmental sustainability...The CIWMB will seek legislation to foster 'cradle-to-cradle' producer responsibility."[95]

On the corporate side, the National Paint and Coatings Association officially passed a Resolution of its Board of Directors in March 2007 that stated the intention of paint manu-facturers to take responsibility for leftover paint management, with certain limitations to be further negotiated. The NPCA resolution was industry-wide and gave government offi-cials the assurance they needed to continue negotiating instead of moving toward legisla-tive initiatives. The resolution followed four years of multi-stakeholder negotiations that included two MOUs signed or endorsed by over 60 entities engaged in the Paint Product Stewardship Initiative.

Product Stewardship, HHW, and Global Warming

In 2007, public attention finally turned toward the potential impacts of global warming, and residents began seeking ways to take personal action to reduce their own impacts. This dynamic creates the opportunity for residents to understand the wider impacts that their consumption habits have on the environment. A much-needed "tipping point" has occurred in public consciousness.[96]

Awareness of the issue presents an opportunity for policies to be developed for prod-ucts that impact global warming. One of the first actions that consumers can take is to change their light bulbs from incandescent to fluorescent. Stepping into the fray, Wal-Mart announced plans to sell millions of compact fluorescent lamps (CFLs) as a gesture to do its part to reduce global environmental impacts. The use of fluorescents will aid in reducing greenhouse gases and mercury emissions since less mercury-containing coal will need to be burned to produce the energy needed to use the new light bulbs.[97] The problem is that the fluorescent bulbs contain mercury, and neither Wal-Mart nor other retailers promot-ing their sale initially informed the public of the need to collect these products when they became waste.

Within a few months of Wal-Mart's sales blitz, numerous initiatives started to address the need to remove CFLs and other fluorescent lamps from the waste stream. EPA held meetings with retailers and manufacturers; the Vermont Department of Environmental Conservation completed a successful pilot project with Ace Hardware and other retail-ers; the Maine Department of Environmental Protection started statewide retail collec-tions; the Product Policy Institute, in conjunction with the Northwest Product Stewardship Council, the British Columbia Product Stewardship Council, and the California Product Stewardship Council, wrote a letter to Wal-Mart seeking a manufacturer take-back pro-gram; Wal-Mart conducted a five-state collection pilot project; and the Product Steward-ship Institute began a national multi-stakeholder dialogue to address a product stewardship solution for all fluorescent lighting. HHW program managers might do well to incorporate global warming messages when the connection can be made between hazardous household products and energy use, conservation, or global impacts. Fluorescent lamps provide the perfect opportunity to engage stakeholders working on global warming with those working on HHW and product stewardship.

Product Stewardship, HHW, and Environmental Groups

Surprisingly, government officials, and not the environmental community, educated the public about HHW impacts. For years, HHW program managers struggled within their own professional community about how to fund and manage programs. Early attempts to engage environmental groups on product stewardship issues were also difficult, as these groups were working on global warming, international environmental issues, and/or large-scale problems, and staff members were stretched thin. Few could be enlisted for national product stewardship dialogues, including NEPSI, which was represented for most of the dialogue by a single but influential organization, the Silicon Valley Toxics Coalition. This group has long been a leader on electronics management issues.

The dynamic is changing, as environmental groups have become major proponents of producer responsibility and have been vocal on both statewide and national initiatives. The growth in the ability of these groups to engage on the issues has created opportunities for other organizations and government agencies to develop strong coalitions in support of product stewardship policies. In addition, as attention has shifted to the role that consumers can play in reducing greenhouse gases, such as buying CFLs, the environmental community is expected to create more partnerships with government and industry stakeholders.

Often though, environmental groups are hesitant to participate in stakeholder dialogues since much of their power is derived through legislative initiatives or high-visibility unilateral tactics. The engagement methods these groups choose will continue to be diverse, at times collaborative and at other times combative, depending on the issue and the stakeholder group.

Corporate Change – By Company and Industry Sector

As mentioned previously, changing corporate America is akin to turning a ship in the harbor: it must be done slowly and carefully, or great collateral damage can occur. But if done right, it can be a smooth experience for all. The barriers that must be overcome are significant, and negotiations require an ongoing positive attitude that change can occur in a way that does not wreak havoc in the marketplace. Government regulations that are barriers must be changed. Long-standing ways of doing business must slowly be undone, and remade.

Corporate change will often take place in two ways. First, it requires one or more industry leaders that understand the business opportunities and innovations needed to service a new market, a new trend, or new consumer demand. Second, it very often requires industry-wide communication through trade associations. These two elements often need to be present for the successful integration of product stewardship in an entire industry sector. In some cases, an industry leader will step out to develop a pilot project to show that a particular program can be accomplished. This was the case when Staples successfully implemented and documented its pilot computer take-back program in 24 retail stores and with 14 commercial customers in the northeast in 2004. Other change occurs through association leadership, such as the National Paint and Coatings Association, which led the industry to develop two MOUs. However, strongest change occurs when companies within a sector take leadership roles but remain a part of the association and the overall initiative.

Corporate change becomes fully integrated when a company's product end-of-life management program becomes a core business interest. Once companies understand this business aspect not as a burden but as a way to meet consumer demand and take a step toward sustainability, they will manage their responsibility with the same efficiencies and best management practices as they manage their core business.

Green Chemistry

Product stewardship began as a means to address the lack of funding for end-of-life management of wastes. The first steps were like putting a finger in a dike to stop the gush of wasted water. A next big step for this movement is to change product chemistries and design better products. There will be no more after-the-fact-scramble to figure out how to collect, transport, recycle, or dispose of a hazardous product. We need to move from reaction to planning. Green chemistry offers a systematic approach to designing products that are environmentally superior. This approach consists of a deliberate consideration of impacts for each material, and can include a multi-stakeholder process to establish criteria for materials use and product development. The movement in green chemistry has been particularly motivated by the "precautionary principle," which is an approach that advocates for the avoidance of potential hazards to save resources in the long term. (See the Appendix B for further discussion of Green Chemistry.)

Three-Legged Stool – Economic, Environmental, and Social Considerations

In his 2007 book, *Blessed Unrest*,[98] Paul Hawken writes that environmentalists are waiting for those in the social movement who fight for workers' rights, child labor, better wages, and related issues to hop on the environmental bandwagon, but that it has to be the other way around. Both movements have a great deal to gain from one another, and over time, their methods and interests are likely to blur. There is little doubt that the two movements have to begin to work more closely together.

In the context of HHW, those involved in the manufacture of toxic products have similar interests to those who manage them at the end-of-life. In both cases, their jobs would be safer and less complicated if those products were made without hazardous materials. Since economic factors are always a consideration in environmental and social policies, that element comprises the third leg of the proverbial stool. For example, the Basel Action Network[99] highlighted the problems that arise when electronic scrap sent to third world countries for recycling is mismanaged in rudimentary recycling operations. While the companies sending this scrap abroad from the U.S. and other nations found a lively reuse and upgrade market for some of these materials and an economical way to recycle, there is no doubt that poorly managed recycling practices in some countries contribute to significant impacts on the health of local workers, the public, and the environment. Environmental groups and those working on social issues will need to jointly address similar issues in the future.

Global Harmonization of Environmental Policies

While product stewardship often encourages local production and consumption, it cannot ignore the market dynamics of international trade. The RoHS Directive not only affected products sold in Europe, but also in the United States and worldwide. It did not make economic sense to manufacture different products for different markets. Now that RoHS is the international standard for restrictions on hazardous materials in electronic products, it should become a legal standard also in the US. Furthermore, any additional changes to RoHS should be considered on a global basis so that implementation of RoHS becomes global practice. This harmonization of environmental policies will begin to occur on an international scale as governments, non-profit organizations, and companies begin to collaborate across borders. Global consistency will result in greater certainty for business, cost savings, and leveling the playing field regarding environmental and social criteria. A coalition of American, Canadian, and European standards might provide the leverage needed to increase the environmental and social standards related to product manufacture in countries such as China, where many products that flood the American market are manufactured under substandard conditions.

Connecting People to Products

In his 1955 classic, *The Sane Society*, social psychologist Eric Fromm unwittingly forecast the future of the product stewardship movement when he said: "The process of consumption is as alienated as the process of production....The act of consumption should be a ... meaningful, human, productive, experience. In our culture, there is little of that. Consuming is essentially the satisfaction of artificially stimulated phantasies ... alienated from our concrete, real selves....We are surrounded by things of whose nature and origin we know nothing....We do not know how bread is made, how cloth is woven, how a table is manufactured, how glass is made. We consume, as we produce, without any concrete relatedness to the objects with which we deal; we live in a world of things, and our only connection with them is that we know how to manipulate or to consume them."[100]

People around the world are disconnected from the products they use, including who made them, how they were made, and how they got to the store where they were bought. Would we buy a television if we knew that a child produced it for fifteen cents a day? Would we buy a toy if we knew the batteries inside contained mercury? Would we want our computer to go to a recycler if we knew that company sent it to locations where metals were extracted using acids that pollute local waterways?

Many products today are manufactured with little thought to the social and environmental impacts they have all along their lifecycle. Government has subsidized the end-of-life management systems needed to reduce these impacts. Product stewardship has enlightened the public about the end-of-life management costs of everyday products. That is only the beginning. We now need to understand and communicate the social and environmental impacts of manufacturing these products, as well as other aspects of a product's lifecycle. We need manufacturers to make superior products that perform as well or better than the current product, are comparable in cost, and readily available. We also need to create a level playing field in product manufacture so that the true costs of making, using, and disposing of a product are evident to the consumer. Only then can sustainable products compete fairly.

Once environmentally and socially superior products are available as alternatives, a major challenge will be to educate the public in a manner that allows people to make informed choices about the products they buy. Consumers will need to differentiate products. Through simplified lifecycle analyses, company and product environmental footprints, and other technical tools, consumers might soon be able to compare companies and their products ... quickly and easily. Ecological labels and product certifications show promise as a means to communicate important information to the consumer about the relative strengths of comparable products. Misleading claims, however, make it necessary for government, business, and environmental groups to work together to ensure that only real claims are allowed and false claims are punished.

Product stewardship has cracked open the old way of thinking about waste management, but we are still a long way from consumer-driven markets based on information about the environmental and social implications of product decisions. But that day will come.

About the Author

Scott Cassel is the Executive Director and Founder of the Product Stewardship Institute, Inc. His professional experiences have focused on product and waste stream management issues at the local, state, and national levels, and the development of product stewardship systems to ensure the environmental sustainability of consumer products throughout their lifecycles.

Acknowledgments

The author would like to thank the following individuals for their time and expertise in providing valuable comments to the draft chapter: Duncan Bury, Environment Canada; Sarah Bolthrunis, Product Stewardship Institute; Ron Driedger, British Columbia Used Oil Management Association; Jim Ferguson, Green Manitoba; Bette Fishbein, formerly with INFORM, Inc.; Dave Galvin, Local Hazardous Waste Management Program in King County, WA; Garth Hickle, Minnesota Pollution Control Agency; Sego Jackson, Snohomish County, WA; Hans Korfmacher, Gillette and European Recycling Platform; David Laws, British Columbia Ministry of the Environment; Clare Lindsay, U.S. EPA; Erin Linsky, Product Stewardship Institute and David Stitzhal, FullCircle Environmental.

Notes

1. The term "producer" is used in Europe to identify those who place a product for the first time on the market, which can be a manufacturer, an importer, or even a retailer that imports products directly.

2. According to Wikipedia, John Elkington, co-founder of the business consultancy Sustain-Ability, coined the phrase "the triple bottom line" in 1994, and expanded and articulated the concept in his 1998 book, *Cannibals with Forks: The Triple Bottom Line of 21st Century Business.* TBL is a business principle that measures corporate performance along three lines: profits, environmental sustainability, and social responsibility, and that a company's responsibility be to stakeholders rather than shareholders.

3. See Basel Action Network video, *Exporting Harm,* available at: http://www.ban.org/main/film.html.

4. Alexis Cain *et al.,* "Substance Flow Analysis of Mercury Intentionally Used in Products in the United States," *Journal of Industrial Ecology,* Volume 11, No. 3, 2007, pp. 61–75.

5. Hans Korfmacher, July 30, 2007, email communication.

6. Beverly Thorpe, Iza Kruszewska, and Alexandra McPherson of Clean Production Action, "Extended Producer Responsibility: A Waste Management Strategy that cuts waste, creates a cleaner environment, and saves taxpayers money," 2004, p.13.

7. Margaret Walls, *Extended Producer Responsibility Policies and Product Design: Economic Theory and Selected Case Studies*, OECD Environment Directorate Report ENV/EPOC/WGWPR(2005)9/FINAL (Paris, France: February 2006).

8. Cradle-to-cradle product management is a concept made accessible to the public by William McDonough and Michael Braungart and in their book, *Cradle-to-Cradle, Remaking the Way We Make Things,* North Point Press, 2002. Available at: http://www.mcdonough.com/cradle_to_cradle.htm.

9. Hans Korfmacher, July 30, 2007, email communication.

10. According to the Battery Council International, more than 98 percent of all battery lead and plastic is recycled. BCI webpage: http://www.batterycouncil.org/environment.html. August 9, 2007.

11. See Maryland's electronics recycling law: Environment Article, Title 9, Water, Ice and Sanitary Facilities, Subtitle 17 Office of Recycling, Part IV Statewide Computer Recycling Pilot Program). The law became effective on July 1, 2005. See Maryland Department of Environment website, at: http://www.mde.state.md.us/Programs/LandPrograms/Recycling/SpecialProjects/ecycling.asp.

12. See Minnesota Session Laws, Chapter 48, available on Minnesota Pollution Control website, at: http://www.pca.state.mn.us/oea/stewardship/electronics-law.cfm, August 9, 2007.

13. The Maine Department of Environmental Protection recycling goals for mercury thermostats in its 2006 law are equivalent to at least 125 pounds of mercury per year from mercury-added thermostats by January 1, 2009, and 160 pounds by January 1, 2010. The rate recycled is a percentage of the number of mercury thermostats estimated to be removed from the wall and replaced with another thermostat.

14. Hans Korfmacher: "Some Learnings from the Establishment of the First Pan-European WEEE Compliance Scheme: The European Recycling Platform," presentation at Product Stewardship Institute Forum, San Francisco, May 2007, http://www.erp-recycling.org.

15. When incorporated in 1998, TRC included three companies. A fourth company, Nordyne, joined in 2007.

16. The European Recycling Platform was established by Hewlett Packard, Sony, Electrolux, and Braun in 2002. By 2007, it represented more than 900 manufacturers with a market share of about 25% in Europe.

17. Historic products are those that have already been sold prior to the date of any newly implemented system.

18. Hans Korfmacher, August 15, 2007, email communication.

19. Hans Korfmacher: "Some Learnings from the Establishment of the First Pan-European WEEE Compliance Scheme: The European Recycling Platform," presentation at Product Steward-ship Institute Forum, San Francisco, May 2007, http://www.erp-recycling.org.

20. For information on the Staples project, see www.productstewardship.us.

21. The national paint dialogue was initially funded by state and local governments, and the U.S. EPA. The collaborative projects included in the MOU were also funded by these entities, but also included funding from the National Paint and Coatings Association and paint recyclers.

22. The 1st MOU included the following projects: the development of a recycled paint stan-dard with Green Seal to increase markets for recycled paint; a lifecycle assessment and cost-benefit analysis that compares drying and disposal of leftover latex paint to reuse and recycling; a study to determine the infrastructure needed (and the cost) to collect, transport, and recycle leftover paint; and several projects to reduce and reuse leftover paint. For more information, see: www.productsteward-ship.us/PaintProjectsandInitiatives.

23. Fishbein, "Industry Program to Collect Nickel-Cadmium (Ni-Cd) Batteries," Section 7.4. Available at: http://informinc.org/recyclenicd.php

24. Hans Korfmacher, August 15, 2007, email communication.

25. Ceres website: http://www.ceres.org/coalitionandcompanies/. 6 July 2007.

26. EPEAT website: http://www.epeat.net/. 6 July 2007.

27. Wal-Mart website, August 15, 2007. http://www.walmartstores.com/GlobalWMStoresWeb/navigate.do?catg=677.

28. Home Depot website: http://www6.homedepot.com/ecooptions/. August 15, 2007.

29. Amy Stodghill, "Whole Foods Unveils Their Own Fair Trade Label," Green Options, March 30, 2007, at: http://greenoptions.com/2007/03/30/whole_foods_unveils_their_own_fair_trade_label.

30. Hans Korfmacher, August 15, 2007, email communication.

31. The Massachusetts beverage return law was enacted in 1981 but implemented in 1983.

32. HP website, August 15, 2007, at: http://www.hp.com/hpinfo/globalcitizenship/environ-ment/recycle/ecoupon.html.

33. Samuel Perkins, "Pollution Prevention and Profitability: A Primer for Lenders," Northeast Waste Management Officials' Association, 1996. For full text see: http://cleanerproduction.com/Training/Banks/Refs/NEWMOA%20P2%20Primer%20for%20Lenders.doc

34. California, Connecticut, Delaware, Hawaii, Iowa, Maine, Massachusetts, Michigan, New York, Oregon, Vermont. www.bottlebill.org.

35. Dr. Jeffery Morris, Bill Smith, Rick Hlavka, "Economic and Environmental Benefits of a Deposit System for Beverage Containers in the State of Washington," 5. (Prepared for the City of Tacoma Solid Waste Management, 2005) Available at: http://www.bottlebill.org/assets/pdfs/legisla-tion/WABottleBillFinalReport.pdf

36. Bill Sheehan and Helen Spiegelman, "Extended Producer Responsibility Policies in the United States and Canada: History and Status" (For publication in *Governance and Sustainability: The Case of Integrated Product Policy*, Heidelberg, Germany, 2005)

37. For current information on state scrap tire laws in the U.S., see: http://www.rma.org/scrap_tires/state_issues/.

38. For current information on lead-acid battery laws in the U.S., see: http://www.batterycoun-cil.org/states.html.

39. Sheehan and Spiegelman, "Extended Producer Responsibility Policies in the United States and Canada," 14

40. The section on the German/European Packaging Ordinance was partially written by Hans Korfmacher, with assistance from Bette Fishbein. It was edited by Scott Cassel.

41. The Ordinance on the Avoidance and Recovery of Packaging Waste came into force in Germany on June 12, 1991.

42. Hans Korfmacher contributed to the writing of this section on the WEEE and RoHS Directives.

43. Directive 2002/96/EC of the European Parliament and of the EU Council of 27 January 2003. For entire text see: http://eurlex.europa.eu/LexUriServ/LexUriServ.do?uri=CELEX:32002L0096: EN:HTML.

44. "Historic" products are those that have already been sold prior to the date of any newly implemented system. Under WEEE, manufacturers also share collective responsibility for "orphan" and "abandoned" products. "Orphan" products are those manufactured by companies that are no longer in business and have not been purchased by another company. "Abandoned" products are those whose brand name cannot be identified.

45. The costs associated with the management of historical WEEE from sources other than private households are borne by producers. "By 13 August 2005, financing is to be covered by producers in the case of waste from holders other than private households and placed on the market after that date. In the case of waste from products placed on the market before 13 August 2005, management costs are to be borne by producers. However, Member States may provide that users be made responsible, partly or totally, for this financing." http://www.weee-forum.org/legislation_eu.htm

46. Press release issued by Greenpeace International, the European Environmental Bureau and Friends of the Earth Europe, September 28, 2006, at: http://www.eeb.org/press/280906_pr_EU_missing_opportunity_innovation_electronics.htm

47. Directive 2002/95/EC of the European Parliament and of the EU Council of 27 January 2003. For entire text see: http://eurlex.europa.eu/LexUriServ/LexUriServ.do?uri=CELEX:32002L0095: EN:HTML.

48. For the status of electronics laws in China and other nations, see: http://www.productstewardship.net/policiesElectronicsIntl.html.

49. Duncan Bury, Environment Canada, Presentation to the Association of Municipal Recycling Coordinators, Extended Producer Responsibility (EPR) Funding and The Future, Hockley Valley, February 14, 2007.

50. Gary A. Davis, Patricia S. Dillon, Bette K. Fishbein, and Catherine A. Wilt, "Extended Producer Responsibility: A New Principle for Product-Oriented Pollution Prevention," (prepared for the U.S. EPA Office of Solid Waste, 1997)

51. Sheehan and Spiegelman, "Extended Producer Responsibility Policies in the United States and Canada," 15.

52. Sheehan and Spiegelman, "Extended Producer Responsibility Policies in the United States and Canada," 16.

53. Fishbein, "Industry Program to Collect Nickel-Cadmium (Ni-Cd) Batteries," Section 4.1. Available at: http://informinc.org/recyclenicd.php.

54. Fishbein, "Industry Program to Collect Nickel-Cadmium (Ni-Cd) Batteries." Available at: http://informinc.org/recyclenicd.php.

55. For an updated list of collection sites, go to: www.rbrc.org.

56. Fishbein, "Industry Program to Collect Nickel-Cadmium (Ni-Cd) Batteries," Section 4.1. Available at: http://informinc.org/recyclenicd.php.

57. The Federal Universal Waste Rule was developed by U.S. EPA to reduce regulatory barriers to collecting particular waste streams, such as batteries, thermostats, and pesticides, which increased recycling and reduced environmental impact. The Universal Waste Rule was amended in 1999 to include some lamps (i.e., fluorescent, high intensity discharge [HID], mercury vapor).

58. Bette Fishbein, telephone communication, August 15, 2007.

59. Aarthi Rayapura, Wireless Waste: The Challenge of Cell Phone and Battery Collection INFORM, Inc., 2005, available at: http://informinc.org/reports_waste.php.

60. RIS International, "Canadian Consumer Battery Baseline Study Final Report," (Submitted to Environment Canada, February 2007.)

61. "Massachusetts Plan for Managing Hazardous Materials from Household and Small Businesses," Executive Office of Environmental Affairs, 5 July 1996. Massachusetts used the term hazardous household products (HHP) to denote that the goal was to reuse and recycle materials and not have them become a waste.

62. Other materials projected to be added were fluorescent lamps, thermometers, mercury switches, and electronic products with cathode ray tubes.

63. "Mercury in Massachusetts: An Evaluation of Sources, Emissions, Impacts, and Controls," Massachusetts Department of Environmental Protection, 1996, available at: http://www.mass.gov/dep/toxics/stypes/hgexsum.htm.

64. At the time, three solid waste combustion facilities in northeast Massachusetts contributed to a high concentration of mercury and other pollution, prompting particular concern in that part of the state.

65. Northeast Waste Management Officials' Association, "Revised Discussion Document: Mercury Education and Reduction Model Act," http://newmoa.org/prevention/mercury/final_model_legislation.doc (5 July 2007) Section 10 (F).

66. For information on the NEWMOA Mercury Reduction Program, including updates on laws, see: http://www.newmoa.org/prevention/mercury/.

67. Municipal Waste Combustor Regulation (M.G.L. c. 111, Sections 142A through 142M and 150A, M.G.L. c. 21A, Section 18), April 1998.

68. Presentation by Mark Smith, Massachusetts Department of Environmental Protection, PSI Networking Conference Call, "The Fate of Excess Mercury in the United States," 13 June 2007.

69. Mercury thermostats contain three grams of mercury per ampoule. Some thermostats contain more than one ampoule. The average thermostat, therefore, contains about four grams of mercury.

70. For up-to-date information, see TRC's website, at: http://www.nema.org/gov/ehs/trc/.

71. Product Stewardship Institute, "Thermostat Stewardship Initiative: Background Research Summary—Final," November 18, 2004.

72. After an initial payment for the collection bin, TRC pays for the replacement collection bins, shipping costs, and the cost of recycling the mercury thermostats.

73. "Review of the Thermostat Recycling Corporation Activities in the Northeast," prepared by the Northeast Waste Management Officials Association, November 2001, available at: http://www.newmoa.org/prevention/mercury/TRCreport.pdf.

74. The national thermostat dialogue was initially funded by state and local governments, and the U.S. EPA. Several of the collaborative projects were also funded by EPA.

75. States that restrict the sale of mercury thermostats did so independent of the national dialogue. These states include California (effective January 2006), Connecticut (effective July 2003, unless the manufacturer submits a plan enabling collection), Louisiana (effective 2008), Maine (effective January 2006), Maryland (effective October 2007), Michigan (effective January 2010), New York (effective 2008), Oregon (effective January 2006, prohibits installation of thermostats containing mercury in commercial and residential buildings), Rhode Island (effective January 2006, labeling requirements, phase-out depending upon mercury content levels, and collection plan requirements), Vermont (effective July 2006), and Washington (unless the manufacturer participates in recycling).

76. Minnesota Pollution Control Agency, "A National Agreement on Carpet Recycling," http://www.pca.state.mn.us/oea/carpet/index.cfm (5 July 2007).

77. Minnesota Pollution Control Agency, "A National Agreement on Carpet Recycling," http://www.pca.state.mn.us/oea/carpet/index.cfm (5 July 2007).

78. The nine states with electronics end-of-life management laws in the United States as of August 2007 are: California, Maine, Maryland, Washington, Minnesota, Texas, Oregon, Connecticut, and North Carolina. The laws in Texas and North Carolina only cover computer equipment.

79. For information on PSI's Staples Pilot Project, go to: http://www.productstewardship.us/displaycommon.cfm?an=1&subarticlenbr=72. For information on the Take-it-Back Network and the Office Depot and Good Guys pilot projects, see: http://www.metrokc.gov/dnrp/swd/takeitback/index.asp

80. For information on EPA's Plug-In To eCycling project, go to: http://www.epa.gov/epaoswer/hazwaste/recycle/ecycling/index.htm.

81. David Stitzhal, "Northwest Product Stewardship Council: A Level Long Enough," *Pollution Prevention Review* (Autumn 2000): 68.

82. Stitzhal, "Northwest Product Stewardship Council: A Lever Long Enough," 69.

83. Stitzhal, "Northwest Product Stewardship Council: A Lever Long Enough," 73.

84. For up-to-date information on the NWPSC, see: http://www.productstewardship.net/index.html.

85. For up-to-date information on PSI, see: http://www.productstewardship.us/index.cfm.

86. PSI mission statement, available at: www.productstewardship.us.

87. For a full list of organizations endorsing PSI's Principles of Product Stewardship, see: http://www.productstewardship.us/displaycommon.cfm?an=1&subarticlenbr=14. These organizations include the Environmental Council of the States, Solid Waste Association of North America, Northeast Recycling Council, Northwest Product Stewardship Council, and North American Hazardous Materials Management Association.

88. PSI research results in a Product Stewardship Action Plan for each product, which forms the basis for a series of face-to-face meetings. This phase includes interviews with key stakeholders, whose perspective is sought on the project problem, focus, goals, issues, and potential strategies. The interviews serve to engage stakeholders and provide them with a level of comfort on the issue and the dialogue process.

89. For a map of the Product Stewardship Institute membership coverage, see: www.productstewardship.us/membershipmap.

90. For up-to-date information on the Product Policy Institute, see http://www.productpolicy.org/

91. The British Columbia Recycling Regulation is at http://www.qp.gov.bc.ca/statreg/reg/E/EnvMgmt/449_2004.htm.

92. For current information on the Manitoba regulations, go to: http://greenmanitoba.ca/cim/1001C1_1T376T3T377.dhtm.

93. Jim Ferguson, Green Manitoba, email communication, August 22, 2007.

94. Senator Barak Obama (D-IL) introduced two bills in 2007 to address this issue. The Mercury Market Minimization Act (M3) would end U.S. exports of elemental mercury by 2010, prohibit Department of Energy and Department of Defense sales of stockpiled mercury, and provide for permanent storage of excess mercury. The M3 bill, coupled with a similar ban in the European Union by 2011, would take substantial amounts of mercury off the world market. The companion Missing Mercury in Manufacturing Monitoring and Mitigation Act (M5) would prohibit the use of mercury in the chlor-alkali process by 2012.

95. For the full text of the CIWMB Strategic Directive, see: http://caproductstewardship.org/state/ciwmb.htm

96. The concept of the tipping point is the focus of a book by Malcolm Gladwell called the *Tipping Point,* published in 2003.

97. Incandescent lamps also contain small amounts of lead. As of August 2007, policymakers were still debating the relative impacts of lead in incandescent lighting.

98. Paul Hawken, *Blessed Unrest,* Penguin Books, 2007.

99. For more information on the work of the Basel Action Network, see: www.ban.org.

100. Erich Fromm, *The Sane Society* (NY, NY: Henry Holt and Company, 1955), pages 131, 133–134.

Summary and a Look Ahead

Jim Hanna

The chapters demonstrate a 25-year history of HHW that runs the gamut from recognition of an unmanaged public health and environmental risk to mature collection and education programs in all 50 states, to further recognition that local government collection programs are simply a transitional service or stopgap to a broader set of comprehensive solutions. What lies beyond that stopgap in the next 5 to 25 years are not unattainable, pie-in-the-sky prophecies, but a series of proven, scientifically based, collaborative, market- and regulatory-driven actions that will lead us in a direction where HHW truly has little-to-no future.

Envisioning an HHW-Free Future

A comprehensive vision of a future free of the burdens hazardous materials place on society is articulated well by the 2007 mission statement of the Local Hazardous Waste Management Program in King County, Washington. It states:

> "Our Vision is that our region is the cleanest in the country – one free of hazardous chemical exposure. More specifically, residents, businesses and government demand, use and produce products that are the least harmful to the environment and all segments of the county's population. Exposure to toxic or otherwise hazardous chemicals is virtually eliminated, essentially reduced to natural background levels. Local residents have the lowest body burden for harmful chemicals of any population in the U.S., and the most disadvantaged are as free of such exposures as the most well off. People's potential is not in any way limited due to chemical exposures, and health disparities due to chemical exposures among different segments of the population are eliminated. Products that still present any risk from chemical content are managed in a closed-loop stewardship system, funded by those who make and sell the products, until such time as they can be replaced with safer ingredients. Waste of all types is minimized, and the area's waste management systems (solid waste, wastewater, storm water) are not compromised in any way due to hazardous chemical content. The local environment is virtually free of hazardous chemicals (approaching natural background levels) and is the cleanest of any urban area in the country. We set a

global example of stewardship and sustainability related to toxic or otherwise hazardous chemicals as we leave a positive legacy for the future."[1]

This book has illustrated, through leaders in the field, a road-map for effectively and efficiently managing HHW and for attaining an HHW-free future.

Transitional Services—
HHW Collection Beyond Today

In reality, despite the vision of an HHW-free future, many local governments are still building their HHW collection infrastructure, not devising ways to dismantle it. In reality, HHW programs still collect stockpiles of lab chemicals from the 1950s, surplus industrial solvents that someone's grandfather brought home from the factory, and carcinogenic pesticides banned over 50 years ago. And, in reality, retailers still sell chemicals that pose a threat to public health and the environment, even when properly used, that must be managed as HHW at their end of life. Additionally, as Bill Lafield of the Consumer Specialty Products Association points out in the Appendix, disagreement between the HHW community and manufacturers still exists as to what chemicals should even be managed as HHW. Consequently, the transition to an idealized product stewardship world still involves a need for discussion and a mechanism of collection that strives to be efficient and as widely available as possible.

In Chapter 5, Bruning demonstrates specific, creative ways that collection programs can reduce their per-pound or per-vehicle costs and capture a larger portion of their local populations than the historical 3, 5, or even 10% participation rate. Multi-jurisdictional programs and purchasing cooperatives help eliminate redundancy across municipal boundaries and reduce costs through "volume" purchasing of management services. Multiple-site, multi-day, and mobile collection events increase participation by reducing travel time for residents and increasing convenience to fit participants' busy schedules. Additionally, strategic decision making by program managers—for deciding which waste streams to collect, what can be collected by other means, and which wastes can safely be disposed in Subtitle D landfills—is key to reducing operating costs.

Shift from Information to
Community-Based Social Marketing

As described throughout this publication, meaningful and motivational public education is critically important to build awareness and encourage behavior change, as well as to foster support for larger institutional and product changes. HHW collection initiatives, regardless of maturity and size, must move beyond traditional "information education" given lack of a direct correlation between knowledge and behavior. Other factors mediate this relationship. To address this, Schultz and Tabanico provide strong support for the community-based social marketing approach, presenting research and case studies. CBSM should be adopted for use in all HHW programs given demonstrated effectiveness and the scarcity of education and outreach dollars in collection program budgets. The CBSM steps, detailed in Chapter 6, include (1) identifying the barriers to a targeted behavior, (2) using behavior change tools to overcome the barriers, (3) piloting the selected tools using empirical research methodology and a control group, and (4) evaluating the project once it has been widely implemented. This is a recipe for success.

Galvin contends that we should think of "public education" efforts as additionally building support for the more sweeping changes that are needed, such as bans of certain chemical ingredients, product stewardship mandates in the legislature, and other changes beyond the traditional message of asking individuals to buy the safer product B over the more hazardous product A. Effective community-based social marketing efforts can help people to understand the larger context of their purchasing decisions and their potential roles in impacting these important government policies.

One of the many things the reader should take away from this book is a mandate to print a brochure or employ other behavior change tools only after the target audience has told you what they need to motivate the desired behavior.

Shift from Hazardous Waste Management to Hazard-Free Products

In Chapter 1, Galvin aptly describes the maturation of many HHW collection programs into comprehensive public services, addressing issues related to hazardous product use, storage, exposure, and safety, in addition to management of the unused residuals at the time of discard. Subsequent sections of the chapter make a case for broadening the purview of HHW programs to address household hazardous products (HHP) and a range of chemical exposure issues. This call to action fosters the natural synergy that exists in local government between the agencies collecting HHW (usually a solid waste division), the local health department, and the municipal sewer district or publicly owned treatment works. If these groups are not already addressing HHPs in your jurisdiction—as a combined public health, environmental health, and solid waste issue—you will want to make it a priority. Remember that HHPs represent an acute health danger through home poisonings, a chronic health danger, and an environmental health risk, whether used and disposed properly or improperly. Chapter 1 cites a number of representative case studies.

In summary, the focus of HHW programs must shift from traditional, end-of-pipe waste management to a prioritization toward reduction of exposure to humans and the environment "upstream" during the production and use of household chemicals. This should serve as a primary motivator to cultivate public-private partnerships between local government operators, regulatory bodies, and the manufacturers of household products. Several of these partnerships, developed around the notion of product stewardship, are cited by Cassel in Chapter 7.

It is heartening that traditional and alternative-thinking consumer products manufacturers are constantly commercializing redesigned products that eliminate (or reduce to a safe threshold) hazardous components of everyday household products, including everything from large technological advances to common natural ingredients such as,

- "Organic Radical Batteries"—a new product invention from NEC that uses a polymer gel and does not require the use of any heavy metal ingredients.[2] There are other trials going on with even more natural ingredients, trying to mimic the old potato battery used by many schoolchildren. Elimination of hazardous constituents, such as mercury, lead, and lithium from batteries minimizes the risk of environmental and human harm and the need to manage them as HHW at their end-of-life.
- "25(b)" pesticides—products such as corn gluten, mint oils, herbs, spices, even table salt, that have pesticidal uses and are considered by EPA to present "minimum risk." They are exempted from many of the FIFRA registration, labeling, and other rules because they pose minimal, if any, hazard. For a complete list, see www.epa.gov/oppbppd1/biopesticides/regtools/25b_list.htm. (9 April 2007)

One needs only to browse the pesticide and home chemical aisles of the nearest big box, home improvement store to realize that "alternatives" and hazard-free products comprise a small minority of available solutions for consumers. The pipeline of hazardous household chemicals that promulgates the need for greater action toward hazard-free products is still wide open. As Galvin notes in Chapter 1, products that are not currently considered hazardous by conventional criteria, such as polycarbonate water bottles, vinyl shower curtains, and furniture containing brominated flame retardants, contain varying amounts of hazardous substances that can leach into drinking water or contaminate indoor air and house dust, providing pathways for human exposures that may be harmful in themselves or in combination with those from other materials. Clearly a new approach to protecting public and environmental health is in order. One such approach, the "Precautionary Principle," is described in this summary.

Shift from Collecting Everything to Setting Priorities

Chapters in this book illustrate a broad range of items collected through the HHW system either at collection events, permanent facilities, "ABOPs" or at other limited collection locations and private entities. Although many programs have started paring down the materials that are collected, such as latex paint or alkaline batteries, it is time to seriously review the range of items collected as HHW and set some clear priorities for focus. The state of Oregon is developing an interesting project as this book goes to press, to establish "a rational method for assessing HHW priorities." Its preliminary findings are that pesticides, strong cleaners, and heavy metals likely represent the greatest HHW threats to human health and the environment in Oregon.[3] The Local Hazardous Waste Management Program in King County, Washington, has also gone through a priority-setting process as it tries to shift its focus upstream and to the more hazardous materials. They now have special projects focusing on mercury, lead, pesticides, high-risk solvents, and bisphenol-A, plus business projects focusing on janitorial services, nail salons, and landscapers. They have also stopped accepting latex paint as household hazardous waste at collection services.

With finite budgets, and with substantive protection of the public health and environment at the top of mind, HHW program managers need to take stock of the items they choose to collect. Research continues, but it is clear that the universe of household substances that cause the greatest harm to humans and the environment is not necessarily the same universe of substances managed by our HHW systems. Expect to see greater attention in the near future to persistent, bioaccumulative toxins, endocrine disruptors, and products that put workers and the environment in jeopardy during their manufacturing, such as polyvinyl chloride. Should HHW programs start collecting these materials instead of paints and cleaners?

Shift from Government Support to Product Stewardship

In Chapter 7, Cassel calls for an end to manufacturers' "unfunded mandate" on local governments to manage products at their end-of-life. He points to successful European models of "extended producer responsibility" or EPR, in which local and EU policies now mandate producer responsibility for product residuals, packaging, and waste after they are used by consumers. Cassel is on target in stating that this movement is a paradigm shift in the way we think about the life of products from creation to disposal. His chapter outlines many of the mechanics of product stewardship laws. Generally, they involve a responsibility to manage whatever remains after consumers finish using their merchandise, accomplished by industry-run collection schemes that are paid by increased product prices, advanced disposal fees or sometimes, by taxes.

This issue will prove to be the most politically charged of all the solutions addressed in this book. Those in industry may argue that product stewardship or EPR laws represent an unfair burden on the business sector. Additionally, the United States and European governments do not share the same attitudes toward regulation versus voluntary standards. Fortunately, at the state level, local governments burdened with the growing costs to their budgets and their citizens' quality of life are recognizing that the purest form of true capitalism is one in which business accounts for all of its operating costs, including externalities.

What we have also recognized from Europe is that EPR mandates work. Over time, rather than simply increasing the prices of their goods to pay for end-of-life management of the wastes, businesses operating in Europe have actually redesigned many of their products to reduce or eliminate packaging, to be easily deconstructed after use, to minimize or eliminate hazardous components (that carry more stringent mandates and higher disposal costs) and to be easily recycled. Generally these businesses have reduced their operating costs and become more competitive among customers and peers.

Cassel points out several successful forays into product stewardship in the United States and Canada, both regulation-mandated and industry-sponsored. These include programs that we all now take for granted, such as lead-acid battery deposit/exchange and leading-edge state programs that include mercury and electronics take-back initiatives.

The sheer number of emerging organizations, commissions, and regulations that Cassel cites paints a clear picture that product stewardship will play a major role in the management of products and HHW in the United States and Canada in the short- and long-term future. It will not eliminate the need for local HHW-type services, but will most likely involve taking advantage of existing collection infrastructures with a shift in financial responsibility.

The author predicts that forward-thinking industries with a strong ethic of corporate social responsibility will actively participate in these stewardship processes and will see a competitive advantage with an increasingly eco- and socially conscious consumer. Those industries that choose to sit out the processes will be subject to regulation of which they had little hand in crafting, and will end up simply responding to enforcement.

Chemical Policies and the
Precautionary Principle

The Green Chemistry appendix offers insight into California's big picture approach to rethinking chemicals from end-of-life or cradle-to-grave, to a "cradle-to-cradle" philosophy. A bit different, but complementary to product stewardship regulations, green chemistry and precautionary principle policies focus on reducing human health and environmental risk at the design phase of chemicals and products. These principles recognize the enormous cost and effort savings associated with eliminating hazards before they are introduced into the biota and must be "dealt with" through increased medical costs, environmental treatment of air, water, and soil, decreased human productivity, and a litany of other societal costs.

The precautionary principle states that it is not society's responsibility to prove that a chemical is dangerous, it is industry's responsibility to prove a chemical is safe. Detractors are numerous, but as with product stewardship, the European Union has taken the lead in integrating the precautionary principle into its regulatory infrastructure.[4] Most applicable to this book, the EU's new REACH legislation mandates registration and testing of a host of legacy chemicals (already in use) plus defines procedures manufacturers must take to prove chemicals are not harmful *before* they are approved for use in the market.

San Francisco adopted the precautionary principle as part of its core environmental policies in 2003, the first U.S. government entity to do so. A three-year progress report is available on the city's website at http://www.sehn.org/sf3year.html

As mentioned, detractors of the precautionary principle are numerous and vocal. However, the author believes that its adoption will continue in the U.S. for two important reasons, in addition to the need to alleviate local government's HHW cost burdens. First, today's global corporations loathe the production inefficiency created by multiple, divergent regulations between countries and states. Tim Shestek, a Sacramento representative for the American Chemistry Council, speaks of his organizations' opposition to "rifle shot" legislation that requires different formulations and procedures in different jurisdictions or that regulate individual chemicals without scientific justification.[5] Since it appears that EU REACH laws will continue to identify a greater number of existing and future chemicals for precautionary legislation, it makes business sense for global companies to adopt REACH-mandated changes universally. Second, as the burden of end-of-life responsibility shifts to manufacturers, those that are able to reformulate chemicals and products to avoid EPR responsibilities will be at a competitive advantage.

Summary

The household hazardous waste system in North America occupies a vast spectrum. To the oldtimers in the field, it is a classic vehicle in need of a good overhaul. To those deciding how to prioritize and streamline their collection systems to face difficult budget implications every year, it is a series of complex give-and-takes. To those who are just starting a program, it is still a primary need to provide a basic service that protects public health and the environment. To everyone, it is also all of these. The facts are that we will have to continue to sweep out a lot of old stuff while we envision a different future for our children and theirs.

This mission of the book is to provide the reader with a history of HHW in the U.S., a comprehensive (though not all-inclusive) how-to manual, some innovative ideas from those who are running programs, and a glimpse of what is on the horizon as we redefine HHW and who should be responsible for its safe management, or more important, its minimization and possible elimination. Wherever the reader sits on the spectrum, the editor and authors hope this book has achieved—in part or full—its mission.

About the Author

As former manager of King County, Washington's HHW collection program, The Wastemobile, Jim Hanna now serves as manager of environmental affairs for Starbucks Coffee Company in Seattle, where he lends his expertise to the company's initiatives to minimize its environmental footprint through green building, energy conservation, international procurement, waste minimization, and collaboration with partner corporations and NGOs.

Notes

1. *Local Hazardous Waste Management Program in King County, Vision & Mission* (Seattle: LHWMP, 19 March 2007).

2. "Organic Radical Battery," *Wikipedia*, http://en.wikipedia.org/wiki/Organic_radical_battery (27 July 2007).

3. Oregon Department of Environmental Quality, *Managing Household Hazardous Waste in Oregon—A Tool for Setting Priorities for HHW Materials, Geographic Areas, and Populations* (Seattle: Cascadia Consulting Group, April 2007).

4. Commission of the European Communities, *Communication from the Commission on the Precautionary Principle* (February 2000)

5. Daniel Weintraub, "'Chemistry' project may neutralize toxic waste" (*The Sacramento Bee,* Sunday, May 13, 2007)

HHW Disposal—
An Industry Perspective

Bill Lafield

The issue of Household Hazardous Waste (HHW) was the subject of extensive debate in the 1980s and '90s. The issue attracted public attention when concerns about the environmental impact of industrial waste disposal practices came to the public's attention. The Consumer Specialty Products Association (CSPA)[1] was an active participant in this debate.

CSPA's Scientific Affairs Committee used the expertise of its members and independent third-party scientific research to examine the impact that the disposal of consumer and institutional products had on the environment and sanitation worker safety. Studies examined the composition of municipal waste and hazards to sanitary workers that resulted from these products. While the committee completed its work on this issue in the late 1990s, its findings are still valid and meaningful since no new credible scientific studies or data on this issue have been generated since that time.

Consumer Specialty Products in the
Normal Household Waste Stream

CSPA members manufacture a variety of products including household cleaning products, floor polishes and waxes, automotive maintenance and appearance products, and consumer pesticides. These products are useful "tools" for a variety of functions necessary to maintain clean and sanitary homes and institutional facilities. Many of these products (*e.g.*, disinfectants, sanitizers) provide significant public health benefits.

Consumer and institutional products are largely consumed in use with very little product and even fewer chemical ingredients entering the waste stream. Once in the waste stream, the small amount of chemicals in these products does not pose a significant problem. Even products that require precautionary labeling such as strong acids (toilet bowl cleaners), strong bases (oven cleaners), and household pesticides are neutralized by other material and buffered within the landfill.

RCRA Exemptions for Household Waste

Households may generate solid wastes (*e.g.*, old solvents, poisons) that, as a technical matter, could fit one of EPA's established four hazardous waste characteristics for industrial wastes (*i.e.*, ignitability, corrosivity, reactivity, toxicity). However, due to the low concentrations of this type of material, household waste is specifically exempt from federal and state laws governing treatment and disposal of hazardous waste.

The United States Congress definitively addressed the issue in 1984 when it enacted amendments to the Federal Resource Conservation and Recovery Act (RCRA). Among other things, these amendments reflect Congress's clear intention to exempt wastes generated by normal household activities from RCRA disposal requirements. State laws modeled on RCRA also include this exemption.

While household waste is exempt from the definition of "hazardous waste" under RCRA Subtitle C, it is regulated as a solid waste under RCRA Subtitle D. Under current law, all municipal waste disposal sites must be "sanitary landfills" as required by Subtitle D. These landfills operate in such a manner that they do *not* pose an unreasonable risk to human health or the environment while accepting all residential and non-hazardous municipal solid waste.

Collection of "Household Hazardous Waste"

The collection and disposal of HHW is a common activity throughout the United States. HHW programs differ in many ways, but they all operate with limited resources. With no generally recognized legal or scientific definition for HHW, it is still worthwhile to examine what materials pose risks substantial enough to merit special treatment and what can best be handled through normal waste disposal systems.

Much has changed since HHW became an issue. Federal and state standards for sanitary landfills have been strengthened to ensure material containment and treatment of leachate; recycling has increased, packaging has been reduced, and the formulas for many consumer products have been modified. Mandatory and voluntary collection programs have diverted high risk materials (*e.g.*, batteries, motor oil and other used automotive fluids, thermostats with mercury, oil-based paints) from landfills.

Although many HHW programs consider post-consumer wastes of many types of consumer specialty products to be candidates for special segregation, collection, and management, an examination of the facts does not support this practice. Consumer specialty products normally contain a very small amount of ingredients that might be of concern.

Despite the fact that federal and most state regulations allow all household wastes to be disposed in RCRA Subtitle D compliant facilities (*i.e.*, landfills, incinerators, or composting operations), careful study and risk assessment of the performance of those facilities do not suggest significant risks deriving from this practice. Waste characterization studies conducted by federal, state, or local agencies indicate that, even given a liberal definition of what product wastes should be considered HHW, the amount of HHW entering the solid waste stream is extremely low (0.2 to 0.4 percent).[2, 3, 4]

Risk to Sanitation Workers

Another concern about HHW is the risk it poses to sanitation workers. CSPA examined the issue of sanitation worker safety in some detail and found that the percentage of product-related injury (*e.g.*, chemical burns or splashes, explosions from flammable products), is very low and there is no substantial risk. Despite anecdotal stories of hazards to sanitation workers, data show that the overwhelming incidence of injuries to sanitary workers had to do with those related to lifting and dumping as well as cuts and punctures from sharp objects.

HHW Policy

Public policy governing the appropriate designation of "HHW" from normal household waste is an important fiscal and environmental protection consideration that should be based on objective and reliable criteria derived from the application of generally accepted scientific risk-assessment practice. Limited resources for HHW collection should be directed toward materials of significant concern.

Household waste, which is non-hazardous, should not be placed in secure hazardous waste facilities since these sites are needed for RCRA hazardous wastes. The great majority of consumer products designed to be used in and around the house and institutions (*e.g.*, office buildings, hospitals, schools) do not pose a risk to the environment or sanitation worker safety, and should *not* be included in HHW collection programs.

HHW programs should focus on the relatively few types of wastes that are truly hazardous. This would include wastes that are disposed in significant volumes and contain ingredients of sufficient toxicity (posing worker safety concerns) and environmental persistence to constitute significant potential risk (such as unforeseen municipal solid waste facility failure and uncontrolled land leachate). Materials such as restricted use pesticides, used motor oil, unused oil-based paints, automotive and other batteries are good examples of materials that merit special handling. A more recent concern is the increasing volume of hazardous materials from electronic components such as televisions, computers, game boxes, and cell phones.

The proper handling and disposal of hazardous material will continue to be an important public policy issue. The public will be best served by HHW programs with clear guidelines defining wastes that require special handling, enabling the efficient use of the limited resources available to address them.

About the Author

Bill Lafield is Vice President of State Affairs and Communications for the Consumer Specialty Products Association. He has more than 25 years of experience in both the non-profit and private sector working on a variety of legislative issues related to consumer products. He was an active participant in the HHW public policy on debate on various state initiatives in the 1990s.

Notes

1. CSPA (formerly known as the Chemical Specialties Manufacturers Association) is a voluntary, non-profit national trade association representing approximately 260 companies engaged in the manufacture, formulation, distribution, and sale of products for household, institutional, commercial, and industrial use. CSPA member companies' wide range of products includes cleaning products, consumer pesticides, antimicrobial products, air care products, automotive specialty products, polishes and floor maintenance products, and various types of aerosol products. CPSA was founded in 1923 by a small group of companies that produced household pesticides.

2. American City and County. (1983). How hazardous are municipal wastes? March: 41–42.

3. Anonymous (1990) Stop hazwaste at the landfill. *World Wastes* February: 18–19.

4. Bertrand H., Oliver D., Tormey M., Cearley, D., Beck, R.W. (1995) Household hazardous waste characterization study for Palm Beach County, Florida: A MITE program evaluation. *EPA/600/R-95/140*. National Risk Management Research Laboratory, Office of Research and Development, USEPA, Cincinnati, OH.

APPENDIX B

Green Chemistry in California

Michael P. Wilson

A key question is whether the chemical industry will start to "go green" by itself, as a few industries are starting to do. "Very unlikely," says Dr. Michael P. Wilson of UC Berkeley's Center for Occupational and Environmental Health. Dr. Wilson is the chief author of a landmark 2006 report to the California Legislature, *Green Chemistry in California: A Framework for Leadership in Chemicals Policy and Innovation*, that articulates a greener vision for the future of the industry and describes how weaknesses in the current chemical management system in the U.S. are impeding the implementation of that vision.[1] The report, developed over a two year period and guided by a 13-member committee of UC faculty, concludes that the 1979 Toxic Substances Control Act (TSCA) (P.L. 94-469) has fallen short of its objectives. TSCA is the only U.S. law that is broadly intended to enable regulation of chemicals before and after they enter commerce, yet according to the UC analysis, it has not served as an effective vehicle for the public, industry, or government to *assess* the hazards of chemicals in commerce or *control* those of greatest concern. As a consequence, the statute has not motivated the U.S chemical industry to invest in cleaner technologies, such as green chemistry: the design, production, and use of chemicals that are safer for human health and ecosystems.

The UC report points to three overarching "Gaps" that have emerged in the U.S. chemical management program as a consequence of TSCA:

- A "Data Gap," because TSCA does not require chemical producers to generate any information on the hazardous properties of the chemicals they produce and disclose that information to the public, government, or downstream businesses and industries;
- A "Safety Gap," because TSCA requires the EPA to meet an excessively high burden of proof before acting to protect public health, even for well-established chemical hazards; and,
- A "Technology Gap," because the lack of both market and regulatory drivers (engendered by the Data and Safety Gaps) has dampened interest by industry in green chemistry research and development.

The UC report points out that as a consequence of TSCA weaknesses, chemicals are marketed in the U.S. almost entirely on the basis of their "function, price, and performance," with much less attention to their toxic and ecotoxic properties. This fact of the chemicals market is reflected in chemistry teaching carried out at universities across the U.S., where chemistry students are not required to gain even a rudimentary understanding of how chemicals affect human health and ecosystems; an understanding of toxicology and ecotoxicology is simply not highly valued in the current chemicals market, according to the UC analysis.

The chemicals market that has emerged in the wake of TSCA has resulted in a chemical production system that is responsible for the great majority of the problems articulated in the previous chapters. The UC report describes an array of problems affecting workers, the public, ecosystems, government, businesses, and industry, and it argues that these problems will broaden and deepen in coming years, along with expanding global chemical production.

The UC report notes, for example, that the EPA has projected the need for over 600 new hazardous waste sites each month of each year in the United States leading up to 2033, with estimated clean-up costs of $250 billion; it describes the appearance of hundreds of industrial chemicals in human tissues and fluids, including those of infants, and the development of chronic diseases and premature death among thousands of California workers as a consequence of chemical exposure in the workplace. It points out that chemical risks fall disproportionately on members of minority, immigrant, and low-income communities, both as residents and workers. And it notes that global chemical production is doubling every 25 years.

On the other hand, the UC report describes unprecedented changes in public environmental health policy in the European Union that are expected to drive global interest in cleaner technologies, including green chemistry, and it describes how a growing number of downstream businesses and local governments in the U.S. are calling for greater transparency and accountability on the part of chemical suppliers and producers. With these and other changes, the UC report argues that the U.S. has a unique opportunity to correct the long-standing weaknesses of TSCA and position itself as a global leader in green chemistry science, technology, and commercial application.

The report illustrates that to fulfill this vision the U.S. will have to fundamentally restructure TSCA so that it closes the Data, Safety, and Technology Gaps. To close the Data Gap, the report calls for new laws that would require the generation, disclosure, and distribution by chemical producers of comprehensive information on the hazardous properties of chemicals in forms that are useful for the public, workers, industry, small businesses, and government. It would require that chemicals now in commerce be assessed to identify those that pose a risk to human health and ecosystems and those that could serve as safer substitutes. To close the Safety Gap, the report calls for policies to expand the capacity of federal and state agencies to efficiently assess the hazards of chemicals in commercial use and take steps to reduce the use of those of greatest concern to public environmental health. To further close the Technology Gap, the report concludes that public investments in green chemistry research, technology development and diffusion, education, and technical assistance will likely be needed.

The report argues that these changes will "raise" the hazardous properties of chemicals to an equal footing with the function, price, and performance of chemicals in the market, that will open opportunities for green chemistry entrepreneurs to market their products on the basis of their greater safety for human and ecosystem health. The report concludes that only through these fundamental changes in the chemicals market will the chemical industry begin to invest in green chemistry as a "core function of the industry," at a level commensurate with the enormous pace and scale of chemical production today, as compared to the niche location where green chemistry currently resides in the chemicals market.

The UC report proposes that a comprehensive U.S. chemicals policy that meets these objectives proactively will build the foundation for new productive capacity in the chemical industry, and it could position the industry to become a global leader in green chemistry innovation. Alternatively, on the current trajectory, the report points out that the U.S. could become a market for hazardous chemicals and materials that are no longer permitted for sale in the European Union and other regions that are implementing modern chemicals policies. This raises the specter of the U.S. becoming a "dumping ground" of sorts for banned chemicals and materials, certainly an unusual turn of events for the U.S. public. The U.S. is already accepting into its market pressed wood products built with formaldehyde-based glues that are banned for sale in the E.U. and Japan due to the carcinogenic properties of formaldehyde.

The UC report articulates a combination of new regulations, targeted research, and bold commitments to innovation that could chart the course for a greener chemical industry and a green, more sustainable future in the U.S.

About the Author

Michael P. Wilson, Ph.D, MPH, is an Assistant Research Scientist at the Center for Occupational and Environmental Health (COEH) at the School of Public Health, University of California, Berkeley, where he conducts research and practice in chemicals policy, occupational safety and health, and sustainable production. Dr. Wilson conducted his doctoral and master's work in environmental health sciences at the University of California, Berkeley, from 1996 to 2003. He earned a bachelor's degree in biology in 1984 from the University of California, Santa Cruz. Dr. Wilson's 2006 report to the California Legislature, *Green Chemistry in California: A Framework for Leadership in Chemicals Policy and Innovation*, (http://coeh.berkeley.edu/news/06_wilson_policy.htm) has formed the basis for renewed attention to chemicals policy and sustainable production in California.

Note

1. Wilson, M., Chia, D., and Ehlers, B. *Green Chemistry in California: A Framework for Leadership in Chemicals Policy and Innovation* (http://coeh.berkeley.edu/news/06_wilson_policy.htm) (accessed March 15, 2007). Special Report to the California Legislature. University of California Policy Research Center, Office of the President (2006).

Household Hazardous Waste Resources

Anne Reichman

Since its inception in 1981, professionals involved in the household hazardous waste (HHW) industry have established and shared an extensive listing of resources on HHW and HHW-related topics. These resources touch on many other areas of the environment and health, including environmental education, water management, recycling, source reduction, and healthcare, to name a few. Products considered HHW are prevalent in our society and they touch almost every aspect of our daily lives, so the proper handling and disposal of these products are of great importance. This resource list serves as a guide for further investigation into the topic.

When searching for HHW-related resources on a particular topic, this appendix can be a useful starting point. It is important to also check with local, state, and federal environmental and solid waste agencies for additional suggestions and resources that may be more localized and applicable. The growth and success of the HHW industry has been greatly influenced by the willingness of HHW and environmental and health professionals to regularly share information, resources, and knowledge.

Books, Articles, Pamphlets, and Presentations

Books

1. *2004 Emergency Response Guidebook: A Guidebook for First Responders During the Initial Phase of a Dangerous Goods/Hazardous Materials Incident;* US Department of Transportation, Transport Canada, and Secretariat of Communications and Transportation of Mexico (SCT); 2004. (Publication: ERG2004) • http://hazmat. dot.gov/pubs/erg/gydebook.htm

2. *Clinical Toxicology of Commercial Products* (5th Edition), Robert E. Gosselin, *et al.,* 1984. Williams & Wilkins • http://www.amazon.com/Clinical-Toxicology-Commercial-Products-Gosselin/dp/0683036327

3. *Hawley's Condensed Chemical Dictionary* (14th Edition), Richard J. Lewis, Sr., 2002. John Wiley & Sons • http://www.knovel.com/knovel2/Toc.jsp?BookID=704

4. *Lessons Learned from Four Years of Household Hazardous Waste Collections: 1995-1998*, Androscoggin Valley Council of Governments (AVCOG) in Auburn, Maine. To obtain a free copy, contact the Maine Department of Environmental Protection at 1-800-452-1942 or the Maine State Planning Office at 1-800-662-4545 • http://www.maine.gov/dep/rwm/homeowner/hhwtowns.htm

5. *The Merck Index: An Encyclopedia of Chemicals, Drugs and Biologicals* (14th Edition), Maryadele J. O'Neil, *et al.,* 2006. Merck & Co., Inc., Rahway, NJ • http://www.merckbooks.com/mindex/

6. *NIOSH Pocket Guide to Chemical Hazards,* National Institute for Occupational Safety and Health, September 2005. (NIOSH Publication No. 2005-149) • http://www.cdc.gov/niosh/npg/

Articles, Pamphlets, and Presentations

1. *Best Management Practices Resources Guide: Chapter 1, Household Hazardous Waste*; Region 4 DoD Pollution Prevention Partnership; Adapted with permission from: Georgia DoD Pollution Prevention Partnership Solid Waste & Recycling Work Team Solid Waste & Recycling Resource Guide, November 2000 • http://www.p2pays.org/ref/13/12935.pdf

2. *Cleaners in the Home: Nontoxic Alternatives for Improved Environmental Quality*, Kansas Department of Health & Environment • http://www.kdheks.gov/waste/fact_sheets/cleaners_in_home.pdf

3. "Collecting Household Toxics: Is It Worth the Effort?," *Waste Age,* Ann Mattheis, February 1987 • http://www.p2pays.org/ref/08/07907.pdf

4. *Consumer's Guide to Household Hazardous Waste*, Mississippi Department of Environmental Quality • http://www.deq.state.ms.us/MDEQ.nsf/pdf/Recycling_ConsumerGuidetoHouseholdHazardousWaste/$File/HHWGuide.pdf?OpenElement

5. *From Chaos to Construction: Lessons Learned When Constructing a Permanent HHWCC on a Landfill*; Sue Gordon and Tim Grogan; County of Orange (CA) Integrated Waste Management Department; March 25, 2004; Powerpoint presentation to the California HHW & Used Oil Conference • http://www.ciwmb.ca.gov/hhw/Events/AnnualConf/2004/Presentation/GroganGordon.pdf

6. *HHW Programs: From One-Day Events to Integrated Strategies*; MSWManagement.com; April 2007; Bruce J. Edmonds III and Chace Anderson • http://www.gradingandexcavation.com/mw_0704_hhw.html

7. *Household Hazardous Waste Collection Programs: An Organizer's Guide to Planning, Orchestrating, and Surviving a Household Hazardous Waste Collection Day*, Center for Hazardous Materials Research, University of Pittsburgh Applied Research Center, 320 William Pitt Way, Pittsburgh, PA 15238, December 1991 • http://www.p2pays.org/ref/36/35230.pdf

8. *Household Hazardous Waste Environmental Fact Sheet* (WMD-HD-3) (2003), New Hampshire Department of Environmental Services, 29 Hazen Drive, Concord, NH 03301 • http://www.des.nh.gov/factsheets/hw/hw-3.htm

9. *Household Hazardous Waste Management: A Manual for One-Day Collection Programs;* U.S. Environmental Protection Agency (EPA), Solid Waste and Emergency Response (OS-305), August 1993, (EPA/530-R-92-026). www.smallbiz-enviroweb.org/pub_video/epadocs/cdocs/c69.pdf

10. *Household HazWaste: Reduction is your first choice*, Wisconsin Department of Natural Resources, PUB-SW-738 95, pamphlet • http://www3.uwm.edu/Dept/shwec/publications/cabinet/pdf/DNR_HHW.pdf

11. *Household Product Management: A Resource Guide for Managing Household Products and Household Hazardous Waste*, Southern States Energy Board (SSEB), September 1998. For a copy of this guide, contact SSEB at sseb@sseb.org • http://www.sseb.org/pubs.htm

12. *Household/Small Business Hazardous Waste: Manual for Sponsoring a Collection Event;* Pennsylvania Department of Environmental Protection, revised June 1999, (2500-BK-DEP2134) • http://www.depweb.state.pa.us/landrecwaste/lib/landrecwaste/hhw/techman.pdf

13. *Hurricane Katrina Disaster Debris Management; Lessons Learned from State and Local Governments—Briefing Report;* Solid Waste Management Association of North America Applied Research Foundation, September 21, 2005 • http://swana.org/pdf/swana_pdf_358.pdf

14. *Janitorial Products P2 Project (JP4) Factsheets;* Western Regional Pollution Prevention Network (WRPPN); http://www.wrppn.org/Janitorial/factsheets.cfm

15. *Little Known But Allowable Ways to Deal With Hazardous Waste;* U.S. Environmental Protection Agency, Small Business Division, Washington, D.C.; May 2000. (EPA 233-B-00-002) • http://www.epa.gov/sbo/pdfs/hazwaste_500.pdf

16. *Learn About Hazardous Products in Your Home Poster,* Idaho Department of Environmental Quality, January 2007 • http://www.deq.state.id.us/waste/assist_citizen_comm/hhw_poster.pdf

17. *National Product Stewardship Forum Presentations held on May 30–31, 2007, in San Francisco, California* • http://www.productstewardship.us/displaycommon.cfm?an=1&subarticlenbr=221

18. *North American Hazardous Materials Management Association (NAHMMA) 2005 Conference Presentations.* ftp://ftp.dep.state.fl.us/pub/hhwprogram/NAHMMA%20Conference%202005/

19. *Planning for a Community Household Hazardous Waste Collection Event,* Alaska Department of Environmental Conservation, Division of Environmental Health, Solid Waste Management Programming Office, October 2005 • http://www.dec.state.ak.us/eh/sw/Factsheets/Household%20hazardous%20waste.pdf

Periodicals

Periodicals—Hardcopy, and On-line

1. *BioCycle,* JG Press, Inc., 419 State Avenue, 2nd Floor, Emmaus, PA 18049.Phone: 641-472-2790 • http://www.jgpress.com/biocycle.htm • BioCycle E-mail alert sign-up: http://www.jgpress.com/signups.html

2. EnvironmentalChemistry.com, 326 Auburn Street, #10, Portland, ME 04103 • Phone: 207-797-8202 • http://www.environmentalchemistry.com

3. *Environmental Health Perspectives* (EHP), c/o Brogan & Partners, 4011 Westchase Boulevard, Suite 150, Raleigh, NC 27607 • Phone: 866-541-3841 • E-mail: ehponline@niehs.nih.gov • http://www.ehponline.org • Newsletter and e-mail update subscriptions: http://www.ehponline.org/docs/admin/newsletter.html

4. *E/The Environmental Magazine,* 28 Knight Street, Norwalk, CT 06851 • Phone: 203-854-5559 • E-mail: Info@emagazine.com • http://www.emagazine.com

5. Environmental News Network, Inc. (ENN), 402 North B Street, Fairfield, IA 52556 • Phone: 800-957-8599 • http://www.enn.com

6. *Environmental Protection,* 5151 Beltline Road, Dallas, TX 75254 • Phone: 972-687-6700 • http://www.eponline.com • Weekly e-newsletter subscription: http://www.eponline.com/subscriptionmagenews.html

7. *MSW Management,* Street Address: 2046 De la Vina Street, Santa Barbara, CA 93105 • Phone: 805-682-1300. Mailing Address: P.O. Box 3100, Santa Barbara, CA 93130 • E-mail: mswinfo@forester.net • http://www.mswmanagement.com

8. Raymond Communications, Inc., 5111 Berwyn Road #115, College Park, MD 20740 • Phone: 301-345-4217. Email: circulation@raymond.com • http://www.raymond.com • Electronic newsletter subscription with service: http://www.raymond.com

9. *Resource Recycling,* P.O. Box 42279, Portland, OR 97242-0270 • Phone: 503-233-1305 • E-mail: Info@resource-recycling.com • http://www.resource-recycling.com • Electronic newsletter subscription: http://www.resource-recycling.com

10. *Recycling Today,* 4020 Kinross Lakes Parkway, Suite 201, Richfield, OH 44286 • Phone: 800-456-0707 • http://www.recyclingtoday.com/

11. *ScienceDaily,* 2 Wisconsin Circle, Suite 700, Chevy Chase, MD 30815 • Phone: 202-558-2103 • E-mail: editor@sciencedaily.com • http://www.sciencedaily.com/ Electronic newsletter subscription available: http://www.sciencedaily.com/

12. *The Scientist,* 400 Market Street, Suite 1250, Philadelphia, PA 19106 • Phone: 215-351-1660 • E-mail: info@the-scientist.com • http://www.the-scientist.com/ • Electronic newsletter subscription is available: http://www.the-scientist.com/

13. *Waste Age,* 6151 Powers Ferry Road NW, Suite 200, Atlanta, GA 30339 • Phone: 770-618-0333 • http://www.wasteage.com • Electronic newsletters subscriptions: http://subscribe.wasteage.com/?tc=NNWEB

14. *Waste Business Journal,* P.O. Box 40034, San Diego, CA 92164-0034 • Phone: 619-793-5190 • E-mail: info@wastebusinessjournal.com • http://www.wastebusinessjournal.com • Electronic weekly bulleting subscription: http://www.wastebusinessjournal.com

15. *Waste Management World,* 1421 South Sheridan Road, Tulsa, OK 74112 • Phone: 918-831-9884 • http://www.waste-management-world.com

16. *Waste News,* 1725 Merriman Road, Akron, OH 44313 • Phone: 330-836-9180 • E-mail: editorial@wastenews.com • http://www.wastenews.com

Federal and State Websites and Resources

Federal

1. The Agency for Toxic Substances and Disease Registry (ATSDR), U.S. Department of Health and Human Services • http://www.atsdr.cdc.gov
2. Centers for Disease Control and Prevention (CDC), U.S. Department of Health and Human Services • http://www.cdc.gov
3. Federal Emergency Management Agency (FEMA), Department of Homeland Security, FEMA, Independent Study Program: IS-55 Household Hazardous Materials—A Guide for Citizens. Online training program for citizens. • http://training. fema.gov/EMIWEB/is/is55.asp
4. FEMA, Household Chemical Emergencies • http://www.fema.gov/areyouready/ household_chemical_emergencies.shtm
5. National Institute Environmental Health Services (NIEHS), National Institutes of Health • http://www.niehs.nih.gov
6. Occupational Safety & Health Administration (OSHA), U.S Department of Labor • http://www.osha.gov
7. OSHA Laws, Regulations and Interpretations • www.osha.gov/comp-links.html
8. Pipeline and Hazardous Materials Safety Administration, Office of Hazardous Materials Safety, U.S. Department of Transportation • http://hazmat.dot.gov
9. Resource Conservation & Recovery Act (RCRA), General Resource Conservation and Recovery Act (RCRA) Hazardous Waste—RCRA Orientation Manual 2006 • http://www.epa.gov/epaoswer/general/orientat
10. RCRA Online • http://www.epa.gov/rcraonline • U.S. EPA RCRA online database providing access to documents and other research materials.
11. U.S. Environmental Protection Agency (EPA) • http://www.epa.gov
    U.S. EPA Regions
    U.S. EPA Region 1 • http://www.epa.gov/NE
    U.S. EPA Region 2 • http://www.epa.gov/region02
    U.S. EPA Region 3 • http://www.epa.gov/region03/index.htm
    U.S. EPA Region 4 • http://www.epa.gov/region4
    U.S. EPA Region 5 • http://www.epa.gov/region5
    U.S. EPA Region 6 • http://www.epa.gov/earth1r6
    U.S. EPA Region 7 • http://www.epa.gov/region7
    U.S. EPA Region 8 • http://www.epa.gov/region8
    U.S. EPA Region 9 • http://www.epa.gov/region09
    U.S. EPA Region 10 • http://www.epa.gov/region10
    Other U.S.. EPA Webpages
    U.S. EPA Environmental Laws • http://www.epa.gov/epahome/laws.htm
    U.S. EPA Executive Orders • http://www.epa.gov/fedrgstr/eo/index.html
    U.S. EPA Federal Register Environmental Documents • http://www.epa.gov/ fedrgstr/index.html
    U.S. EPA Household Hazardous Waste Webpage • http://www.epa.gov/msw/ hhw.htm • http://www.epa.gov/epaoswer/non-hw/muncpl/hhw.htm

U.S. EPA, Office of Solid Waste • http://www.epa.gov/osw/

U.S. EPA Recycling Management Tool • http://www.epa.gov/epaoswer/non-hw/recycle/recmeas/

U.S. EPA Toxics Release Inventory (TRI) Program • www.epa.gov/tri/tridata/tri05/index.htm

U.S. EPA Universal Waste Laws & Regulations • www.epa.gov/epaoswer/haz-waste/id/univwast/laws.htm

U.S. EPA Waste Climate Change Tools (Greenhouse Gas Impact calculator) • http://epa.gov/climatechange/wycd/waste/tools.html

State

Alabama

1. Alabama Department of Economic and Community Affairs (ADECA), 401 Adams Avenue, Suite 560, P.O. Box 5690, Montgomery, AL 36103-5690 • Phone: 334-242-5100 • E-mail: ADECA.webmaster.Info@adeca.alabama.gov • http://www.adeca.alabama.gov

2. Alabama Department of Environmental Management (ADEM), 1400 Coliseum Boulevard, Montgomery, AL 36110-2059 • Mailing Address: P.O. Box 301463, Montgomery, AL 36130-1463 • Phone: 334-271-7700 • http://www.adem.state.al.us • http://www.adem.state.al.us/LandDivision/HazWaste/HazWasteMainInfo.htm

3. Other Alabama Resources:
    a. Alabama Environmental Council, 2717 7th Avenue, South, Birmingham, AL 35203 • Phone: 205-322-3125 • http://www.aeconline.ws
    b. Alabama Environmental News (BEN), Pat Byington, Publisher • 205-999-4390 • E-mail: pkbyington@aol.com • http://www.bamanews.com
    c. Alabama League of Action Environmental Voters, P.O. Box 1987, Montgomery, AL 36102-1987 • Phone: 334-221-5882 • E-mail: voter98@aol.com • http://www.alaleavs.org
    d. Project ROSE (Recycled Oil Saves Energy), Alabama Department of Economic and Community Affairs (ADECA) • http://prose.eng.ua.edu

Alaska

1. Alaska Department of Environmental Conservation (ADEC), Division of Environmental Health, Solid Waste Management Program, 410 Willoughby Avenue, Suite 105, Juneau, AK 99801-1795 • Phone: 907-465-5150

2. Other Alaska Resources:
    a. Alaska Environmental Links • http://www.alaska.net/~jrc/alaska.html
    b. Environmental Education Outreach Program (EEOP) • http://www4.nau.edu/eeop/ak_region10.html
    c. Solid Waste Alaska Network (SWAN) • http://www.ccthita-swan.org/main/index.cfm

Arizona

1. Arizona Department of Environmental Quality (ADEQ), 1110 West Washington Street, Phoenix, AZ 85007 • Phone: 602-771-2300 • Toll-free 800-234-5677 • http://www.azdeq.gov
2. Other Arizona Resources:
   a. Arizona Association for Environmental Education • http://www.arizonaee.org
   b. Arizona Climate Change Advisory Group (CCAG) • http://www.azclimat-echange.us
   c. The University of Arizona Udall Center for Studies in Public Policy • http://www.udallcenter.arizona.edu/programs/enrp/index.html

Arkansas

1. Arkansas Department of Environmental Quality, Solid Waste Management Division—Recycling Branch, 8017 Interstate 30, Little Rock, AR 72209 • Mailing Address: P.O. Box 8913, Little Rock, AR 72219-8913 • Phone: 501-682-0600 • ADEQ Helpline: 501-682-0923 • http://www.adeq.state.ar.us/solwaste/branch_recycling/hhwcc.htm
2. Other Arkansas Resources:
   a. Arkansas Center for Environmental Studies • http://www.uams.edu/aces/Files/Links.html
   b. Arkansas Environmental Education Association • http://www.uca.edu/org/aeea
   c. Arkansas Recycling Coalition • http://www.recycleark.org

California

1. California Department of Toxic Substances Control (DTSC), DTSC Headquarters (Joe Serna Jr. Cal/EPA Headquarters Building), 1001 I Street, Sacramento, CA 95814-2828 • Mailing Address: P.O. Box 806, Sacramento, CA 95812-0806 • http://www.dtsc.ca.gov
2. California Integrated Waste Management Board (CIWMB), 1001 I Street, P.O. Box 4025, Sacramento, CA 95812-4025 • Phone: 916-341-6000 • http://www.ciwmb.ca.gov
3. Other California Resources:
   a. The Association for Environmental and Outdoor Education • http://aeoe.org
   b. Californians Against Waste (CAW) • http://www.cawrecycles.org
   c. California Environmental Health Association • http://www.ceha.org
   d. California Office of Environmental Health Hazard Assessment (OEHHA), http://www.oehha.ca.gov
   e. California Resource Recovery Association (CRRA), http://www.crra.com
   f. California Universal Waste Rules • http://www.ciwmb.ca.gov/WPIE/HazSub/UniWaste.htm
   g. eRecycle.org • http://www.erecycle.org

h. eRecycle.org is a partnership between government, manufacturers, retailers, and the environmental community to provide guidance and information to consumers about recycling electronic waste in California.

i. Northern California Association of Law Libraries (NOCALL), Environmental Law Resources • http://www.nocall.org/links/environment.html

Colorado

1. Colorado Department of Public Health and Environment (CDPHE), Hazardous Materials and Waste Management Division, 4300 Cherry Creek Drive South, Denver, CO 80246-1530 (Located in Glendale, Colorado) • Phone: 303-692-2000 or 1-800-886-7689 (In-state) • http://www.cdphe.state.co.us/hm/hhw/index.htm

2. Other helpful information:
   a. Colorado Association for Recycling (CAFR) • http://www.cafr.org
   b. Colorado Alliance for Environmental Education • http://www.caee.org
   c. Colorado Bar Association, Environmental Law • http://www.cobar.org/listservs.cfm
   d. Colorado Conditionally Exempt Small Quantity Generator (CESQG) Waste Consolidation Programs • http://www.cdphe.state.co.us/hm/cesqgwaste.htm
   e. Colorado Environmental Coalition • http://www.ourcolorado.org

Connecticut

1. Connecticut Department of Environmental Protection, 79 Elm Street, Hartford, CT 06106-5127 • Phone: 860-424-3000 • http://www.ct.gov

2. Other Connecticut Resources:
   a. Connecticut Outdoor & Environmental Education Association (COEEA) • http://coeea.org
   b. Northeast Recycling Council (NERC) • http://www.nerc.org/connecticut.html

Delaware

1. Delaware Department of Natural Resources & Environmental Control (DNREC), 89 Kings Highway, Dover, DE 19901• Phone: 302-739-9400 • http://www.dnrec.delaware.gov

2. Delaware Solid Waste Authority, 1128 South Bradford Street, Dover, DE 19901 • Phone: 302-739-5361 • http://www.dswa.com • Citizens' Response Line 800-404-7080

3. Other Delaware Resources:
   a. Northeast Recycling Council (NERC) • http://www.nerc.org/delaware.html

District of Columbia

1. Government of the District of Columbia, Department of Public Works, Franklin D. Reeves Center, 2000 14th Street, NW, 6th Floor, Washington, DC 26009 • Phone: 202-727-1000 • E-mail: dpw@dc.gov • http://dpw.dc.gov/dpw

2. Other DC Resources:
    a. District Department of the Environment (DDOE) • http://ddoe.dc.gov/ddoe/
        site/default.asp

Florida

1. Florida Department of Environmental Protection, Bureau of Solid & Hazard-
    ous Waste, Division of Waste Management, 2600 Blair Stone Road, Mail Station
    #4550, Tallahassee, FL 32399-2400 • Phone: 850-245-8707 • http://www.dep.state.
    fl.us/waste/categories/hazardous/default.htm
2. Other Florida Resources:
    a. Recycle Florida Today (RFT) • http://www.recyclefloridatoday.org
    b. William W. "Bill" Hinkley Center for Solid and Hazardous Waste Manage-
        ment • http://www.floridacenter.org

Georgia

1. Georgia Department of Community Affairs, 60 Executive Park South, NE, Atlanta,
    GA 30329 • Phone: 404-679-4940 • Toll-free: 800-359-4663 • http://www.dca.
    state.ga.us
2. Other Georgia Resources:
    a. Environmental Education in Georgia • http://eeingeorgia.org
    b. Georgia Recycling Coalition • http://www.georgiarecycles.org

Hawaii

1. Hawai'i Department of Health, Solid and Hazardous Waste Branch, 919 Ala Moana
    Boulevard #212, Honolulu, HI 96814 • Phone: 808-586-4266 • http://www.hawaii.
    gov/health/environmental/waste/p2wastemin/index.html
2. Other Hawai'i Resources:
    a. Sustainable Hawai'i, University of Hawai'i at Manoa • http://www.sustain-
        ablehawaii.hawaii.edu/index.html

Idaho

1. Idaho Department of Environmental Quality, Waste Management and Remediation
    Division, DEQ State Office, 1410 North Hilton, Boise, ID 83706 • Phone: 208-
    373-0502 • http://www.deq.state.id.us/waste
2. Other Idaho Resources:
    a. Idaho Environmental Education Association • http://idahoee.org

Illinois

1. Illinois Department of Commerce and Economic Opportunity (DECO), 620 East
    Adams, Springfield, IL 62701 • Phone: 217-782-7500 • http://www.commerce.
    state.il.us/dceo

2. Illinois Environmental Protection Agency, Bureau of Land, 1021 North Grand Avenue East, P.O. Box 19276, Springfield, IL 62794-9276 • Phone: 217-782-3397 • http://www.epa.state.il.us/land/hazardous-waste/household-haz-waste
3. Other Illinois Resources:
   a. Chicago Recycling Coalition • http://www.chicagorecycling.org
   b. Environmental Education Association of Illinois • http://www.eeai.net
   c. Greening Schools • http://www.greeningschools.org
   d. Illinois Recycling Association • http://www.illinoisrecycles.org
   e. Illinois Waste Management and Research Center • http://www.wmrc.uiuc.edu

Indiana

1. Indiana Department of Environmental Management, Source Reduction and Recycling Branch, Office of Pollution Prevention & Technical Assistance, 100 North Senate Avenue, MC 64-01, Indianapolis, IN 46204-2251 • Phone: 317-232-8172 or 800-988-7901 • http://www.in.gov/idem/programs/oppta/index.html
2. Other Indiana Resources:
   a. Association of Indiana Solid Waste Management Districts, Inc. • http://www.aiswmd.org
   b. Environmental Education Association of Indiana • http://www.goshen.edu/eeai
   c. Indiana Department of Natural Resources • http://www.in.gov/dnr
   d. Indiana Economic Development Corporation • http://www.in.gov/iedc
   e. Indiana Household Hazardous Waste Regulations, Recycle Indiana • http://www.in.gov/recycle/topics/hhw/regulations.html
   f. Indiana Materials Xchange (IMX) • http://www.in.gov/recycle/imx/index.html
   g. Indiana Recycling Coalition • http://www.indianarecycling.org
   h. Indiana Watershed Leadership Program • http://www.ces.purdue.edu/water-quality/iwlp.html
   i. Keep Indianapolis Beautiful • http://www.kibi.org/recycle/index.htm
   j. Recycle Indiana • http://www.in.gov/recycle/index.html

Iowa

1. Iowa Department of Natural Resources, Energy & Waste Management Bureau, Wallace State Office Building, 502 East 9th Street, Des Moines, IA 50319-0034 • Phone: 515-281-5918 • http://www.iowadnr.com/waste/index.html
2. Other Iowa Resources:
   a. Iowa Environmental and Natural Resources Law Section • http://members.aol.com/JurTerra/section
   b. Iowa Recycling Association • http://iowarecycles.org
   c. Iowa Society of Solid Waste Operations • http://www.isoswo.org
   d. Iowa Waste Reduction Center • http://www.iwrc.org
   e. Keep Iowa Beautiful • http://www.keepiowabeautiful.com

f. Metro Waste Authority • http://www.mwatoday.com

g. Recycle Iowa • http://www.recycleiowa.org

Kansas

1. Kansas Department of Health and Environment (KDHE), Bureau of Waste Management, 1000 SW Jackson Street, Suite 320, Topeka, KS 66612-1366 • Phone: 785-296-1600 • http://www.kdheks.gov/waste/bwm_hhw.html

2. Other Helpful Resources:

   a. Kansas Business & Industry Recycling Program (BIRP) • http://www.kansasbirp.com

   b. Kansas Legislative Update on the Environment (KLUE) • http://www.knrc.ws/klue.htm

   c. Kansas Natural Resource Council (KNRC) • http://www.knrc.ws

   d. Kansas Organization of Recyclers (KOR) • http://www.kskor.org

   e. Students for Environmental Action (SEA) • http://www.k-state.edu/environment

   f. Johnson County Environmental Department, Buddy the Recycler. Created by Johnson County • http://jced.jocogov.org/hazardous_materials/khhw/kids_page.htm

Kentucky

1. Kentucky Department of Environmental Protection, Division of Waste Management, 14 Reilly Road, Frankfort, KY 40601 • Phone: 502-564-6716 • E-mail: waste@ky.gov • http://www.waste.ky.gov

2. Other Kentucky Resources:

   a. Kentucky Environmental Education Council (KEEC) • http://keec.ky.gov

   b. Kentucky Institute for the Environment and Sustainable Development (KIESD) • http://louisville.edu/org/kiesd

Louisiana

1. Louisiana Department of Environmental Quality, 602 North Fifth Street, Baton Rouge, LA 70802 • Phone: 225-219-5337 • http://www.deq.louisiana.gov

2. Other Louisiana Resources:

   a. Louisiana Environmental Action Network • http://leanweb.org

   b. Louisiana Office of Environmental Education • http://www.gov.state.la.us/enved/default.htm

   c. Recycle Louisiana • http://www.recyclelouisiana.com

Maine

1. Maine Department of Environmental Protection, Bureau of Remediation & Waste Management, 17 State House Station, Augusta, ME 04333-0017 • Phone: 207-287-7688 or 800-452-1942 • http://www.maine.gov/dep/rwm/homeowner/household-hazwaste

2. Maine State Planning Office, Waste Management & Recycling Program, 38 State House Station, 184 State Street, Augusta, ME 04333 • Phone: 207-287-3261 or 800-662-4545 • http://www.maine.gov/spo/recycle
3. Other Maine Resources:
   a. Environmental Health Strategy Center • http://www.preventharm.org
   b. Maine Environmental Education Association • http://www.meeassociation.org
   c. Maine Resource Recovery Association (MRRA) • http://www.mrra.net
   d. Maine Department of Environmental Protection, Toxics and Hazardous Waste Reduction Program (THWRP) • http://www.maine.gov/dep/oia/thwrp

Maryland

1. Maryland Department of the Environment, 1800 Washington Boulevard, Baltimore, MD 21230 • Phone: 410-537-3000 or 800-633-6101 • http://www.mde.state.md.us/Programs/landPrograms
2. Other Maryland Resources:
   a. Maryland Recyclers Coalition • http://www.marylandrecyclers.org
   b. Maryland Association for Environmental & Outdoor Education • http://www.maeoe.org

Massachusetts

1. Massachusetts Department of Environmental Protection, One Winter Street, Boston, MA 02108 • Phone: 617-292-5500 • http://www.mass.gov/dep
2. Other Massachusetts Resources:
   a. MassRecycle • http://www.massrecycle.org
   b. Toxic Use Reduction Institute • http://www.turi.org
   c. WasteCap of Massachusetts • http://www.wastecap.org

Michigan

1. Michigan Department of Environmental Quality, Waste and Hazardous Materials Division, 525 West Allegan Street, P.O. Box 30473, Lansing, MI 48909-7973 • Phone: 517-373-7917 • http://www.michigan.gov/deq
2. Other Michigan Resources:
   a. Ecology Center • http://www.ecocenter.org
   b. Michigan Alliance for Environmental and Outdoor Education • http://www.michiganenvironmentaled.org
   c. Michigan Environmental Council • http://www.mecprotects.org
   d. Michigan Recycling Coalition • http://www.michiganrecycles.org
   e. Michigan State University, Knight Center for Environmental Journalism • http://www.ej.msu.edu
   f. State Bar of Michigan, Environmental Law • http://www.michbar.org/environmental/deskbook.cfm

Minnesota

1. Minnesota Pollution Control Agency, 520 Lafayette Road, St. Paul, MN 55155-4194 • Phone: 651-296-6300 or 800-657-3864 (in Minnesota only) • http://www.pca.state.mn.us/waste
2. Other Minnesota Resources:
   a. Bridges: Environmental Information Access in Minnesota • http://www.bridges.state.mn.us
   b. Minnesota Sustainable Communities Network • http://www.nextstep.state.mn.us
   c. Recycling Association of Minnesota • http://www.recycleminnesota.org
   d. Sharing Environmental Education Knowledge (SEEK) • http://www.seek.state.mn.us
   e. University of Minnesota, Duluth, Center for Environmental Education (CEED) • http://www.d.umn.edu/ceed

Missouri

1. Missouri Department of Natural Resources, Division of Environmental Quality, P.O. Box 176, Jefferson City, MO 65102 • Phone: 573-751-3176 • E-mail: haz-waste@dnr.mo.gov

2. Other Missouri Resources:
   a. Household Hazardous Waste Project, University of Missouri Extension, Office of Waste Management • http://extension.missouri.edu/owm/hhw.htm
   b. Missouri Environmental Education Association • http://www.meea.org
   c. Missouri Recycling Association • http://www.mora.org

Montana

1. Montana Department of Environmental Quality, Air, Energy & Pollution Prevention Bureau, Planning, Prevention and Assistance Division, 1520 East Sixth Avenue, P.O. Box 200901, Helena, MT 59620-0901 • Phone: 406-444-4643 • http://www.deq.state.mt.us/Recycle
2. Other Montana Resources:
   a. Montana Environmental Education Association • http://www.montanaeea.org
   b. Montana Material Exchange • http://www.montana.edu/mme/links.php
   c. Montana Pollution Prevention Program • Montana State University • http://www.montana.edu/wwwated
   d. Recycle Montana • http://recyclemontana.org

Nebraska

1. Nebraska Department of Environmental Quality, 1200 "N" Street, Suite 400, P.O. Box 98922, Lincoln, NE 68509 • Phone: 402-471-2186 • http://www.deq.state.ne.us

2. Other Nebraska Resources:
   a. Keep Nebraska Beautiful • http://www.knb.org
   b. Nebraska Alliance for Conservation and Environment Education • http:// www.nacee.org
   c. Nebraska Environmental Trust • http://www.environmentaltrust.org
   d. Nebraska State Recycling Association • http://recyclenebraska.org
   e. WasteCap Nebraska • http://www.wastecapne.org

Nevada

1. Nevada Department of Conservation & Natural Resources, Division of Environmental Protection, 901 South Stewart Street, Suite 401, Carson City, NV 89701-5249 • Phone: 800-597-5865 • http://ndep.nv.gov/mercury/mercury_recycling.htm
2. Other Nevada Resources:
   a. Nevada Natural Resource Education Council • http://www.nnrec.org

New Hampshire

1. New Hampshire Department of Environmental Services, Waste Management Division, 29 Hazen Drive, Concord, NH 03301-6509 • Phone: 603-271-2900 • E-mail: hhw@des.state.nh.us • http://www.des.state.nh.us/hhw
2. Other New Hampshire Resources:
   a. New Hampshire Environmental Educators Association • http://www.neeea. org/nh
   b. New Hampshire Office of Energy and Planning • http://www.nh.gov/oep
   c. New Hampshire the Beautiful • http://www.nhthebeautiful.org
   d. Northeast Recycling Council • http://www.nerc.org/newhampshire.html

New Jersey

1. New Jersey Department of Environmental Protection, Solid & Hazardous Waste Department, P.O. Box 414, 401 East State Street, Trenton, NJ 08625 • Phone: 609-633-1418 • http://www.state.nj.us/dep/dshw
2. Other New Jersey Resources:
   a. Association of New Jersey Household Hazardous Waste Coordinators (ANJHHWC) • http://www.njhazwaste.com
   b. Association of New Jersey Recyclers (ANJR) • http://anjr.com
   c. New Jersey State League of Municipalities • http://www.njslom.org
   d. Solid Waste Policy Group, Rutgers University • http://aesop.rutgers.edu/ ~wastemgmt

New Mexico

1. New Mexico Environment Department, 2290 St. Francis Drive N4050, P.O. Box 26110, Santa Fe, NM 87505 • Phone: 505-827-2855 or 800-219-6157 • http://www. nmenv.state.nm.us

2. Other New Mexico Resources:
   a. Environmental Education Association of New Mexico • http://www.eeanm. org
   b. New Mexico Clean & Beautiful • http://www.nmcleanandbeautiful.com
   c. New Mexico Recycling Coalition • http://www.nmrecycle.org
   d. New Mexico Environmental Finance Center, New Mexico Institute of Mining & Technology • http://129.24.3.38/home.php

New York

1. New York Department of Environmental Conservation, 625 Broadway, Albany, New York 12233-0001 • Phone: 518-402-8013 • http://www.dec.ny.gov
2. Other New York Resources:
   a. Environmental Education Advisory Council • http://www.eeac-nyc.org
   b. Federation of New York Solid Waste Associations • http://www.nyfederation. org
   c. New York City Department of Sanitation • http://www.nyc.gov/html/dsny/html/home/home.shtml
   d. New York State Association of Solid Waste Management • http://www.new yorkwaste.org
   e. New York State Association of Reduction, Reuse and Recycling • http://www. nysar3.org

North Carolina

1. North Carolina Department of Environment and Natural Resources, Division of Waste Management, 401 Oberlin Road, Suite 150, Raleigh, NC 27605 • Phone: 919-508-8400 • http://www.wastenotnc.org/swhome/hhw.asp
2. Other North Carolina Resources:
   a. Carolina Recycling Association (CFA) • http://www.cra-recycle.org
   b. Land-of-Sky Regional Council • http://www.landofsky.org
   c. North Carolina Cooperative Extension Service • http://www.ces.ncsu.edu/depts/fcs
   d. North Carolina Office of Environmental Education • http://www.eenorthcar-olina.org
   e. University of North Carolina-Chapel Hill, Environmental Finance Center • http://www.efc.unc.edu

Ohio

1. Ohio Environmental Protection Agency (EPA), Division of Solid & Infectious Waste Management, 50 West Town Street, Suite 700, Columbus, OH 43215 • Phone: 614-644-3020 • http://www.epa.state.oh.us
2. Ohio Department of Natural Resources (DNR), Division of Recycling & Litter Prevention, 2045 Morse Road, Building C-2, Columbus, OH 43229-6693 • Phone: 614-265-6333 • http://www.dnr.state.oh.us/recycling

3. Other Ohio Resources:
   a. Association of Ohio Recyclers (AOR) • http://www.aor-omex.org
   b. Eco City Cleveland • http://www.ecocitycleveland.org
   c. Environmental Education Council of Ohio (EECO) • http://www.eeco-online.org
   d. Great Lakes Environmental Finance Center • http://urban.csuohio.edu/glefc
   e. Solid Waste Authority of Central Ohio • http://www.swaco.org
   f. Summit/Akron Solid Waste Management Authority • http://www.saswma.org
   g. Sustainability-Involved Organizations in Southeast Ohio • http://www.gasp.athens.oh.us/susorgs.shtml
   h. Sustainable Cincinnati • http://www.sustainablecincinnati.org
   i. Sustainability Roundtable of Central Ohio • http://www.swaco.org/SRCO.aspx

Oklahoma

1. Oklahoma Department of Environmental Quality (DEQ), Land Protection Division, P.O. Box 1677, Oklahoma City, OK 73101-1677 • Phone: 405-702-5100 • http://www.deq.state.ok.us/LPDnew
2. Other Oklahoma Resources:
   a. INCOG (Council of Governments for Tulsa Area) • http://www.incog.org
   b. Keep Tulsa Beautiful • http://www.tulsabeautiful.com
   c. The Metropolitan Environmental Trust (M.e.t.) • http://www.metrecycle.com/computer.htm
   d. Oklahoma Association of Environmental Education • http://www.okaee.org
   e. Oklahoma Recycling Association • http://www.recycleok.org
   f. Oklahoma Sustainability Network • http://www.oksustainability.org
   g. Sustainable Tulsa • http://www.sustainabletulsa.org

Oregon

1. Oregon Department of Environmental Quality (DEQ), Land Quality Division, 811 SW 6th Avenue, Portland, OR 97204-1390 • Phone: 03-229-5696 • http://www.oregon.gov/DEQ
2. Other Oregon Resources:
   a. Association of Oregon Recyclers (AOR) • http://www.aorr.org
   b. Metro (Portland) • http://www.metro-region.org
   c. NW MaterialSmart Exchange • http://www.nwmaterialsmart.org
   d. Oregon Biofuels Network • http://www.biofuels4oregon.org
   e. Oregon Department of Environmental Quality, Publications and Forms http://www.deq.state.or.us/pubs/reports.htm
   f. SOLV • http://www.solv.org
   g. Water Watch • http://www.waterwatch.org

Pennsylvania

1. Commonwealth of Pennsylvania, Department of Environmental Protection, Bureau of Waste Management, Rachel Carson State Office Building, P.O. Box 8471, Harrisburg, PA 17105-8471 • Phone: 717-787-7382 • E-mail: recyclepa@state.pa.us
    Pennsylvania Recycling Hotline: 1-800-346-4242 • http://www.depweb.state.pa.us/landrecwaste
2. Other Pennsylvania Resources:
    a. Environmental Fund of Pennsylvania • http://www.greenworks.tv/efp/about_us.htm
    b. Keep Pennsylvania Beautiful • http://www.keeppabeautiful.org
    c. Northeast Recycling Council (NERC) • http://www.nerc.org/pennsylvania.html
    d. Pennsylvania Center for Environmental Education (PCEE) • http://www.pcee.org
    e. Pennsylvania Cleanways • http://www.pacleanways.org
    f. Pennsylvania Department of Conservation and Natural Resources (DCNR) • http://www.dcnr.state.pa.us
    g. Pennsylvania Environmental Council (PEC) • http://www.pecpa.org
    h. Pennsylvania Resources Council, Inc. (PRC) • http://www.prc.org/community_hhw.html
    i. PRC administers the Southwestern PA Household Hazardous Waste Task Force • http://www.swpahhw.org
    j. The Professional Recyclers of Pennsylvania (PROP) • http://www.proprecycles.org

Rhode Island

1. Rhode Island Department of Environmental Management (DEM), Office of Waste Management, 235 Promenade Street, Providence, RI 02908-5767 • Phone: 401-222-2797 • http://www.dem.ri.gov/programs/benviron/waste
2. Rhode Island Resource Recovery Corporation, 65 Shun Pike, Johnston, RI 02919 • Phone: 401-942-1430 • info@rirrc.org • http://www.rirrc.org
3. Other Rhode Island Resources:
    a. Rhode Island Environmental Education Association • http://www.rieea.org

South Carolina

1. South Carolina Department of Health and Environmental Control (DHEC), Division of Waste Management, 2600 Bull Street, Columbia, SC 29201 • Phone: 803-898-3432 • http://www.scdhec.gov/eqc/lwm/html/haz.html
2. South Carolina Department of Health and Environmental Control (DHEC), Office of Solid Waste Reduction and Recycling, 2600 Bull Street, Columbia, SC 29201 • Phone: 800-768-7348 • http://www.scdhec.gov/recycle/index.html
3. Other South Carolina Resources:
    a. Carolina Recycling Association (CFA) • http://www.cra-recycle.org

    b. Environmental Education Association of South Carolina (EEASC) • http://
alpha1.fmarion.edu/~scenvedu/EEASC.html

    c. DHEC Compliance Assistance Program, Land & Waste Management Program Area Assistance • http://www.scdhec.net/environment/admin/compass/
CompassLWM.htm

South Dakota

1. South Dakota Department of Environment & Natural Resources, Waste Management Program, Joe Foss Building, 523 East Capitol, Pierre, SD 57501 • Phone: 605-773-3153 • http://www.state.sd.us/denr/DES/WasteMgn/WMPpage1.htm

Tennessee

1. Tennessee Department of Environment and Conservation, Division of Solid and Hazardous Waste Management, 401 Church Street, 1st Floor, L&C Annex, Nashville, TN 37243-0435 • Phone: 615-532-0109 • E-mail: ask.tdec@state.tn.us • http://www.state.tn.us/environment/swm/hhw

2. Other Tennessee Resources:

    a. Appalachian Resource Conservation and Development Council • http://www.
appalachianrcd.org

    b. Tennessee Environmental Council • http://www.tectn.org

    c. Tennessee Pollution Prevention Partnership (TP3) • http://tennessee.gov/
environment/ea/tp3

    c. Tennessee Recycling Coalition (TRC) • http://www.trc-online.org

    d. The University of Tennessee - Knoxville, Energy, Environment and Resource Center (EERC) • http://eerc.ra.utk.edu

    e. Vanderbilt Center for Environmental Management Studies, http://www.vanderbilt.edu/htdocs/VCEMS/links.html

Texas

1. Texas Commission on Environmental Quality (TCEQ), 12100 Park 35 Circle, Austin, TX 78753 • Phone: 512-239-1000 • E-mail: recycle@tceq.state.tx.us • http://www.tceq.state.tx.us/assistance/hhw/hhw.html

2. Other Texas Resources:

    a. Central Texas Recycling Association • http://www.cash4trash.com

    b. Clean Water Clear Choices • http://www.cleanwaterclearchoice.org

    c. North Texas Corporate Recycling Association • http://www.ntcra.org

    d. Recycling Alliance of Texas • http://www.recycletx.com

    e. Texas Campaign for the Environment • http://www.texasenvironment.org

Utah

1. Utah Department of Environmental Quality, Division of Solid and Hazardous Waste, P.O. Box 144880, Salt Lake City, UT 84114-4880 • Phone: 801-538-6170 • http://www.hazardouswaste.utah.gov

2. Other Utah Resources:
   a. Utah Center for Multicultural Health Network • http://www.health.utah.gov/cmh/LHD.htm
   b. Utah State Universal Waste Resources • http://www.h2e-online.org/uw.cfm?st=UT

Vermont

1. Vermont Department of Environmental Conservation (DEC), Waste Management Division, 103 South Main Street, West Office Building, Waterbury, VT 05671-0404 • Phone: 802-241-3888 • http://www.anr.state.vt.us/dec/wastediv/R3/WReduct.htm
2. Other Vermont Resources:
   a. Association of Vermont Recyclers (AVR) • http://www.vtrecyclers.org
   b. University of Vermont Environmental Council • http://www.uvm.edu/greening/envcouncil
   c. Vermont Business Materials Exchange (VBME) • http://www.vbmx.org
   d. Vermont Earth Institute • http://www.vtearthinstitute.org

Washington

1. Washington Department of Ecology, P.O. Box 47600, Olympia, WA 98504-7600 • Phone: 360-407-6000 • http://www.ecy.wa.gov/ecyhome.html
2. Other Washington Resources:
   a. Green Seattle Guide, City of Seattle (WA) • http://www.seattle.gov/environment/cag
   b. King County (WA) HHW Program • http://www.govlink.org/hazwaste
   c. Urban Pesticide Education Strategy Team (UPEST), Washington Department of Ecology • http://www.ecy.wa.gov/programs/swfa/upest
   d. Washington Biodiversity Council • http://www.biodiversity.wa.gov
   e. Washington State Recycling Association • http://www.wsra.net

West Virginia

1. West Virginia Department of Environmental Protection, Division of Water and Waste Management, Environmental Enforcement, 601-57th Street, Charleston, WV 25304 • Phone: 304-926-0495 • http://www.wvdep.org
2. Other West Virginia Resources:
   a. National Environmental Services Center (NESC), West Virginia University • http://www.nesc.wvu.edu

Wisconsin

1. Wisconsin Department of Natural Resources (WDNR), 101 South Webster Street, P.O. Box 7921, Madison, WI 53707-7921 • Phone: 608-266-2621 • http://www.dnr.state.wi.us/org/aw/wm/household.htm

2. Other Wisconsin Resources:
    a. Environmental Resources Center (ERC), University of Wisconsin-Madison •
        http://www.uwex.edu/erc
    b. WasteCap, Wisconsin, Inc. • http://www.wastecapwi.org
    c. Wisconsin Clean Sweep Program, Wisconsin Department of Agriculture,
        Trade and Consumer Protection • http://www.datcp.state.wi.us/arm/agricul-
        ture/pest-fert/pesticides/clean-sweep
    d. Wisconsin Pollution Prevention Partnership, University of Wisconsin Exten-
        sion • E-mail: wip2@uwm.edu • http://wip2.uwex.edu

Wyoming

1. Wyoming Department of Environmental Quality, Solid and Hazardous Waste Divi-
    sion, 122 West 25th Street, Cheyenne, WY 82002 • Phone: 307-777-7164 • http://
    deq.state.wy.us/shwd/Old%20Stuff/aboutrecycle.asp
2. Other Wyoming Resources:
    a. Wyoming Environmental Quality Council (EQC) • http://deq.state.wy.us/eqc
    b. Wyoming Solid Waste and Recycling Association • http://www.wswra.com

Listservs

The Internet is expediting the dissemination of information among hazardous waste professionals across the country and the world. Listservs provide an efficient way to reach a
large number of industry professionals on a wide range of topics. Listservs generally are by
region or topic and may have specific membership requirements.

1. Alabama Environmental Council Listserv • http://groups.yahoo.com/group/ala-
    bamaenvironmentalcouncil/?yguid=84407131#ans
2. California Air Resources Board Listserv • http://www.arb.ca.gov/listserv/listserv.
    php
3. California Environmental Protection Agency (Cal/EPA) Listservs • http://www.
    calepa.ca.gov/Listservs
4. California Environmental Protection Agency (Cal/EPA) DTSC Listservs • http://
    www.calepa.ca.gov/Listservs/dtsc
5. California Integrated Waste Management Board Listservs • http://www.ciwmb.
    ca.gov/listservs/
6. California Office of Environmental Health Hazard Assessment (OEHHA) Listserv
    • http://www.oehha.ca.gov/Listservs/ListSubscribe.asp?LID=11
7. California Product Stewardship Listserv • E-mail: CAProductStewardship@yahoo-
    groups.com
8. Campus Safety Health and Environmental Management Association, A Division of
    the National Safety Council • http://www.cshema.org/communicate/listserv.htm
9. Children's Environmental Health Network Listserv • http://www.cehn.org/cehn
10. Colorado Bar Association Environmental Law Listserv • http://www.cobar.org/list-
    servs.cfm

11. College and University Environmental Management (CUE) Listserv • http://www.p2ric.org:81/read/about/?forum=CUE

12. Commission for Environmental Cooperation (CECnet) Listserv • http://www.udallcenter.arizona.edu/programs/usmex/cecnet/index.html

13. Connecticut Green Party (CTGP) Listserv • http://www.ctgreens.org/listservs.shtml

14. Florida Household Hazardous Waste Listserv • flhhw@lists.dep.state.fl.us • *Note: This Listserv is only open to Florida HHW community coordinators.*

15. Georgia Recycling Coalition Listserv • E-mail: GA-RECYCLERS@HOME.EASE.LSOFT.COM

16. Great Lakes Regional Pollution Prevention Roundtable Listservs • http://www.glrppr.org/listservs/#glrppr_private • *Note: This listserv includes links to public, private, and national listservs.*

17. Greening Schools Listserv • http://www.greeningschools.org/services/listserv.cfm

18. GreenYes Listserv • www.greenyes.grrn.org

19. Hospitals for a Healthy Environment (H2E) Information Exchange Listserv • http://cms.h2e-online.org/listserv/join

20. Household Hazardous Waste Resource Exchange Listserv • http://hhwlist.org/listserv

21. Indiana Watershed Listserv, Purdue University • http://www.ces.purdue.edu/water-quality/listserv.html

22. International Society for the History, Philosophy, and Social Studies of Biology (ISHPSSB) Listserv • http://www.ishpssb.org/listserv.html

23. Mercury Policy Project Listserv • http://www.mercurypolicy.org/org/lists/index.shtml

24. MassRecycle Listserv • E-mail: MassRecycle@yahoogroups.com

25. Minnesota Department of Health, The Lead Link Listserv (lead issues) • http://www.health.state.mn.us/divs/eh/lead/listserv.html

26. Montana Environmental Education Association Listserv • http://www.montanaeea.org/meealistserv.html

27. MSW Management TrashTalk Listserv • http://www.mswmanagement.com/trash-talk.html

28. National Drinking Water Clearinghouse News Listserv http://www.nesc.wvu.edu/ndwc/ndwc_listserv.htm

29. National Small Flows Clearinghouse News Listserv • http://www.nesc.wvu.edu/nsfc/nsfc_listserv.htm

30. NEWMOA Listservs • http://www.newmoa.org/prevention/listserv.cfm

31. North Carolina Office of Environmental Education Listserv • http://www.eenorth-carolina.org/whatisoffice/listserv.htm

32. Northeast Recycling Council (NERC) Environmentally Preferable Products Procurement (EPPnet) Listserv • http://www.nerc.org/eppnet.html

33. P2 (U.S. EPA) Region 7 Listserv • http://www.p2ric.org:81/read/about/?forum=p2r7

34. P2Rx™ Centers National, Regional & State Listserv List • http://www.p2rx.org/Networking/Listserves.cfm#State

35. Pharmaceutical Listserv (National) • E-mail: pharmwaste@lists.dep.state.fl.us

36. Pollution Prevention Resource Exchange (P2Rx) Listservs • http://www.p2rx.org/Networking/Listserves.cfm#State • *Note: This includes a list of state, regional, and national listservs.*
37. Product Stewardship Institute (PSI) Listservs • http://www.productstewardship.us/displaycommon.cfm?an=1&subarticlenbr=30 • *Note: These listservs are available to government officials only.*
38. PSI Electronics Listserv • E-mail: PSIElectronics-subscribe@yahoogroups.com
39. Sierra Club Listserv Archive • http://lists.sierraclub.org/archives/index.html
40. University of Kentucky, College of Education Professional Listservs: • http://www.uky.edu/Education/kylists.html • See Environmental Education Listserv (KYENVED)
41. University of Vermont Environmental Council GREENUVM Listserv • http://www.uvm.edu/greening/envcouncil/
42. University of Vermont, Safety List Listserv. Discusses regulatory interpretation, safety management issues and chemical safety. • http://list.uvm.edu/cgi-bin/wa?A0=SAFETY
43. Urban Environmental Management Listserv. The Global Development Research Center • http://www.gdrc.org/uem/email-lists.html
44. U.S. EPA Environmental Justice Listserv • https://lists.epa.gov/read/all_forums/subscribe?name=epa-ej
45. U.S. EPA Federal Register Listserv • http://www.epa.gov/fedrgstr/subscribe.htm • Receive daily Federal Register updates on one to twelve environmental EPA topics.
46. Utah Department of Environmental Quality Listserv List • http://www.deq.utah.gov/ListServ/index.htm
47. Vermont Business Material Exchange Listserv • http://www.vbmx.org/listserv.php
48. Washington Department of Ecology Household Hazardous Waste Listserv • http://listserv.wa.gov/archives/hhw-information.html
49. Washington Department of Ecology Environmental Listserv List • http://www.ecy.wa.gov/maillist.html
50. Washington State All Topic Listserv List • http://listserv.wa.gov
51. Western Regional Pollution Prevention Network (WRPPN) Listserv • http://www.wrppn.org/listserv.cfm

Organizations

Organizations associated with hazardous materials have been important catalysts and resources for the developing field of household hazardous waste management. This section includes a variety of organizations involved in or related to HHW, recycling or specific-HHW topics and/or materials.

1. Academy of Certified Hazardous Materials Managers (ACHMM), 9650 Rockville Pike, Bethesda, MD 20814, Phone: 800-437-0137 or 301-634-7430 • E-mail: academy@achmm.org • http://www.achmm.org

ACHMM is a professional association promoting the environment, health and safety, advancing the field of hazardous materials management, and promoting the Certified Hazardous Materials Manager® (CHMM®) credential.

2. Air & Waste Management Association (A&WMA), One Gateway Center, 3rd Floor, 420 Fort Duquesne Boulevard, Pittsburgh, PA 15222-1435 • Phone: 412-232-3444 or 800-270-3444 • E-mail: info@awma.org • http://www.awma.org

   The Air & Waste Management Association (A&WMA) is a non-profit, non-partisan professional organization that provides training, information, and networking opportunities to thousands of environmental professionals in 65 countries.

3. Association of State and Territorial Solid Waste Management Officials (ASTSWMO), 444 North Capitol Street, NW Suite 315, Washington, DC 20001 • Phone: 202-624-5828 • http://www.astswmo.org

   The Association of State and Territorial Solid Waste Management Officials (ASTSWMO) provides environmental state and trust territory agencies with support in the areas of hazardous waste, recycling, sustainability, waste minimization, and reduction programs.

4. Beyond Pesticides, 701 E Street, SE, Suite 200, Washington, DC 20003 • Office Hours: 9 AM-5 PM EST STD • Phone: 202-543-5450 • Fax: 202-543-4791 • Email: info@beyondpesticides.org • http://www.beyondpesticides.org

   Beyond Pesticides is a non-profit organization working to protect the health of the public through the elimination of toxic pesticides. This organization was formerly known as the National Coalition Against the Misuse of Pesticides.

5. Bio-Integral Resource Center (BIRC), P.O. Box 7414, Berkeley, CA 94707 • Phone: 510-524-2567 • E-mail: birc@igc.org • http://www.birc.org

   BIRC is a non-profit organization specializing in the development and communication of environmentally preferable Integrated Pest Management (IPM) practices.

6. Children's Environmental Health Network, 110 Maryland Avenue NE, Suite 505, Washington, DC 2002 • Phone: 202-543-4033 • E-mail: cehn@cehn.org • http://www.cehn.org/cehn

   The Children's Environmental Health Network is a national multi-disciplinary organization whose mission is to protect the fetus and the child from environmental health hazards and promote a healthy environment.

7. Environmental Council of States (ECOS), 444 North Capitol NW, Suite 445, Washington, DC 20001 • Phone: 202-624-3660 • E-mail: ecos@sso.org • http://www.ecos.org

   The Environmental Council of the States (ECOS) is the national non-profit, non-partisan association of state and territorial environmental agency leaders. The purpose of ECOS is to improve the capability of state environmental agencies and their leaders to protect and improve human health and the environment of the United States of America.

8. Environmental Hazards Management Institute (EHMI), Oyster River Parsonage, 10 Newmarket Road, Durham, NH 03821 • Phone: 800-558-EHMI • http://www.ehmi.org

   EHMI is a non-profit organization dedicated to environmental, health, and safety education and resolving problems through education and consensus.

9. Environmental Health Coalition (EHC), 401 Mile of Cars Way, Suite 310, National City, CA 91950 • Phone: 619-474-0220 • E-mail: ehc@environmentalhealth.org • http://www.environmentalhealth.org
    Environmental Health Coalition empowers communities with social change strategies to achieve long-term environment solutions and environmental justice.
10. Environmental Law Institute (ELI), 2000 L Street, NW, Suite 620, Washington, DC 20036 • Phone: 202-939-3800 • E-mail: law@eli.org • http://www.eli.org
    The Environmental Law Institute provides information services, advice, publications, training courses, seminars, research programs and policy recommendations to engage and empower environmental leaders around the world.
11. Environmental Working Group (EWG), Headquarters, 1436 U Street, NW, Ste. 100, Washington, DC 20009 • http://www.ewg.org/
    The Environmental Working Group is a nonprofit organization that researches and advocates the use of public information to protect public health and the environment.
12. Great Lakes Regional Pollution Prevention Roundtable (GLRPPR), One East Hazelwood Drive, Champaign, IL 61820, 800-407-0261 • E-mail: glrppr@wmrc.uiuc.edu • http://www.glrppr.org
    GLRPPR provides pollution prevention professionals with a forum to exchange information specific to the Great Lakes regions of the United States and Canada. This area consists of Illinois, Indiana, Michigan, Minnesota, New York, Ohio, Ontario, Pennsylvania, and Wisconsin.
13. Green Seal, 1001 Connecticut Avenue, NW, Suite 827, Washington, DC 20036-5525 • Phone: 202-872-6400 • E-mail: greenseal@greenseal.org • http://www.greenseal.org
    Green Seal is an independent, non-profit organization that strives to achieve a healthier and cleaner environment by identifying and promoting products and services that cause less toxic pollution and waste, conserve resources and habitats, and minimize global warming and ozone depletion. Green Seal has no financial interest in the products that it certifies or recommends nor in any manufacturer or company. Green Seal provides credible, objective, and unbiased information to direct the purchaser to environmentally responsible products and services.
14. Health Care Without Harm (HCWH), 1755 S Street NW, Suite 6B, Washington, DC 20009 • Phone: 202-234-0091 • E-mail: info@hcwh.org • http://www.noharm.org
    Health Care Without Harm (HCWH) is an international coalition of more than 400 organizations in 52 countries working to transform the health care industry so it is no longer a source of harm to people and the environment.
15. Hospitals for a Healthy Environment (H2E), P.O. Box 376, One Lyme Common, Lyme, NH 03768 • Phone: 603-795-9966 • www.h2e-online.org
    H2E is dedicated to educating health care professional on the resources and methods to make hospitals environmentally sustainable.
16. League of Conservation Voters (LCV), 1920 L Street, NW, Suite 800, Washington, DC 20035 • Phone: 202-785-8683 • http://www.lcv.org
    The League of Conservation Voters is an independent organization providing a pro-environmental voice to our politicians. It provides the National Environmental

Scorecard and Presidential Report Card, which inform the public on the voting records of their congressional representatives.

17. Local Government Environmental Assistance Network (LGEAN), LGEAN is managed and operated by the International City/County Management Association • E-mail: lgean@icma.org • Phone: 877-865-4326 • http://lgean.org

18. Mid-Atlantic Consortium of Recycling and Economic Development Officials (MACREDO) • http://www.macredo.org

    MACREDO promotes recycling and economic development in Delaware, Maryland, Pennsylvania, Virginia, West Virginia, and the District of Columbia.

19. Mid-America Council of Recycling Officials (MACRO) • http://www.epa.gov/epaoswer/non-hw/recycle/jtr/state/macro.htm

    MACRO is a 501(c)(3) organization composed of 14 states: Illinois, Indiana, Iowa, Kansas, Kentucky, Michigan, Minnesota, Missouri, Nebraska, North Dakota, Ohio, Pennsylvania, South Dakota, Wisconsin. The organization's goal is to encourage, educate, and develop regional programs on recycling, market development, source reduction, and recycled-content purchasing.

20. National Association of Environmental Managers (NAEM), 1612 K Street, NW, Suite 1102, Washington, DC 20006 • Phone: 202-986-6616 or 800-391-NAEM • E-mail: programs@naem.org • http://www.naem.org

    National Association of Environmental Managers is a non-profit, education association promoting Environmental, Health, & Safety management.

20. North American Association for Environmental Education (NAAEE), 2000 P Street NW, Suite 540, Washington, DC 20036 • Phone: 202-419-0412 • http://www.naaee.org or http://www.eelink.net

    Find HHW resources through NAAEE's site EE-Link, the most widely used environmental education search engine on the Web, or in person at NAAEE's annual conference, www.naaee.org/conference

21. National Association of Regional Councils (NARC), 1666 Connecticut Avenue, NW, Suite 300, Washington, DC 20009 • Phone: 202-986-1032 • http://www.narc.org

    The National Association of Regional Councils (NARC) is dedicated to advocating for environmental policies and programs that meet the economic and social needs of our communities, regional councils, metropolitan planning organizations, and local elected officials.

22. National Environmental Services Center (NESC), Box 6064, West Virginia University, Morgantown, WV 26506-6064 • Phone: 304-293-4191 or 800-624-8301 • E-mail: info@mail.nesc.wvu.edu • http://www.nesc.wvu.edu/nesc

    The National Environmental Services Center consolidates and provides small and rural communities and homeowners with information about drinking water systems, wastewater treatment systems, and solid waste management. NESC offers a toll-free technical assistance hotline, referrals, educational products, publications, environmental training, and other helpful resources.

23. National Recycling Coalition (NRC), 805 15th Street, NW, Suite 425, Washington, DC 20005 • Phone: 202-789-1430 • E-mail: info@nrc-recycle.org • http://www.nrc-recycle.org

The National Recycling Coalition is a non-profit advocacy organization promoting the advancement and improvement of recycling, waste prevention, composting, and reuse.
24. North American Hazardous Materials Management Association (NAHMMA), 3030 W. 81st Ave., Westminster, CO 80031-4111 • Phone: 303-433-4446 or 877-292-1403 • E-mail: nahmma@imigroup.org • http://www.nahmma.org

North American Hazardous Materials Management Association is an organization for hazardous materials management professionals dedicated to advanced education, fostering communication, encouraging policy development, recognizing exemplary programs and providing professional development opportunities.
25. Northeast Recycling Council (NERC), 139 Main Street, Suite 401, Brattleboro, VT 05301 • Phone: 802-254-3636 • E-mail: info@nerc.org • http://www.nerc.org

The Northeast Recycling Council is a regional, non-profit organization dedicated to promoting source and toxicity reduction, recycling, and the purchasing of environmentally preferable products (EPP) and services.
26. Northeast Resource Recovery Association (NRRA), 2101 Dover Road, Epsom, NH 03234 • Phone: 603-736-4401 • E-mail: info@nrra.net • http://www.nrra.net

NRRA is a co-op that provides technical and marketing assistance in the areas of waste reduction and recycling to over 300 municipalities, individuals, and businesses in New Hampshire, Vermont, Massachusetts, Connecticut, and Southern Maine.
27. Northeast Waste Management Officials' Association (NEWMOA), 129 Portland Street, Suite 602, Boston, MA 02114-2014 • Phone: 617-367-8558 • http://www.newmoa.org

The Northeast Waste Management Officials' Association (NEWMOA) is a non-profit, non-partisan interstate association that has a membership composed of the hazardous waste, solid waste, waste site cleanup, and pollution prevention program directors for the environmental agencies in Connecticut, Maine, Massachusetts, New Hampshire, New Jersey, New York, Rhode Island, and Vermont. NEWMOA's mission is to develop and sustain an effective partnership of states to explore, develop, promote, and implement environmentally sound solutions for the reduction and management of materials and waste, and for the remediation of contaminated sites, in order to achieve a clean and healthy environment.
28. Northwest Coalition for Alternatives to Pesticides, P.O. Box 1393, Eugene, OR 97440-1393 • Phone: 541-344-5044 • E-mail: info@pesticide.org • http://www.pesticide.org

The Northwest Coalition for Alternatives to Pesticides protects the health of people and the environment by advancing alternatives to pesticides.
30. Poison Control Center Hotline – 1-800-222-1222 and http://www.1-800-222-1222.info
31. American Association of Poison Control Centers, 3201 New Mexico Avenue, Suite 330, Washington, DC 20016 • Phone: 202-362-7217 • E-mail: info@aapcc.org

The American Association of Poison Control Centers (AAPCC) is a nationwide organization of poison centers and interested individuals.
32. Product Stewardship Institute (PSI), 137 Newbury Street, Suite 700, Boston, MA 02116 • Phone: 617-236-4855 • http://www.productstewardship.us

The Product Stewardship Institute (PSI) is a national non-profit membership-based organization located in Boston, Massachusetts. PSI works with state and local government agencies to partner with manufacturers, retailers, environmental groups, federal agencies, and other key stakeholders to reduce the health and environmental impacts of consumer products. PSI takes a unique product stewardship approach to solving waste management problems by encouraging product design changes and mediating stakeholder dialogues.

33. Silicon Valley Toxics Coalition, 760 North First Street, San Jose, California 95112 • Phone: 408-287-6707 • E-mail: svtc@svtc.org • http://svtc.etoxics.org

Silicon Valley Toxics Coalition is a diverse organization engaged in research, advocacy, and grassroots organizing to promote human health and environmental justice in response to the rapid growth of the high-tech industry.

34. Solid Waste Association of North America (SWANA), 1100 Wayne Avenue, Suite 700, Silver Spring, Maryland 20910 • Phone: 800-467-9262 • http://www.swana.org

SWANA is a membership association for professionals in the solid waste industry.

35. Southeast Recycling Development Council (SERDC) • http://www.serdc.org

SERDC is a coalition of eleven states including Alabama, Arkansas, Florida, Georgia, Kentucky, Louisiana, Mississippi, North Carolina, South Carolina, Tennessee, and Virginia. Its goal is to bring together those involved in recycling to promote sustainable programs and coordinate public education activities.

36. Southeast Watershed Assistance Network (SWAN) • http://swan.southeastwaterforum.org

The Southeast Watershed Assistance Network is a clearinghouse for land and water protection resources.

37. Toxics Action Center, Massachusetts Office, 44 Winter Street, 4th Floor, Boston, MA 02108 • Phone: 617-292-4821 • http://www.toxicsaction.org

Toxics Action Center assists neighborhood groups across New England to combat toxic pollution and issues in their communities.

38. Union of Concerned Scientists (UCS), National Headquarters, 2 Brattle Square, Cambridge, MA 02238-9105 • Phone: 617-547-5552 • http://www.ucsusa.org

Online newsletters are available at: http://ucsaction.org/ucsaction/join.tcl?qp_source=wacucs%5fheads The Union of Concerned Scientists is a science-based non-profit organization made up of scientists and citizens working to achieve practical environmental solutions.

39. Washington Toxics Coalition (WTC), 4649 Sunnyside Avenue N, Suite 540, Seattle, WA 98103 • Phone: 206-632-1545 • E-mail: info@watoxics.org • http://www.watoxics.org

Washington Toxics Coalition protects public health and the environment by eliminating toxic pollution. WTC promotes alternatives, advocates policies, empowers communities, and educates people to create a healthy environment.

40. Worldwatch Institute, 1776 Massachusetts Avenue, N.W., Washington, DC 20036-1904 • Phone: 202-452-1999 • E-mail: worldwatch@worldwatch.org • http://www.worldwatch.org

Worldwatch is an independent, globally focused environmental and social policy research organization.

Trade Organizations

Batteries

1. Battery Council International, 401 North Michigan Avenue, 24th Floor, Chicago, IL 60611-4267 • Phone: 312-644-6610 • E-mail: info@batterycouncil.org • http://www.batterycouncil.org
2. Portable Rechargeable Battery Association (PRBA), 1776 K Street, 4th Floor, Washington, DC 20006 • Phone: 202-719-4978 • http://www.prba.org
3. Rechargeable Battery Recycling Corporation (RBRC), 1000 Parkwood Circle, Suite 450, Atlanta, GA 30339 • Phone: 678-419-9990 • E-mail: recycling@rbrc.com • http://www.rbrc.org/

Chemicals—General

1. American Chemistry Council, 1300 Wilson Boulevard, Arlington, VA 22209 • Phone: 703-741-5000 • http://www.americanchemistry.com
2. Chemical Specialty Products Association, 900 17th St. NW, Suite 300, Washington, DC 20006 • Phone: 202-872-8110, Fax: 202-872-8114 • http://www.cspa.org/ CSPA (formerly known as the Chemical Specialties Manufacturers Association).
3. National Association of Chemical Distributors (NACD), 1560 Wilson Boulevard, Suite 1250, Arlington, VA 22209 • Phone: 703-527-6223 • E-mail: nacdpublicaffairs@nacd.com • http://www.nacd.com
4. Synthetic Organic Chemical Manufacturers Association (SOCMA), 1850 M Street NW, Suite 700, Washington, DC 20036-5810 • Phone: 202-721-4100 • http://www.socma.com

Cosmetics

1. Cosmetic, Toiletry, and Fragrance Association (CTFA), 1101 17th Street, NW, Suite 300, Washington, DC 20036-4702 • Phone: 202-331-1770 • http://www.ctfa.org
2. Society of Cosmetic Chemists (SCC), 120 Wall Street, Suite 2400, New York, NY 10005-4088 • Phone: 212-668-1500 • http://www.scconline.org

Electronics

1. Electronic Industries Association (EIA), 2500 Wilson Boulevard, Arlington, VA 22201 • Phone: 703-907-7500 • http://www.eia.org
2. Information Technology Industry Council (ITI), 1250 Eye Street, NW, Suite 200, Washington, DC 20005 • Phone: 202-737-8888 • http://www.itic.org
3. International Association of Electronics Recyclers (IAER), P.O. Box 16222, Albany, NY 12212-6222 • Toll-free in the U.S. & Canada: 888-989-IAER (4237) • Email: info@IAER.org • http://www.IAER.org

4. National Electrical Manufacturers Association (NEMA), 1300 North 17th Street, Suite 1752, Rosslyn, VA 22209 • Phone: 703-841-3200 • http://www.nema.org
5. USTelecom, 607 14th Street NW, Suite 400, Washington, DC 20005 • Phone: 202-326-7300 • http://www.usta.org

Mercury

1. Association of Lighting and Mercury Recyclers (ALMR), 2436 Foothill Boulevard, Suite B, Calistoga, CA 94515 • Phone: 707-942-2197 • E-mail: mail@almr.org • http://www.almr.org
2. Thermostat Recycling Corporation (TRC) • Phone: 800-238-8192 • http://www.nema.org/gov/ehs/trc

Oil Filters

1. Filter Manufacturers Council, 10 Laboratory Drive, P.O. Box 13966, Research Triangle Park, NC 27709-3966 • Phone: 919-406-8817 • http://www.filtercouncil.org

Paint

1. National Aerosol Association (NAA), P.O. Box 5510, Fullerton, CA 92838 • Phone: 714-525-1518 • E-mail: naa@nationalaerosol.com • http://www.nationalaerosol.com
2. National Paint and Coatings Association (NPCA), 1500 Rhode Island Avenue, NW, Washington, DC 20005 • Phone: 202-462-6272 • E-mail: npca@paint.org • http://www.paint.org

Pesticides

1. Pesticides, Ag Container Recycling Council (ACRC), 1156 15th Street, NW, Suite 400, Washington, DC 20005 • Phone: 202-861-3144 • E-mail: information@acrecycle.org • http://www.acrecycle.org
2. Association of American Pesticide Control Officials (AAPCO), P.O. Box 466, Milford, DE 19963 • Phone: 302-422-8152 • E-mail: AAPCO-SFIREG@comcast.net • http://aapco.ceris.purdue.edu
3. CropLife America, 1156 15th Street, N.W., Washington, DC 20005 • Phone: 202-296-1585
4. National Pesticide Information Center (NPIC), Oregon State University, 333 Weniger Hall, Corvallis, OR 97331-6502 • Phone: 1-800-858-7378 (6:30am to 4:30pm PST 7 days a week) • E-mail: npic@ace.orst.edu • http://npic.orst.edu
5. The Pesticide Stewardship Alliance (TPSA), P.O. Box 5204, Takoma Park, MD 20913 • Phone: 877-920-6772 • E-mail: contact@tpsalliance.org • http://tpsalliance.org

Pharmaceuticals

1. PhRMA, 950 F Street, NW, Washington, DC 20004 • Phone: 202-835-3400 • http://www.phrma.org

Propane and Gas Cylinders

1. National Propane Gas Association (NPGA), 4901 Forest Avenue, Downers Grove, IL 60515-3509 • Phone: 630-769-1986 • E-mail: info@npga.org • http://www.npga.org
2. Propane Education & Research Council, 1140 Connecticut Avenue, NW, Suite 1075, Washington, DC 20036 • Phone: 202-452-8975 • http://www.propanecouncil.org

Used Motor Oil and Liquids

1. American Petroleum Institute (API), 1220 L Street, NW, Washington, DC 20005-4070 • Phone: 202-682-8000 • http://www.api.org
2. NORA, the Association of Responsible Recyclers, 5965 Amber Ridge Road, Haymarket, Virginia 20169 • Phone: 703-753-4277 • http://www.noranews.org

HHW-Related Databases

1. California Pesticide Database, California Department of Pesticide Regulation • http://www.cdpr.ca.gov/dprdatabase.htm
   The Department of Pesticide Regulation (DPR) has a number of collections of data and other information related to pesticide registration, licensing, pesticide use, environmental effects, enforcement, and other elements of our program.
2. Canadian Centre for Occupational Health and Safety (CCOHS), Academic Support Program Databases • http://www.istl.org/04-fall/databases.html
   The CCOHS provides universities and colleges with information and data on environmental, occupational health, and safety issues.
3. Chemical Abstracts Service (CAS) • http://www.cas.org
   CAS, a division of the American Chemical Society, provides databases of chemical information.
4. ChemIDplus Advanced Database, U.S. National Library of Medicine (NLM) • http://chem.sis.nlm.nih.gov/chemidplus
   This database allows users to search the NLM ChemIDplus database of over 370,000 chemicals.
5. Chemfinder.com • http://chemfinder.cambridgesoft.com
   Chemfinder.com is a portal of free and subscription scientific databases including the following: reference, chemical, reaction, and safety databases.

6. The Collaborative on Health and the Environment (CHE), CHE Toxicant and Disease Database • http://database.healthandenvironment.org
   The CHE Toxicant and Disease Database provides correlations between chemicals and over 180 human diseases and conditions based on certain toxicants.

7. Earth 911, http://www.Earth911.org / 1-800-CLEANUP
   Earth 911 provides community-specific environmental information to residents and businesses for recycling, reuse, and household hazardous waste disposal locations in the U.S. and Canada. It also provides information on a broad range of environmental topics.

8. European Chemicals Bureau (ECB), Toxicology and Chemical Substances • http://ecb.jrc.it
   The European Chemicals Bureau (ECB) collects data and provides analysis of dangerous chemicals, and monitors policy with regards to dangerous chemicals in Europe.

9. EXTOXNET – Pesticide Information Profiles • http://extoxnet.orst.edu/pips/ghindex.html
   EXTONET provides information profiles on pesticides and is a cooperative effort of the University of California-Davis, Oregon State University, Michigan State University, Cornell University, and the University of Idaho.

10. Haz-Map: Occupational Exposure to Hazardous Agents, U.S. National Library of Medicine • http://hazmap.nlm.nih.gov

11. HealthcareFreeware.com • http://www.healthcarefreeware.com/chem_hz_an.htm
    Healthcare Freeware is an online resource of databases, freeware software, and other helpful resources for those in the healthcare field and the general public.

12. Household Products Database, National Institutes of Health • http://hpd.nlm.nih.gov
    This database is accumulated from a variety of publicly available sources including brand-specific labels and Material Safety Data Sheets (MSDS). It links over 7,000 consumer brands to health effects from MSDS and enables scientists and consumers to research products based on chemical ingredients.

13. Integrated Risk Information System (IRIS), U.S. Environmental Protection Agency • http://www.epa.gov/iris/subst/index.html
    IRIS is an electronic database containing information on the human health effects that may result from exposure to various chemicals in the environment.

14. Mercury-Added Products Database, Interstate Mercury Education & Reduction Clearinghouse (IMERC) • http://www.newmoa.org/prevention/mercury/imerc/notification/#note

15. National Institute of Occupational Safety and Health (NIOSH) Databases and Information, Centers for Disease Control • http://www.cdc.gov/niosh/database.html
    The NIOSH website includes database and information resources on chemicals, injuries, & hazardous, publications, respirators and personal protection equipment, agriculture, and construction.

16. National MSDS Repository • http://ww.msdssearch.com
    The National MSDS Repository provides no cost access to over 2.5 million Material Safety Data Sheets (MSDSs), and links to the manufacturers.

17. National Small Flows Clearinghouse (NSFC) Regulations Database and Reposi-
    tory, National Environmental Service Center • http://www.nesc.wvu.edu/nsfc/
    nsfc_regulations.htm
18. Skin Deep Cosmetic Safety Database, Environmental Working Group • http://www.
    cosmeticdatabase.com/index.php?nothanks=1
        Skin Deep provides ratings of almost 25,000 personal care products and 6,500
    ingredients with 50 toxicity and regulatory databases.
`19. Specialized Information Services (SIS), National Library of Medicine
        Specialized Information Services (SIS) provides access to a variety of data-
    bases and resources associated with toxicology, environmental health, chemistry,
    and minority health topics.
20. TOXMAP Web Search, National Institutes of Health • http://toxmap.nlm.nih.gov/
    toxmap/main/index.jsp
        TOXMAP uses maps of the United States to help users visually explore data
    from the EPA's Toxics Release Inventory (TRI) and Superfund Programs. Maps
    indicate where TRI chemicals are released on-site into the air, water, and ground.
21. Toxics in Packaging Clearinghouse (TPCH), Northeast Recycling Council (NERC)
    • http://www.toxicsinpackaging.org
        The TPCH mission is to develop public policy actions which reduce the amount
    of toxicity of packaging at the source, before it enters the solid waste stream.
22. TOXNET Web Search, National Institutes of Health • http://toxnet.nlm.nih.gov
        TOXNET provides access to numerous databases on toxicology, hazardous
    chemicals and substances, environmental health, and toxic releases.
        TOXNET Hazardous Substance Data Bank (HSDB) • http://toxnet.nlm.nih.
    gov/cgi-bin/sis/htmlgen?HSDB
        TOXNET Toxic Release Inventory (TRI) • http://toxnet.nlm.nih.gov/cgi-bin/
    sis/htmlgen?TRI
23. Washington Department of Ecology, Searchable Databases • http://www.ecy.
    wa.gov/database.html
24. Washington Department of Ecology, 1-800-Recycle Database • http://1800recycle.
    wa.gov

About the Author

Anne Reichman is Director of Public Affairs and former Director of Earth 911 (www.
Earth911.org/1-800-CLEANUP), the environmental information portal and toll-free hotline for the United States and Canada.

Acknowledgments

A special thank-you to the following individuals and organizations for generously pro-
viding resources for this important resource section: Amy Cabaniss, Dave Galvin, Irene
Gleason, Meryl Klein, Bill Lewry, the North American Hazardous Materials Management
Association (NAHMMA), and the Florida Department of Environmental Protection.

Index